Misha Strittmatter

A Reference Structure for Modular Metamodels of Quality-Describing Domain-Specific Modeling Languages

The Karlsruhe Series on Software Design and Quality
Volume 31

Chair Software Design and Quality
Faculty of Computer Science
Karlsruhe Institute of Technology

and

Software Engineering Division
Research Center for Information Technology (FZI), Karlsruhe

Editor: Prof. Dr. Ralf Reussner

A Reference Structure for Modular Metamodels of Quality-Describing Domain-Specific Modeling Languages

by
Misha Strittmatter

Scientific
Publishing

Karlsruher Institut für Technologie
Institut für Programmstrukturen und Datenorganisation

A Reference Structure for Modular Metamodels of Quality-Describing Domain-Specific Modeling Languages

Zur Erlangung des akademischen Grades eines Doktors der Ingenieurwissenschaften von der KIT-Fakultät für Informatik des Karlsruher Instituts für Technologie (KIT) genehmigte Dissertation

von Misha Strittmatter

Tag der mündlichen Prüfung: 22. Juli 2019
Erster Gutachter: Prof. Dr. Ralf Reussner
Zweiter Gutachter: Prof. Dr. Bernhard Rumpe

Impressum

KIT Scientific Publishing

Karlsruher Institut für Technologie (KIT)
KIT Scientific Publishing
Straße am Forum 2
D-76131 Karlsruhe

KIT Scientific Publishing is a registered trademark of Karlsruhe Institute of Technology.
Reprint using the book cover is not allowed.

www.ksp.kit.edu

Print on Demand 2020 – Gedruckt auf FSC-zertifiziertem Papier

ISSN 1867-0067
ISBN 978-3-7315-0982-0
DOI: 10.5445/KSP/1000098906

Acknowledgment

First, I thank my adviser (Doktorvater) Professor Ralf Reussner for his supervision and input. I thank him for having faith in me and my work and for giving me this opportunity. The work and research I did, entailed a great degree of responsibility and freedom. Although this was not easy, from these aspects I benefited the most. I thank my direct adviser Robert Heinrich for his supervision and input. Especially for the cooperation in the main paper of my thesis, his commitment improved the paper greatly.

By using his characteristic leadership style, Professor Reussner built the SDQ chair in a way that fostered a cooperative and constructive work atmosphere with many great colleagues. This chair was a great support to me and my work. Therefore, my thanks also go out to all of my current colleagues. You are awesome, and I wish you all the best for your research. One part of me would have really liked to stay longer, but now is the time for me to move on. For most of the time I worked at the chair, I shared an office with Axel and then with Kiana. It really was a great time. Thank you both. I also thank all of my former colleagues, many of which I miss dearly. Lucia Happe, I thank for supervising me when I was still a diploma student and for motivating me to go into research. For a long time, I participated actively in the MDSD research group of the SDQ chair. I thank them for the fertile discussions, their input, and their preciseness. Thanks to Professor Jörg Kienzle for his cooperation and for inviting me to his workshop. My research greatly benefited from both. Thanks to Professor Bernhard Rumpe and Professor Hannes Hartenstein for taking an interest in my work. I also thank all the students with whom I worked in the scope of my research. Especially Amine Kechaou was an invaluable help. For that, I thank him and wish him all the best for his future.

I thank all of my friends for their patience during the time I neglected them. My family, I thank for supporting me and for giving me the chance to pursue this path in the first place. Last but not least I thank my partner Janine for her patience, understanding, love, and support.

Abstract

Research Context In model-driven engineering and software development, domain-specific modeling languages (DSMLs) are used to model systems. Models are created during system design or reengineering. They can be used for analysis, verification, simulation, code generation, documentation, communication, and so on. Modeling languages can be defined by metamodels.

Challenges The challenges posed by the use of metamodels are twofold. They stem from metamodel maintenance (see my paper [SH16b]) and metamodel reuse.

Maintenance Like all software artifacts, metamodels have to evolve to remain useful. Over time, changes can lead to a degradation of the structure of a metamodel. This includes a decline in understandability, maintainability, and reusability. Subsequent evolution gets more time-consuming and can potentially cause even more harm. These effects do also negatively affect the development of tools that work on the metamodel (e.g., editors, analyses, transformation, and simulators).

Reuse Often, metamodels are not built with reusability in mind. They mostly support all-or-nothing reuse. Further, the reusability of a metamodel is hampered by improper evolution. If new requirements arise, these problems may lead to intrusive additions, branching of languages, or newly developed languages to be built from scratch instead of reusing existing language parts or extending an existing language. Intrusive additions bring the problems as mentioned above. Branches and new languages are incompatible to the original language, even if they could be in part compatible where they share common concepts. Additionally, they have to be maintained on their own.

State of the Art Language engineering approaches are great to quickly build new languages from existing languages or language fragments. They are, however, not concerned with the compatibility of the newly formed language to the original nor other derivations of the original language. There are several approaches for modularizing or extending metamodels. They do, however, not focus on the restructuring of dependencies. They, therefore, do not utilize the full potential to improve the reusability of a metamodel. Further related works investigate reoccurring negative patterns in metamodels (i.e., bad smells), as well as ways to detect and correct them. These works, however, mostly focus on errors that harm a the validity or correctness of metamodels and less on problems to metamodel evolvability.

Solution To close this gap in state of the art, this thesis offers three contributions.

This thesis presents an **investigation of bad smells** in metamodels. Bad smells were identified in the review of a metamodel [Str+16a] and by a transfer from object-oriented software design. For 12 of the bad smells, automatic detections were developed.

The core contribution of this thesis is the **reference structure** [HSR19; Str+15; SH16a], which enables design, evolution, and extension of metamodels for modeling languages that are used for quality analysis in a modular and layered way. Applied to a metamodel, the reference structure approach helps with the typical reuse scenarios from the domain of quality analysis. Applying this reference structure will help counter the degradation of the metamodel due to long-term evolution. By doing so, the reference structure addresses several bad smells of the first contribution.

Applying the reference structure approach yields a modular metamodel. To be able to couple the modules of metamodels in a meaningful way, this thesis investigates **metamodel extension mechanisms**. The extension mechanisms are also needed to extract parts of existing metamodels and to remodel dependencies to make them conform to the reference structure.

Validation The automated bad smells detections are evaluated by executing them and manually investigating the reported occurrences for adverse effects. By performing corrections and rerunning the detections, the effectiveness of the corrections is evaluated. To evaluate the reference structure approach, four metamodels were refactored according to the reference structure. A scenario-based evaluation shows an improvement of evolvability by determining complexity, coupling, and cohesion using metrics that are rooted in information theory. A second evaluation shows that the utilization of the metamodel increases. It, therefore, can be concluded that the refactored metamodels are more suited for need-driven use and reuse. The metamodel extension mechanisms are evaluated according to a catalog of comparison criteria and compared with each other. For each extension scenario, this enables to determine the most suited extension mechanism.

Zusammenfassung

Kontext In der modellgetriebenen Entwicklung werden domänenspezifische Modellierungssprachen verwendet, um unter anderem Systeme zu entwerfen, zu analysieren, zu simulieren und Code zu generieren. Solche Modellierungssprachen können durch Metamodelle definiert werden.

Problemfelder Bei der Verwendung von Metamodellen ergeben sich aus deren Wartung (siehe hierzu mein Artikel [SH16b]) und Wiederverwendung spezifische Herausforderungen.

Wartung Wie jedes andere Software-Artefakt auch, sind Metamodelle sich ändernden Anforderungen ausgesetzt. Die Struktur von langlebigen Metamodellen, welche über die Zeit viele Änderungen und Ergänzungen erfahren, verschlechtert sich mehr und mehr. Nachfolgende Wartungsarbeiten werden dadurch umso aufwendiger und potenziell noch nachteiliger. Diese Auswirkungen beschränken sich nicht nur auf die Wartungsarbeiten des Metamodells, sondern behindern auch die Entwicklung und Wartung von Software-Werkzeugen, welche auf dem Metamodell aufbauen (z. B. Editoren, Analysen, Transformationen und Simulatoren).

Wiederverwendung Oft werden Metamodelle nicht im Hinblick auf Wiederverwendung entworfen, wodurch eine bedarfsgerechte Teilwiederverwendung nicht möglich ist. Neue Anforderungen an den Sprachumfang oder der Einsatz in einem anderen Kontext führen entweder zum intrusiven Erweitern des Metamodells, zur Bildung eines Dialekts oder sogar zur Entwicklung einer neuen Sprache. Die intrusive Erweiterung bringt die oben genannten Probleme mit sich. Für Dialekte und neuen Sprachen fällt jeweils eigener Wartungsaufwand an. Zudem sind diese nicht mehr ohne Weiteres mit dem ursprünglichen Metamodell kompatibel.

Stand der Forschung Verwandte Sprachentwicklungsansätze konzentrieren sich darauf neue Sprachen zu erstellen, teils indem sie Sprachfragmenten wiederverwenden. Diese Ansätze haben den Nachteil, dass die Sprachen, welche sie erzeugen, im Allgemeinen nicht miteinander kompatibel sind, selbst wenn sie viel gemeinsam haben. Es gibt mehrere Ansätze zur Modularisierung und Komposition von Metamodellen. Diese Ansätze behandeln allerdings nicht die Umgestaltung von Abhängigkeiten und schöpfen daher nicht das volle Potenzial der Verbesserung der Wiederverwendung aus. Weitere verwandte Arbeiten untersuchen wiederkehrende negative Muster in der Metamodellierung (sogenannte Bad Smells) und Möglichkeiten diese zu erkennen und zu beheben. Diese Arbeiten beschränken sich hauptsächlich auf Modellierungsfehler, welche die Validität oder Korrektheit des Metamodells betreffen, und somit weniger auf Probleme der Evolvierbarkeit.

Beiträge Um die Lücke im Stand der Forschung zu schließen, bietet diese Arbeit drei Beiträge.

Zum ersten wird eine **Untersuchung der Bad Smells** der Metamodellierung präsentiert. Diese Bad Smells wurden bei der Durchsicht eines bestehenden Metamodells identifiziert [Str+16a] sowie aus der Objektorientierung übertragen. Für 12 der Bad Smells wurde eine automatische Erkennung entwickelt.

Die **Referenzstruktur** [HSR19; Str+15; SH16a] für Metamodelle von Modellierungssprachen für Qualitätsanalysen ist das Herzstück dieser Arbeit. Wird solch ein Metamodell nach der Referenzstruktur gestaltet oder umgestaltet, hilft dies bei den typischen Wiederverwendungsszenarien in der Domäne der Qualitätsanalyse. Das Metamodell wird modularer und somit für Entwickler einfacher zu verstehen. Zudem macht es das Metamodell langfristig evolvierbarer, indem Ursachen für strukturelle Verschlechterung ausgeschlossen werden. Die Referenzstruktur adressiert somit einige der Bad Smells des ersten Beitrags.

Das Anwenden der Referenzstruktur ergibt modulare Metamodelle. Um die Module solcher Metamodellen sinnvoll koppeln zu können, untersucht diese Arbeit **Metamodellerweiterungsmethoden**. Diese werden benötigt um Teile aus bestehenden Metamodellen zu extrahieren und zudem Abhängigkeiten so umzuformen, dass sie mit der Referenzstruktur konform sind.

Validierung Die automatischen Bad-Smell-Erkennungen wurden evaluiert, indem sie angewandt und die resultierenden Vorkommen manuell nach ihren negativen Auswirkungen begutachtet wurden. Durch das Beheben von Vorkommen und das erneute Ausführen der automatischen Erkennungen, wurde die Wirksamkeit der vorgeschlagenen Korrekturen evaluiert. Um die Referenzstruktur zu evaluieren, wurden vier Metamodelle nach der Referenzstruktur restrukturiert. Durch eine szenariobasierte Evaluation mit informationstheoretischen Metriken konnte gezeigt werden, dass sich die Evolvierbarkeit der modularisierten Metamodelle verbessert. Zudem verbessert sich der Metamodellnutzungsanteil, woraus sich folgern lässt, dass eine bedarfsgerechtere Nutzung und Wiederverwendung möglich ist. Die Metamodellerweiterungsmethoden wurden nach einem Kriterienkatalog bewertet und miteinander verglichen.

Contents

Part I.

Prologue

1. Introduction

Research Context In Model-driven Engineering (MDE) [Sch06], domain-specific modeling languages (DSMLs) are used to capture the concepts and reoccurring patterns of the domain. MDE is used in many domains like aviation [FGH06], automotive [Cue+10; Für+09], automation [Dra+08], mechatronics [Bec+14], business information systems [Reu+16], and business processes [Obj14].

An instance of a DSML is a model. Besides documentation and communication, models are used constructively in MDE. They are the result of the design or reengineering of a software-intensive system. During the development of a system, models are not a byproduct of the engineering process. They are central first-class artifacts. From these models, parts of the software can be generated. In MDE, models are also used analytically. They can be validated to test a static property that the system has to fulfill.

More complex aspects can be investigated by analyses and simulations that are developed for the DSML. Such analyses and simulations usually evaluate some quality properties. A metamodel that, in addition to domain concepts, also captures quality properties is referred to as a quality-describing metamodel. Quality characteristics may purely concern the software aspects of the system (e.g., performance and maintainability). They may also refer to the interplay between the software and other aspects of the system (e.g., the timing of an automated production unit), or even to aspects that do not involve software.

DSMLs can be defined by metamodels or grammars. The focus of this thesis is metamodels (Section 1.3 gives the rationale). If they are used, metamodels are the central artifact in MDE. All tools (e.g., analyses, simulators, editors, generators) depend on them. Quality properties and the results of analyses and simulators may be included in a metamodel. If they are not included, they have to be stored externally from the models in another format. The same holds for additional information that a tool needs like configuration and input data.

Challenges There is, however, the open question of how to implement multiple qualities and the data of multiple tools in a metamodel. Some tools may share parts the information they require; other tools may require completely different definitions in the metamodel. From an initial glance, there are two opposing solutions. The first solution is to integrate all information into one DSML. The second solution proposes to create a new DSML for each quality or tool. Both approaches have shortcomings, which will now be outlined.

To integrate all information into one language creates monolithic metamodels and can degrade the structure of these metamodels. This problem can be generalized into the challenge of long-term evolution. To create a new DSML for each tool poses a different set of problems. If, for example, the same system should be analyzed for two quality characteristics, and these need different languages, the system has to be modeled twice. Depending on how different the two languages are, the translation of the model into the other language may require great manual effort. This problem can be generalized into the challenge of reuse. The following paragraphs outline these two challenges. The problems that this thesis addresses are elaborated in much more detail by Chapter 3.

Evolution The long-term use of DSMLs and metamodels brings several challenges (as outlined in my past publication [SH16b]). These can be motivated by Lehman's laws. Software has to evolve to adapt to changing requirements in order to stay useful [Leh80]. Software that evolves tends to become more complex, and more effort has to be spent in its maintenance [Leh80]. As metamodels are software artifacts too, these laws also apply to metamodels. Metamodel evolution has several types of causes: new features should be expressed, features have to be adapted, and errors corrected.

The long-term evolution of a metamodel may degrade its inner structure. Amongst others, this degradation manifests in: uncontrolled growth of dependencies, feature scattering, feature lumping, inconsistent feature integration, and concept erosion. The metamodel gets more complex and looses its clear internal structuring. This leads to a decline in understandability and maintainability.

The repeated intrusive addition of features (e.g., quality or analysis information) leads to monolithic metamodels. Because of their lack of modularity, they suffer from several shortcomings. They only allow all-or-nothing reuse. The increased local complexity and feature overload make them hard to understand.

As any software artifact, metamodels should also be documented to preserve the knowledge about their elements. If this is omitted, or keeping the documentation up to date is neglected, the risk to lose essential knowledge about the metamodel rises as development team changes. By partitioning the metamodel into a meaningful package structure, some information can be encoded into the metamodel. This approach is, however, susceptible to the repercussions of long-term evolution. As the package structure degrades, so does this information.

Reuse Metamodels are often not built with reusability in mind. Lacking modularity and hard coupling within a metamodel often lead to all-or-nothing reuse. These problems can often be caused or worsened by improper evolution. Coarse-grained reuse tends to be inappropriate, as it increases the probability that the reused parts contain unnecessary constructs. This may incite developers to develop a metamodel from scratch or to branch the metamodel instead of reusing it as it is. Branches and new metamodels, however, have to be maintained on their own. This approach, thus, cause additional effort in the long run. A further problem is that branches and new metamodels are not compatible with the original metamodel, not even the parts that they may have in common. This leads to the above-mentioned drawbacks of either double modeling or translation.

A further challenge to metamodel reuse is posed by a classical tradeoff that is also known in software development. An artifact has to be general enough in order to be used in different contexts. On the other hand, it has to be specific enough to be useful. In the context of this thesis, the above-mentioned challenges of the field of quality analyses tie in. To base an analysis on a metamodel, it should not contain unnecessary details (i.e., be general enough). If, however, the concepts that are needed by the analysis are intrusively integrated into the language, the language is no longer suited as a basis for other analyses. This calls for another solution apart from all-or-nothing reuse, branching, intrusive addition, and development from scratch.

State of the Art The main fields of related work of this thesis can be categorized into metamodel composition, modularity, problem detection, and quality assessment approaches.

Language composition approaches build new languages by composing language fragments, or modifying and composing existing languages. They are well suited to reduce the effort of creating new languages. They usually strive to give as many options to modify the languages that are reused. This has the drawback, that there is, in general, no compatibility between related languages that are the result of such compositions. A set of independent languages is, unfortunately, not the solution to the problems that are stated above. Further, these language composition approaches do not take the evolution scenarios into account that are common to the field of quality analyses.

There are several approaches towards **modularity** of metamodels. They can be used to break down big metamodels in an attempt to increase their modularity and, therefore, to reduce local complexity Some may be useful as initial suggestions on how to modularize a metamodel. They, however, do not consider how the language is used that is defined by the metamodel. The internal separations that are imposed by the different ways the metamodel can be used are a much more relevant factor for modularizations. If the ways a metamodel is used are disregarded, a modularization does not improve a metamodels reusability. Another drawback is that some approaches merely partition metamodels. They do not restructure any dependencies. This does not achieve proper modularity, as often partitions are still strongly coupled and can only be used and understood together, even if that is not meaningful.

Several **problem detection** approaches, automatically inspect metamodels for metamodeling problems. Most of them do, however, not focus on maintainability, as they mainly report validity and semantic errors. Another drawback is that these approaches work reactively. They address problems after they have arisen. While this is useful, they cannot be the single final solution, even if they also addressed maintainability problems. A proactive solution is still needed to prevent the degradation of metamodels.

Approaches that provide metamodel **quality assessment** by metrics also tackle metamodel maintainability. These approaches suffer from the same drawback as error detection approaches: they work reactively. They are, nonetheless, useful for tracking the development of the quality of a metamodel. They, however, mostly do not report actual points of improvement.

Solution This thesis addresses shortcomings of the related work by providing three contributions, which build upon each other: (1) an investigation of maintainability problems in metamodels, (2) an evaluation of how to properly couple parts of metamodels, and (3) the reference structure approach for modular metamodels. The contributions (1), (2), and a large part of (3) apply to EMOF-based metamodels in general. Contribution (3) also features a specific reference structure that applies only to quality-describing metamodels. The three contributions are now briefly presented.

Metamodeling Bad-Smells To this thesis, it is essential to understand the problems that hinder metamodel evolution. It should be investigated what exactly the drawbacks of lacking modularity and monolithic metamodels are, and which problems arise from intrusive additions and long-term maintenance. This understanding is essential to solve the problems of metamodel maintenance. To achieve this, the concept of bad smells [Fow+99] is investigated. A bad smell is a symptom for a possible design flaw that degrades maintainability.

This thesis presents a collection of metamodel bad smells. They were collected from two sources. Firstly, a monolithic, long-living metamodel was reviewed that was subject to many intrusive additions. Secondly, bad smells from object-oriented design were investigated whether they are also meaningful in the scope of metamodeling. For each smell that was collected, its effect, detection, and correction are discussed. Not all smells are automatically detectable. The metamodel quality assurance tool EMF Refactor [Are14] was extended to detect a subset of these metamodel bad smells.

Metamodel Extension Mechanisms Modularity is the key to a kind of metamodel reuse that enables compatibility of the parts that are shared between languages. The parts of a metamodel, however, have to be coupled appropriately in order to form a truly modular and reusable metamodel. Unsuited dependencies between metamodel parts lead to strong coupling, which diminishes the possibilities of fine-grained reuse. This thesis investigates a particular kind of coupling: one directional extension. It can be used to add new features to existing classes without having to modify them. By doing so, it enables refactorings that are essentials to properly modularize a metamodel (e.g., dependency inversion and class split). Depending on the needs of the user, an extension can be enabled or disabled. This can be used to establish a variable language. As extension enables modularity, it addresses several of the bad smells that were identified before. Leveraging this mechanism is also beneficial to the specific field of quality analysis. Having a common core of the metamodel that is used by several qualities and analyses solves the challenge of double modeling and translation. The data that are needed to model the quality characteristics and extensions can be placed in optional extensions.

This thesis presents a list of extension mechanisms and assembles a set of comparison criteria. These also include criteria that are derived by the challenges of reuse. Those criteria enforce, for example, unintrusiveness, compatibility of instances, and independent extensibility.

Reference Structure for Quality Analyses As a basis for quality analyses, a modular and variable language is already a move in the right direction. Such a modular structure is, however, also subject to long-term maintenance and erosion. Instead of an unstructured set of extensions, a more explicit structuring is required. To prevent the development of harmful couplings over time, the dependencies have to restricted, and the developer properly guided.

To establish this, this thesis transfers modularity concepts (e.g., modules, layers), and best-practices (e.g., acyclicity, dependency inversion) from related disciplines. These modularity concepts are enabled by the metamodel extension mechanisms. This thesis proposes an approach to metamodel modularization that divides a metamodel according to its language features. A language feature represents a unit of use. The features of a language are explicitly expressed by a feature model. The individual features are linked to the modules of the metamodel. This feature model is utilized by the user to select the metamodel modules s/he wants to use in his model. It is also used by the metamodel developer to navigate the metamodel, to place new extensions, and to align new dependencies. The feature model and its metamodel modules are partitioned according to layers, which further restrict dependencies.

The aforementioned approach applies to metamodels in general. This thesis also provides a reference structure for metamodels of the field of quality analysis. It proposes four layers that separate fundamental patterns, domain, quality, and analysis information. This separation supports the common evolution scenarios of the field by leveraging the variability that is enabled by metamodel extension. It supports multiple quality characteristics and analysis data and does not fall into the trap of intrusive addition, branching, or all-or-nothing reuse.

Validation The three contributions of this thesis are evaluated as follows.

The implemented bad smell detections were applied onto a metamodel. The detection hits were manually investigated for whether they are correct and harmful. All hits represent occurrences according to the definitions of their smells. This can be seen as a partial confirmation of the correctness of the detections. Except for one detection, meaningful corrections could be manually identified that improved the metamodel at the reported occurrences. This can be seen as an argument that these smells can indicate improvement potential. For each smell, corrections were performed on its occurrences. After each correction, the bad smell detections were performed a second time. Each correction resulted in the addressed occurrence no longer being detected. This demonstrates that the applied corrections are effective and evaluates the correctness of the detections a second time.

The metamodel extension mechanisms were evaluated according to the comparison criteria. This enables a comparison of the ext mechanisms. For a set of scenarios that occur in metamodel extension, it allowed determining the extension mechanisms that fit best for the individual scenarios.

Four case study metamodels were refactored to adhere to the reference structure. On these four metamodels, two evaluations were conducted.

A scenario-based evaluation used information-theory-based metrics to analyze the effect of the reference structure on the evolvability of the metamodels. For each metamodel, a set of evolution scenarios were collected. Based on each scenario, the part of the metamodel was determined that is relevant for the scenario. On these metamodel parts, the information-theory-based metrics were applied. The evaluation shows that the evolvability of the metamodels improved by applying the reference structure approach.

The second evaluation investigates how the reference structure influences the degree to which the metamodels allow need-driven usage and reuse. For each case study metamodel, a set of models were collected. The evaluation analyzed the ratio of how much of a metamodel has to be deployed and how much is used by the individual models. This allowed concluding the reference structure approach enables fine-grained use and reuse.

Outline The remainder of this introduction is structured as follows. Section 1.1 explains the scope of this thesis. Section 1.2 motivates the case for good metamodel design. Section 1.3 elaborates on the commonalities and differences of metamodeling and object-oriented design.

This thesis is structured into four parts. The first part is the Prologue, which contains this introduction. Chapter 2 presents the foundations and terminology on that this thesis is based. Chapter 3 presents the problems that this thesis addresses. The Contribution part contains the chapters for the three contributions of this thesis. Chapter 4 presents the contribution about bad smells in metamodeling. Chapter 5 contains the metamodel extension contribution. Chapter 6 presents the the reference structure approach. The Validation part contains the evaluations of the contributions. Chapter 7 features the detection and correction evaluation of the metamodel bad smells contribution. Chapter 8 evaluates and compares the extension mechanisms from the metamodel extension contribution. Chapter 9 presents the four case studies that were refactored according to the reference structure approach. Chapter 10 validates the reference structure approach on the basis of the case studies from the previous chapter. The Epilogue part concludes this thesis. Chapter 11 elaborates on related work. Chapter 12 summarizes the contributions and their validation, discusses limitations, and presents future work. The Appendix contains supplementary material. Appendix A contains the full result of the evaluation of the bad smell contribution.

Appendix B explains how the modularization concepts of the reference structure are mapped to technical concepts. Appendix C presents the tool that was used for the evaluation of the reference structure approach. The index is a powerful resource to find the location where a term is explained.

1.1. Scope

The contribution of this thesis is focused on EMOF-based metamodels. This section explains the rationale behind this decision.

A language can be defined by a metamodel or a grammar. Both approaches are equal in expressiveness. This means every language can be expressed by a metamodel or a grammar. Metamodel- as well as grammar-based languages can both feature textual as well as graphical syntaxes. There are, however, subtle differences. Metamodels focus on classes, their relations, and attributes. They are convenient for the construction of graphical syntaxes, as usually graphical diagram elements are mapped onto most classes. Grammars, on the other hand, emphasize the containment of terminals. They are well suited to provide textual syntaxes. In the field of modeling languages, however, metamodels are widely used. Therefore, this thesis focuses on metamodels. As grammars and metamodels are similar, some parts of the approach of this thesis may also apply to the technical space of grammar-based modeling language engineering. This is, however, not the focus of this thesis.

There are several metalanguages, that can be used to express metamodels. This thesis focuses on MOF-based metamodels (see Section 2.2.1). The reason for this is, MOF is an open international standard, that is widely used. EMOF is one of two compliance level of the MOF standard. This thesis focuses on EMOF, as it is much more established than the other compliance level CMOF. EMF's Ecore[1] is a free implementation of EMOF for Eclipse. As EMF is open source, many supporting tools and frameworks were developed for EMF (e.g., code generators, transformation languages, editor frameworks). In contrast to CMOF, EMOF has no practical shortcomings (see Section 2.2.1).

[1] `https://www.eclipse.org/modeling/emf/` (last visited 23.08.2019)

However, most contributions of this thesis are also applicable to non-EMOF metamodels that support concepts that are similar to or can be mapped to EMOF concepts (classifiers, attributes, references, and the ability to depend on classifiers of other metamodels). This is, however, not the focus of this thesis.

1.2. Why Good Metamodel Design is Important

This section[2] briefly motivates why a particular focus should be put on metamodels. A good metamodel design is essential, as metamodel debt (technical debt in metamodels) accumulates over time and is the costlier, the more dependencies exist onto the metamodel. There are four reasons why good design is crucial: tight coupling, much dependent software, modifications in generated code, and challenges in regeneration.

By the nature of metamodels, software that is dependent on it is tightly coupled with it. From the outside, every class of a metamodel can be referenced, and every concrete class can be instantiated. This means that in principle, each intrusive modification of a metamodel has implications onto external code. The more code depends on the metamodel, the higher is the impact of the change.

The challenge of tight coupling is intensified by the fact, that in metamodel-centric systems, many modules or programs are dependent on the metamodel. Examples of such code can be editors, transformations, validators, analyzers, and simulators. When changing the metamodel intrusively, all these programs have to be adapted. Depending on the type of program, this can be done with relatively little effort if the logic of the program is oriented heavily on the structure of the metamodel (e.g., editors, validators). However, if an external functionality is implemented (e.g., a model is interpreted), the change impact can be grave. A related issue is the migration effort for models that are instances of the metamodel that was modified. The more modifications were applied to the metamodel, the more effort is necessary to update its models.

[2] This section is based on [SH16b].

Modifications that were made to generated code (e.g., model code, editor code) pose another challenge. For changes of the metamodel to take effect, it is necessary to regenerate the code from the metamodel. In general, manual changes to the generated code are lost, as soon as the code is regenerated from the metamodel. These changes then have to be reapplied to the generated code. The more changes have been made to the generated code, the more of a burden it becomes to regenerate and reapply the changes. This can go as far that the process of regeneration is delayed until a certain number of changes to the metamodel has accumulated. It is even possible that changing the metamodel is avoided at all. As a workaround, it is possible to automate the reapplication of the changes. However, this reapplication is dependent on the metamodel structure. If the structure changes, the reapplication mechanism has to be co-evolved.

The challenge of modified generated code is intensified by generated code remnants. When regenerating generated code, only existing classes are regenerated (they overwrite existing code). However, if a class is deleted or renamed, the deleted class or the class with the old name is not automatically deleted in the model code. If there were no changes to the generated code, the complete code could just be manually deleted and regenerated, thereby ensuring a consistent code base. If this is done with a modified code base, the changes are lost. When generating over existing code, these code remnants have to be kept in mind. External code is still able to compile, but will not incorporate the metamodel changes if remnant classes are used. The resulting errors are masked by the outdated code and thus are not easily identified.

1.3. The Relation of Metamodeling and Object-oriented Design

Metamodeling is related to object-oriented design. Both fields describe classes, their attributes, relations, inheritance hierarchies, and partitioning into packages. As object-oriented design is more mature, several useful concepts were established there. One goal of this thesis is to transfer concepts from object-oriented design and related disciplines to metamodeling.

On the other hand, however, object-oriented design and metamodeling are not the same. Concepts for reuse and design principles cannot be simply transferred from object-oriented design as they are. Their benefit cannot just be assumed but has to be evaluated. To substantiate this claim, the remainder of this section explains the differences between metamodeling and object-oriented design.

In object orientation, the sum of classes defines a program. The classes are used by instantiation. Their objects contain data, which is manipulated through methods. These objects reside in the heap memory and are referenced by variables. A developer operates mostly on the internals of a class and its methods through a textual view. For a user of the software, its classes and objects are not visible.

In metamodeling, the sum of classes defines a language. In contrast to object-orientation, the classes have to form a containment hierarchy. This means each class that is not contained has instances that are roots of separate model files. The classes are not used to be instantiated, but to generate code. The generated code is then instantiated, to represent models in the memory. The data that is carried by the objects is also important in metamodeling. In contrast to object orientation, however, the object itself and its relation to other objects are much more relevant than its methods. The objects are persisted in model files. The developer interacts with metamodels mostly through inter class views, which are either graphical diagrams or tress of classes and packages. The user interacts with the instances of the classes of a metamodel directly through graphical or textual representations.

In conclusion, metamodeling and object-oriented design are similar but not the same. Object-orientation has a strong focus on the internals of a class (e.g., its attributes and methods). Metamodeling focuses more on the inter-class level (i.e., dependencies). These differences determine differences in what is relevant for the maintainability of metamodel and object-oriented designs.

2. Foundations and Terminology

This chapter introduces the foundations of this thesis. It defines terminology that is important to this thesis. The index at the end of this thesis can also be used for a quick look-up of terms. This chapter is structured as follows. Section 2.1 explains the fundamental concepts of languages and models. Section 2.2 provides the foundations of metamodeling. Section 2.3 describes the concept of quality-describing DSMLs and metamodels. Section 2.4 explains feature models. Section 2.5 provides several topics that are relevant to the validation of this thesis. Section 2.6 presents the graphical notation that this thesis uses.

2.1. Languages and Modeling

In contrast to natural languages, computer languages are formalized to make their instances machine processable. For the sake of brevity, this thesis refers to a computer language simply as *language*. Languages can be further subdivided into programming languages and modeling languages. The main purpose of a *programming languages* is for their instances (i.e., code) to be executed. The purpose of *modeling languages*, on the other hand, is to specify information about a subject. Instances of a modeling language (i.e., models) are used for various purposes: design, documentation, communication, analysis, and generation of other artifacts. The boundary between programming and modeling languages is, however, blurry. Lately, executable modeling languages are being researched [Rum02; May+13]. On the other hand, a programming language can also be seen an abstraction (i.e., a model of computation).

Instances of modeling languages are *models*. The term model also has a more general meaning, which is also applicable to instances of modeling languages. According to Stachowiak [Sta73], a model represents a subject, leaves out unnecessary details and has a purpose.

Models and modeling languages are heavily used in Model-Driven Engineering (MDE) and Model-Driven Software Development (MDSD). In MDSD [SV06], modeling languages are created to capture reoccurring code in the domain. Instances of such modeling languages are then used for code generation. The generated code has to usually be completed with code that is individual to the current software product and, therefore, cannot be generated. In MDE [Sch06], on the other hand, code generation is not the main goal of the use of models. Modeling languages are used for designing and reasoning about systems (i.e., analysis, simulation, verification). MDE is not intended for pure software projects, but the development of software-intensive systems.

In addition to programming and modeling, there is another distinction dimension that is orthogonal to the former. *General-purpose languages* (GPLs) are opposed to special-purpose or *domain-specific languages* (DSLs) [FP10]. A GPL is general enough to be applied for any purpose. A DSL has a limited scope of application and expressiveness. It is, however, much more specialized on its purpose and should, therefore, be more efficient in its used. Examples for the different language variant are Java as a programming GPL, SQL as a programming DSL, UML as a modeling GPL, and PCM as a modeling DSL.

A domain-specific modeling language is also referred to as a *DSML*. DSMLs are the main scope of this thesis; even though some concepts may also apply to the other variants (especially modeling GPLs). A DSML captures reoccurring patterns and concepts of a domain and makes them reusable.

A language consists of abstract syntax, concrete syntax and semantics. An *abstract syntax* can be defined by a grammar or a metamodel. It defines what valid instances of a language are. The *concrete syntax* defines how an instance of the language is displayed. Usually, a concrete syntax of a language is either textual or graphical. A *graphical syntax* is usually a diagram with two-dimensional shape and connectors. Lately, however, more special kinds of concrete syntaxes appeared. Examples are the tabular syntax and the formulaic syntax as featured by MPS [VS10]. A language also has semantics. The *static semantics* imposes further constraints onto the instances of the language that cannot be expressed in the abstract syntax. The *dynamic semantics* describes how the elements of an instance are executed.

There can exist several tools that operate on a language. For grammar-based programming languages, these are usually tools like compiler and interpreter. For metamodel-based languages, there can be analyses, simulators, transformations, validators. In the scope of this thesis, these are referred to as *metamodel-based tools*. An *analysis* processes an instance of a language and produces a set of metrics. A *simulator* [Ban+00] is similar to an analysis, with the distinction that a simulator has a concept of time and an internal state that changes over the simulated time. *Transformations* [CH03; MG06] process instances and produce another artifact based on the input. Depending on the type of transformation the result may be an instance of the same metamodel, another metamodel or even something completely different. In this regard, the definition of a transformation overlaps with the definition of analysis. A transformation that produces code is also named a *generator* [Jun16a]. A transformation that adds elements to an instance and only alters existing elements to include the new elements is named a *completion* [Hap+14]. A *validator* traverses the structure of an instance and checks for the compliance to one or multiple characteristic or constraints. Validators are often defined by the static semantics that is in-built in a metamodel. There can, however, also be other external validators that check for something else. A validator can be seen as a special kind of analysis that produces one or multiple Boolean results.

This thesis uses a particular terminology to address what is expressed by a modeling language. A *modeling concept* (or concept in short) is a subject that is expressed by a modeling language. Examples for concepts are a person, a software component, a building, or an action in a business process. A concept can either be first- or second-class. A *first-class* concept can exist on its own. A *second-class* concept cannot exist on its own. Its existence is either directly bound to a first-class concept or indirectly bound to a first-class concept via one or multiple other second-class concepts. A *core concept* is a concept that is always instantiated in a model when the language is used. An *abstraction* is the specification of a concept in a metamodel (or grammar) in a way that leaves out unnecessary details. The notion of first- and second-class does also apply to abstractions, as abstractions relate one-to-one to concepts.

2.2. Metamodeling

This section presents the foundations of metamodeling. It is structured as follows. Section 2.2.1 presents the Meta Object Facility metamodeling framework that is fundamental to this thesis. Section 2.2.2 explains metamodels and their terminology. Section 2.2.3 elaborates on metamodel use and reuse. Section 2.2.4 introduces terminology from view-driven modeling. Section 2.2.5 provides the foundations of metamodel evolution. Section 2.2.6 elaborates on metamodel quality. Section 2.2.7 introduces the term bad smell. Section 2.2.8 elaborates on metrics. Section 2.2.9 presents the EMF Refactor approach. Section 2.2.10 explains the roles that are involved in metamodeling and the use of metamodels.

2.2.1. Meta Object Facility

The *Meta Object Facility (MOF)* [Obj16] is an international standard of the Object Management Group (OMG) that defines a metamodeling framework. It provides two levels of compliance: *Complete MOF (CMOF)* and *Essential MOF (EMOF)*. CMOF includes EMOF and makes some extensions on it. It enhances its reflection and tagging capabilities. MOF does only make one constraint regarding the number of modeling levels. There have to be at least two: the MOF level and the level containing MOF instances. Usually, however, three explicit modeling levels are used: the meta-metalevel M3 that contains MOF, the metalevel M2 that contains metamodels, and the model level M1. As MOF does not constrain the number of levels, even more levels may be possible. M1 could be used to instantiate another level. Usually, however, M1 is the level that is utilized by the user. EMOF has been implemented by the *Eclipse Modeling Framework (EMF)*. EMF extends the integrated development environment (IDE) Eclipse. It provides the EMOF conformant metamodel format *Ecore*. It further provides an Ecore editor and a code generator for Ecore metamodels. Applied on a metamodel M1, the code generator generates its model code and rudimentary editors. The editor can be used to create instances of M1 (i.e., models). The model code is needed to programmatically create models and represent them in-memory. EMF provides the functionality for the serialization and deserialization of models.

2.2.2. EMOF-based Metamodels

As already mentioned, EMOF defines a metamodeling language. This means its instances are metamodels. EMOF provides concepts similar to that of class diagrams. An EMOF-based metamodel implements the abstractions that the language provides by classifiers and their properties. A *classifier* is either a metaclass, data type or enumeration.

In the scope of this thesis, a metaclass is merely referred to as a *class*. Classes can own several class properties. This thesis refers to the properties of classes as class properties to distinguish them from properties in the general sense. The types of *class properties* are attribute, reference, inheritance, operations, and constraints. All of these class properties introduce dependencies to other classifiers. In EMOF, an *abstraction* is implemented either by a class, multiple classes with relations, or even a class property. An instance of a class in an *object*. Classes can be abstract. An *abstract* class cannot be instantiated.

An *attribute* is typed by a data type or enumeration. It has a lower and upper multiplicity bound. For example, a lower and upper bound of 1 means that the attribute holds precisely one value. A lower bound of 0 and an upper bound of $*$ means that there may be an arbitrary number of values.

A *reference* from a class C1 to class C2 establishes a "knows a" relation from C1 to C2. C1 and C2 may be the same class. A reference also has a lower and upper multiplicity bound. Two references can be assigned as their respective *opposites*. This establishes a bidirectional reference.

An *inheritance* relation points to another class. In the context of the inheritance relation, the class that owns the inheritance relation is named the *subclass*. The class to that the inheritance relation points is named the *superclass*. The inheritance relation establishes an "is a" relation from the subclass to its superclass. The subclass inherits all class properties from its superclasses. In EMOF, multiple inheritance is allowed. In Ecore, the conflicts that can be caused by multiple inheritance are prevented by forbidding two attributes or relations from having the same name. In this thesis, the graph that is constituted by classes and inheritance relations is referred to as the *class hierarchy* of a metamodel. A further inheritance related term is *intermediate class*. Consider the classes C1 and C2 that are connected via a chain of inheritance relations. C1 indirectly inherits from C2. This means there is at least one more class between C1 and C2. In the scope of this thesis, these classes are refered to as intermediate classes. From the viewpoint of C1, they are *intermediate superclasses.* From the viewpoint of C2, they are *intermediate subclasses.*

A special type of reference is the *containment* reference. It establishes a "has part" relation. A class that has a containment to a second class is referred to as the *container* of the second class. A non-abstract class that is not contained anywhere but has outgoing containments is named a *root container.* A containment implies that instances of the contained class can be contained in an instance of the container. In this thesis, the graph that is constituted by classes and containments is referred to as the *containment hierarchy* of a metamodel.

A containment reference may have an opposite reference. This opposite is named a *container reference*, as it references a container. The multiplicity bounds of a container reference can either be "0..1" or "1..1". Higher bounds are not possible, as an object can only be contained within one other object at a time. If a class has a container reference with "1..1" multiplicity bounds, its instances can only be contained in the container that is referenced.

A class that is the target of a containment is considered as *directly contained* by its container (i.e., the class that owns the containment). A class that can be reached from another class by following a path of at least two containment relations and reversed inheritance relations is referred to as *indirectly contained* by the second class. In most cases, in which the distinction is not relevant, classes that are directly or indirectly contained will be referred to simply as contained. The concept of indirect containment is meaningful, as the effect of containment is transitive. Consider three classes C1, C2, and C3. C1 contains C2. C2 contains C3. An instance of C1 contains an instance of C2, which may contain an instance of C3. The instance of C3 is therefore indirectly contained in C1. Subclasses in the containment chain do also contribute to the indirect containment. Consider C4 that inherits from C2. Instances of C4 are therefore also instances of C2. As an instance of C1 can contain instances of C2 it can also contain instances of C4. C1 is, therefore, an indirect container of C4.

A class can also contain constraints and operations. Constraints can be expressed, for example, with the Object Constraint Language (OCL) [Obj06], and constitute the static semantics of the language. Operations are not explicitly supported by MOF. Its tagging extension mechanism, however, supports the addition of arbitrary information to metamodels. The EMF code generator supports specific types of tags, which enable to express operations. Operations have a name, a parameter list, and an operation body. During code generation, operations are inserted into the model code. They may carry helper functions to process the data of the class, or may even implement parts of the dynamic semantics of the language.

Generics are a further feature, which is not specified by MOF but added by EMF. They work the same way as generics in object-oriented programming. Classes may have type parameters. These can be referred to by the properties of the class. When inheriting, the type parameters may be assigned a concrete type by a type argument. Type parameters can also have type bounds, which specify that the used type has to be more general or more specific as another type.

In this thesis, *class dependency* is the umbrella term for a relation from a class to a classifier. If the context is unambiguous, class dependencies are referred to merely as dependencies. All class properties cause dependencies. Attributes, references, inheritances, cause a dependency to the classifier that is the target of the class property. Generics contribute further dependencies to the classifiers that are referred to by type bounds and type arguments. Operations and constraints also cause dependencies to the classifiers that they use in the constraint and operation body, and the operation's parameter list. If a figure illustrates a dependency but it is irrelevant what kind of class property causes the dependency, the *arbitrary dependency* arrow is used.

In addition to classes, there are two other classifiers: data types and enumerations. A *data type* expresses a primitive type (e.g., a Boolean or a number). *Enumerations* or enums function analogously to their counterpart from object orientation. An enum specifies a list of literals. An attribute or variable that is typed with the enum holds one of the literals as a value.

The classifiers of a metamodel are organized in a *package structure* (by some referred to as package hierarchy). A *package* can contain classifiers and other packages. In the simplest case, the hierarchy of a metamodel consists of one package. The package structure of a metamodel does not influence its semantics. A package gives its elements a namespace. In addition to that, it is used by metamodel developers to group classifiers that are related.

In the scope of this thesis, a *metamodel element* is any constituent. This includes classifiers, packages, and class properties.

EMOF-based metamodels are persisted in files. This thesis refers to these files as *metamodel files*. A metamodel file usually has one package as a root element that in turn may contain further packages and classifiers. It is, however, possible for a metamodel file to contain multiple root packages. Although the terms metamodel and metamodel file are often blurred, this thesis draws a distinction. In the scope of this thesis, a metamodel consists of one metamodel file or of several metamodel files that depend upon each other. A dependency from one metamodel file F1 to another metamodel file F2 is caused by a class of F1 being dependent on a classifier of F2. As mentioned above, on the classifier level, a dependency is caused, for example, by a reference, inheritance, or attribute. For a dependency between two metamodel files to exist, the number of dependent classifiers and the type of dependency is irrelevant. It is merely sufficient if one classifier of F1 depends on a classifier of F2. In the scope of this thesis, the term *structure* of a metamodel refers to the metamodel files, their dependencies amongst each other, and their package structures.

The concept of metamodel files does also translate to the model level. A *model* consists of one or multiple model files. A *model file* contains objects (i.e., instances of classes). In this thesis, the objects of a model are referred to as *model elements*. A model file has a *root object*, which is the instance of a root container. This root object directly or indirectly contains all other elements of the model.

2.2.3. Metamodel Use and Reuse

A metamodel is *used* by tool user through the tools that are based on the metamodel. They create and modify models using editors or transformations. Many more types of tools can be used to process models. These types of tools were mentioned by Section 2.1. Tools depend on metamodels by referring to their classes in their code. For a user to be able to use a metamodel-based tool, the tool has to be installed, and the metamodel files on that the tool depends on have to be deployed. In the scope of this thesis, *deploying* a metamodel file means to install its compiled model code. In order to deploy a metamodel file, all metamodel files on that it depends on have also to be deployed. In EMF, the model code is compiled into an Eclipse plugin, which has to be installed in the Eclipse instance of the user.

When developing a new metamodel, there are several ways to *reuse* other metamodels or parts thereof. One way is to depend on a metamodel file of another metamodel by references, containments, attributes, or inheritances. The drawback of this approach is that the whole metamodel file and all of its dependencies have to be used as is. Possibly unneeded metamodel elements are still present in the reused metamodel files. Another approach to metamodel reuse is simple copy and paste. The copied metamodel elements are inserted into a metamodel file of the new metamodel. This decouples the development of these metamodel elements from their original metamodel, and they can be modified as needed. For example, unnecessary metamodel elements can be removed. This approach, however, suffers from the usual drawbacks that are also known from code duplication. Maintenance tasks that are meaningful in the context of both languages have to be performed in both metamodels. The third approach to metamodel reuse are language composition approaches, which weave together metamodel files or possibly parametrized metamodel fragments. Section 11.3.1.1 presents such approaches in detail.

2.2.4. Views and View Types

In view-based modeling, models are not interacted with directly but through views. Examples for view-based modeling approach are Vitruvius [Kra+15] and OSM [ASB10], which are presented by Section 11.3.1.1. This thesis does not build on view-based approaches. It, however, relies on some of their terms [GBB12].

A *view* offers access to one or multiple models. A view is usually tailored to the concern of a role, a specific task of a role, or even the needs of a tool. It may limit access to a model, merge several models, and alter model elements. A *view type* provides the type system for views. This means a view is an instance of a view type.

Views are transient, which means that they are usually not persisted. The underlying models persist the relevant data. Modifications of views are propagated into the underlying models. Views may be persisted for the purpose of caching to increase performance.

In the metamodel-based technology space, a view type is a metamodel, and a view as an instance of a view type is a model file. There is a transformation between the view type and the metamodel or metamodels that the view operates on to propagate changes.

Looking at non-view-based modeling in terms of view-based modeling, a model file can be seen as a simple view. A root container provides root objects for model files. As a metamodel may have multiple root containers, it can also have multiple kinds of model files. In the literature, these are sometimes referred to as sub-model [Bus+16]. Examples for such simple views or sub-models are the repository, assembly and resource environment of the PCM.

2.2.5. Metamodel Evolution

This section[1] presents several aspects of metamodel evolution. First, the causes of metamodel evolution and a coarse classification of metamodel modifications are presented. Section 2.2.5.1 presents a detailed classification according to its impact. Section 2.2.5.2 explains the notion of refactorings.

There are several types of *causes for metamodel maintenance.* If new requirements arise after the metamodel has been specified, content may have to be added. This is also the case if requirements did not change, but have not been met yet and have to still be implemented. Fixing an error or implementing the change of a requirement does also necessitate metamodel modifications.

Regarding how *modifications* can be realized and how they affect metamodel files, they can be classified into two categories: changes and additions. A *change* alters (deletion, property change) the content of a metamodel, while an *addition* adds new metamodel elements.

Sometimes, changes are unavoidable, especially if errors have to be fixed in the metamodel. A change can either be implemented intrusively in the metamodel or as a branch. The benefit of intrusive modification is that the shared metamodel is kept identical for all dependent software. However, the

[1] This section is based on my past publication [SH16b].

modification also affects all dependent software artifacts, which have to be adapted to be again compatible with the metamodel. In contrast, creating a branch and applying the modification only to that branch has the benefit that only the software has to be adapted that is of interest to that modification. The development of the branch is decoupled from the development cycle of the main branch. Modifications in the main branch's metamodel do not impose any modifications of the software which works on the separate branch. However, this has the disadvantage that the branch and software that uses it gradually get more and more incompatible to the main branch.

An addition can be implemented intrusively, in a branch, or externally in a new metamodel file. External additions have the advantage that the original metamodel is not altered.

The effort caused by metamodel changes increases the later the changes are carried out. E.g., it is easy to change a metamodel while it is being designed or initially implemented. It gets more and more costly to modify it after it has been implemented and further software is developed on top of it. Thus, delaying refactorings has dormant consequences. If modifications are not carried out, new functionality cannot be supported, and bugs cannot be fixed which leads to an increase in technical (metamodel) debt.

2.2.5.1. Metamodel Modification Types

In his dissertation [Her11b], Herrmannsdörfer classifies metamodel modification types into primitive and composite modifications. A primitive modification is atomic; a composite modification is a sequence of primitive modifications. For this thesis, only the primitive modification types are relevant. The primitive modification types are further subdivided into structural and non-structural modification types. Structural modifications add or remove metamodel elements; Non-structural modifications manipulate metamodel elements.

In their paper [BG10], Burger and Gruschko present a metamodel that describes modifications of MOF-based metamodels. They first classify modifications into existence modifications, property changes, and link changes. They also do this from the viewpoint of model metamodel co-evolution.

This thesis slightly alters the classification, because of two reasons. First, it is only concerned with the effect of modifications on the metamodel level and not with their influence on models. Second, this thesis focuses on EMOF, which is a subset of MOF. Thus, not all modification types of Burger and Gruschko are relevant to this thesis. One major difference is that EMOF does not support first-class associations, but the concept of second-class references that belong to the source class. Adjusting the classification of Burger and Gruschko allows to later make statements about groups of modification types that have the same impact on the metamodel. The list of modification operations by Burger and Gruschko is further complemented with the help of the dissertation of Herrmannsdörfer [Her11b] and by inspecting the Ecore meta-metamodel. In this thesis, modification types are also classified into existence modifications and value changes. Figure 2.1 illustrates the classification.

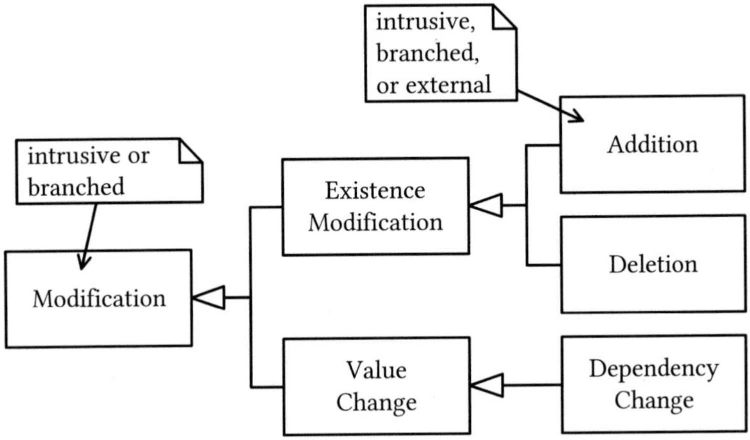

Figure 2.1.: Metamodel Modification Classification

Existence modifications are additions and deletions of metamodel elements. In Ecore, there are existence modifications of the following metamodel elements: packages, classes, data types, enumerations, enumeration literals, attributes, references, operations, and constraints. The addition of References, Attributes, and Operations does not establish a dependency to another metamodel element. This is not done until the value of the type is set to the class to which the dependency should point to. Setting the type does not belong to the existence modifications category, but to the dependency changes category. On the other hand, a deletion of a metamodel element E will remove all dependencies that are held by E. If these dependencies are unset or removed by dependency changes before the deletion of E, no dependencies are changed by the deletion itself. Without loss of generality, deletions are defined to have no effects on dependencies. The same principle applies for incoming dependencies. Before a classifier can be deleted, all dependencies that point to the classifier have to be unset.

Value changes modify the value of a metamodel element that does not establish, remove or modify dependencies between metamodel elements. In Ecore, the relevant properties for the metamodel element types are as follows.

Package Name, Namespace Prefix, Namespace URI

Classes Name, IsAbstract, IsInterface

Enumerations and DataTypes Name, IsSerializable, and Default Value

Enumeration Literals Name, Value, and Literal

Attributes and References Name, IsChangeable, Default Value, IsDerived, Ordered, IsTransient, IsUnique, IsUnsettable, IsIdentifier (only for Attributes)

Operations and Constraints Name, IsOrdered, IsUnique

Dependency changes establish, redirect, or remove dependencies between metamodel elements. These changes concern the following values: supertypes of classes, the package of classifiers, and exception references of operations. For attributes, references, operations, type bounds, and type arguments this includes the type. For references the following values are included: IsContainment, IsContainer, and Opposite. For references, attributes, operations, and constraints this includes the lower multiplicity bound and the upper multiplicity bound.

2.2.5.2. Metamodel Refactoring

Refactoring is a term that stems from object orientation [Fow+99]. It means to modify code to improve its quality without altering its functionality and semantics. Mens and Tourwe [MT04] provide a survey of the field of software refactoring. When transferred to metamodeling, a *metamodel refactoring* modifies a metamodel without changing its semantics and expressiveness. Conceptually, this means that there has to exist a bidirectional transformation between the initial and the modified metamodel versions that fulfills the following requirement. Figure 2.2 illustrates the requirement. The transformation has to be able to transform all possible instance of one metamodel version into the other and back again. The initial and the transformed version of the instance have to be identical for a set of modifications to be considered a refactoring. This must be possible for instances starting from the initial and the modified version of the metamodel. Iovino, Di Ruscio, and Pierantonio provide a catalog[2] of metamodel refactorings. Metamodel refactorings can either be performed manually or by using tools (e.g., EMF Refactor as described by Section 2.2.9, or Edelta [Bet+17]).

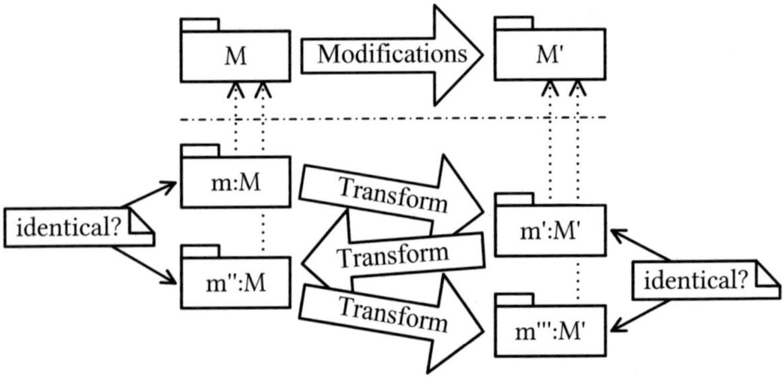

Figure 2.2.: Requirement for Modifications to be Considered a Refactoring

[2] `http://www.metamodelrefactoring.org/` (last visited 23.08.2019)

2.2.6. Metamodel Quality

Metamodel quality can be subdivided into several quality characteristics. There are several works that either address metamodel quality in general, elaborate specific characteristics, or implement ways to inspect characteristics. This section, first, presents these works. It then discusses the characteristics that are relevant for this thesis and refers to these sources. Metamodel quality is, however, still a research field and characteristics are still discussed and adjusted. Therefore, the characteristics are adapted, extended or linked to other characteristics, where it is meaningful.

Bertoa and Vallecillo [BV10] transfer the quality model for software from the ISO/IEC standard 9126 [ISO01] to modeling. Their classification is staged into characteristics, sub-characteristics, and attributes. They substantiate the entries of their classification by further sources. The characteristics are functionality, reliability, usability, efficiency, maintainability, and portability. Their classification is extensive. Only a subset, however, applies to the metamodel level. Some characteristics and sub-characteristics are described very briefly, which makes it hard to operationalize them. In our past publication, Hinkel [Hin+16] adapted the quality characteristics of Bertoa and Vallecillo [BV10] into complexity, understandability, conciseness, modularity, consistency, completeness, correctness, changeability, instance creation, and transformations. The publication, however, only contains descriptions for some characteristics. The ISO/IEC standard 25010 [ISO11] superseded 9126 [ISO01]. Like its predecessor, it proposes a quality model for software in general. Therefore, not all of its characteristics and sub-characteristics can be transferred to metamodeling. In our past publication [HSR19], Heinrich breaks metamodel evolvability down into modifiability and analyzability.

The *correctness* of a metamodel refers to whether a metamodel expresses the abstractions it is supposed to. This means whether it is able to express all the instances it is supposed to without any unnecessary information. Correctness can be further split into two dimensions: completeness and preciseness. To be able to describe these terms, the term *set of intended models (IM)* has to be introduced. IM contains all models that the metamodel should be able to express. It is, therefore, potentially infinite. A correct metamodel is complete as well as precise. An incorrect metamodel is incomplete, imprecise, or both.

The *preciseness* [GBS12] of a metamodel specifies to which degree a metamodel is able to only allow models from IM. E.g., an imprecise metamodel allows to model irrelevant concept. A precise metamodel does not allow any models that are not in IM. Preciseness is also related to the relevance and correctness sub-characteristics of Bertoa [BV10].

The *completeness* [BV10] of a metamodel specifies to which degree a metamodel is able to express the models of IM. A complete metamodel can express all models of IM. For an incomplete metamodel, there are models in IM that it cannot express. Metamodel completeness can be seen as an adaption of the functional completeness sub-characteristic of software products [ISO11]. The completeness characteristic is addressed by the approach of Ferdjoukh and Mottu [FM18].

The *reusability* of a metamodel refers to how well parts of the metamodel can be reused for other languages. For example, it is detrimental for the reusability of a metamodel if the metamodel is too specific. If parts of the metamodel are reused by other languages, they contain irrelevant abstraction. This means they are imprecise in their new context. The problem of too high specificity can be alleviated by improved modularity. By separating abstract concepts from their specifics, the concepts are more suited for reuse. The definition of metamodel reusability is an adaption of the reusability sub-characteristic of the ISO/IEC 25010 standard [ISO11].

A the *extensibility* of a metamodel refers to how well it lends itself to be the basis of extensions. A metamodel is suited for extensions if the extension can be applied in the metamodel in a way that includes no irrelevant abstractions when the extension is used. In this regard, metamodel reusability is analogous to metamodel reusability. A monolithic metamodel with many specifics has bad extensibility. A modular metamodel that separates the specifics from its abstractions offers a proper basis for extensions.

The *modularity* of a metamodel is "the extent that its parts are systematically structured and separated such that they can be understood in isolation" [BV10, p. 9]. Strong coupling of many parts of a metamodel degrades its modularity. Parts of a metamodel should only be coupled if it is necessary. This is the case when dependencies cannot be avoided or modeled differently. One way to measure the perceived modularity of a metamodel is given by Hinkel in our publication [HS18].

The *evolvability* of a metamodel refers to how well the metamodel can be evolved. In our past publication [HSR19], Heinrich elaborates on evolvability. Starting from the evolvability model ob Breivold [BCE08] and the ISO/IEC standard 25010 [ISO11], he transfers the characteristics to metamodeling that are meaningful in this context. He breaks evolvability down into analyzability and modifiability. He argues that these two characteristics correspond to structural complexity, which also includes complexity-based measures of cohesion and coupling.

The *analyzability* [BV10] of a metamodel refers to how easy it is to inspect it for deficits or to identify parts of the metamodel that have to be modified. Analyzability is influenced by modularity [BV10]. This makes sense, as proper modularity of a metamodel limits the amount of information a developer is exposed to when examining the parts of a metamodel. This definition of analyzability also corresponds to the analyzability sub-characteristic of the ISO/IEC standard 25010 [ISO11].

The *understandability* is "the degree in which a metamodel is self-describing", as stated by Hinkel in our past publication [Hin+16, p. 3]. The understandability of a metamodel is influenced by its complexity [BV10]. Understandability and analyzability are related, as an understandable metamodel is also easier to analyze. By the same argumentation as for analyzability, the understandability of a metamodel is also influenced by its modularity.

The *modifiability* of a metamodel refers to how well its structure supports modifications (see maintainability and changeability by Bertoa [BV10]). The modifiability of a metamodel is influenced by its modularity [BV10].

2.2.7. Bad Smells

In object-oriented software development, a *bad smell* [Fow+99] is considered an indicator for a possible problem in the software's design or code. Some bad smells are always problematic. For example, identical code should always be consolidated. Other bad smells do not always indicate problems. E.g., a class or interface with allegedly too many methods can often point to an insufficient modularization. Sometimes, however, it is the result of the use of a facade design pattern [Gam+95]. The evaluation whether a part of a program has a bad smell is often dependent on the context of the software project. For example, what is considered an adequate length and complexity of methods in an algorithmically heavy software project might be a bad smell in a business information system project. In general, bad smells are only indicators or symptoms. This means they are not problems, but they point the developers to problematic spots in the code This is the case for the divergent change bad smell [Fow+99] and the shotgun surgery bad smell [Fow+99]. Divergent change occurs if a class changes because of different reasons. Shotgun surgery occurs if the implementation of a new feature modifies many classes. With some other bad smells, however, the distinction between the bad smell and the underlying problem is not as clear. For example, this is the case for duplicated code and large methods.

An anti-pattern was originally defined as being "... just like pattern, except that instead of a solution it gives something that looks superficially like a solution, but is none." [Ris98]. However, the meaning of *anti-patterns* changed over time to mean a recurring pattern that has negative consequences [SW00; Jul13], regardless if it was purposely used or not.

When transferring these terms to the domain of metamodeling, some bad smells can be defined as anti-patterns [ABT10]. Other bad smells may be indicated by metrics [ABT10]. Some are only detectable through a manual investigation. The remainder of this thesis is only concerned with bad smells in metamodels. Therefore, it addresses metamodeling bad smells simply as bad smells or just smells.

2.2.8. Metrics

A *software metric* or metric, in short, is the result of a quantification of a property of a software artifact. Metrics are often used as heuristics to assess the quality of software artifacts. Examples for software quality metrics are cyclomatic complexity [McC76] or can be found in the ISO/IEC standard 25023 [ISO16]. Metrics that merely analyze the software artifact are popular for quality assessments, as they can be computed automatically. In general, however, the value of a metric does not provide a clear statement about the quality of the software artifact. They have to be interpreted in the context of the software project in that they were measured. A metric can also be computed based on other metrics. These are named composed metrics.

The term metric can be transferred to metamodeling. A *metamodel metric* measures a property of a metamodel. Some metrics provide measures about elements in a metamodel or the metamodel as a whole. Examples for metrics for classes are the number of class properties, and the number of direct subclasses. Examples for metamodel level metrics are the average number of properties per class or the maximum number of classifiers in a package. Metrics that provide a measure for a whole metamodel do not provide direct indicators for improvement potential.

2.2.9. EMF Refactor

EMF Refactor [Are14; AT13] is a metamodel quality assurance tool. It can be used to automatically evaluate metamodel metrics, detect bad smells, and perform refactorings. Bad smell detections can either be specified by an anti-pattern, or a metamodel metric and its threshold. If an occurrence of an anti-pattern is found or a measure of the metric exceeds the threshold, a bad smell is detected. It supports UML- and Ecore-based metamodels. The tool can be extended by new metrics, bad smell detections, and refactorings. For Ecore, EMF Refactor provides bad smell detections for the following bad smells: Large EClass, Speculative Generality EClass, Unnamed EClass. It features an even longer list for UML anti-patterns. A Large EClass is detected if a class contains more attributes and operations than the specified threshold. A Speculative Generality EClass is detected if an abstract class has only one concrete subclass. An Unnamed EClass is detected if a class lacks a name. In the scope of this thesis, this is, however, a validity error rather than a bad smell. This is because it prohibits code generation for the metamodel.

2.2.10. Roles

There are three roles that work with metamodels: metamodel developers, tool developers, and tool users. This section[3] briefly explains these roles.

[3] This section is based on [HSR19] (©2019 IEEE).

2.2.10.1. Developer

Two developer roles can be distinguished depending on how they work with metamodels: metamodel developer and tool developer. The *metamodel developer* implements, maintains, and extends metamodels. For example, s/he creates the metamodel, fixes bugs, specifies constraints, modifies classifiers according to changing requirements, and extends the metamodel by new features. The *tool developer* develops and maintains tools that work on the metamodel. S/he writes and modifies code that uses the metamodel. This thesis uses the term *developer* hereafter to refer to both roles at the same time.

2.2.10.2. User

This thesis also refers to the role of the users of a metamodel. The user employs a metamodel via tools that operate on instances of the metamodel. Thus, this role is addressed as the *tool user*. Tool users create and modify models using editors. They process models with simulators and analyzers. Further, they transform models into other formats (e.g., code, databases). A tool user has specific needs regarding the abstractions that are implemented by the metamodel. This thesis refers to specific sets of abstractions that are usually used together and have a common theme as a *concern* of the tool user. Examples of concerns are the modeling of static software design, software behavior, software performance, and security.

2.3. Quality-Describing DSMLs and Metamodels

DSMLs are used to express various subjects. As they are domain-specific, they usually describe the structure or behavior of concepts of their domain. Some DSMLs define quality properties for their concepts. This thesis refers to such languages as *quality-describing DSMLs*. As Section 2.1 explains, quality-describing DSMLs are used in MDE to evaluate the quality of systems.

A quality-describing DSML may feature quality properties of one multiple quality dimensions. Alone for the domain of software, there are numerous quality dimensions (see, e.g., the ISO/IEC standard 25010 [ISO11]). A DSML may describe a quality dimension descriptively. This serves, for example, documentation and communication purposes. A DSML may also define properties that are used as an input or output of quality analyses. How quality properties are specified cannot be generalized. They can be different for different quality characteristics and can even differ when the same characteristic is modeled for different domains or subjects. For the scope of this thesis, the term of quality-describing DSMLs should be generalized. This thesis is also concerned with *DSMLs that are used for quality analyses.* Such DSMLs do not have to explicitly feature quality properties. A quality assessment should, however, be deductible from such a DSML by an analysis. The metamodel that defines a quality-describing DSMLs is referred to as *quality-describing metamodel* or more general as a *metamodel for quality analysis.* This thesis provides a reference structure, which applies to such metamodels.

An example of a quality-describing metamodel is the Palladio Component Model (PCM). The PCM is a DSML for the design and analysis of software-architecture. Performance and reliability properties are inbuilt into the metamodel. It also contains a basic notion of performability, which is a combination of performance and reliability. For the PCM, several addons exist that add support for more quality characteristics. These bring their metamodels, that add expression capabilities for their quality properties. Examples for such addons are KAMP [Ros+15], which analyzes maintainability; IntBIIS, which analyzes the performance of business processes in conjunction with the software architecture; and PASE, which analyzes security rules.

A simplified explanation of the definition of performance properties in the PCM is given as an example. The PCM models services that are provided by components in a formalism that is similar to flow charts. Some of the actions in the flow chart are specified with resource demands. Components have to be deployed on a resource container, which is equipped with resources. A resource has a specified processing rate. If, in the simulation of the system, the service of a component is called, the flow chart is processed. Each time, an action with a resource demand is encountered, the resource demand is served by the respective resource of the component's resource container. This potentially creates contention on the resources if services are called concurrently. As an output, the simulator of the PCM delivers, for example, the response time and throughput of services. Resource demands of actions and the processing rates of resources are the performance properties in the PCM, which serve as an input for the performance analysis.

There are many more examples of metamodels from the field of quality analysis. KAMP4Aps [Hei+18] evaluates the maintainability of automated production systems. The Descartes Modeling Langauge [KBH14] can be used to analyze the performance of self-adaptive systems during their runtime. KLAPER [Gra+08; GMS05] is an intermediate language for transformations between several component system models and several performance models. In his survey of performance analyses for component-based software systems [Koz10], Koziolek explicitly lists metamodel-based approaches. His survey can be seen as a guide to select metamodels for the desired analysis approach.

2.4. Feature Models

The reference structure approach of this thesis uses feature models to express the features of a language. Based on a feature model, subsets of the given features are selected to specify which features of a language are of current interest for model instantiation and tool development. Feature models are known from Feature-oriented Domain Analysis (FODA) [Kan+90] and from the SPL community. A *feature model* [CE00] is a formalism to capture the variability and interdependencies of features of a specific subject. A feature model consists of *feature nodes* (in the following referred to as features) and their relations. Each feature model has one *root feature*. Except for the root feature, each feature has precisely one parent. These parent-child relations form a tree. Parent-child relations are either of the type mandatory or optional, or can be part of an alternative set or OR set [CE00]. A *mandatory* child feature has to be selected if its parent feature is selected. An *optional* child feature may be selected. From the features in an *alternative set*, exactly one feature has to be selected. From the features in an *OR set*, at least one feature has to be selected. In contrast to the usual use of feature models, in the scope of this work, feature sets with only one feature are allowed. A set with one feature (regardless of alternative or OR) has to always be selected. The benefit is that later, more features can be added to the feature set, without having to change the child relation type. Features can also have *requires relations* and *excludes relations* to other features. Requires relations are directional. Excludes relations are mutual. Feature relations are not allowed to point to parent features or parents thereof. A required relation would be redundant. A excludes relation would be contradictory.

A *feature selection* is a subset of the features from the feature model that adheres to the constraints imposed by the feature relations. The root node is always selected. Except for the root node, a feature can only be selected if its parent is also selected. If a feature is selected that has children, the following rules apply. Mandatory child features have to be selected. Optional child features may be selected. From an OR set, one or more features have to be selected. From an alternative set, exactly one feature has to be selected. If a feature has required dependencies, these required features have to be also selected. If a feature excludes other features, these features cannot be selected.

As this thesis relies heavily on feature models, the following introduces terms that allow a more concise description of feature models. *Grouping features* are feature nodes that do not represent a language feature but only serve as the parent for a group of related features or a feature set. *Feature dependency* is the umbrella term for child relations and the requires relation, as both establish a dependency to another feature. *Sibling features* of a feature are all other features that share the same parent feature. A *descendant features* of a feature are all direct and indirect child features. This means feature A has feature B as a child; feature B has feature C as a child; thus, B and C are descendants of A. Analogously, *antecedent features* are all direct and indirect parent features.

This thesis is not strictly dependent on feature models. There are also other variability modeling approaches (e.g., the Common Variability Language [Hau+08]). The reference structure approach of this thesis will also work with other variability languages, provided they support sufficiently similar concepts to the ones it depends on from feature modeling (dependencies, feature selection).

2.5. Concepts and Approaches Relevant to the Validation

This section presents concepts that are essential to the validation of this thesis. Section 2.5.1 presents the Goal Question Metric approach. Section 2.5.2 elaborates on the types of validity of a validation. Section 2.5.3 explains the hypergraph metrics of Allen, which are used by the evolvability evaluation of the reference structure contribution of this thesis.

2.5.1. Goal Question Metric Approach

The *Goal Question Metric (GQM) approach* is an approach to derive metrics from goals. It was initially developed by Basili [BCR94] and aimed towards software projects and products. Koziolek [Koz08] points out that the approach can also be applied in other contexts. Basili postulates that when a subject should be evaluated, the metrics should not be chosen directly (bottom-up). They should rather be chosen in a goal driven top-down manner. This avoids evaluating metrics that later turn out to not measure what is relevant.

The result of an application of the GQM approach is referred to as a *GQM plan*. The definition of a GQM plan is performed top-down. First, the goals of the subject that ought to be evaluated are defined. E.g., the use of the new library should speed up user requests. For a goal, one or more questions are specified. E.g., does the performance of function f42 improve? For a question, one or more metrics are specified. E.g., throughput and response time. After the measurement, the GQM plan is evaluated bottom-up. By observing the metrics, the questions are answered. How the questions were answered gives conclusions about their goal.

2.5.2. Types of Validity

In their book [Run+12], Runeson et al. present four types of validity in case study research in the field of software engineering. The validities are internal validity, external validity, construct validity, and reliability. The stronger these validities are for a case study, the stronger are the conclusions that are drawn from it. This thesis refers to these validity types, when it discusses the validity of a case study evaluation.

Internal validity is concerned with whether the effects that are observed stem from the cause that they are attributed to. Internal validity is compromised if there are unknown causes for the effects that are observed. *External validity* refers to the ability to generalize the conclusions that are obtained by a case study. External validity is compromised if the sample for the case study is not diverse enough to draw valid conclusions for the scope for which is claimed the conclusions should apply for. *Construct validity* addresses whether a construct (in the context of this thesis a metric) measures what it is supposed to measure. *Reliability* is concerned with the repeatability, i.e., whether the evaluation can be repeated by other researchers and the same results be achieved. Reliability is compromised, for example, if data or tools are not obtainable or the evaluation process is not known.

2.5.3. Graph and Hypergraph Metrics According to Allen

Allen et al. propose several metrics for graphs [All02] and hypergraphs [AGG07]. This thesis utilize these metrics for its validation. They are based on measures of information size in bits. In contrast to counting metrics, the metrics of Allen take into consideration that reoccurring patterns in the relations between entities require less effort from a developer to be understood. *Hypergraphs* are similar to standard graphs, except that instead of edges it features hyperedges. A *hyperedge* connects two or more nodes. Coupling, complexity, and information size are evaluated on hypergraphs [AGG07]. Cohesion is graph-based [All02]. How Allen's metrics are calculated is explained by Heinrich in our paper [HSR19]:

> "We use a hypergraph partitioned into several hypergraph modules we denote as modular hypergraph H. A *hypergraph module* is a set of nodes. Each node can only be contained in one of the hypergraph modules of H. We denote hyperedges crossing hypergraph module boundaries as inter-module hyperedges. Hyperedges that do not cross hypergraph module boundaries are named intra-module hyperedges.

For calculating the *complexity* of a modular hypergraph, we performed a procedure taken from [Jun16a] based on the size metric by Allen et al. In order to calculate the size of a hypergraph, we establish a pattern for each node describing the hyperedges connected or not connected to the node in form of ones and zeros. The pattern (i.e., sequence of ones and zeros) for several nodes may be identical. In that case, we aggregate them and remember the number of occurrences. Then, we calculate the probability of each pattern p by the ratio of number of occurrences and number of nodes in H [AGG07]. Equation 2.1 and Equation 2.2 depict the metrics for size and complexity. G is the modular hypergraph. G_i is the modular hypergraph containing node i and all nodes which are connected to this node. $p_L(j)$ provides the pattern probability of node j. The size metric is first used on all G_i partial hypergraphs and then on the complete hypergraph G. Therefore, H indicates that different hypergraphs are passed to the size metric.

$$Size(H) = \sum_{j=1}^{n}(-log_2\, p_L(i)) \qquad (2.1)$$

$$Complexity(G) = \left(\sum_{i=1}^{n} Size(G_i)\right) - Size(G) \qquad (2.2)$$

The *coupling* of a modular hypergraph is specified as the complexity of the hypergraph with only inter-module hyperedges [AGG07]. Following the procedure for the computation of coupling in [Jun16a], we construct a modular hypergraph H^* containing only inter-module hyperedges. Then, we calculate the complexity of H^*.

Allen [All02] defines *cohesion* as the ratio of the complexity of the intra-module graph MG^o and the complexity of the complete graph $MG^{(n)}$. A complete graph is a graph for which all nodes are interconnected by edges [All02]. We cannot construct a meaningful complete graph for a hypergraph. This is because a complete hypergraph would not only contain hyperedges between two nodes but also all other hyperedges for a given set of nodes [Jun16a]. Therefore, we apply the cohesion metric by Allen [All02] to graphs, not hypergraphs. We follow the procedure described in [Jun16a]. First, we map the modular hypergraph H to a modular graph MG. We replace each hyperedge by a set of edges connecting all nodes that were previously connected by the hyperedge. Based on MG, we then derive a graph containing only intra-module edges MG^o and construct a complete graph $MG^{(n)}$. Cohesion is calculated as shown in Equation 2.3."

$$Cohesion(MG) = \frac{Complexity(MG^o)}{Complexity(MG^{(n)})} \tag{2.3}$$

2.6. Graphical Notation

Figure 2.3 shows the graphical notation that this thesis uses in its figures. The notational elements are grouped after the themes in which they mostly appear. The elements that are depicted in the legend are introduced in the foundations or contribution chapters. It is not the purpose of this section to explain these concepts. It merely presents the graphical notation and explains some details. For a proper introduction, refer to the respective chapter. To find the location where a concept is introduced, the index, which is placed at the end of this thesis, should be used.

To express metamodels, this thesis uses the UML class diagram notation [Obj17]. The extends relation uses the notation of UML stereotype application. Like classes, objects are depicted in rectangles. The difference is that object names are written in lower case and are underlined. The "is instance" relation illustrates that an object is the instance of a class. The arbitrary dependency illustrates a dependency induced by any class property. The module boundary illustrates that classes are in different metamodel modules.

This dissertation also presents concepts with the UML class diagram notation. Like a class, a concept is also illustrated by a rectangle. Relations

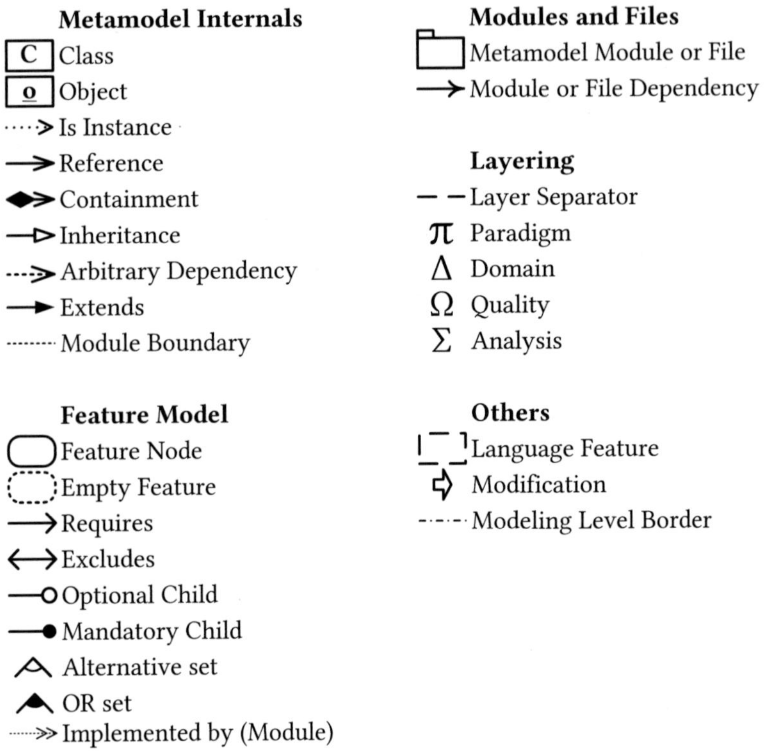

Figure 2.3.: Graphical Notation

between concepts are expressed by the standard class diagram arrows (reference, containment, and inheritance).

This dissertation uses the standard feature model diagram notation. The excludes relation is displayed as a two-headed arrow, as it works mutually. The "implemented by" arrow refers to a metamodel module, that implements the feature.

Metamodel files and metamodel modules share the same notation. They are conceptually similar. Some figures are valid for metamodel modules and files. If it is relevant whether a file or module is meant, this is made explicit by the context of the figure.

The reference structure proposes a layering of the modules of a metamodel. The layer separator shows the border between two layers. The Greek symbols are shortcuts for the names of the four layers that are proposed in the reference structure.

A modification arrow symbolizes that the entities that are depicted on its left side are transformed into those that are depicted on its right side. It can express modifications of classes, modules, and features. The modeling level border indicates that the objects or concepts on one side are instances of classes or concepts of the other side.

3. Problem Areas and Challenges

This chapter[1] presents the problems and challenges this thesis tackles. From these problems and challenges, the chapters of the contributions derive their research questions. Instead of presenting the challenges and problems in the chapters of the contributions, they are presented here, as some of them are addressed by multiple contributions.

This chapter explains most problems by the example of the PCM, as the PCM is a good representative for large and historically-grown metamodels. This does not mean that these problems only affect the PCM. They concern metamodels in general, e.g., other metamodels show similar weak spots[2]. Thus, the PCM is used as concrete evidence where possible.

The PCM is an established and widely used metamodel. It provides various features for quality modeling and analysis of component-based software architectures as described by Reussner et al. [Reu+16]. The PCM consists of 24 packages that contain 203 classes. It is divided into five metamodel files. Around 73 % of its classes reside in the largest metamodel file. Starting in August 2006, the PCM has a long history of evolution. In the time from spring 2007 to fall 2012, the PCM grew from under 100 to over 200 classes (as reported in my paper [Str+16a]). There are at least 12 metamodel extensions for the PCM[3]. However, many more exist that are not publicly documented (e.g., student theses, experimental, incubation). Due to its historically grown structure, the PCM exhibits some shortcomings described hereafter.

[1] This section is based on [HSR19] (©2019 IEEE) and [SH16b].

[2] `https://sdqweb.ipd.kit.edu/wiki/EMOF_Bad_Smells` (last visited 23.08.2019)

[3] `https://sdqweb.ipd.kit.edu/wiki/PCM_AddOns` (last visited 23.08.2019)

3.1. Package Structure Erosion and Uncontrolled Growth of Dependencies

Repeated maintenance and intrusive addition of new features over time is detrimental to the internal structure metamodels. The results are twofold, the deterioration of the package structure and uncontrolled dependencies.

When new features are implemented intrusively, their classes have to be placed consistently in the package structure. If this is not done, the package structure suffers. This is usually the case with long-living metamodels, as their development teams change and design rationale is lost. It is caused by implementing new features in packages of similar features or scattering them in the packages of multiple related features. This is often the case with cross-cutting concerns.

Language features are hard to grasp if they are not adequately reflected in the package structure. In case a package contains classifiers of multiple features or features are scattered over the package structure, it is not easy for the developers to narrow down the part of the metamodel that is relevant for their current task. Thus, the erosion of the package structure worsens the understandability and therefore also the evolvability of a metamodel.

The fact that package structures allow free creation of new dependencies to other packages within the same metamodel file causes another related shortcoming: the accumulation of superfluous inter-package dependencies and dependency cycles between packages.

Such uncontrolled growth of dependencies worsens the understandability of a metamodel. This is because developers, while trying to understand the semantics of a class, may follow dependencies to packages that are irrelevant to their current goals. Uncontrolled growth of dependencies further increases the complexity of the metamodel. Unnecessary inter-package dependencies increase coupling which impedes evolving the metamodel and hinders developers who try to identify the parts of the metamodel that are relevant to their tasks.

The problems of package structure erosion and uncontrolled dependencies can be observed in the PCM (see my paper [SL14]). They were caused by repeated intrusive additions and maintenance. The PCM was originally tailored for performance analysis. However, the scope of the PCM broadened, and more structural features and quality properties were incorporated. Initially, new features were intrusively implemented in the metamodel. Examples for such new features are the modeling of reliability [Bro+12], event-based communication [Rat13], and infrastructure components and middleware [Hau09]. As a consequence, the PCM suffers from all of the above explained cases of package structure erosion, unnecessary dependencies, and dependency cycles (as stated in my paper [Str+16a]).

3.2. Loss of Knowledge

A further problem that plays into the erosion of structure over time is the loss of knowledge. If a metamodel is modified, the developer who carries out the change should have sufficient knowledge of the metamodel or else the change could be implemented incorrectly. If s/he has no prior knowledge, s/he has to then spend time to learn and understand the metamodel. As development teams change, knowledge of rationale about the design of the metamodel is lost. Decisions that have been intentionally made at one point may later seem counter-intuitive to someone else. If the modeling is then changed or a workaround implemented, the initial good intention may be lost and the stringency and consistency of the metamodel impaired.

The problem of loss of knowledge applies also to the PCM. Over time, almost the complete team of developers changed. There are documentation texts annotated onto the elements of the metamodel. From these, even a technical report was generated automatically. They are, however, not complete. Although the packages are mostly documented with non-trivial annotations, they often do not cover strategic decisions about language features. The history of inconsistent intrusive additions of the PCM demonstrates that the documentation was not sufficient (argued by my papers [SL14; Str+16a]).

3.3. Monolithic Metamodels

Many conventionally developed metamodels are too large and lack separation of concerns on the level of metamodel files. This applies especially to metamodels that were maintained and extended over longer periods of time. This causes two main problems.

Monolithic metamodels do not support to create dependencies in a need-specific way, but offer only all-or-nothing dependence. The problem of all-or-nothing dependence impacts the development of new languages, language extensions, and metamodel-based tools. If a related language is developed, it is not possible to only depend on a part of the original language. The whole language has to be depended on, which causes a bloating of the implementation of the new language. The same applies to the development of language extensions. If an extension only needs a part of the original metamodel, still the whole metamodel has to be depended on. Lastly, this problem also concerns the development of tools that are based on a monolithic metamodel.

The second problem is a consequence of the all-or-nothing dependence issue, which is explained above. Due to the lacking modularity and the depending on unneeded parts of metamodels, the understandability of the metamodel suffers. When new languages are developed that use a monolithic metamodel, new extensions, or metamodel-based tools are created, metamodel developers are confronted with the full extent of the monolithic metamodel. During development, they stumble over features that are irrelevant to them. These irrelevant features may confuse them, as it is not always apparent at first glance what a set of classifiers is representing.

These problems can be observed with the PCM. Although the PCM consists of several metamodel files, one of them contains with 148 most of the classes. All these classes can only be used together, as the whole metamodel always has to be deployed. For new developers, it is overwhelming to investigate the metamodel, as it contains many language features.

3.4. Commonalities in Related Languages

To model and analyze certain qualities, a particular language is required that provides the modeling of the concepts for which the quality is evaluated. If multiple qualities should be analyzed for the same subject, it has to be modeled multiple times. As a consequence, some parts of the subject are modeled multiple times in different languages. This causes unnecessary effort.

For example, a software architecture has been modeled in the PCM and enriched with resource demands to conduct performance evaluation. To document and analyze, for example, security, the system has to be remodeled with UML[4] and supplied with security properties [Jür02]. A large part of the software is modeled multiple times, which should be avoided considering that the utilized concepts of the PCM and UML are related.

3.5. Tool-specific Metamodel Content

Another challenge in metamodel design as in maintenance is the compromise between a clean and clear metamodel and on the other side incorporating auxiliary content for tooling. A metamodel that only contains the necessary information to model a particular subject matter is precise, easy to understand and to evolve. However, the complexity and the efficiency of tooling that works on the metamodel can be improved by including utility content in the metamodel. If a metamodel becomes too tool specific, however, it impedes its usability for specific tooling or its reusability in other contexts.

3.6. Generality Compromise

Another trade-off that the metamodel developers have to tackle, even in maintenance, is implementing the right degree of extensibility and generality. Some extensions have to be provided with extension points beforehand

[4] Although there currently is research towards security in the scope of the PCM, there is no mature security specification and analysis approach at the time of writing this thesis.

to be able to implement them in a clean way. A metamodel for a very specific purpose may be very precise. However, as requirements change, such a precise metamodel may turn out to be inflexible and not well suited for extension. On the other side, too many predefined extension points increase the complexity of the metamodel. Making a metamodel too general makes it too abstract, which impedes its usability, as the necessary concepts are not modeled.

One end of this problem can be observed in the PCM. The PCM was designed specifically for performance and reliability prediction. These aspects are hard-coded into the metamodel. The reusability of the PCM for other quality dimensions is limited, as this specific content always has to be depended and deployed.

3.7. Metamodel Coupling

The practice of externally extending a metamodel, is not yet adequately understood. The same mechanisms apply when two metamodels are coupled in general. There are several types of coupling, and some types have different ways of how they can be implemented. It is not clear how they compare and in which situations they should be used.

3.8. Instance Incompatibility

One way to unintrusively implement additions to the metamodel is to branch it and implement the addition in the branch. The advantage is that the master branch does not need to be altered, and the development of master and other branches is decoupled. The addition branches, however, need to be maintained to be up-to-date with the master. Further, instances of metamodels from branches are not necessarily compatible with the master metamodel nor the tools that operate on instances of the master metamodel. As a consequence, tools have to be branched and maintained in specific branches as well. Alternatively, a transformation between both metamodel branches needs to be developed. It transforms parts of instances of the branched metamodel to the original metamodel so that the original tools can still be used. However, these transformations have to be maintained as well. In summary, it should be possible to prevent incompatibilities on instance level between closely related languages without explicit manual effort.

Concerning the PCM, the problem of instance incompatibility is relevant. Some additions to the PCM that were developed in branches have never been included in the PCM master branch (e.g., [Hei+17; KBK15; WBK14]). These addition either cause additional maintenance effort to the maintainer or were discontinued due to that extra effort.

In the scope of this thesis, *instance compatibility* refers to the instances of an extended or modified metamodel still being instances of the original metamodel (i.e., being compatible with the original model code). This also means that tools that operate on the original metamodel can operate on the instances of the extended or modified metamodel.

3.9. Incompatible Extensions

One option to implement an extension is to use inheritance to add new class properties to an existing class. Inheritance is problematic as two different extensions that subtype the same class cannot be used in combination. It is only possible to create an instance of the subclass of one extension or the other. The only way to use the combination of both extensions is to create another extension that extends both existing extensions and creates one class that inherits from both subclasses. This, however, means that extensions cannot be developed independently, as all conflicting extensions have to be extended to make them compatible.

The problem of incompatible extension can be observed in the PCM. Some extensions to the PCM (e.g., [Hei+17]) use inheritance to introduce new class properties to existing classes.

3.10. Feature Overload in Metamodel-based Tools

The intrusive addition of metamodel elements over time has further disadvantages. Users of tools that are based on a monolithic metamodel are usually confronted with the full extent of its features. Especially optional features that are not of interest to specific tool users can distract and confuse them.

Such a feature overload is especially the case with the PCM, which is mainly used for performance prediction. The metamodel features several concepts that are not performance related (e.g., reliability) and many advanced features that are not relevant to basic performance prediction (e.g., infrastructure interfaces and events). When tool users create PCM models for basic performance prediction, they have to use the whole metamodel. Further, they are confronted with the full extent of the GUI of the Palladio Bench tool. An inexperienced user is not able to identify the modeling concepts that are relevant to him.

The problem of overburdening users by feature overload in tools brings a related problem to the surface. It is not a primary problem but is a consequence of applying the approach of this thesis. The overall complexity of a metamodel that is modularized and coupled increases. Such an increase brings disadvantages to metamodel-based tools that take a monolithic approach. The code of these tools gets more complex, but it does not bring any direct benefits. Furthermore, if a metamodel is modular and extensible, but this software is not, the software has to be modified to be able to support new metamodel extensions.

Part II.

Contribution

4. Bad Smells and Anti-Patterns in Metamodeling

Like in conventional software, there are problems in metamodels that do not impede their functionality but degrade their maintainability. These are named bad smells. They arise in the initial design of metamodels, but also accumulate over time when new features are added. The more bad smells accumulate, the more effort is caused in the maintenance of the metamodel. Related work covers the detection of various types of problems in the metamodel. However, these works either provide minimal support for EMOF [Are14], focus on metamodel defects [Ela12] or address semantic errors [GBS12; FM18]. This chapter[1] presents the following contributions, to address these problems. It defines the underlying fundamental regarding problems in metamodeling, with a focus on bad smells. It presents bad smells that stem from a manual metamodel review and a literature review of bad smells from object orientation. Amongst other aspects, for each smell, its effect, detection, and correction are explained. Automated detections are implemented for several bad smells. Metamodel developers should be aware of these bad smells. For the ones that can be automatically detected, a detection should be performed regularly. This contribution is evaluated in an explorative study. In this study, the harmfulness, detection, and correction are inspected for the smells for which detections were implemented. The subject metamodel on which the detections are performed is the Palladio Component Model (PCM) [Reu+16].

Section 4.1 presents the research questions that this contribution addresses. Section 4.2 introduces the terms and definitions that are fundamental to this contribution. Section 4.3 explains the research approach for finding the bad

[1] This chapter is in parts based on a master's thesis that I supervised [Hah17]. The smell description and the detection of smells were revised where necessary.

smells. Section 4.4 presents the collection of bad smells. Section 4.5 briefly presents the implementation of the automatic detection of bad smells.

This chapter is continued in subsequent parts of this thesis. Chapter 7 present the detection and correction evaluation. Section 11.1 elaborates on related work. Section 12.1 concludes this chapter.

4.1. Research Questions

This section derives the research questions for this contribution from the problems that Chapter 3 presented. Problem 1 states that the package structure of metamodels erodes over time and that dependencies within metamodel files can grow unconstrained. Problem 3 states that the understandability and reusability of monolithic metamodels are impaired. Although these problems, some causes, and their effects were already outlined, a systematic investigation should be conducted. It is essential to understand what exactly makes a metamodel less evolvable and how these problems can be detected. Therefore, this section specifies the research questions that are concerned with evolvability problems in metamodeling.

RQ Ia (Bad Smells): *What are the types of problems that may impair the evolvability of metamodels and what are their effects?*

RQ Ib (Smell Identification): *How can these problems be detected? Which problems can be detected automatically?*

RQ Ic (Smell Resolution): *How can these problems be resolved?*

4.2. Terms and Definitions

The problems and errors that are made by metamodel developers or that manifest themselves throughout maintenance can be classified into validity errors, semantic errors, and bad smells.

A *validity error* occurs if a metamodel is no longer conform to its meta-metamodel. This means it is not considered a valid instance of its meta-metamodel. Validity errors are the most basic type of error and are usually detected by the metamodeling framework. A validity error prevents the generation of code that compiles, and, therefore, renders the metamodel unusable in its current state. Examples of validity errors are attributes and references without types, references that point to a no longer existing class, and even simple errors like metamodel elements without names.

A *semantic error* occurs if a metamodel does not correctly reflect the subject matter it represents. A semantic error damages the correctness of the metamodel in that it occurs. It makes the metamodel either imprecise or incomplete. Examples of semantic errors are missing or superfluous references between classes, wrong attribute types, and wrong multiplicities.

A metamodel *design flaw* is a problem in a metamodel that does not introduce semantic errors but impairs the evolvability of the metamodel. This can happen, e.g., by introducing complexity because of unnecessary elements, increasing the coupling of the metamodel because of conceptually flawed or unnecessary dependencies, or reducing its cohesion by lacking or improper division. Design flaws can be refactored without changing the semantics of the metamodel.

This contribution builds upon the definition of bad smells in Section 2.2.7. Figure 4.1 illustrates the concept of *bad smells.*

A bad smell usually has one *indicator*. An *occurrence* of a bad smell is the positive evaluation of an indicator. The occurrence includes the element that violates the metric or the elements that are involved in the anti-pattern. Some smells may have more than one indicator. An indicator is either the violation of a metric threshold or the detection of an anti-pattern. All metric violations can be automatically detected by evaluating the metric on the metamodel. An anti-pattern can be purely syntactical. This means that at least a portion of its occurrences can be automatically detected by analyzing the metamodel solely. For example, a class that inherits from a class from that one of its other superclasses already inherits. Some anti-patterns may also involve the semantics of metamodel elements. The semantic of metamodel elements is not formalized in the metamodel but is either interpreted by a developer or persisted in the documentation of the metamodel. Occurrences of semantic-based anti-patterns can, therefore, only be detected by a manual investigation of the metamodel. For example, if a package contains classifiers that implement concepts of many different language features, the package and its content are difficult to understand

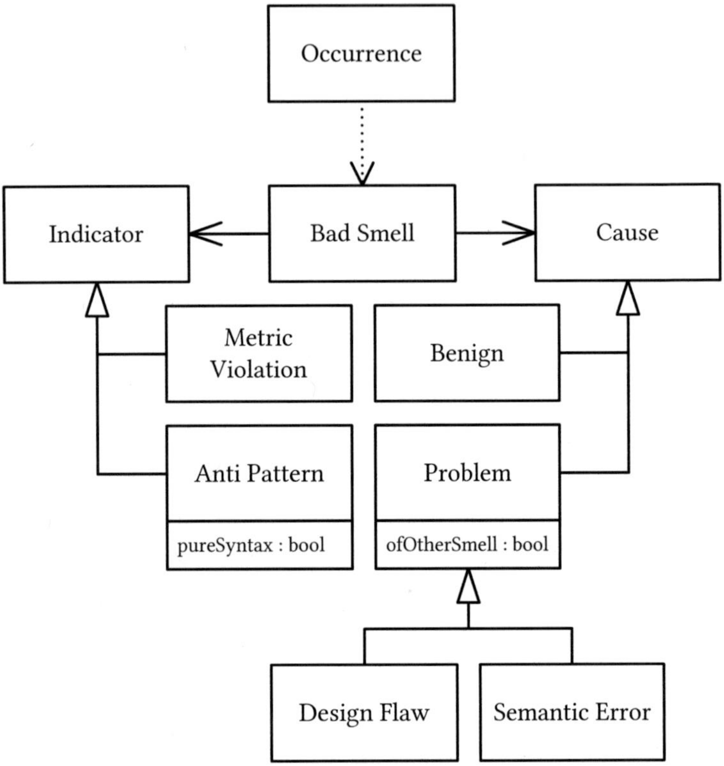

Figure 4.1.: Metamodeling Bad Smells

in contrast to a properly modularized packaging. As the knowledge about the meaning of the classifiers is not persisted in the metamodel, such anti-pattern occurrences cannot be found automatically.

A bad smell has either a problematic or a benign *cause*. A problematic cause is a design flaw or a semantic error. A bad smell that has a problematic cause, is refered to as *harmful* in the scope of this thesis. It is possible that a bad smell occurs because of the cause of another smell. In such cases, the occurrence can be seen as secondary, and the bad smell which is primary for the cause should be treated.

4.3. Research Approach

The bad smells that this chapter presents were inferred in two ways. First, from a manual review [Str+16a] of the PCM. Second, from a transfer [Hah17] of bad smells from a literature review in the domain of object-oriented design.

Manual Metamodel Review The actual goal of the metamodel review of the PCM was to understand its semantics. The metamodel was considered package by package, class for class. Flaws in the design, especially ones that hindered the understanding of the metamodel, were documented.

Transfer from Object Orientation Object-oriented smells cover a wide range of abstraction levels and effects. Not all of these are relevant to metamodeling. Thus, the scope of the literature review had to be set.

There are object-oriented smells on different levels of abstractions [GSS13]: code, design, and architecture. Only design smells are relevant for a transfer to metamodeling. Code smells might be relevant for code that is embedded in metamodels through operations if the bodies of the operations get sufficiently large. The development of large operation bodies is considered to be coding rather than metamodeling. Therefore, this thesis focuses on the design of classifiers and their relations, rather than the bodies of operations. Architecture smells do not apply to metamodels, as this layer of abstraction is not existent in metamodeling.

Another dimension of object-oriented smells is their effect [GSS13]: creational, structural, behavioral. Only structural smells are transferable to metamodels. Creational smells are not applicable, as the creation of instances is handled by the metamodeling framework. Behavioral smells might be relevant to the bodies of large operations. However, as already stated above, the development of large operation bodies is considered to be coding rather than metamodeling.

For each remaining smell that was found in the literature, it was considered if and how it can be transferred to metamodeling and if it is still an indicator for a problem.

4.4. Bad Smells

This section presents the metamodel bad smells types. The smells are grouped according to a classification of structural design smells by Ganesh [GSS13]. Some smells are even named according to it. This is, however, only the case when the expressiveness of the name is not limited. When the classification is applied to metamodels, the smells are classified into abstraction, modularization, hierarchy, and relation. Abstraction is concerned with generalization and boundaries of concepts, and inadequate or unnecessary details. Modularization is concerned with cohesion, coupling, and the boundaries of language features. Hierarchy is concerned with classification, hierarchical organization, and commonalities of concepts. Relation is concerned with dependencies and their constrainment.

Table 4.1 provides an overview of the bad smells. The first two columns provide the source of the bad smell: was it discovered in the metamodel review or the transfer from object orientation. The next three columns show the granularity level that the smell affects: classes, packages, or metamodel files. The last five columns give an overview of how the smells can be detected. The Automatic Detection column specifies whether the smell can be automatically detected. The remaining detection columns do only apply if an automatic detection is possible. They specify whether the detection produces false positives and false negatives and whether the detection is anti-pattern or metric-based. The last two columns show the effect of the smells. The first show a check mark if a smell impairs the maintainability of the metamodel. The second column specifies whether a smell weakens the semantic correctness of a metamodel. If a non-benign smell occurrence always weakens correctness, it is denoted with a check mark (✓). If a non-benign smell occurrence sometimes weakens correctness, it is denoted with a swung dash (~). If a non-benign smell occurrence does not affect correctness, the cell is empty.

	Source		Level			Detection					Effect	
Bad Smell Name	Metamodel Review	Object Orientation	Classes	Packages	Metamodel Files	Autom. Detection	False Positives	False Negatives	Anti-pattern	Metric	Maintainability	Semantic
Missing Class		✓	✓			✓	✓	✓		✓	✓	~
Dead Classifier	✓	✓	✓			✓	✓		✓		✓	✓
Inconsistent Abstraction	✓	✓	✓	✓	✓						✓	
Language Feature Scattering	✓			✓							✓	
God Class		✓	✓			✓	✓			✓	✓	~
Blob Package	✓			✓		✓		✓		✓	✓	
Metamodel Monolith	✓				✓	✓	✓	✓		✓	✓	
Missing Hierarchy	✓	✓	✓			✓	✓	✓	✓		✓	~
Instance Data by Inheritance		✓	✓			✓	✓	✓		✓	✓	
Redundancies in Hierarchy	✓	✓	✓			✓	✓	✓	✓		✓	
Wide Hierarchy		✓	✓			✓	✓			✓	✓	
Speculative Hierarchy		✓	✓			✓	✓	✓	✓		✓	
Deep Hierarchy		✓	✓			✓	✓	✓		✓	✓	
Multipath Hierarchy		✓	✓			✓			✓		✓	
Concrete Abstract Class	✓	✓	✓			✓	✓		✓		✓	✓
Dependency Cycles	✓	✓	✓	✓	✓	✓			✓		✓	
Container Relation	✓		✓			✓			✓		✓	
Obligatory Container Relation	✓		✓			✓			✓		✓	~
Specialized Relation		✓	✓			✓	✓		✓		✓	✓

Table 4.1.: Bad Smell Overview

The smells are presented according to the following template:

1. Related smell definitions from object orientation are mentioned if the smell was transferred from object orientation.

2. A description of the smells is supplied.
3. The effect of the smell is explained.
4. Reasons for an accidental forming and rationale for a deliberate creation are provided.
5. Ways to correct the smell are provided.
6. The detection of the smell is discussed.
7. Automatic treatment is discussed if a treatment is possible in a fully automatic way. This is only the case if there are no false positives and each occurrence of the bad smell is a problem.
8. The relation to object orientation is discussed if no related object-oriented smell was found.

4.4.1. Abstraction

The bad smells of the abstraction category are concerned with the encapsulation of concepts and the adherence to levels of abstraction. The category features the Missing Class, Dead Classifier, and Inconsistent Abstraction smells.

4.4.1.1. Missing Class

The Missing Class smell is known in object orientation as Primitive obsession [Fow+99; Are14] and Data Clumps [Fow+99; Are14]. It is further related to the Large Class [Fow+99; CU06] and Divergent Change [Fow+99] smells.

Description Missing Class occurs if groups of class properties (mainly references and attributes) are used that would be better modeled in their own class, as they represent a concept on their own. A less adverse case is when the group of properties is only present in one class. It gets more severe if the same group of properties is present in multiple classes. If multiple classes need the group of properties, but it is not duplicated, it leads to inadequate references. This means a class references another class not because of the concept the class implements but only because of the group of properties.

Effect Missing Class impedes the understandability and changeability of the metamodel. Understandability is affected, as the group of properties is not immediately recognizable as an own concept. If inadequate references exist, they can be misleading to developers. The changeability is affected if multiple occurrences of the property group exist, as they have to be evolved together.

Reason and Rationale There is no occasion where this bad smell could be utilized on purpose. It is a mistake that was made in the design or implementation of the metamodel. Sometimes a metamodel developer just does not recognize when s/he implements an additional concept in a class.

Correction A Missing Class occurrence can be corrected, by creating a class that holds the group of properties. This new class is then referenced by all classes that contained the group of properties and all classes that referenced another class merely because of the group of properties.

Detection It is possible to detect some Missing Class occurrences automatically. Two heuristics can be applied.

The first heuristic is to identify classes that have many attributes of primitive types. The count of primitive attributes is defined as a threshold. False positives occur, as in the modeling of certain subject matters, it is necessary to create classes with many primitive attributes. This heuristic focuses on primitive types instead of class properties in general. This differentiates it from the God Class smell (see Section 4.4.2.2).

The second heuristic checks for identical groups of properties between classes. Properties are identical if their name, type, and multiplicity are equal. The size of a group of properties is also defined as a threshold. The threshold should not be set to one, as there are usually many identical properties that belong to several classes. On the other side, a concept could be encoded in only one duplicated attribute. Further, if the types or names of properties do just slightly vary, these occurrences also cannot be detected. Thus, this detection suffers from false negatives. It does also suffer from false positives, as it is possible that two groups of properties do not model the same concept. The probability of this, however, drops with increasing size of the groups.

4.4.1.2. Dead Classifier

Dead Classifier is known in object orientation as Speculative generality [Fow+99], and Unused classes [LR06; Are14]. The tool metaBest [LGL14b] provides a property (D02) that is related to this smell. This smell description, however, considers more circumstances that make a class unusable than pure isolation.

Description A dead classifier is a classifier that cannot be used (see also my paper [Str+16a]). There are two types of dead classifiers: Dead Classes and Dead Enums. A Dead Class has no incoming containments. Its super- and subclasses also have no incoming containments. It is further not a root container and has no subclass that is a root container. A dead enum is not used as an attribute value by any class.

To identify dead classifiers, it is essential to not merely focus on the metamodel file in which the classifier resides. It might be that a possible Dead Class is contained by a class of another metamodel file or has a child in another file that is a root container. In these cases, the class is not dead. The same holds for the search for dead enums. Enums could be used by classes of another metamodel file.

Effect There are two cases of Dead Classifiers. First, a dead classifier is a classifier that is unnecessary and could be simply deleted. Second, it is a classifier that is essential to the language but cannot be used because of a missing containment or attribute. In this second case, the cause of the bad smell is a semantic error, as it compromises the correctness of the metamodel. In the first case, the understandability of the metamodel is impaired, as metamodel developers might waste time to consider the classifier as they stumble upon it. If the dead classifier is a class, the correctness of the metamodel is impaired, as the Dead Class could be mistakenly used as the root for a model.

Reason and Rationale There is no occasion where this bad smell could be utilized on purpose. It is a mistake that was made in the design or implementation of the metamodel. Regarding the first case that the effect section mentioned, it is possible that a metamodel developer abandoned the implementation of a classifier and simply forgot to delete it. Another possibility is that a metamodel developer deleted a container, containment, or attribute and did not realize or check whether the referenced classifier is still needed. Concerning the second case, it is merely a mistake of a metamodel developer who did not model the essential containment or attribute. This is also true for situations where a class that carried such a containment or attribute is deleted, and it is forgotten to recreate the containment or attribute in another class.

Correction Dead classifiers that are unnecessary should just be deleted. If a language actually needs a dead classifier, a containment or attribute has to be created that points to the dead classifier.

Detection All dead classes can be automatically detected, by determining all classes that have no incoming dependencies. Therefore, this detection has no false negatives. However, in EMF dead classes cannot be technically distinguished from root containers and their parents. Therefore, a metamodel developer still has to check whether the detected classes are actually dead. Thus, this detection produces some false positives.

Dead enums can be automatically detected, by determining all enums that are not used by attributes. This detection has no false negatives. It also has no false positives, assuming all relevant metamodel files that might use the enum are being analyzed.

4.4.1.3. Inconsistent Abstraction

This problem is known in object orientation as a violation of the dependency inversion principle [Mar03].

Description The dependency inversion principle [Mar03] is a design principle from object orientation. When translated to metamodeling (in my paper [Str+16a]), it states that high-level classes should not depend on low-level classes. A high- and a low-level are regarding the degree of abstraction.

The principle also applies to packages and metamodel files. The dependencies of a package and metamodel are regarded as the combined dependencies of their elements. The cause of the violation is a dependency that crosses the boundary between packages or metamodel files. If the dependency points into a more abstract package or metamodel file, the two packages or metamodel files suffer from Inconsistent Abstraction.

Part (a) of Figure 4.2 shows an Inconsistent Abstraction on the class and package level. Package H contains high-level concepts, relative to which the content of package L is low-level. Class A has a dependency (relation, inheritance or containment) to K. Thus, a high-level class is dependent on a low-level one. Class K contains further information about A (indicated by the data attribute). Although it is illustrated as a single attribute, this information may come in the form of attributes, relations, and containments.

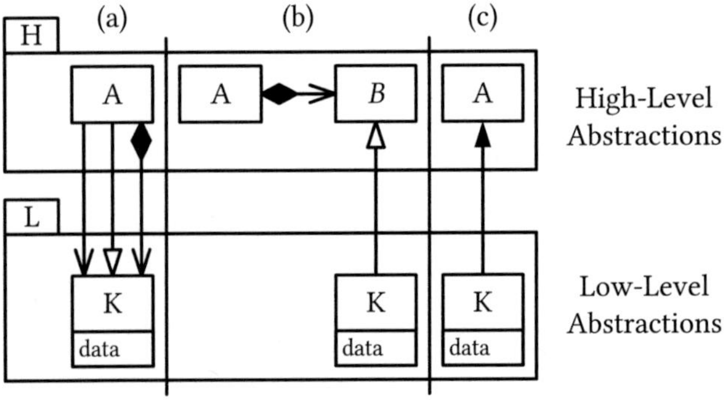

Figure 4.2.: The Inconsistent Abstraction Smell and its Correction [Str+16a]

Effect An Inconsistent Abstraction may have detrimental effects on the maintainability of the metamodel. During evolution, modifications of a language feature may influence a more low-level language feature. Such violations do also hinder understanding the metamodel. If a developer tries to understand a language feature, s/he may trace the outgoing relations to more high-level language features. Thus, s/he may examine language features which are not necessary for understanding the low-level language feature and even irrelevant to her/his intent. On the metamodel file level, an Inconsistent Abstraction impairs the reusability of the low-level metamodel file. The low-level file erroneously depends on the high-level file. Thus, if the low-level file is used, the high-level file also has to be deployed, even if it does not provide any necessary concepts.

Reason and Rationale Occurrences of Inconsistent Abstraction are flaws in the design of the metamodel and often stem from the intrusive addition of language features. It is most convenient for a developer to extend an existing class hierarchy by adding dependencies that point to the new content. However, there is a difference between object-oriented design and metamodels. In object orientation, it is easier and more natural to introduce new abstraction layers. In metamodels, on the other hand, interfaces cannot be used similarly; because usually, it is not similar functionality that is added, but new and different data. At first glance, it seems to be a good solution just to create a new subclass, which adds the needed properties. However, when multiple new independent properties are added this way, they cannot be combined. Therefore, in metamodeling, it can be reasonable to violate the dependency inversion principle in certain cases. A possible rule would be to do so for core concepts of the language. A concept is considered a core concept if it is used in every use case of the language and for every possible kind of tool user. Core concepts should be integrated intrusively into the metamodel with a violation of the dependency inversion principle. This has the following advantages: type safety, adherence to cardinality without having to resort to constraints and retrieval in $O(1)$ (constant time). In contrast, concepts that are only for special use cases or are generally less often used, should not be added intrusively into the language.

Correction When implementing non-core concepts, it is important to adhere to the dependency inversion principle. By performing dependency inversion on the relation between A and K, the Inconsistent Abstraction can be corrected. As the possibilities that replace the relation between A and K are subject of Chapter 5 and the dependency inversion refactoring is subject of Section 6.5.1.2, this section will only briefly discuss the most prominent solutions. Figure 4.2 shows the solutions.

In (b), the new abstract class B is created as well as a containment from A to B. Class K then inherits from B. Thus, the dependency is reversed and now goes from L to H. This solution has some benefits. The instances of K are contained in instances of A. This enables direct navigation and thus retrieval in constant time. In addition, the cardinality can be controlled directly without having to specify complex constraints. However, type safety is not guaranteed, as the extended data is not placed in B but K. This solution has to be enabled in the initial development, as the class B is required. This is no issue if K is also already created during the initial development or if the future extension of K can be foreseen. The main disadvantage of this solution is that H has to be modified if this solution is implemented in hindsight.

In (c), an alternate solution is shown, which does not require a modification of H. It uses the metamodel extension relation, which is presented in Chapter 5, to associate instances of K to instances of A. The relation can be implemented in several ways, e.g., by stereotype application [Lan+12; Kra+12] or referencing [Jun+14; JHH16]. Compared to (b) this has the disadvantage, that the lookup is in $O(k)$, where k is the number of instances of K; or a register of reversed pointers has to be stored and maintained in memory. For more information, which includes pros and cons, refer to Chapter 5 and Chapter 8.

Detection Inconsistent Abstraction occurrences are not automatically detectable. An algorithm is not able to deduce if concepts are higher- or lower-leveled compared to others.

4.4.2. Modularization

The bad smells of the Modularization category are concerned with the cohesion, coupling, and boundaries of language features. The category features the smells Language Feature Scattering, God Class, Blob Package, and Metamodel Monolith.

4.4.2.1. Language Feature Scattering

Description The package structure of a metamodel is used for logical partitioning of its content. The Language Feature Scattering smell (see my paper [Str+16a]) occurs if the classes that constitute a feature of a language are spread over multiple packages that do not share a meaningful parent. Even cross-cutting language features can be modularized in a more meaningful way.

Effect This bad smell has negative consequences on the understandability and thus maintainability of metamodels. When a developer tries to understand a metamodel, s/he examines its packages and from their content and documentation (if there is any) tries to conclude its purpose. If a language feature is scattered, the purpose of the package cannot be fully comprehended without tracing relations that leave the package. The smell may also increase coupling between affected packages and reduce the cohesion within the packages.

Reason and Rationale Language Feature Scattering occurs mostly when new language features are implemented in an already existent metamodel. The new language feature is related to the purpose of multiple other packages. Parts of the new language feature are then placed in related packages. So, the new language feature is ripped apart.

Correction A better approach would be to place the new language feature in its own package. The package should further contain sub-packages for each related package, which then contain the related classes of the new language feature. If there are larger groups of classifiers within the implementation of the language feature, that are closer related, they should be placed into their own subpackage (e.g., a class with its many subclasses).

The package of the new language feature should be placed meaningfully. If it is a first-order language feature, it should be placed below the root package. If it is a cross-cutting language feature, it should be placed on the same level, as the language features with which it is intersecting. If it is a second-order language feature, its package should be placed as a subpackage of the parent language feature.

Moving classes can be done through refactorings. Even the code, which depends on the classes, may be automatically fixed. A mere moving of affected classes may lead to other bad smells if the dependencies are not modified. The new dependencies between packages may lead to package dependency cycles (see Section 4.4.4.1) and Inconsistent Abstractions on the package level (see Section 4.4.1.3). This is not the fault of consolidating a language feature, but of dependencies that were improper in the first place.

Detection This bad smell is not automatically detectable. An algorithm is not able to automatically infer the semantics of parts of the metamodel.

Relation to Object Orientation In object orientation, there are issues similar to Language Feature Scattering, e.g., when cohesive classes are scattered over packages or assemblies. To my knowledge, however, there is no explicit smell that covers the problem on this level. Object orientation smells are more concerned with the internals of packages: relations between classes and the internals of classes and methods.

4.4.2.2. God Class

God Classes are known in object orientation as The Blob [Bro+98], Fat Interface [Mar03], and God Class [TT07]. EMF Refactor [Are14] detects classes with many attributes and operations. The tool metaBest [LGL14b] provides properties (M01 and M02) that are related to this smell. This bad smell description, however, considers more class properties that contribute to a God Class.

Description A God Class is a class with too many properties. It represents a symptom and overlaps with several smells. Improper separation of several concepts might cause it. It might coincide with the missing class smell if a big group of properties is not encapsulated in their own class. It might also appear together with the Missing Hierarchy smell as properties that would typically reside in the superclass are located in the affected class.

Effect A large number of properties may make the class challenging to understand. This is especially the case if a class implements two concepts. If another smell causes a God Class occurrence, please refer to the respective effect description.

Reason and Rationale There is no occasion where this bad smell could be utilized on purpose. Usually, a God Class arises if a class is extended over time, the number of its class properties grows, and it is not split.

Correction To resolve a God Class, some properties of the class have to be factored out. If the class implements more than one concept, the metamodel developer has to split the class. If another smell causes a God Class, please refer to the respective correction description.

Detection God Classes can be automatically detected by scanning the metamodel for classes that have more properties than a defined threshold. What number of properties is appropriate, however, always depends on the subject matter. Some circumstances necessitate a large number of properties. Others do not. Thus, this detection may produce false positives.

4.4.2.3. Blob Package

Description Conversely to the scattered language feature smell, a package that contains classes of multiple language features is an occurrence of the Blob Package smell (see also my paper [Str+16a]).

Effect Having multiple language features in one package, increases the effort to understand the package because the developer has to identify the contained language features and their respective classes. Simply put, the package is needlessly complex. This bad smell also decreases the cohesion within the package.

Reason and Rationale Developers tend to place classes in packages that hold their container or implement a closely related language feature. It is just more convenient to use the existing package structure than to come up with a new structure by oneself.

Correction How to modularize and package language features is already well explained in the resolution part for the Scattered Feature Scattering smell (see Section 4.4.2.1). As already suggested, new language features should be placed in their own package. If a language feature is secondary, its package should be placed as a subpackage. Often, a deeper subdivision of a language feature in subpackages is meaningful.

Detection Blob Packages can be automatically detected. In general, a package that contains multiple concerns has a higher number of classifiers. To search for packages that contain more than a defined threshold can point out some Blob Packages. However, if packages are used to finely subdivide language features into their constituents, a package might only contain a small number of classifiers, to begin with. If another small language feature is then integrated into such a package, the overall number of classes is still relatively low. Thus, this heuristic suffers from false negatives.

Relation to Object Orientation The relation of the Blob Package smell to object orientation is analog to the Scattered Language Feature smell. Insufficient modularization on the package level is also an issue in object orientation. However, I am not aware of an explicit smell definition.

4.4.2.4. Metamodel Monolith

Description A Metamodel Monolith is the analog of the Blob Package on the level of metamodel files. A metamodel file that implements multiple language features is an occurrence of the Metamodel Monolith smell. It is even worse if a metamodel contains essential and optional language features in combination. Optional language features are not relevant to all tool users and therefore not always needed.

Effect Metamodel Monolith impacts the reusability of the metamodel file, as it can only be depended on as a whole. If only a subset of language features is needed, it is not possible for other metamodels, extensions, and tools to selectively depend on the necessary language features. Due to the lacking modularity, the complexity of the metamodel files is unnecessarily high. This impacts the understandability of the metamodel during evolution, reuse, and tool development. A Metamodel Monolith might even lead to a low cohesion between the classifiers in the metamodel file.

Reason and Rationale There is no reason to create a Metamodel Monolith on purpose. It develops because of ignorance of best practices, carelessness, and intrusive additions over time. Metamodel files grow, and it is not noticed that they should be split although they implement multiple language features.

Correction Metamodel Monoliths can be corrected by splitting metamodel files according to their language features. Refactorings and a process for the modularization of metamodels are presented in Section 6.5 and Section 6.6.2.

Detection Metamodel Monoliths can be automatically detected. This is because, a metamodel that implements many language features tends to be large. The size of a metamodel is best measured by the number of its classifiers. If a metamodel exceeds the set threshold, it is considered a Metamodel Monolith. This detection, however, suffers from false positives and false negatives. The appropriate size of a metamodel file does vary depending on the language feature that it implements. A language feature might be complex enough to exceed the threshold on its own, thereby causing a false positive. On the other hand, two simple language features that would be better implemented in separate metamodel files may not exceed the threshold if they are implemented in one metamodel file. Thereby they cause a false negative.

Relation to Object Orientation The relation of the Metamodel Monolith smell to object orientation is analog to the Blob Package smell. Compared to object orientation, a metamodel file is analogous to a unit of compilation (e.g., a project that results in a jar or exe). Insufficient modularization on the level of compilation units is also an issue in object orientation. However, I am not aware of any explicit smell definitions.

4.4.3. Hierarchy

The Hierarchy category is concerned with the classification, hierarchical organization, and commonalities of concepts. It includes the smells Missing Hierarchy, Instance Data by Inheritance, Redundancies in Hierarchy, Wide Hierarchy, Speculative Hierarchy, Deep Hierarchy, Multipath Hierarchy, and Concrete Abstract Class.

4.4.3.1. Missing Hierarchy

The Missing Hierarchy smell is known in object orientation as Missing Inheritance [DDN02], Collapsed Type Hierarchy [Tri08], and Embedded Features [Tri08].

Description A Missing Hierarchy occurs if type information is encoded into attributes of a class. The attributes could be typed with basic data types like boolean, string, or integer, or with an enum (see my paper [Str+16a]).

Effect In contrast to the proper use of inheritance, by decoding type information in attributes, it is not possible to add features to parts of the classification selectively. This might lead to the developer adding features to the base class, which are only used for specific values of the attributes. By doing that, the complexity of the class increases unnecessarily, and its understandability suffers. In the special case of using an enum for additional classifications, the classification is impossible to be extended externally.

Reason and Rationale Using attributes for classification is one possible solution of how to model multiple orthogonal classifications. Figure 4.3

illustrates the problem. It should be possible to classify the class Base as either A1 or A2 and additionally either as B1 or B2. This is not possible by using an class hierarchy of the depth of just one. Figure 4.4 shows a solution by using an enum for the second classification dimension. This is an occurrence of the Missing Hierarchy smell. A classification by a data type works analogously.

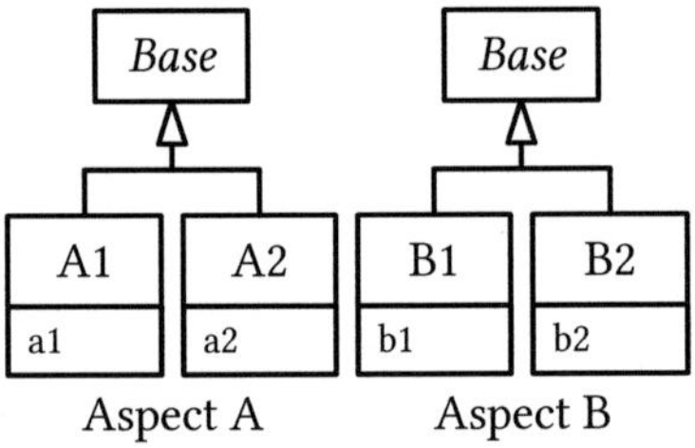

Figure 4.3.: The Problem of Orthogonal Classifications [Str+16a]

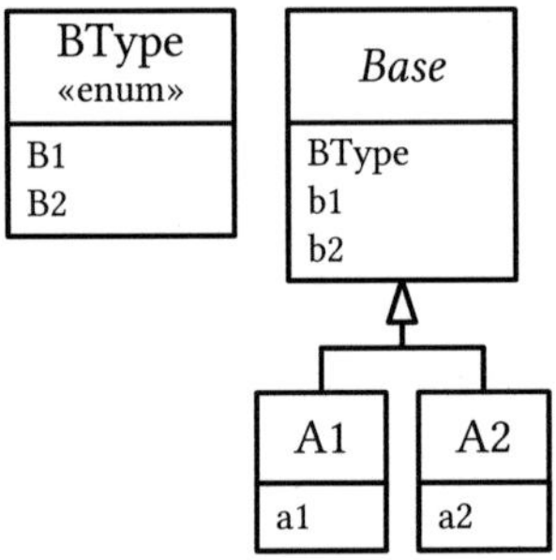

Figure 4.4.: Missing Hierarchy Smell Occurrence: Classification by Enum [Str+16a]

The naive solution to modeling orthogonal classifications is shown in Figure 4.5. There, every possible combination is explicitly modeled by inheritance. This has several disadvantages. It produces a high number of classes. Although a single classification dimension is externally extensible, it is not possible to develop independent extensions, as every combination of every dimension has to be modeled.

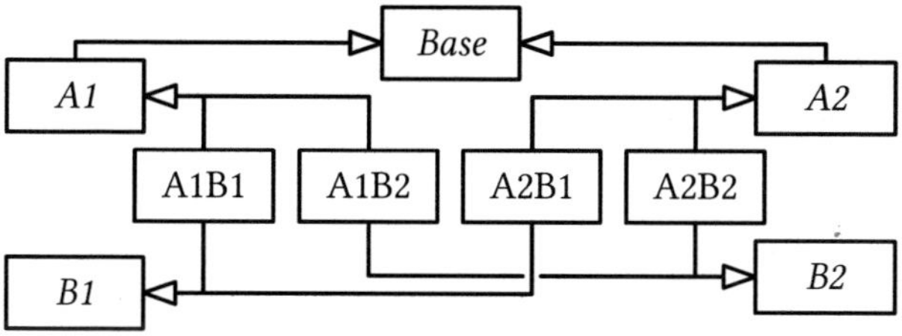

Figure 4.5.: Naive Solution to Orthogonal Classifications [Str+16a]

Developers utilize classifications by class properties because of lack of knowledge of more appropriate solutions. In addition, it looks simple and little intrusive compared to the naive approach (see Figure 4.5). If, however, the developer wants one classification to be closed for extension, s/he might consciously go for a classification by enum or boolean. If a classification does not carry any new features that vary for its subtypes, classifications by basic types might be legitimate if they are intuitive.

Correction There are two ways to resolve a Missing Hierarchy. If the classification is already known when the metamodel is initially implemented, or it is possible to modify the metamodel, the *composition over inheritance principle* [Fre+04] should be applied. This is shown in part (a) of Figure 4.6. If not, an extension should be created (see Chapter 5). This is shown in part (b).

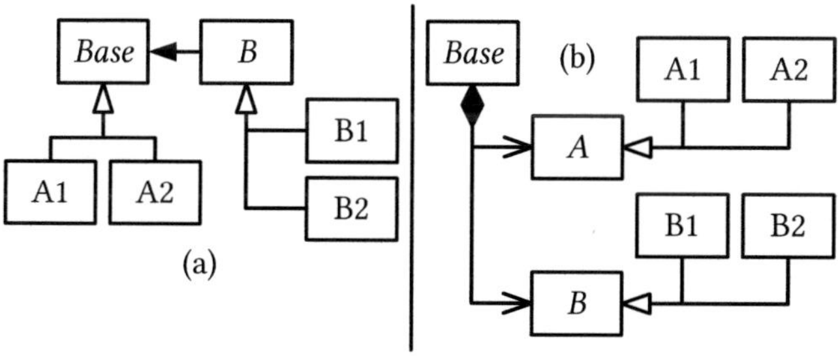

Figure 4.6.: Solutions to Orthogonal Classifications [Str+16a]

Detection Missing Hierarchies are not automatically detectable. One could scan for each usage of an enum to at least detect classifications by enum. However, not every usage is a classification. Therefore, each enum usage has to be checked manually. Classifications by data type referencing attributes cannot be detected.

4.4.3.2. Instance Data Modeled by Inheritance

The Instance Data Modeled by Inheritance smell is known in object orientation as Object Classes [LP09].

Description Instance Data Modeled by Inheritance occurs if inheritance is used to model non-type information. Type information does not change during the lifetime of an object. If it does, however, a new object of a sibling class has to be created to replace the former object. This is a reliable indicator that the inheritance does not model type information but state information and should be replaced by one or multiple attributes.

Effect Instance Data Modeled by Inheritance affects tools that are based on the metamodel. As new objects have to be created to perform changes in the state that is modeled by the unnecessary hierarchy, the code of these tools gets more complex. A Instance Data Modeled by Inheritance occurrence is also bad for the understandability of the metamodel. As usually, only type information is modeled using inheritance, a developer might wrongfully assume that the unnecessary hierarchy models proper type information.

Reason and Rationale This bad smell is merely a flaw in the design of the metamodel. The responsible metamodel developer simply did not realize that the inheritance does not model type information.

Correction The inheritance should be replaced by one or multiple attributes. It must be possible to cover the state that is covered by the subclasses before the refactoring using the attributes. For example, two subclasses can be replaced by one Boolean attribute; however, it cannot replace three subclasses.

Attribute types with a closed value range should only be used if the state space that is to be modeled is also closed and will not be expanded in the future. Closed attribute types are, e.g., booleans and enums. Open ones are, e.g., numbers[2] and strings.

Note that it is not considered a good practice to encode complex state information into strings. Instead, the state space should be modeled with an additional class hierarchy. If the state classes do not carry any additional attributes or references, they should be used as singletons. This approach does not cause an occurrence of the Instance Data Modeled by Inheritance smell, as the state information is modeled externally.

Detection Instance Data Modeled by Inheritance occurrences are not reliably detectable. A rough heuristic is to look for classes with many subclasses that do not possess any properties. The number of subclasses is defined as a threshold. This, however, produces false positives, as proper inheritances are also detected. It also suffers from false negatives, as unnecessary hierarchies could be smaller than the threshold or even feature some class properties in the child classes.

4.4.3.3. Redundancies in Hierarchy

Redundancies in Hierarchy is known in object orientation as Orphan Sibling Attribute [TT07], Incomplete Inheritance [Bie06], and Redundant Variable Declaration [CU06]. It is related to the duplicate code smell [Fow+99]. The tool metaBest [LGL14b] provides a property (B01) that is identical to this smell.

Description Redundancies in Hierarchy appear in two cases. In the first case, class properties are duplicated in sibling classes (see in my paper [Str+16a]). Classes are sibling if they share a common superclass. In the second case, class properties are duplicated in a class and its direct or indirect superclass.

Effect Redundancies in Hierarchy introduce redundancy. It impedes the evolvability of a metamodel, as the class properties have to be evolved together. By not doing so, inconsistencies may compromise the correctness of the metamodel. The smell is also bad for the understandability of a

[2] Technically, numbers are limited by the amount of memory that is used to represent the specific data type. It is, however, unlikely that a class hierarchy exceeds the value range of a numeric data type. For example, on most platforms the maximal integer value is $2^{31} - 1$.

metamodel, as the duplication of the properties unnecessarily increases its complexity. When they inspect the metamodel, developers have to recognize that the redundant properties model the same thing.

Reason and Rationale Redundancies in Hierarchy may result as a mishap in the design or implementation of the metamodel. Another reason is the repeated addition of class properties by metamodel developers. Class properties could be introduced without noticing that they are already present in a super or sibling class.

Correction If the class property is shared across all sibling classes, and they are appropriate to the superclass, a pull-up refactoring should be conducted [LR13]. If the class properties do not fit the semantics of the superclass, a new superclass may be introduced. If only some siblings share the class properties, a new superclass should be introduced only for them. New superclasses may or may not inherit from the former superclass. This depends on the semantics of the class properties that are factored out. If class properties are shared between a class and its superclass, the properties should be removed from the child class.

Detection Automated detection of Redundancies in Hierarchy is possible but suffers from false negatives. Only duplicated class properties can be detected that have identical names and types. As soon as there is a discrepancy, the duplication can only be found manually. This detection may even produce false positives. This is the case if two class properties are identical but represent different concepts. This case could itself be considered to be a bad smell. At least one of the properties should be renamed to indicate that the properties represent different concepts.

4.4.3.4. Wide Hierarchy

The Wide Hierarchy smell is known in object orientation as Missing Levels of Abstraction [MHK99], Coarse Hierarchies [MHK99], Getting Away from Abstraction [CU06], and Fat Class Hierarchies[3]. Inheritance width is also analyzed by the metaBest tool [LGL14b] (D05).

[3] `http://wiki.c2.com/?FatClassHierarchies` (last visited 23.08.2019)

Description A class with many subclasses is considered a wide hierarchy. Wide hierarchies might be an indicator for missing intermediate superclasses. Intermediate superclass refers to a class that lies in between two classes in the inheritance hierarchy. Wide Hierarchies might occur together with the Redundancies in Hierarchy smell, as intermediate superclasses are missing that could provide common class properties.

Effect A wide inheritance hierarchy can be hard to understand. Especially, if there are meaningful partitions, that could be implemented using intermediate superclasses. The code of metamodel-based tools may become complexer. Considering a case where a meaningful intermediate superclass could be referenced by the tool. As the intermediate superclass does not exist, type safety is lost. The code has to refer to the next superclass that is too general. To ensure type safety, type checks for the desired subclasses have to be put in place.

Reason and Rationale Wide hierarchies are a flaw in the design or implementation of the metamodel. They can be caused by a metamodel developer who repeatedly adds subtypes without considering or noticing the opportunity to introduce an intermediate superclass.

Correction A metamodel developer can correct Wide Hierarchies by inserting intermediate superclasses and redirecting the inheritance accordingly. If there are common class properties in the subclasses of the intermediate superclass, the metamodel developer should pull them up. The correction of the Redundancies in Hierarchy smell already explained this (see Section 4.4.3.3).

Detection Wide Hierarchies can be automatically detected with the metric for the number of child classes. All classes of the metamodel are iterated and reported if the metric exceeds a certain threshold. Of course, this is prone to false positives. The appropriateness of the broadness of an inheritance depends on the context. Sometimes, there just are many sibling classes, and no meaningful partitioning by intermediate superclasses is possible.

4.4.3.5. Speculative Hierarchy

Speculative Hierarchy is known in object orientation as Extra Subclass [CU06] and Speculative Generality [Fow+99]. The tool metaBest [LGL14b] provides a property (D03) and EMF Refactor offers a smell detection that are identical to this smell.

Description The Speculative Hierarchy smell occurs if an abstract class only has one subclass. Concrete superclasses with only one subclass are no problem, as the superclass can be used on its own by instantiation. The sole purpose of an abstract class, on the other hand, is to be the target of inheritance. It is essential to not only examine the metamodel file in that the class resides but also dependent metamodel files; dependent metamodel files could very well add new subclasses into the inheritance hierarchy.

Splitting a class into a superclass and a subclass is sometimes done for the sake of modularization. As long as the superclass and its subclass provide meaningful semantics, the constellation is legitimate. A class without properties and only one subclass, however, is definitely a design flaw that should be corrected.

Effect An unnecessary intermediate class brings unnecessary complexity, as there is one more class for the developer to consider. It is even worse for the understandability of the metamodel if the semantics of the superclass and its child are not meaningful.

Reason and Rationale Occurrences of Speculative Hierarchy are either flaws in the design of the metamodel or introduced on purpose. A design flaw occurred if the metamodel developer who introduced the abstract intermediate class anticipated to add further subclasses or attributes, but did not do so, as it was not necessary. On the other hand, a metamodel developer introduces the smell on purpose if the intermediate superclass is intended to serve as an extension point and extensions are expected in the future. In such cases, the smell occurrence is benign.

Correction A Speculative Hierarchy is corrected by removing the intermediate superclass (S). If S has superclasses, the child of S (C) has to inherit from all superclasses of S. If S has properties, they are moved to C. All incoming dependencies on S are redirected on C.

Detection Speculative Hierarchies can easily be automatically detected by scanning a metamodel for abstract classes with only one subclass. For the stricter version of Speculative Hierarchy, the detection ignores classes with properties. As already mentioned, it is essential to not only analyze single metamodel files but all files of a metamodel including metamodel extensions.

In both detection modes, the normal and the strict variant, the detection produces false positives, as the intermediate class could be a meaningful extension point. The less strict detection mode of Speculative Hierarchy produces more false positives, as it is unlikely that a large portion of intermediate classes is unnecessary. The strict detection mode results in false negatives, as flawed intermediate classes with properties are not detected.

4.4.3.6. Deep Hierarchy

Deep Hierarchy is known in object orientation as Deep Class Hierarchies[4]. Inheritance dept is also analyzed by the metaBest tool [LGL14b] (M04).

Description A Deep Hierarchy occurs if there is an excessively deep inheritance hierarchy. Depth refers to the number of classes in a chain of classes that are related through inheritance relations. The depth of the inheritance chain of the furthest down subclasses and its highest superclass is relevant to the Deep Hierarchy smell.

A deep inheritance hierarchy is not always problematic. For example, it is legitimate if all classes in a chain of inheritances are meaningful on their own. It can, however, be an indicator for problems like unnecessary or poorly cut superclasses. A Deep Hierarchy may occur together with the Speculative Hierarchy and the Instance Data Modeled by Inheritance smell, but may also appear independently.

Effect Unnecessarily deep inheritance hierarchies damage a metamodels understandability. Unnecessary divisions of superclasses create unnecessary complexity, and semantically inappropriate superclasses may confuse developers.

The claim that it is difficult to discern all the features of a class if they are scattered over many superclasses [Hah17] is false. With proper tool support, all features of a class can be viewed at once. Such tool support is available in EMF (e.g., the EClass Information view and the Contextual Explorer view).

Reason and Rationale As a Deep Hierarchy may occur together with the Instance Data Modeled by Inheritance and Speculative Hierarchy smell, their reasons and rationale coincide in these cases. To summarize, it is

[4] `http://wiki.c2.com/?DeepClassHierarchies` (last visited 23.08.2019)

either a flaw in the design of the metamodel or caused by intentionally placed extension points that are not yet needed. If a Deep Hierarchy occurs independently of those smells, there are two reasons left. First, the occurrence is harmless, as the depth of the class hierarchy is needed and appropriate to model the subject matter. Second, the hierarchy is unnecessarily deep, and the depth is caused by semantic modeling errors that lead to unnecessary classes in the hierarchy.

Correction If a Deep Hierarchy coincides with the Instance Data Modeled by Inheritance or Speculative Hierarchy smell, refer to the correction description of the respective smell. In summary, non-type information should be transformed into attributes or references, and unnecessary intermediate classes should be fused with sub- or superclasses. If the Deep Hierarchy smell occurs on its own and is not the result of a complex subject matter, the semantic errors have to be identified and fixed. How this is done depends on the concrete circumstance. It often entails the fusion of levels in the class hierarchy.

Detection To automatically detect a Deep Hierarchy, the superclasses of each class are crawled. Starting from a class, the inheritance relations to its superclasses span a tree with the initial class as the root. Each branch of the tree has to be traversed until a class is reached that does not have a superclass. This means it is a leaf. While traversing the branches, the distance of each superclass to the root is counted in terms of inheritance relations. If a leaf reaches the defined threshold, it is a Deep Hierarchy occurrence.

This detection suffers from false positives, as not all deep hierarchies are necessarily problematic, as mentioned in the description of this smell. This detection also suffers from false negatives, as unnecessarily deep hierarchies can exist that are shorter than the depth threshold.

4.4.3.7. Multipath Hierarchy

The Multipath Hierarchy smell is known in object orientation as Degenerate Inheritance [BL03], Repeated Inheritance [Mey09], and Diamon Inheritance [Are14].

Description Multipath Hierarchy describes a setting in which there are multiple paths of inheritance from a class C to one of its superclasses S. There are two cases of Multipath Hierarchy. Figure 4.7 illustrates both cases.

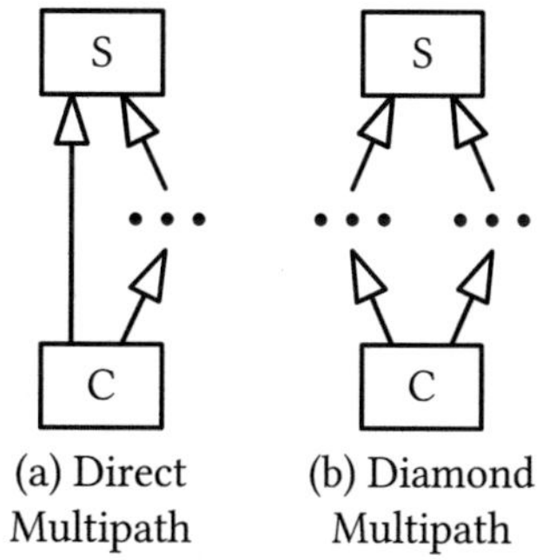

Figure 4.7.: The Multipath Hierarchy Smell

In the first case (a), there is a direct inheritance from C to S. If C then also inherits from another class that has S as a direct or indirect superclass, this is referred to as a Direct Multipath Hierarchy. The inheritance from C to S is redundant.

In the second case (b), C inherits from two or more classes that have S as a direct or indirect superclass. This is referred to as a Diamond Multipath, in reference to the diamond problem from object orientation. Compared to the Direct Multipath Hierarchy, this setting is of a more benign nature. If all inheritance relations from the superclasses of C to S are necessary, this the Diamond Hierarchy cannot be avoided.

Effect In the Direct Multipath Hierarchy, the direct inheritance from C to S is redundant. This unnecessarily increases the complexity of C. If a developer inspects C, s/he may consider the direct inheritance as well as the inheritance to the intermediate superclass. However, the information from the direct inheritance is already contained in the inheritance to the intermediate superclass.

Reason and Rationale The reason for a Multipath Hierarchy occurrence is simply carelessness. It results from a metamodel developer who adds a new superclass via inheritance and not being aware that the superclass is already an indirect superclass.

Correction To resolve a Direct Multipath Hierarchy, the direct inheritance can just be deleted. The deletion has no adverse side effects.

As already mentioned, a Diamond Inheritance may be the only way to abstract a specific subject matter. In such cases, it should not be removed. On the other hand, a Diamond Hierarchy is resolvable if there are one or multiple unnecessary inheritances between the superclasses of C and S. The unnecessary inheritances can just be deleted.

Detection Multipath Hierarchies can be automatically detected by analyzing every class in a metamodel for multiple inheritance paths. To find multiple inheritance paths of a class, the direct and indirect superclasses have to be crawled and collected in a set. Before a superclass is added to the set, it has to be checked if the set already contains the superclass. If so, a Multipath Hierarchy is found. To detect all multipaths, all superclasses have to be crawled. By storing information about the inheritance path for the classes that are stored in the set of superclasses, the exact paths can be reported that contribute to the Multipath Hierarchy.

Automatic Resolution A Direct Multipath Hierarchy can be detected with full accuracy and can always be resolved without adverse effects. This means this variant of the Multipath Hierarchy can be automatically resolved. Each inheritance that points to the superclass that is already inherited via another class can automatically be deleted.

Diamond Inheritances cannot be automatically resolved as it cannot be automatically determined if an inheritance is unnecessary.

4.4.3.8. Concrete Abstract Class

Concrete Abstract Class is known in object orientation as Late Abstraction [TT07], and Concrete Superclass [Are14]. The tool metaBest [LGL14b] provides a property (D05) that is related to this smell.

Description Concrete Abstract Class is concerned with classes that should be abstract, but are not (see my paper [Str+16a]). In a class hierarchy, a class with subtypes is often abstract. However, not every occurrence is necessarily bad design, as sometimes even a concrete class might have concrete subclasses. A concrete class that has abstract subclasses is an even more severe case of this smell.

Effect If a class that should be abstract is not declared as such, this has a negative impact on the metamodels correctness and understandability. Due to the fact, that an instance of the metamodel may validly contain direct instances of a class that should not have any instances, the metamodel is less correct. Usually, this problem is hidden by self-built editors, which just do not offer any possibility to create direct instances of the affected class. When using entirely generated model editors (like the EMF tree editors), however, this problem does manifest.

Further, the understandability of the metamodel is slightly reduced by a Concrete Abstract Class. A developer, who investigates the metamodel, cannot instantly identify the class as abstract and has to reflect.

Some claim [TT07] that a Late Hierarchy occurrence violates Liskov's Substitution Principle [LW94], as an abstract subclass cannot be instantiated in contrast to its concrete superclass This is, however, dependent on the interpretation of the principle, as originally it only applies to objects and is therefore not applicable to an abstract and a concrete class.

Reason and Rationale A Concrete Abstract Class appears because of carelessness mistakes.

Correction The correction of a Concrete Abstract Class is trivial. The affected class has to merely be declared as abstract.

Detection Occurrences of Concrete Abstract Class can only partly be detected automatically. If a concrete class has subclasses, it might be a pathological case of Concrete Abstract Class [ABT10]. If any of the subclasses are abstract, it is even more likely that there is an issue. However, manual evaluation is still required, as it might be the case that the superclass is validly concrete. Therefore, this detection suffers from false positives. In constellations, where all subclasses of the concrete superclass are in external metamodels, the smell can only be detected if the external metamodels are considered in the detection. If they are not considered, the concrete superclass might be wrongfully detected as a Dead Class (Section 4.4.1.2). This is the case if the class and its superclasses are never used within the metamodel but carry the information of an abstract concept that should be specialized in other metamodel files.

4.4.4. Relation

The Relation category is concerned with dependencies and their constrainment. The category features the bad smells Dependency Cycles, Container Relation, Obligatory Container Relation, and Specialized Relation.

4.4.4.1. Dependency Cycle

The Dependency Cycle smell is known in object orientation as Cyclic Dependencies [Pag88], Bidirectional Relation [CU06], and Dependency Cycle [Are14]. It is further related to the object-oriented smells Knows of Derived [TT07; GSS13] and Curious Superclasses [BL03].

Description In metamodeling, dependency cycles (see my paper [Str+16a]) can appear on different levels: between classes, packages and metamodel files. Dependencies between classes are caused by references, containments, inheritance, type parameters, and type bounds (see also Section 2.2). Dependencies between packages are caused by the dependencies of classes of the package that point to classes of another package. This is analogous to metamodel files. The dependencies of a metamodel file are caused by the classes that reside in the packages of the metamodel file. Dependencies form a cycle when starting from one element (class, package, or metamodel file) it is possible to follow dependencies to elements of the same type (class, package, or metamodel file) and eventually reach the starting element again. The cycle has to involve at least two elements. A dependency from an element to itself does not constitute a cycle. A bidirectional dependency causes a dependency cycle with two affected elements.

On the class level, dependency cycles are sometimes unavoidable to model an interdependent relationship between concepts. Often, however, dependency cycles and especially bidirectional dependencies are created to mirror another dependency.

To explain this, a small toy example from the automotive domain is presented. Consider hardware controllers and sockets on which a controller can be placed. A socket knows which controller is placed on it. If a controller also knows on which socket it is placed, this information is redundant.

Such bidirectional dependencies are unnecessary, as, in models, there is enough information to navigate dependencies in the opposite direction. This can be done in three ways. Firstly, in many cases, an object is reached by following references. To navigate a reference in the opposite direction, one can simply backtrack. For this, the objects that were visited have to be kept in memory, which is usually the case. The second option is by navigating to the source of the dependency via the root. This is, however, more expensive, as the containment tree has to be crawled. The third option is to create and maintain cross-referencing information for all or selected references in either the memory or the model.

A special case of the Dependency Cycle smell is known in object orientation as Knows of Derived. It is considered a bad practice if a superclass is dependent on one of its subclasses. Figure 4.8 illustrates the problem. The superclass has either a reference or a containment to at least one subclass. A Knows of Derived occurrence violates the dependency inversion principle.

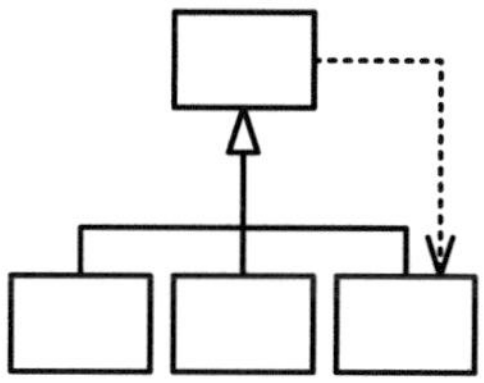

Figure 4.8.: Superclass is Dependent on Subclass

Effect Dependency cycles impede the understandability of a metamodel, as for a full understanding it might be required to consider all elements in the cycle. The modularization of a metamodel is encumbered by dependency cycles. They have to be resolved if they couple the parts of the metamodel that should be separated.

Cycles between metamodel files are always harmful. They reduce the reusability of the metamodel files, as the files within the cycle can only be reused together. They even lead to compiler errors when code from the metamodels is generated into separate units of compilation (e.g., two jars or projects).

Dependency cycles between classes are sometimes bad, sometimes benign. Classes on the same level of abstraction that describe the same concept can be involved in a cycle. These classes are then strongly coupled. This is not a bad thing if they can only be used together from a conceptual standpoint. If this does not apply, the cycle is harmful, and the drawbacks that are described above apply.

The same principle from cycles between classes can also be applied to packages. If the packages are intended to be used together, dependency cycles are benign. This is the case in metamodel files that are appropriately modularized. Metamodel files that are not adequately modularized tend to contain many unnecessary dependencies and dependency cycles between their packages. This is the case as in Ecore the creation of new dependencies between packages within a metamodel file is not constrained.

A cycle violates the dependency inversion principle [Mar03] if elements in the cycle are of different degrees of abstraction. This is also the case for Knows of Derived occurrences, as the superclass is of a stronger abstraction compared with its subclasses, it should not depend on them. Violations of the dependency inversion principle are described by the Inconsistent Abstraction smell. For more details on the effects of Inconsistent Abstraction, refer to Section 4.4.1.3.

Reason and Rationale A problematic class cycle is a design flaw that is either introduced on purpose but without being aware of the adverse side effects or unintentionally by adding a dependency and not being aware that the new dependency closes a cycle. There is no rationale to utilize metamodel file and package cycles deliberately. They are introduced by ignorance of the best practice or an intrusive addition that introduces a dependency to another metamodel file or package and the metamodel developer being unaware that the new dependency closes a cycle. Regarding package cycles, in EMF, this is a drawback of using packages for modularization, as packages do not constrain the creation of dependencies to other packages.

Correction Dependency cycles can be broken by splitting a class (see Section 6.5.1.1), package, or even a metamodel file (see Section 6.5.2). To resolve a cycle between packages or metamodel files, it may be sufficient to move one or more inadequately placed classes. If a Dependency Cycle is caused by an Inconsistent Abstraction, the respective dependency should be reversed (see Section 4.4.1.3). Sometimes, a cycle is merely caused by an unnecessary or erroneous dependency. In such cases, the dependency can be deleted or should be redirected. An example of an unnecessary dependency is a back-reference that is only present for the ease of navigation, as explained earlier.

Detection The detection of Dependency Cylces can be performed automatically. Dependency Cycles between classes, packages, and metamodel files can be found by transforming the respective metamodel elements into a directed graph and applying a cycle detection algorithm (e.g., Floyd's cycle detection algorithm [Flo67]). For example for packages, packages are transformed into nodes, and dependencies between packages are transformed into edges.

4.4.4.2. Container Relation

Description Containment in metamodeling is essential, as models form a tree of objects that contain other objects. Containment relations are needed to define this hierarchical structure and to build complex types. When tools process models, it is often necessary to navigate from an object to its container. In EMF, each object carries the generic eContainer reference that points to its container. Except for model root objects, this reference is always set. It is, however, also possible to create a new reference and declare it as the opposite of a containment relation. This makes the reference a container relation. In EMF, there is even a flag that indicates whether a reference is a container relation. Container relations are considered a bad smell (see my paper [Str+16a]).

Container relations have either a lower multiplicity bound of 0 or 1. Higher values are not possible, as an object can only be contained in one other object at any time. The Container Relation smell is concerned with container relations with a lower bound of 0. A lower bound of 1 has further implications and is discussed in the next section.

Effect Container relations create unnecessary complexity. The explicit container relation is not needed, as the information is already present in the eContainer reference. The unnecessary complexity is especially bad if a class is contained from several other classes and, thus, has many container relations. Only one of the container relations is set at a time. The unnecessary container relations clutter the class. In the PCM, there is a particularly severe case. One class carries 17 container relations.

As a container relation opposes a containment relation, it creates a dependency cycle between the contained class and its container. This comes with all the drawbacks of dependency cycles (see Section 4.4.4.1). It is detrimental to reusing the metamodel, as the container always has to be deployed with the contained class. Even if another container is used and the container to which the container relation exists is unnecessary. This gets more severe if the container and the containee are in different metamodel files. This establishes a hard coupling between both metamodel files and, thus, the modularization is in vain.

Container relations do some harm to the maintainability of a metamodel. Depending on the editor that is used to modify the metamodel if the container is deleted, the container relations remains and points nowhere. The contained class has then to be adapted.

Reason and Rationale There are two reasons for Container Relations. First, metamodel developers might consciously use explicit container relations, as they think that they ensure type safety. The second reason are transformations from other meta-languages. These reasons are discussed in the following.

At first glance, one may think that an explicit container relation ensures type safety when it is used in the code of tools. This is, however, only the case if there is only one type of container. In these cases, the explicit container is always correctly set and typed. On the other hand, the eContainer reference has to be cast to the container type. However, in this situation, the eContainer reference can always be successfully cast to the container type. Thus, in this case, the only benefit from the explicit container reference is the avoidance of the cast. This could, however, also be achieved by a helper method that casts eContainer.

The other case that has to be considered regarding type safety is the existence of multiple types of containers. In such situations, the explicit container relation might point to a container object of the type of the container relation, or it is not set. This means before working with the container relation, it has to be tested if it is set. To find the container, it is necessary to test different container relations until the proper container is found. In contrast, the eContainer relation is always set but has to be checked for the type of the container. Checking the type of the eContainer is similar to testing whether the container relations are set or not. Thus, also in the case of multiple types of containers, explicit container relations bring no benefit.

The second reason for container relations is the translation of a metamodel from another meta-language. For example, in UML class diagrams, both ends of relations can be named. To informal models, this affects, that they become more explicit. If such models are transformed into metamodels, however, relations with two named ends are usually translated into two opposing references. If the relation in UML is a composition, this results in a Container Relation smell occurrence.

Correction The solution to Container Relations is simply to delete the container reference. In the code of tools that work with the metamodel, access to the container relation has to be replaced with the eContainer reference. If the explicit container was not checked for null, eContainer can be cast to the container type. In this case, the cast can be replaced by a call to helper method. If, on the other hand, the container relation is checked for null, eContainer has to be checked and cast to the expected container type.

Detection Container Relations can be automatically detected. For each reference, it has to be checked if the container flag is set to true.

Automatic Resolution Container Relations can be detected with full accuracy and can always be removed without implications onto the metamodel. Thus, Container Relations can be automatically resolved. Each Container Relation that is detected to have a lower multiplicity bound of 0 can be deleted.

Relation to Object Orientation Container Relations do not exist in object orientation, as there are in general no explicit containers. Objects are contained in the heap memory and are merely referenced by other objects or the stack. If no more references to an object exist, the object is eventually deleted. In metamodeling and modeling, on the other hand, each object except for the model root must have a container. If that container is deleted, all contained elements are also deleted, and all references to the deleted elements are unset.

4.4.4.3. Obligatory Container Relation

Description A Obligatory Container Relation is a special case of the Container Relation smell (see Section 4.4.4.2). If a containment relation has an opposite reference that has a lower multiplicity bound of 1, it is an Obligatory Container Relation (see my paper [Str+16a]). Figure 4.9 illustrates the smell. Class C1 contains A, and the container relation is obligatory.

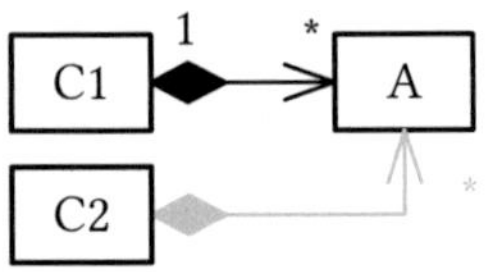

Figure 4.9.: The Obligatory Container Relation Smell [Str+16a]

Effect A cannot be used in any other context. E.g., although C2 has a containment relation to A, an instance of C2 can never contain any instances of A. An object can only be contained in at most one other object. This means only one container relation can be set. As the container relation to an instance of C1 has a lower bound of 1, it always has to be set. In such cases, the EMF framework does not even allow code generation for C2.

Even if it is foreseeable that the class will not be reused in other metamodels, an obligatory container relation should not be used. It may still be necessary to instantiate the class independently of a proper complete model. E.g., this is the case when fragments are created for documentation or as alternatives for automatic optimization[5].

Reason and Rationale There are some reasons why one might want to use an obligatory container reference. It ensures type safety when navigating to the container, as it prohibits any other type of container. It is also possible that the metamodel developer wants to restrict reuse explicitly. In most circumstances, however, the metamodel developer was most likely unaware of this consequence. Like the Container Relation smell, Obligatory Container Relations can also be the result of a translation from another format or language (e.g., UML) by a transformation. Especially when informal

[5] https://sdqweb.ipd.kit.edu/wiki/Architecture_as_Connection_between_Requirements_and_Quality_Prediction (last visited 23.08.2019)

class diagrams are designed, there is a tendency to explicitly specify both directions of a containment relation.

Correction To fix a Obligatory Container Relation, remove the container reference. Regarding code that uses A, the eContainer reference of A can be cast to C1, as long as there are no other containers like C2. If there are other containers, the type of the eContainer reference has to be checked.

Detection Obligatory container relations can be automatically detected. For each reference, it has to be checked if the container flag is set and if the lower multiplicity bound is 1. There are no false positives and no false negatives.

Relation to Object Orientation As with Container Relation, the Obligatory Container Relation smell is not relevant in object orientation, as there is no explicit containment.

4.4.4.4. Specialized Relation

Specialized Relation is known in object orientation as Specialization Aggregation [PS16; Are14].

Description The Specialized Relation smell is concerned with references that are respecified in a subclass with a more specific target class. Figure 4.10 (a) illustrates the Specialized Relation smell on an abstract level. Class A references B through reference r1. The subclass A' of A provides the reference r2 that points to B', which is a subclass of B. There may be further intermediate classes between A and A' as well as between B and B'. In the simplest case, A' and B' are direct subclasses. To specialize a reference means that in a subclass a reference expresses the same relationship but is limited in its type range. For a simple example, consider part (b) of the figure. A System references Software, but its subclass EmbeddedSystem references EmbeddedSoftware. EmbeddedSystem does not need r1, as it has r2 as a more specific alternative. In MOF, the specialization of references without any further arrangements is considered a bad smell. This is a limitation of MOF in contrast to other meta-languages that support the refinement of references (e.g., NMF [Hin18]). If r2 is flagged as derived and transient or A' features a constraint that prohibits the use of r1, r2 is not considered a Specialized Relation smell occurrence. More information about this is provided in the correction section.

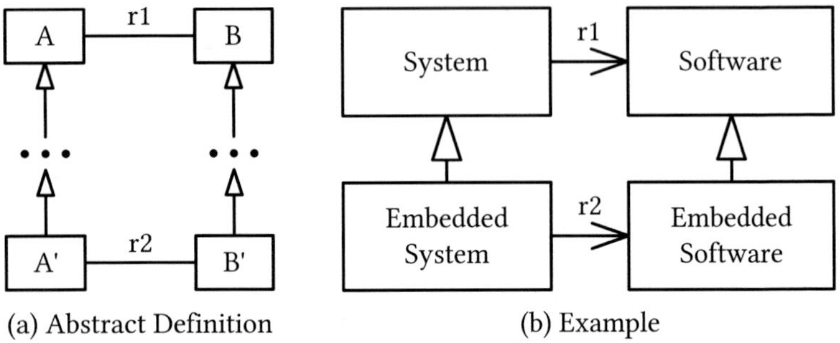

Figure 4.10.: The Specialized Relation Smell

Effect The main problem with specialized references is that the original relation still exists and can be used independently from the specialized one. This introduces redundancy.

It impacts the correctness of the metamodel as it leads to errors while using the metamodel. If it is assumed that with an instance of A' only r2 is used, but r1 is used, the referenced instances of B' are stored in different sets. This is the case if code of a metamodel-based tool either accidentally uses r1 or an instance of A' is treated as A and, thus, only r1 is accessible.

A specialized reference also impedes the understandability of a metamodel. r2 does not declare any ties to r1. From the metamodel, it is not apparent that two references model the same thing. To discover this relation might cost a metamodel developer some time.

A specialized reference also slightly impacts the maintainability of the metamodel. On deletion of the target class, the specialized reference loses its type and has to be adapted.

Reason and Rationale A Specialized Relation occurs either because the metamodel developer has overlooked that a more general reference already exists in a superclass that could have been used instead. It is also possible that the metamodel developer was aware of the more general reference but wanted to specialize it nevertheless to constrain its type range. In that case, s/he was not aware that there are better ways to support this implementation. This is explained in the next section.

Correction If the specialized reference is unnecessary, it can just be removed, and the more general reference can be used. This solution reduces complexity, but also loses the limitation on the more specific class B'.

An alternative solution is to flag r2 as derived and transient and provide a custom implementation that accesses the entries of r1 that are of the type B'. When the values of the r2 are read, the values of r1 are filtered for instances of B'. Additions and removals are also delegated to r1, as r1 can handle instances B'. Alternatively to a custom derived reference, a feature map can be used [EMF04]. In A, a feature map has to be already present or has to be set up instead of the reference r1. Based on that feature map, further derived references can be created in A and its subclasses.

It is also possible to create a constraint for A' that does not allow instances of classes except B' in r1. This can be combined with making r2 derived and transient. This solution violates Liskov's substitution principle [LW94], as A' can no longer be used like its superclass A. Depending on the circumstances, however, this can be legitimate in modeling. E.g., A is not referenced in external code, as it is only used to provide class properties through inheritance.

Detection Specialized Relations can be automatically detected by iterating over all classes and comparing inherited references with local references. A local reference is defined in the class, in contrast to an inherited one. Considering the references r1 and r2 from the figure, the following conditions have to be fulfilled for r2 to be a Specialized Relation smell occurrence:

- r2 has a more specific class than an inherited reference (i.e., r1). This means it references a subclass of B.
- r1 and r2 have to both be either a normal reference or a containment. If one of them is a containment and the other is not, they model different relations and are, therefore, not a smell occurrence.
- r2 is not flagged as derived and transient.

Not all references that are detected this way are problematic. If the references model different relations, the detection of the smell is a false positive.

4.5. Automatic Bad Smell Detection

To enable automatic detection of bad smells, the metamodel quality assurance tool EMF Refactor (see Section 2.2.9) was migrated to the current Eclipse version. The source code can be found online[6]. It was further modified to handle the input of multiple metamodel files at once to be able to process modular metamodels efficiently. Using the predefined extension points, the following 14 bad smell detections were implemented. The list is divided into quantity- and anti-pattern-based smell detections.

The Speculative Hierarchy detection was already implemented in EMF Refactor. It was, however, adjusted only to detect abstract classes that have one subclass. Before the adjustment, it detected abstract classes that had one concrete subclass. Abstract subclasses were ignored. An abstract class with one concrete subclass and further abstract subclasses is, however, not problematic. The abstract subclasses could provide further meaningful subclasses. This would mean, that the abstract superclass is not speculative but meaningful. The detection was further adjusted to be able to process modular metamodels.

Metric-based Bad Smell Detections:

- Missing Class – Primitive Obsession: Classes with many attributes of primitive data types
- Missing Class – Shared Properties: Classes that share a specific number of identical attributes (name, type, multiplicity)
- God Class
- Wide Hierarchy
- Deep Hierarchy

[6] `https://github.com/kit-sdq-emf-refactor-fork` (last visited 23.08.2019)

Quantity-based Bad Smell Detections:

- Dead Classifier – Dead Class
- Dead Classifier – Dead Enum
- Multipath Hierarchy
- Concrete Abstract Class
- Dependency Cycles
- Container Relation
- Obligatory Container Relation
- Specialized Relation
- Speculative Hierarchy

5. Metamodel Extension

Reuse in DSL engineering is not yet very prevalent. There are several approaches to reuse (see Section 11.3.1). These approaches include embedding, composition, merging, and extension. In contrast to the other approaches, extension aims to preserve compatibility to the tools of the extended metamodel.

The practices of externally extending a metamodel and the coupling of several metamodel files, however, are not yet adequately understood (see Problem 7: Metamodel Coupling). It is not clear what the advantages and disadvantages of the individual extension mechanisms are. It is unknown whether there is a single extension mechanism that can be used universally. If not, it is not clear which extension mechanisms should be used under which circumstances.

This chapter[1] presents a catalog of EMOF-based extension mechanisms and a catalog of comparison criteria. The extension mechanisms are evaluated according to the comparison criteria. From this evaluation, a decision process is derived, which guides a developer when s/he develops external extensions.

There is not much related work that surveys and evaluates EMOF-based extension mechanisms. Richard Braun, however, did extensive work in this field. He created his dissertation [Bra17] partly in parallel to the research that is presented in this chapter. The release of his dissertation, on the one hand, helps to confirm the findings that are identical. On the other hand, his dissertation opened the door to go further into detail by building on his findings. In this part, this chapter presents novel research. Section 11.2 provides a detailed differentiation to his work.

[1] This chapter is in parts based on [HSR19] (©2019 IEEE) and a bachelor's thesis [Her17], which I supervised.

This chapter is structured as follows. Section 5.1 presents the research question and presents further challenges. Section 5.2 clarifies the concept of external extension and defines essential terminology. Section 5.3 specifies the selection criteria that a mechanism has to fulfill in order to be considered an extension mechanism and to be evaluated in the scope of this thesis. Section 5.4 presents the extension mechanisms. Section 5.5 briefly lists the mechanisms that were dismissed and explains why they did not fulfill the selection criteria. Section 5.6 presents the list of comparison criteria.

This chapter is continued in subsequent parts of this thesis. Chapter 8 presents an evaluation and comparison of the extension mechanisms according to the comparison criteria. Section 11.2 presents related work. Section 12.2 concludes the metamodel extension contribution.

5.1. Research Question and Challenges

In contrast to the research questions of the first contribution from Chapter 4, which were focused on treating problems retroactively, this chapter explores the means to externally extend metamodels in order to circumvent the drawbacks of intrusive evolution and to strengthen their separation of concerns.

RQ II (Extension Mechanism Comparison): Problem 7 states that the mechanisms of extending a metamodel are not yet sufficiently understood. Therefore, this chapter explores the research question:

What are the advantages and disadvantages of different metamodel extension mechanisms?

Beyond this research question, this chapter addresses several challenges.

This contribution classifies the types of external additions of metamodels on a conceptual level. It investigates how the types of external additions can be implemented.

Problem 1 states that intrusive evolution over time erodes the internal structure of the metamodel. Therefore, this contribution investigates how to add properties to existing classes without modifying the metamodel. By doing so, a metamodel can be extended without violating separation of concerns and without causing a feature overload.

Problem 3 states that monolithic metamodels are plagued by several issues like bad understandability and all-or-nothing reuse. The metamodel can be modularized to fix such issues. To achieve this, it is sometimes necessary to separate concerns in a class in a way that fulfills the DIP. With the standard means of EMOF, this is difficult to achieve. This contribution provides an approach to achieve this.

Problem 8 states that extensions should not make an instance incompatible to the original metamodel and its tooling. Therefore, this contribution investigates how a metamodel can be extended to still ensure the compatibility of extended instances.

Problem 9 states that for some extension mechanisms it is not possible to independently develop compatible extensions for the same class. Therefore, this contribution examines how to extend metamodels in a way that allows extensions to be developed independently of each other and still be used in combination?

5.2. Terms and Definitions

This section presents several terms and definitions that are essential to this contribution. At first, it explains how external additions and extensions fit in with the classification of metamodel modifications. Next, it presents an illustration of the notation of external additions and extensions. Lastly, the concept of extensions is defined.

Figure 5.1 shows how external additions fit into the classification of metamodel modifications of Section 2.2.5. To recapitulate, an addition is an existence modification that can either be performed intrusively, in a branch, or externally. The figure explicitly shows the two types of external additions: the addition of a new subclass and the addition of a new property to an existing class. This thesis refers to the latter as a class extension.

When adding new elements to a metamodel, external extension is, however, not always the right approach. It depends on the nature of the features that should be added to the language. If the features are always used when the language is used, they should be added intrusively. Optional features, which are not always used, should indeed be implemented externally.

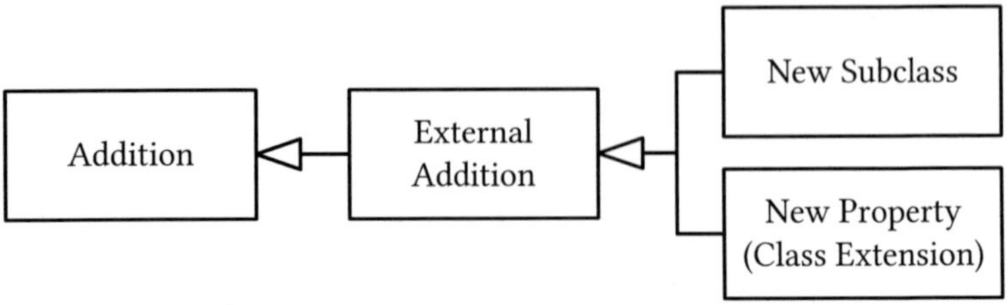

Figure 5.1.: Concept Overview: External Additions

Figure 5.2 (a) shows an illustration of the notation of external additions of subclasses. The external addition of new subclasses is supported by EMOF through the inheritance relation. The figure shows a subclass that inherits from a superclass. The subclass resides in a separate metamodel file. Thus, it implements an external addition.

Figure 5.2 (b) shows an illustration of the notation of class extensions. The external addition of new properties is not supported by EMOF. There are, however, several ways to implement it using the means of EMOF or addons to EMOF. In the figure, a base class is extended by an extension class. The notation that is used for the extends relation is taken from UML stereotypes. Both classes reside in separate metamodel files. The extended metamodel file is named the base metamodel file. The metamodel file of the extension class is named extension metamodel file. The extension class carries an arbitrary number of class properties. These are indicated by the arbitrary dependency arrow that is labeled d. Class properties are, for example, references and attributes. The extends relation implies that the properties of the extension class are added to the base class. Together, the extends relation and the extension class are named a class extension.

The labels extension class and extension metamodel file are context dependent. In the figure, they relate to the extends relation that is shown. There could be another class C in another metamodel file, that, in turn, could extend the extension class. Concerning this other extends relation, the extension class in the figure would be the base class, and C would be the extension class.

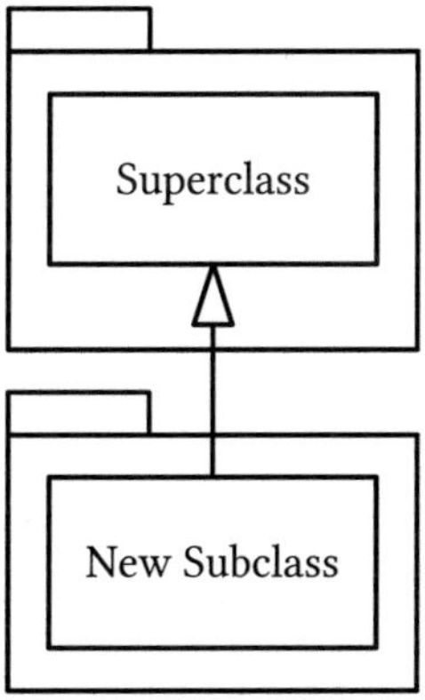

(a) External Addition of a new Subclass

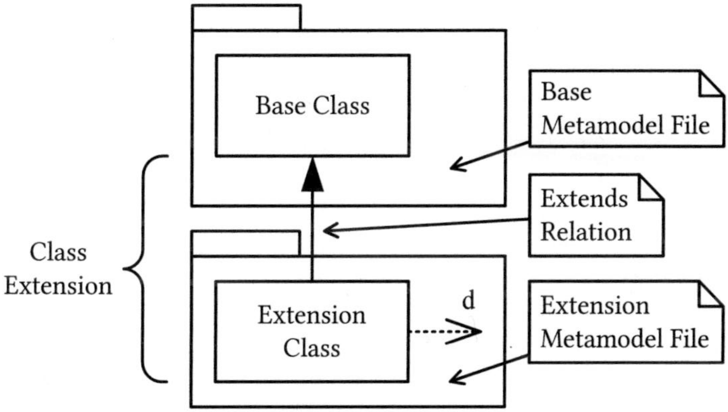

(b) Extension

Figure 5.2.: Illustration of External Additions

Figure 5.3 shows a conceptual description of class extensions. An *extension class* owns at least one extends relation that points to exactly one other class. The instance of an extension class is an *extension object*. It adds its extension content to the base object. A *base object* is an instance of the base class. Base objects are located in base model files. Depending on the extension mechanism, extension objects are either located in the *base model file* or in *extension model files*, which are separate from the base model file. This is indicated by the gray coloring of the extension model file concept and the containment from the base model file to the extension object. *Extension content* are the values of the class properties of an extension object's extension class. As already mentioned, a *class extension* consists of one extension class and one of its extends relations. Like any class, an extension class carries class properties. For a class extension to be meaningful, the extension class must carry at least one class property. An *extends relation* is implemented by an *extension mechanism*. For a metamodel file to be an *extension metamodel file*, it has to contain at least one extension class. A *metamodel extension* is a set of extension metamodel files that contains at least one file. This thesis uses the term *extension* to refer to a class extension, an extension metamodel file, or a metamodel extension in cases where all terms apply. For example, the creation of an extension means the creation of an extension metamodel file that contains an extension class; together, both constitute a new metamodel extension. The creation of an extension object and assignment of its extends relation is named *extension instantiation*.

Instead of externally, a class extension can also be implemented intrusively or in a branch. In these cases, the extends relation does not cross metamodel file boundaries. Such intrusive extensions are, however, not meaningful. Instead of implementing an intrusive extension, the class properties that are to be extended should better be intrusively added to the base class. If an intrusive extension is used to separate concerns of a class, the extension class should better be referenced by the base class. As they are not meaningful, they are not further considered in this thesis.

Some extension mechanisms need *extension points* in order to be used. They are prerequisites that a base class has to fulfill.

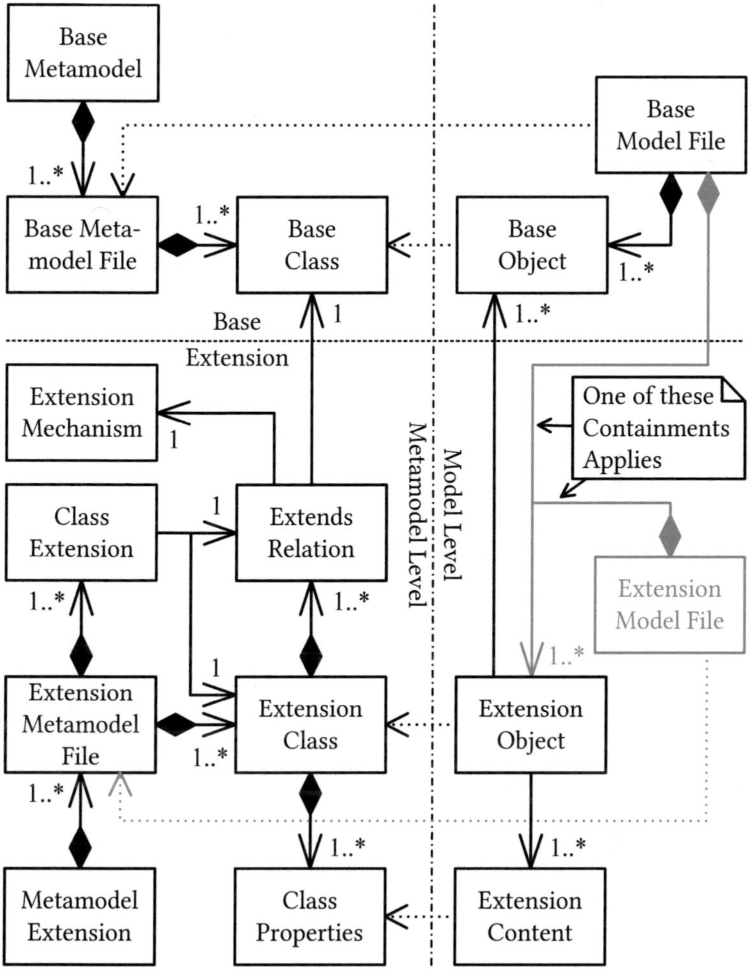

Figure 5.3.: Concept Overview: Metamodel Extension

5.3. Mechanism Selection Criteria

For this contribution, only mechanisms that fulfill specific criteria are relevant. E.g., the mechanisms should enable external extensions. Therefore, a mechanism had to fulfill several criteria in order to be evaluated. Extension mechanisms that do not fulfill these criteria are briefly presented in Section 5.5.

S1) Unintrusiveness Intrusive mechanisms were dismissed, as they do not enable an external extension. Extension mechanisms were still allowed to require extension points in the base metamodel. This is a slight degree of intrusiveness, as a metamodel that does not feature extension points has to be modified in order to support such an extension mechanism. If, on the other hand, extension points are already present in the base metamodel, the extension mechanism is not intrusive. This selection criterion helps to address Problem 1 (Package Structure Erosion and Uncontrolled Growth of Dependencies) and Problem 3 (Monolithic Metamodels). By implementing extensions externally and not intrusively, the effect of structural erosion over time can be avoided; monolithic metamodel can be modularized and coupled using external extensions. Intrusive additions, on the other hand, are not the solution, but the reason for monolithic metamodels.

S2) Instance Compatibility Language Composition approaches that either perform in-place modifications of a metamodel or produce a new metamodel to which models of the original metamodel are no longer compatible are dismissed in the scope of this evaluation. There are cases of less severe instance incompatibilities that are allowed. Some extension mechanisms add objects to a model whose classes are not known to the metamodel of the model. Usually, at least one of the superclasses of their class is from the extended metamodel. In such cases, runtime errors may occur in tools, as the direct type of the objects is not known. These errors can, however, be caught and meaningfully handled, e.g., by ignoring the unknown content. This selection criterion addresses Problem 8 (Instance Incompatibility).

S3) Metamodel Independent This evaluation only investigates extension mechanisms that work for all EMOF-based metamodels. Some extension mechanisms were explicitly developed for one metamodel. They are not of interest for this contribution.

S4) Novel and Non-Composite This evaluation only investigates extension mechanisms that were not yet investigated. Combinations of other extension mechanisms are less interesting, as they inherit the properties of these extension mechanisms.

S5) Availability In order to evaluate an extension mechanism, it must be possible to apply it. Without the option to use the extension mechanisms, several comparison criteria cannot be assessed. If an extension mechanism requires an extension to the meta-metalanguage or the modeling framework, but no implementation is available, the extension mechanism cannot be applied and investigated.

5.4. Metamodel Extension Mechanisms

This section presents a collection of metamodel extension mechanisms. They stem from experience and a literature review. To the best of my knowledge and except for the dismissed mechanisms of Section 5.5, this list is complete. In the future, however, new extension mechanisms may be developed, that are not yet included in this list.

Figure 5.4 shows what the extension should accomplish. Subfigure (0) shows the initial situation. It is simply the class B (short for base class). Subfigure (1) shows what should be emulated by an external extension. It is the result of an intrusive addition. An arbitrary dependency d is added to B. Arbitrary dependencies (dotted arrows) represents one of the dependencies that were introduced in Section 2.2 (attribute, reference, containment, inheritance, type bound or argument). The goal is, however, to extend B externally. This is shown in (2). The extension class E has an extends relation to B. It carries the extension content, which in this case is d. The notation of the extends relation is a filled arrow. It is taken from UML stereotyping. This extends relation can be implemented in several ways by the extension mechanisms that are presented in this section. Subfigure (1) could even be the starting point of a modularization where one wants to factor out

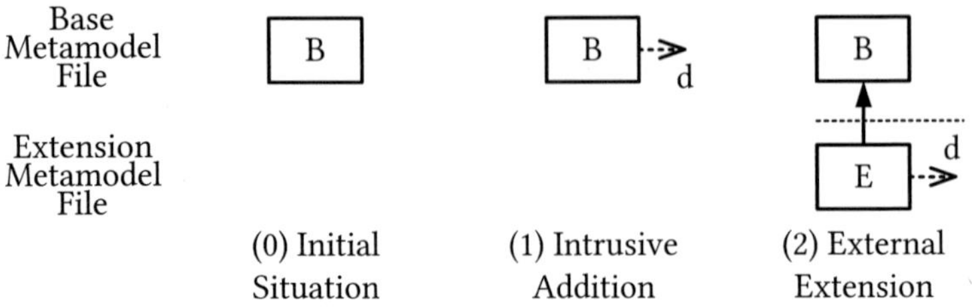

Figure 5.4.: Intrusive Addition and External Extension

the dependency d. To separate concerns, d is extracted into the new class E and placed in another metamodel file.

5.4.1. Intrusive Addition

Intrusive Addition is not a mechanism for external extension. It is, however, mentioned here for comparison. Figure 5.4 (1) shows an intrusive addition. The arbitrary dependency d is added to B. Before the addition, B did not contain d.

5.4.2. Direct Inheritance

Extension by Direct Inheritance is implemented by using a cross-module inheritance relation from the extension class to the base class. Figure 5.5 (2) shows an application of Direct Inheritance. The extension class E inherits from the base class B. E carries the extension content. If the extension is instantiated, E is instantiated instead of B. An instance of E can then be used like an instance of B with the addition that it also carries the extension content.

It is important to differentiate Direct Inheritance against the addition of new subtypes. Direct Inheritance is not used to add true subtypes to a containment but only to add new class properties to existing classes.

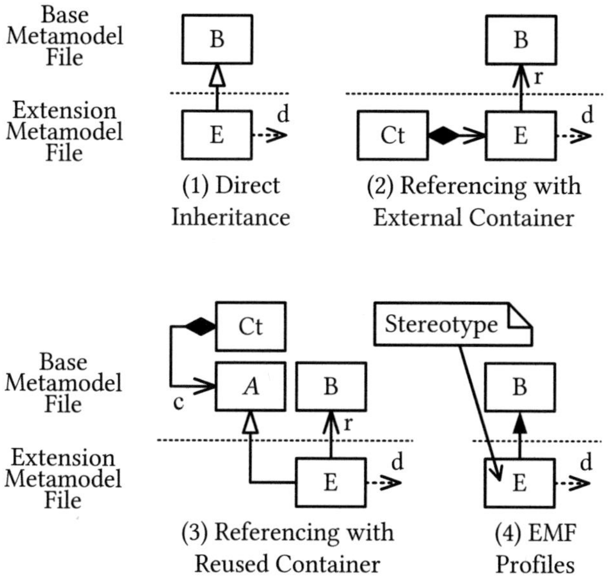

Figure 5.5.: Extension Mechanisms: Direct Inheritance, Referencing, EMF Profiles

IntBIIS [Hei+17; Hei14], for example, uses Direct Inheritance to establish extensions.

5.4.3. Referencing with External Container

An extension relation can also be realized by a reference (as explained in a paper in which I collaborated [Jun+14]). When doing so, there are several options to contain the extension class. This section first explains these options and then focuses on the first one. The next option is presented in Section 5.4.4.

As already mentioned, there are several options to contain the extension class. It could be a root container itself. This means, however, that each of its instances produces a new model file. This is only reasonable if there are only one or very few instances. This applies only to some special cases. In general, it is beneficial to provide a container for the extension class. There are two ways to achieve this: (1) by providing a new container in the extension metamodel, (2) by reusing an existing container in the base metamodel. The second option is not always feasible, as a suitable superclass has to exist.

Figure 5.5 (2) illustrates the first option. The base class B is referenced by the extension class E. E is contained by the new container Ct. Ct is located in the same metamodel file as E. The extension is instantiated as follows. For a model file that ought to be extended, a new model file with an instance of Ct as the root object is created. Tools that use the extension have to locate this extension model file. This can be done, e.g., by depositing it in the same location as the base model file and naming it accordingly. Each instance of E is contained in the root Ct object. To find an extension of a B object, the content of the root object must be iterated until one is found that points to the B object in question.

The PASE extension[2] to Palladio uses Referencing with External Container to establish extensions.

5.4.4. Referencing with Reused Container

When using a reference to realize a class extension, the second option to contain the extension objects is to reuse an existing container in the base metamodel. This is shown in Figure 5.5 (3). The extension class E references the base class B. E also inherits from A, which is contained by Ct. Ct and A are located in the base metamodel. A has to be a meaningful superclass of E. Instances of E are stored in instances of Ct. Tools that operate on the extension have to know where the Ct instance that contains the extension objects is located.

5.4.5. EMF Profiles

There is no native support for stereotypes in EMOF and EMF. EMF Profiles [Lan+11; Lan+12] is an extension to EMF that provides functionality similar

[2] `https://sdqweb.ipd.kit.edu/wiki/PASE` (last visited 23.08.2019)

to UML profiles and stereotypes [Obj17] (see also an adaption by Braun [BE15a]). This evaluation considers the current version[3] [Kra+12] of EMF Profiles. Figure 5.5 (4) shows the application of a stereotype. In this case, E is not a class but a stereotype. It is not contained in a metamodel file but in a profile. A profile contains a set of stereotypes. The arrow from E to B is a stereotype application arrow. Its notation is identical to the notation of the extends relation that is shown in Figure 5.4 (2). Attributes and references can be specified in the stereotype. Addition of containments is not possible in the current version. New complex data must be therefore defined in a separate metamodel. Tools can instantiate stereotypes on base objects and access their extension content via an API that is part of EMF Profiles. The instance of a profile is contained in the base model file as an additional root object. Such a profile instance contains instances of its stereotypes.

5.4.6. Extension Point Inheritance

In addition to Direct Inheritance, there is another way to leverage cross-module inheritance to implement extensions. This extension mechanism, however, requires an extension point in the base metamodel. Figure 5.6 shows the application of this extension mechanism. There are two variants. Both variants have in common that the extension class E inherits from a class A that is contained by B. In the local variant (1), B contains A directly. In the global variant (2), B inherits from the superclass S that contains A. S is the common superclass of all classes in the base metamodel, so all classes can be extended this way if needed. In both variants, A has to be a proper superclass to E. This means if A has any class properties, they must suit E. To instantiate the class extension, an E instance is created and stored in the B object. Tools that operate on the extension need to iterate the instances that are contained in the B instance to find the proper extension object.

Kitalpha [LEZ14] uses Extension Point Inheritance with a global extension point to establish extensions.

[3] `https://sdqweb.ipd.kit.edu/wiki/MDSDProfiles` (last visited 23.08.2019)

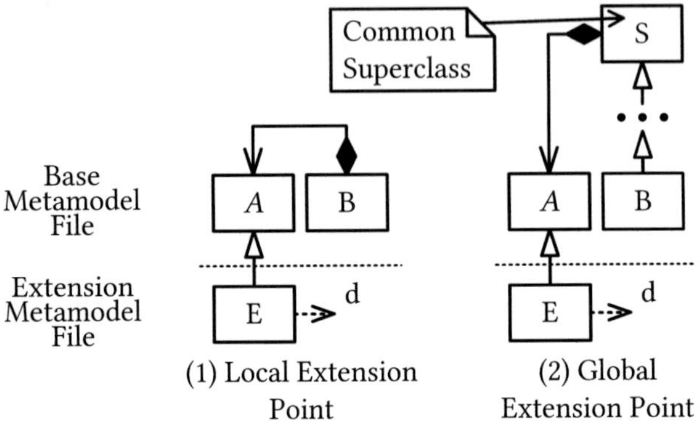

Figure 5.6.: Extension Mechanisms: Extension Point Inheritance

5.4.7. Decorator Pattern

The decorator pattern is used to enrich an object by new class properties [Gam+95]. When used correctly across metamodel module boundaries, it also functions as an extension mechanism. Figure 5.7 illustrates the application of two variants of the decorator pattern. Both variants have several things in common. AD stands for abstract decorator. It is the superclass for all decorators. More decorators may be provided by further metamodel extensions. The concrete decorator E, which is the extension class, inherits from AD. Through the containment of AD, a decorator can contain a B instance or another decorator. This way, an arbitrary number of decorators can be nested. When instantiating a decorator-based extension, an E instance is placed in the containment c in which the extended B instance would reside. The B instance is then contained by the decorator. This way, the B instance is extended by the extension content of E. Tools that operate on the extension follow c to retrieve the outermost decorator. The decorators are then iterated until the data in question is found. This is either the extension content of a decorator or the property values of the B instance.

Variant (1) requires a superclass to exist that fits the scope of the extension. This means that the set of its subclasses contains all classes that should be extended but no further classes. In the usual descriptions of the decorator

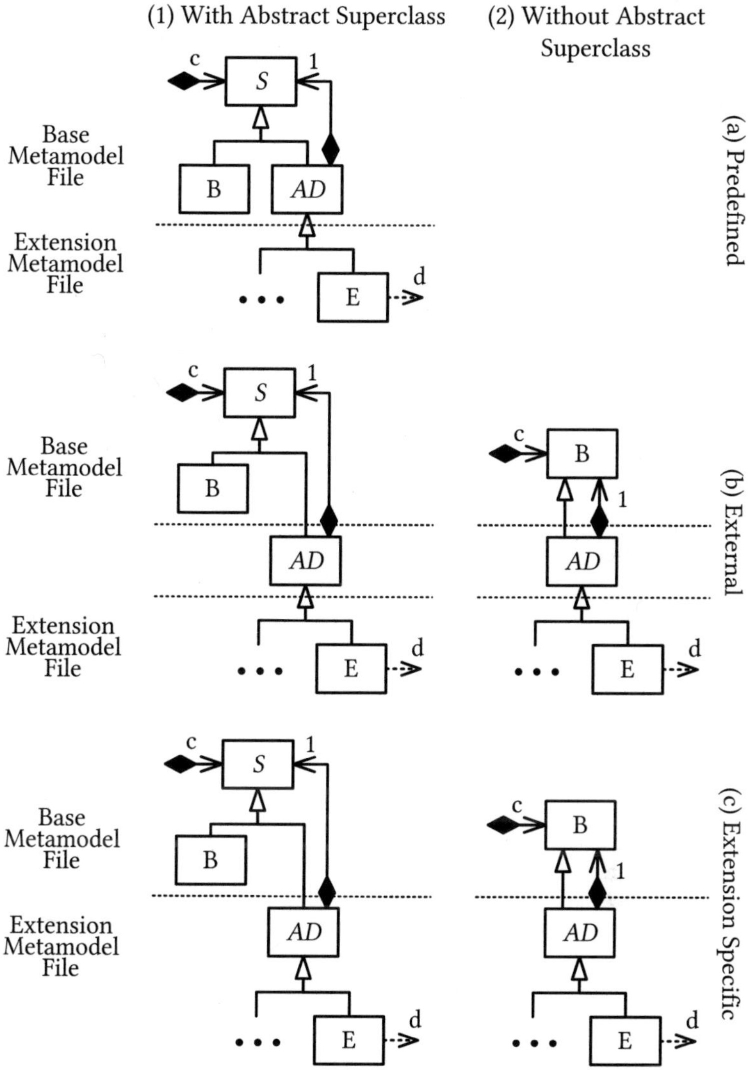

Figure 5.7.: Extension Mechanisms: the Decorator Pattern

pattern, S has only the class that ought to be decorated (B) and the superclass for all decorators (AD) as subclasses. Other sibling classes of B that can also be decorated are, of course, allowed. As a further requirement, all incoming references and containments have to refer to S and not to B. If this is not the case, some part of the model may refer to the B instance directly and, thus, bypass the decorators.

If no such S exists as a superclass, variant (2) may be used. In this variant, AD inherits directly from B. This includes all class properties of B. This has the advantage that if only one decorator is instantiated, no instance of B is necessary, as all class properties of B are already present in the decorators. It, however, also has the disadvantage that class properties are redundant if multiple decorators are instantiated. One decorator carries the values of the class properties and the others are redundant and not needed. Either they are left empty, which is only possible if their multiplicities have a lower bound of 0, or their values are duplicated. In the case where only the properties of one decorator are used, the outermost decorator should carry the values. New decorators should be added to the innermost decorator as not to displace the outermost decorator. In the case of duplication, all modifications of a value have to be propagated to all other decorator instances.

The classes that are necessary to realize a decorator-based extension may be placed in metamodel files in various constellations. Of course, B and S (only for the first variant) always reside in the base metamodel file. E is always located in the extension metamodel file. In variant (1), AD may be located either in the base metamodel file (a), an own metamodel file (b), or the extension metamodel file (c). Regarding variant (2), AD can be located in an own metamodel file (b) or in the extension metamodel file (c).

If AD is located in the base metamodel, it is named a *predefined decoration* (a). Predefined decoration only makes sense for variant (1), as variant (2) does not prepare a decoration. If a decoration had been prepared, there would have been a proper superclass for the decorator to inherit from, which is the case for variant (1). The benefit of predefined decoration is that the tools that operate on the base metamodel expect a decoration and therefore can handle decorated model files. This is not the case for the other (b) and (c), as the tooling expects an instance of B in the containment c. If a decoration is instantiated in (b) and (c), there is no B instance in c but a decorator instance, which cannot be processed by the tooling of the base metamodel.

If the base metamodel does not feature an abstract superclass for decorators (AD), it can be added externally. One way to do so is named an *external decoration* (b). AD resides in its own metamodel file, which is separate from the extension metamodel files. This option should be chosen if multiple independent extensions are expected.

If only one extension is expected, AD can also be defined within the extension metamodel file. This is named *extension specific decoration*. This has the benefit that fewer metamodel files are required. If further decorator-based extensions ought to be developed, there are two options: the extensions inherit from the existing AD class, or they define their own AD class. Both options have a drawback. If the AD class is reused, the modularity of the extensions is impaired. Further metamodel extensions depend on the metamodel extension that defines AD, which contains further classifiers that are not relevant for the depending metamodel extension. If the AD class is respecified, the class is duplicated and, therefore, unnecessary complexity is introduced.

5.5. Dismissed Mechanisms

This section presents mechanisms that have been dismissed. They do not fulfill the selection criteria that were presented in Section 5.3. Each mechanism is briefly presented; the reason for its dismissal is explained. This list is not complete. Some research fields were not further explored when it became apparent that they, for example, only pursue intrusive mechanisms. The dismissed mechanisms are grouped into the following categories: intrusive mechanisms (violating S1 and S2, see Section 5.5.1), metamodel-specific mechanisms (violating S3, see Section 5.5.2), duplicate and composed mechanisms (violating S4, see Section 5.5.3), and unavailable mechanisms (violating S5, see Section 5.5.4).

5.5.1. Intrusive Mechanisms

Several approaches that are not considered by this evaluation, as they are intrusive or do not provide instance compatibility. Therefore, they do not fulfill the selection criteria S1 or S2.

A model transformation [CH03; MG06] takes a model as an input and automatically produces another model as output. A model completion [Hap+14] is a special case of model transformation. It only adds new model elements. Existing elements cannot be deleted. Values (i.e., the target of a reference) are only modified to include the new elements. As a metamodel is also a model, model transformations and completions can also be applied to metamodels. A completion could be used to perform an addition of class properties. If the completion is performed in-place, it is an intrusive addition. Such a mechanism does not fulfill the selection criterion S1. If the completion produces a new metamodel, it can be considered to be a branch. Instances of the branched metamodel are, in general, not compatible with the original version. As soon as the new class properties are used (e.g., an object provides a value for a new attribute), the model is no longer compatible with the original version of the metamodel. Such a mechanism, therefore, does not fulfill the selection criterion S2.

Aspect-oriented modeling (e.g., [KAK09]) uses a technique which is named model weaving to insert new model elements. Model weaving is similar to performing additions of class properties by using completions. It, therefore, does not fulfill either S1 or S2 depending on whether it is used in-place or produces a branched metamodel. Language composition approaches for metamodel-based languages (e.g., Melange [Deg+15], metamodel merging [ES06; Léd+01], template instantiation [ES06]) have the same problem. An addition of class properties could be achieved by merging a small metamodel that contains only the desired class properties into the base metamodel. Analogously to completions, however, S1 or S2 are not fulfilled.

5.5.2. Metamodel-specific Mechanisms

Architectural Templates [Leh18] is an extension mechanism for the PCM. It is used to define architectural templates (i.e., patterns) and annotate them to PCM models. Based on annotated templates, a PCM model is automatically completed. Such templates, therefore, reduce the modeling effort of PCM models. Architectural Templates does not fulfill the selection criterion S3 as it cannot be applied onto other metamodels without further ado. Further, it uses EMF Profiles to establish extensions. Architectural Templates, therefore, does not fulfill criterion S4.

5.5.3. Duplicate and Composed Mechanisms

The Role pattern [Küh17] is a design pattern known from object orientation. The pattern describes that objects can take part in different kinds of roles and thereby relate to other objects. Figure 5.8 shows two possible application of the Role pattern as an extension mechanism. Both do not fulfill the selection criteria S4, as explained in the following paragraphs.

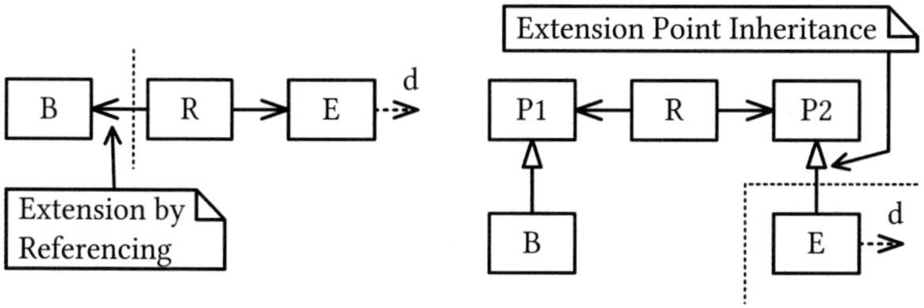

(1) External Role Pattern (2) Internal Role Pattern

Figure 5.8.: Extension Mechanisms: the Role Pattern

Subfigure (1) shows a variant in which the base metamodel does not prepare the use of roles. The base metamodel only contains the base class B. The role class R has to be implemented in the extension metamodel. It references the base class B and the extension class E. E is located in the extension metamodel and carries the extension content d. This variant does not fulfill the selection criteria S4, as it uses a referencing extension mechanism. Depending on the container of R, the Referencing with Reused Container or (Section 5.4.4) or External Container (Section 5.4.3) extension mechanism is used. It is also possible for R to reference a superclass of E in order to enable other extension classes to use the same role. This, however, does not affect the decision whether this Role pattern variant is a novel extension mechanism.

Subfigure (2) shows a variant in which the base metamodel provides classes for a role-based extension. The base metamodel contains the base class B, the role class R, and two abstract superclasses for the participants for the role (P1 and P2). In order to relate the participants, R references P1 and P2. In order to participate in the role, B inherits from P1. The external extension is implemented by a metamodel file crossing inheritance from E to P2. This is, however, the same mechanism as Extension Point Inheritance. This variant, therefore, does not fulfill the selection criteria S4.

Emerson and Sztipanovits [ES06] present metamodel composition methods. These include Metamodel Interfacing and Class Specialization. As metamodel composition methods, they are more general compared to metamodel extension mechanisms. Transferred to an application as an extension mechanism, they are identical to the Referencing with External Container (Section 5.4.3) and the Direct Inheritance (Section 5.4.2) extension mechanisms.

5.5.4. Unavailable Approaches

Braun developed four extension mechanisms [BE15b; Bra17]: Hooking, Aspects, Plugins, and Addons. They require an extension to EMOF and presumably an extension to the modeling framework runtime. For the Hooking mechanism, the metamodel developer defines hooking points in the base metamodel. With the help of these hooking points, class properties can be added and modified, classes can be specialized, and classifiers can be renamed. Aspects support the addition of reoccurring abstractions without the need for prearrangement. Plugins enable the coupling of standalone metamodels. Addons are related to plugins, but are less complex and may depend directly on the base metamodel.

In the scope of this thesis, however, Braun's extension mechanisms are not considered, as the do not fulfill the selection criteria S5. In his paper [BE15b], Braun specifies the extension of EMOF. To be usable, however, an extension to a modeling framework runtime is missing. There is no publicly available implementation, nor could the author provide one when requested. Thus, it is not possible to evaluate these mechanisms.

Without the option to use the extension mechanisms, several comparison criteria cannot be assessed. From the information that is available in publications, it cannot be reliably determined whether Braun's mechanisms really are extension mechanisms according to the definition given in Section 5.2. As Braun mentions merging in the context of applying his mechanisms, it may be more appropriate to classify them as language composition mechanisms. At least the Hooking mechanism in its entirety does not fulfill S2, as it is possible to change types and rename classes.

5.6. Comparison Criteria Catalog

This section presents the comparison criteria that are used to evaluate the extension mechanisms. This catalog could also be expressed as a QGM plan. The goal, however, which is derived from **RQ II** (Extension Mechanism Comparison), is too broad. The **goal** is to find the advantages and disadvantages of the extension mechanisms. This does not really fit the QGM approach. If applied regardless, the criteria can be seen as evaluation questions, which have only one metric. This metric is the metric that is presented for each criterion.

Some of these criteria were derived from the challenges this contribution addresses (see Section 5.1). The remaining criteria were specified from experience. When experimenting with the extension mechanisms, one notices characteristics that put them apart from other mechanisms. This list contains the criteria most relevant to this thesis. It, however, is not exhaustive. Some of the criteria overlap with the descriptions of Braun [Bra17]. For a proper differentiation, see Section 11.2.

The criteria with a binary result are stated in a way that the TRUE result is positive. This does not necessarily apply for the Extension Object Deletion criterion. Whether an automatic deletion is desired is dependent on the purpose of the extension.

These criteria were set up before the evaluation. As a consequence, they contain causal relations. The causal relations that were discovered during the evaluation are discussed in Section 8.2.3. These relations are, however, not a weakness of the comparison criteria, even if some of them produce identical or negated results. The comparison criteria express an effect, which is a merit in itself.

5.6.1. Metalanguage Support

This criterion checks whether an extension mechanism is supported by the EMOF meta-metamodel. Some extension mechanisms can be used with a standard EMOF Framework (e.g., EMF). Other extension mechanisms require an extended EMOF meta-metamodel or additional libraries. Tools that operate on content of extensions that are implemented by these extension mechanisms are dependent on the meta-metamodel extensions and additional libraries.

The results of this criterion are:

Yes The extension mechanism is supported by standard EMOF.

No The extension mechanism requires some form of an addon to be installed.

5.6.2. Applicable without Preparation

This criterion assesses whether an extension mechanism needs to alter the base metamodel in order to be applicable. Some extension mechanisms can be applied in any case. Other extension mechanisms need predefined extension points in the base metamodel.

This comparison criterion addresses Problem 1 (Package Structure Erosion and Uncontrolled Growth of Dependencies). An extension mechanism that requires preparation enriches the base metamodel a little. Compared with an intrusive addition the effect is minimal. However, many extension points may still clutter the metamodel. A completely unintrusive extension mechanism that does not require preparation does not worsen the erosion of a metamodel at all.

Heavyweight language composition methods that either do in-place modifications of the base metamodel or produce a new metamodel are considered to be intrusive. Their intrusiveness is higher compared with extension mechanisms that merely require extension points. In general, such heavyweight language composition methods, however, do not provide backward compatibility and are therefore excluded from this investigation.

The results of this criterion are:

Yes The extension mechanism can be applied to any class in any metamodel and does not need any preparation in the metamodel.

No The base metamodel has to be prepared for the extension mechanism to be applicable.

5.6.3. Model Level Unintrusiveness

This criterion rates if the instantiation of an extension on a base object alters the model file of the base object. Some extension mechanisms persist their instance data in separate files. Others add it to the model file that contains the base object.

This criterion addresses Problem 8 (Instance Incompatibility). In EMF, the loading of models is implemented to fail fast. This means a program is interrupted on the detection of unknown objects, even if they are subtypes of known classes. This leads most tools to be unable to load models with unknown extension content. This can be counteracted only by manual effort that is spent on implementing the handling of unknown extension content in the tools. E.g., the Sirius framework for graphical editors ignores unknown extension content. In general, however, the forward compatibility of tools depends on whether the extension mechanism is unintrusive on the model level. Figure 5.9 illustrates the problem of model level intrusiveness and forward compatibility of tools. A tool that can operate on an instance of B might not be able to operate on an extended instance of B. As already mentioned, the compatibility of tools is not determined on the object level, but on whole model files. A tool could be unable to load a whole model file that contains an extended base object.

The results of this criterion are:

Yes The extension method is unintrusive regarding the model level.

No The model that is extended is altered by the application of the extension mechanism.

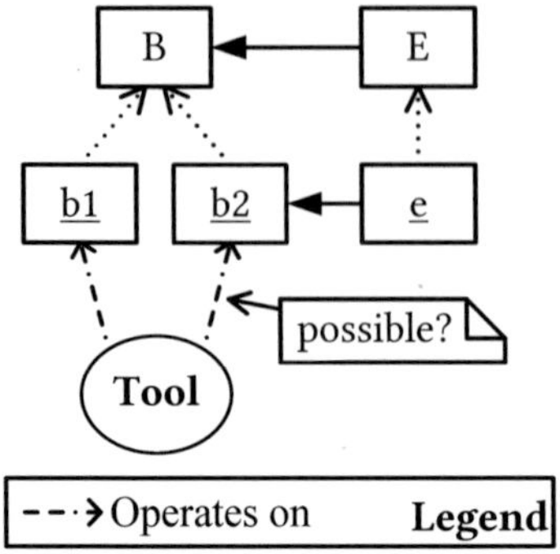

Figure 5.9.: Forward Compatibility of Tools

5.6.4. Content Retrieval Computational Complexity

This criterion assesses the computational complexity of the retrieval of the extension content of a base object. It uses the Bachmann–Landau notation [Bac94; Lan74] to provide an upper bound for the growth in response time as specific numbers of objects in the model or extension model increase.

Some extension mechanisms support the navigation from a base object directly to its extension objects. In these cases, the response time is constant as it is not influenced by the number of other objects in the base and extension model. The computational complexity of the content retrieval of such extension mechanisms lies in $O(1)$. For the other extension mechanisms, objects have to be iterated and tested if they refer to the base object in question. For some of these extension mechanisms, the number of objects that have to be iterated in the worst case is the number of extension objects of the metamodel extension (n). For other extensions, the number of extension objects (m) that have been applied to a base object possibly by multiple metamodel extensions is relevant. To the remaining extensions, the number of instances (k) that are contained by a containment in the base metamodel is relevant. This number is constituted by several factors: extension objects of the extension, of other extensions, and instances from the base metamodel.

If the search for the correct extension object is implemented explicitly on every access in the code of a tool, the code complexity of the tools increases.

Thus, helper methods should be provided by the developers of either the extension mechanism or the metamodel extension to encapsulate this complexity and ease the retrieval of the extension objects. Often, however, such helper methods only hide the fact that the retrieval time grows linearly with the number of objects that have to be searched. A workaround to achieve better performance is to build an in-memory hash maps to retrieve extension objects. Such hash maps can be implemented for every extension mechanism that does not offer constant retrieval time. Hash maps, however, take up additional memory, have to be maintained as the model and the extension content changes, and are transient. Transient means that they are not persisted and have to be build again if the model is loaded.

The results of this criterion are:

1 Extension content retrieval is possible in $O(1)$ without any additional maintenance overhead.

n The worst case extension content retrieval time grows linearly with the number of extension objects of the metamodel extension. The computational complexity of the operation lies in $O(n)$.

m The worst case extension content retrieval time grows linearly with the number of extension objects that are applied to the base object. The computational complexity of the operation lies in $O(m)$.

k The worst case extension content retrieval time grows linearly with the number of objects in the utilized containment. The computational complexity of the operation lies in $O(k)$.

5.6.5. Applies to Subclasses

This criterion evaluates if a class extension that extends a class B can also be instantiated on the subclasses of B. Figure 5.10 illustrates the criterion. Usually, a class obtains all class properties from its superclass. If, however, class properties are externally extended, it depends on the extension mechanism whether the extended class properties are also inherited. Extension mechanisms that rely on inheritance cannot be instantiated on subclasses usually.

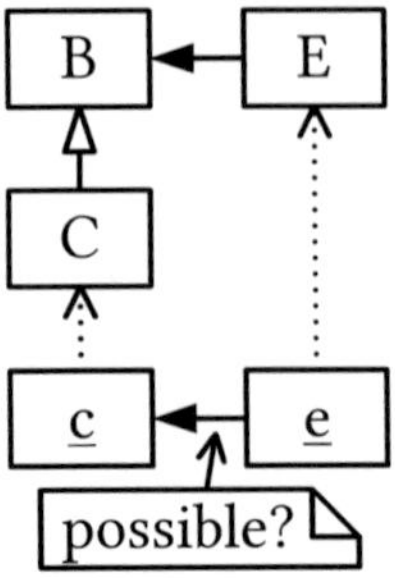

Figure 5.10.: The Applies to Subclasses Comparison Criterion

The results of this criterion are:

Yes The extension mechanism can also be applied on subclasses of the base class.

No The extension only applies to precisely the class it extends.

5.6.6. Orthogonality

The orthogonality criterion states whether multiple class extensions can refer to the same base class and be instantiated on the same base object. Orthogonality should not be confused with multiplicity, which addresses whether the same extension can be instantiated multiple times. Figure 5.11 illustrates the orthogonality criterion. In general, it is desirable to be able to independently develop an arbitrary number of extensions for a class. Some extension mechanisms, however, only support the instantiation of one class extension on an extension object. This criterion addresses Problem 9 (Incompatible Extensions).

As a workaround, some extension mechanisms can support the instantiation of multiple extensions on one class if the class extensions know each other. This is, however, undesirable. Extension developers should be able to develop extensions independently. Extensions should not depend on other extensions for technical reasons, but only if the contents of the extensions are conceptually required. Thus, this workaround of making the extensions

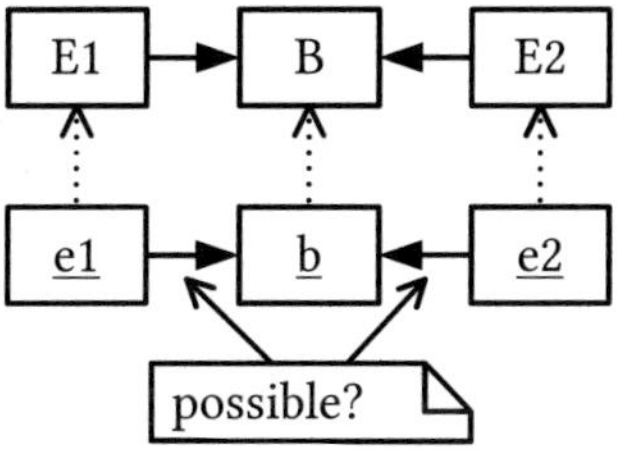

Figure 5.11.: The Orthogonality Comparison Criterion

compatible amongst each other does not count as the extension mechanism supporting orthogonality.

The results of this criterion are:

Yes Multiple extensions developed independently using the extension mechanism can be instantiated on one extension object.

No It is not possible to instantiate multiple extensions on one extension object, or the extensions must know each other to be able to be combined.

5.6.7. Multiplicity

The Multiplicity criterion is concerned with whether an extension that has been defined can be instantiated multiple times on one base object. Figure 5.12 illustrates the criterion. Extension mechanisms that cannot be instantiated multiple times have to specify higher upper multiplicity bounds to emulate multiple instantiations.

The results of this criterion are:

Yes The extension mechanism supports multiple instantiation on the same base object.

No It is only possible to instantiate an extension once on a base object.

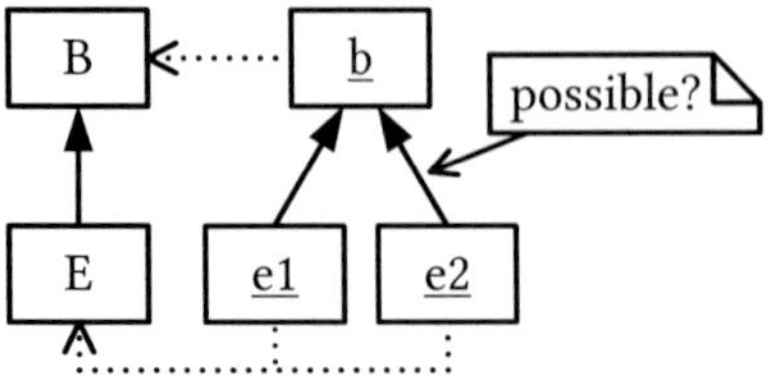

Figure 5.12.: The Multiplicity Comparison Criterion

5.6.8. Model File Integrity

This comparison criterion is concerned with the integrity of model files on which an extension has been instantiated. Some extension mechanisms deposit their extension content in the base model files. Other mechanisms create new model files to hold the extension objects and their content. This is named *model fragmentation*. When model fragmentation occurs, tools that operate on the metamodel and the extension have to know the location of the extension model files. This can be done, e.g., by naming the extension model file accordingly.

The results of this criterion are:

Yes The instantiation of the extension mechanism does not produce any new model files.

No The instantiation of the extension mechanism causes model fragmentation.

5.6.9. Containment Tree Integrity

This comparison criterion is concerned with the integrity of the containment tree of models for which an extension has been instantiated. A metamodel forms a hierarchy concerning its containment relations. This also translates to the instances (models) of a metamodel. E.g., if class A contains class C, a is an object of A, and c is an object of C, then c can also be contained by a. Figure 5.13 illustrates the criterion. Subfigure (1) shows the containment tree of a model on that an extension should be instantiated. The b object should be extended. Subfigure (2) shows an extension that leaves the containment tree intact. The extension object e is contained by the base object b. Subfigure (3) shows an extension that does not leave the containment tree intact. This is named *containment tree fragmentation.* The extension deposits its extension objects in a separate root container. This container may reside in the base model file or a separate model file.

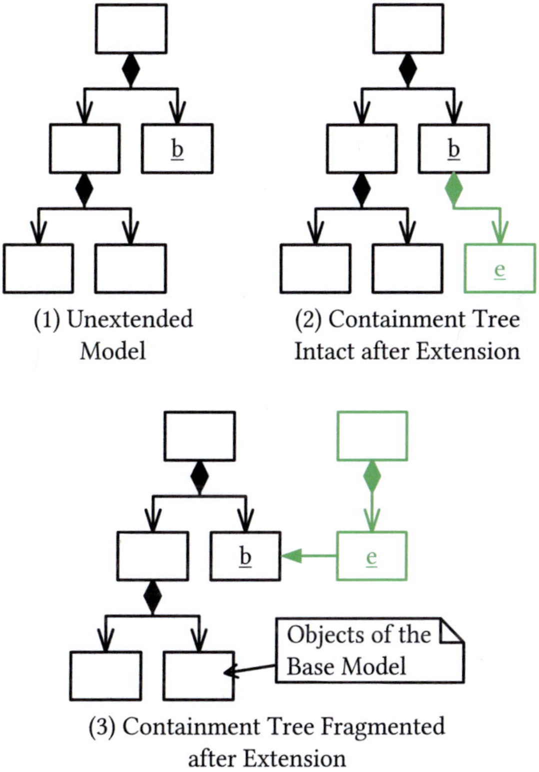

Figure 5.13.: The Containment Tree Integrity Comparison Criterion

The results of this criterion are:

Yes The containment tree of a model stays intact if the extension mechanism is instantiated.

Depends Whether the containment tree of a model stays intact depends on the circumstances.

No The instantiation of the extension mechanism fragments the containment tree of a model by creating further roots.

5.6.10. Extension Object Deletion

This comparison criterion is concerned with whether extension objects are automatically deleted if their base object is deleted. An automatic deletion occurs, e.g., with extension mechanisms with which the extension object is contained by the base object. The extension content is lost on the deletion of the base object. This may be undesirable if a tool or tool user that is unaware of the extension deletes base objects for which the extended information should remain. If extension objects are not deleted, they remain in the extension model file with a void relation with which they used to point to the base object. Tools that operate on the base metamodel and its extension may explicitly delete extension objects if the respective objects are deleted. If this is not done, extension objects with void references remain and accumulate.

The results of this criterion are:

Yes Extension objects and extension content is deleted on the deletion of the base object.

Depends Whether extension objects are deleted depends on the implementation of the helper methods of the extension mechanism.

No Extension objects and extension content remain even if the base object is deleted.

5.6.11. Adds a Type

The Adds a Type criterion rates whether the instantiation of a class extension using the extension mechanism makes the base object b an instance of the extension class E. Figure 5.14 illustrates the criterion.

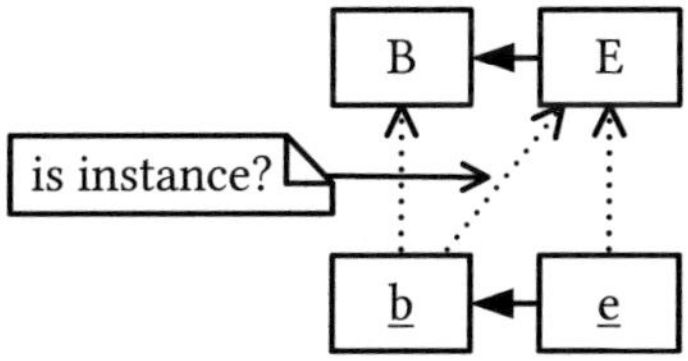

Figure 5.14.: The Adds a Type Comparison Criterion

The results of this criterion are:

Yes An instantiation of a class extension makes the base object an instance of the extension class.

Depends If multiple different class extensions are instantiated on a base object, only one applies its type to the base object.

No There is no type added to the base object on the instantiation of a class extension.

6. A Reference Structure to Enforce Modularity in Metamodels

In the context of MDE and domain modeling, metamodels are created to describe specific subjects. Conventional metamodel design, however, produces metamodels that tend to have certain shortcomings. They lack modularity and are neither designed for reuse nor extension. The lack of modularity leads to a high complexity of the constituent metamodel files. Lacking modularity and high complexity severely impede a metamodel's understandability. An improper modularization favors problematic dependencies that deteriorate the evolvability of a metamodel due to higher coupling. The potential for reuse is diminished because of monolithic metamodels. When languages that describe the same subject matter from different points of view are developed, the developers are forced to implement large parts of the metamodel from scratch or clone parts of other metamodels. It would be more favorable for these languages to share a common core. This reduces effort and brings partial interoperability. This is also beneficial for metamodels that are used for quality analysis. Fundamental patterns could be reused in different domains but are not. On a domain model, several quality dimensions could be specified and analyzed, but a lacking separation of concerns hinders this endeavor. For some analyses, their specific input and output data is integrated into the language, which further convolutes its metamodel.

Some approaches pursue various goals to tackle the challenges that were mentioned above. An approach proposes the creation of languages by reusing patterns [Pes+15; CG11], others offer operations that transform and combine existing metamodels to form new languages [Deg+15], and further ones compile metamodel fragments into complete metamodels

[Com+18]. These types of approaches, however, have the shortcoming that, in general, they do not enable partial interoperability between the languages even though they share a common core. Other approaches deal with metamodel modularization [Gar+14] and refactorings [Are14] in general. These approaches, however, do not provide guidelines on how to organize the overall structure of the metamodels.

This chapter[1] presents the core contributions of this thesis, an approach to structure metamodels to improve their reusability and evolvability. This contribution consists of two parts. One is beneficial to metamodels in general. The other is specific for metamodels that are used for quality analysis. In contrast to contribution **I** (Bad Smells and Anti-Patterns in Metamodeling), this chapter takes a more proactive approach to properly structure a metamodel to protect it from erosion over time. This chapter transfers several concepts and best practices from related disciplines to metamodeling. The approach of metamodel extension from the previous contribution is necessary to apply some of these concepts and best practices in metamodeling. This chapter proposes to structure metamodels to reflect their language features to achieve proper separation of concerns. This is achieved with the help of feature models. This chapter further presents a specific layering as a reference structure for metamodels that are used for quality analysis. A layering partitions a metamodel and only allows layer-crossing dependencies in one direction. Layering is useful, as the dependency direction restriction decouples more basic layers from more advanced ones. This reference structure supports evolution scenarios that are common for metamodels that are used for quality analysis.

This chapter is structured as follows. Section 6.1 provides an overview of concepts and best practices that are transferred to metamodeling from related disciplines. Section 6.2 specifies the research questions and challenges that the reference structure contribution addresses. Section 6.3 describes metamodel modularization concepts that are fundamental to this contribution and can be applied to metamodels in general. Section 6.4 proposes the reference structure for metamodels that are used for quality modeling and analysis. Section 6.5 describes refactorings of classes, modules and feature models that are necessary to apply the reference structure approach. Section 6.6 presents three processes of how to apply the reference structure

[1] This chapter is partly based on [HSR19] (©2019 IEEE) and [SH16a; Str+15].

approach in the scenarios: designing a modular metamodel, modularizing a legacy metamodel, and extending a modular metamodel.

This chapter is continued in subsequent parts of this thesis. Chapter 9 presents case studies in which the reference structure was applied to metamodels. Chapter 10 performs evaluations on the case studies to validate the reference structure approach. Section 11.3 presents related work. Section 12.3 concludes this chapter. Appendix B explains the mapping of the modularization concepts onto the technical foundation and presents tool support for the reference structure approach.

6.1. Concepts and Best Practices of Related Disciplines

This contribution takes established concepts and best practices from related disciplines and transfers them to metamodeling. Thus, this section first justifies and motivates the transfer. Amongst the disciplines that are related to metamodeling, there are object-oriented design, software architecture, and Software Product Line development. Some of them are older and more mature compared to metamodeling. Concepts and best practices have been established that are not applied in metamodeling. These are modules, reference architectures, the layered architecture pattern, feature models, the acyclic dependency principle, the dependency inversion principle, the separation of concerns principle, and the single responsibility principle. For each concept and best practice, the following paragraphs provide a brief explanation, a description of how it is transferred to metamodeling, and a quick motivation for the use in metamodeling. A full explanation of the rationale behind the concepts, however, cannot be provided until the concepts were fully presented. This is done in Section 6.3.7 and Section 6.4.5. The full explanation of how they are utilized in metamodeling is presented in Section 6.3, Section 6.5, and Section 6.6.

A *module* [Par72] is a partition of a program. Originally, a module was a set of subroutines that features an explicit interface for these routines. In contrast to a component, it does not provide multiple instantiation. The concept of *modules* can loosely be transferred to metamodeling. Metamodels (i.e., their classifiers) can also be partitioned. As a metamodel provides types, a multiple instantiation is not always desired, as a it would result in multiple different types with the same properties. The concept of explicit interfaces can also be loosely transferred to making the metamodel files that a metamodel file requires explicit. In order for a metamodel developer to introduce a new dependency to another metamodel file that was not yet depended on, s/he has to manually and explicitly allow the new dependency. This approach is also related to the import of packages or the loading of libraries in software development. The rationale of the transfer of the module concept to metamodeling is to enforce more conscious handling of dependencies.

A *reference architectures* proposes a template solution for software architectures of a specific domain or purpose. It suggest a specific partitioning of the architecture and may even propose concrete components, modules, interfaces, or data types. As a metamodel has no architecture as software does, the term is adopted to metamodeling as reference structure. Applying the concept of a reference structure to the internals of metamodels is not meaningful, as this scope is already covered by metamodel design patterns. It can, however, be applied to metamodel files and their relations. The benefit of a reference structure is that it provides an explicit structure as well as guidance to developers.

The *layered architecture pattern* [Bus+96] also establishes a partitioning and enforces a directionality of relations between the layers. The concept of a layer can be transferred to a set of metamodel files and their dependencies. The dependencies of the metamodel files of a layer are only allowed to go into metamodel files of the same layer or to metamodel files of more basic layers. The benefit of such an approach is to decouple more base layers from more specific ones. This makes basic layers reusable and more specific layers easier to exchange.

Feature models (see Section 2.4) are used to explicitly and hierarchically express functionality, its interdependencies, and variability. Feature models can be used in arbitrary domains to map feature nodes to software artifacts of said domain. By doing so, the mapped artifacts of selected feature nodes can be further processed after a selection has been performed on the feature model. This approach can also be applied to metamodels. Feature nodes can be mapped to, for example, metamodel files. If a feature node is selected, its metamodel file is deployed. The motivation behind using feature models is to explicitly model the relation of the language features and impose that structure onto the larger structure of a metamodel. It also serves as a means to give tool users an interface to select the features of a metamodel they want to instantiate in a model.

The *acyclic dependency principle* [Fow03] from object-oriented design states that the dependencies of packages or similar high-level partitions should not form cycles. The principle can be transferred, for example, to metamodel files and their dependencies. All metamodel files in a cycle can only be used, reused, and understood together. Forbidding cycles breaks this coupling, and some of the metamodel files no longer depend on all other files of the former cycle. This enables a more fine-grained use, reuse, and understanding.

The *dependency inversion principle* [Mar03] states that abstractions should not depend on specifics, but specifics should depend on abstractions. As the concepts of metamodeling also feature dependencies and express varying degrees of abstraction, the principle can be transferred to metamodeling. This is possible on several levels of granularity (e.g., classes and metamodel files). By transferring the dependency inversion principle to metamodel concepts, more abstract concepts can be decoupled from more specific ones. This should increase the reusability of these concepts.

Separation of concerns [Dij82] and *single responsibility* [Mar03] are two principles that propagate a modularization and encapsulation. These principles can be transferred to metamodeling, as also a metamodel expresses concerns and responsibilities on several levels of granularity. The concerns or responsibilities in a metamodel can be seen as the definition of an abstract pattern and the definition of a feature of the metamodel's language. By enforcing these principles, the metamodel should become more modular and by that better understandable and reusable.

6.2. Research Questions and Challenges

This section presents the research questions of this contribution. For each research question, it describes how it derives from the problem areas that Chapter 3 presents. Next, this section presents further challenges that this contribution addresses. These did not result in research questions as they are not validatable or could not be validated in the scope of this thesis. Nevertheless, they represent questions that were important drivers of this thesis.

The following presents the research questions of this contribution. The common theme for all research questions of this contribution is that they proactively counteract problems that Chapter 3 presented.

RQ IIIa (Improve Evolvability): Problem 1 states that the erosion of the package structure and uncontrolled growth of dependencies damage the evolvability of a metamodel. The purpose of this research question is to find an approach to structure a metamodel in a more meaningful way. Therefore, a contribution of this chapter is to explore the following research question:

Can concepts from related disciplines be transferred to metamodeling to improve the evolvability of metamodels?

RQ IIIb (Understandability): Problem 3 states, that conventionally developed metamodels suffer from structural shortcomings. These have two effects. (1) they expose more internals to developers than necessary. (2) they structure the abstractions that implement the features of a language unfavorably. This damages the understandability of such metamodels. Therefore, this chapter explores the following research question:

Can concepts from related disciplines be transferred to metamodeling to improve the understandability of metamodels?

RQ IIIc (Need-specific Dependence): Problem 3 states that large conventionally developed metamodels do not enable developers to create dependencies to parts of the metamodel in a need-specific way. Only on whole metamodel files can be depended. Therefore, this chapter explores the following research question:

Can concepts from related disciplines be transferred to metamodeling to improve the potential to depend only on the desired parts of a metamodel?

RQ IIId (Selective Use): When a tool user uses a metamodel, s/he is usually only interested in specific language features. Problem 10 states that with conventionally developed metamodels, the tool user is not able to choose which parts of a metamodel to use according to her/his needs. Therefore, this chapter explores the following research question:

Can concepts from related disciplines be transferred to metamodeling to improve the ability of tool users to selectively use parts of a metamodel according to their needs?

Beyond these research questions, this thesis addresses several challenges.

One of the main drivers of this thesis was to find a way to harden a metamodel against degradation over time (addresses Problem 1: Package Structure Erosion and Uncontrolled Growth of Dependencies). This went hand in hand with an effort to provide more explicit information to a metamodel to ensure that structural design rationale is not lost (addresses Problem 2: Loss of Knowledge) and to ensure that developers perform maintenance more consistently (addresses Problem 1: Package Structure Erosion and Uncontrolled Growth of Dependencies).

This contribution satisfies the need for a systematic process of how to proceed when working with modular metamodels. This includes the scenarios of designing modular metamodels from scratch, refactoring legacy metamodels into a modular form, and extending modular metamodels. Such a systematic process is necessary to address Problem 3 (Monolithic Metamodels).

When metamodels are modularized in an unsystematic way, it is often not clear how to prioritize the modularization of orthogonal dimensions that are present in the metamodel. For example, a metamodel may define several structural formalisms and quality properties. If these two dimensions are orthogonal, each formalism has support for each quality property. The metamodel could be first divided by formalisms or quality dimensions. It is unclear how to start the modularization. The systematic process that was mentioned above answers this question of orthogonal modularization dimensions. This is necessary to address Problem 3 (Monolithic Metamodels) adequately.

Problem 4 states that there is insufficient reuse between related languages. This contribution aims to provide means to consolidate shared parts of related languages to form a common base on which both languages can then build extensions.

The problems in Chapter 3 include two seemingly contradicting trade-off decisions. Problem 6 explains that a general metamodel is very versatile but may lack essential constructs for specific situations. A very specific metamodel, on the other hand, is well suited for its purpose, but less so for other purposes. Problem 5 reports that tool-specific content in a metamodel is beneficial for the implementation of that exact tool. It is, however, unnecessary if the metamodel is used with another tool or in another context. By using the concepts from related disciplines as mentioned above, this contribution proposes a decomposition and decoupling of general and specific concepts. By doing this, this contribution addresses both of the trade-off problems (Problem 6 and Problem 5).

6.3. Metamodel Modularization Concepts

Before describing the layered reference structure, this section defines the fundamental concepts of this approach. These concepts are independent of the purpose and the semantics of the language and therefore can be applied to metamodels in general. They are language features, metamodel modules, module dependencies and their restrictions, as well as layers. This section also explains how feature models are involved with the modularization concepts.

Figure 6.1 shows how the concepts relate on the type level. For the sake of clarity, the figure does not completely define feature models. For a full definition, refer to Section 2.4.

6.3.1. Language Features

Like a software product implements a set of functional requirements, a language implements a set of language features. The term of language features is introduced for the metamodel architect to be able to specify what a language should be able to express on a conceptual level. In this thesis, a *language feature* is an implementation-independent first-class concept. This means, although a language feature may be implemented by metamodel elements (e.g., packages, classifiers, references), it also exists if there is no or multiple implementations of the language. A language feature

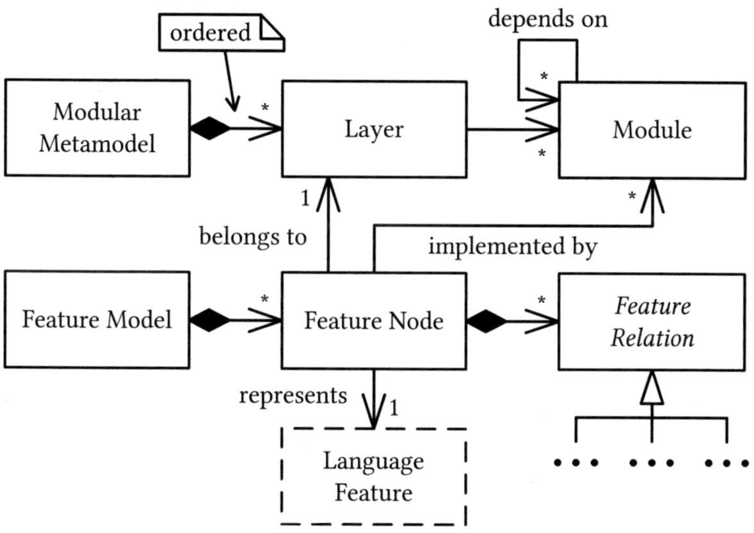

Figure 6.1.: Metamodel Modularization Concepts

contains one or multiple concepts that ought to be modeled. It represents a part of the language that is a unit of use. This means that a tool user either needs the whole language feature or s/he does not need it at all.

An example from the embedded domain is a language feature that defines types of microcontrollers. Also included in this language feature is information about the pins of the microcontroller. A microcontroller is always modeled with the information about its pins. Vice versa, it does not make sense to model pins without a microcontroller. This means, that it is a legitimate language feature. Considering the additional concept of socket types, it makes sense to model a socket type independent of a microcontroller. Therefore the socket type concept is not in the same language feature as the microcontroller type concept.

Language features can have *feature dependencies* to other language features. Like the language features, their dependencies are also implementation-independent. This means that the target and the direction of a dependency are determined by what is conceptually correct in this context. Considering language features A and B. There is a dependency from A to B, but no dependency from B to A. The relation between A and B is *conceptually correct* if concepts from A depend on concepts from B and no concept from B depends on any concept from A. The implication of the language feature dependency for the tool user is, that if s/he wants to use A, s/he also has to use B.

As an example from the embedded domain, consider a language feature A to contain the concept of microcontroller types and B to contain the socket type concept. The concept of a microcontroller type owns the information on which type of socket it fits. Therefore, the microcontroller type concept is dependent on the socket type concept. However, a socket type does not need to know which microcontroller types fit on it. Assuming A and B do not contain any further concepts with conflicting dependencies, the language feature dependency from A to B is conceptually correct.

There are two specific types of language features. A *standalone language feature* has no feature dependencies and can, therefore, be used on its own. Usually, most language features that implement view types are standalone language features. A language feature that only adds new properties and abstractions to other language features is addressed as an *extension language feature*. A *cross-cutting language feature* is a language feature that depends on many other language features.

6.3.2. Feature Modeling

In this thesis, language features and their dependencies are expressed using feature models[2]. This achieves several goals: (1) to structure the dependencies of language features hierarchically and more explicitly, (2) to express variability, and (3) by using feature selections, tool users are given an interface for model creation.

Almost every feature node in the feature model represents a language feature. Those that do not, have no implementation. They are addressed as *empty features*. Often, the root feature node and grouping feature nodes are empty features. This is not necessarily always the case. By compacting

[2] This approach is inspired by a diploma thesis that I supervised [Kan17] and the use of feature models by the CORE [Sch+15] software engineering approach, which was used in the thesis.

and simplifying a feature model by using refactorings (see Section 6.5.3), root and grouping features can be consolidated with other features. If the other feature is non-empty, the resulting feature is also non-empty.

For the sake of simplicity, this thesis does not distinguish between a language feature and the feature node that represents the language feature. Such cases will simply be addressed as a feature.

All language feature dependencies have to be covered by dependencies in the feature models. As a reminder, dependencies in the feature model are the child relations (optional and mandatory), the feature sets (OR and alternative), and the requires relation. Figure 6.2 shows how language feature dependencies can be covered by the feature model dependencies. For reasons of clarity, the figure does not show feature sets, although they also cover dependencies. (a) shows the dependency d from language feature B to A. d can be directly covered by a feature model dependency from feature node B to A. This is shown in (b). Only one of the dependencies is necessary. More than one dependency is disallowed anyway. The dependency direction of child relations and feature sets points from the child to the parent. This means the child is dependent on its parent. (c) shows how the dependency can be indirectly covered. There has to exist a path of dependencies in the feature model that connects B to A. Note that feature dependencies are not allowed to form cycles.

As already mentioned, tool users can use feature models to select the language features they want to use. In contrast to a mere graph of language features and their dependencies, a feature model forces the language features into a hierarchical structure regarding the child/parent relation. Such a feature hierarchy helps tool users during the feature selection, as tool users can start at the root feature and only follow down on branches that are relevant to them.

6.3.3. Metamodel Modules

In the reference structure approach, all language features are implemented by metamodel modules. This thesis defines a *metamodel module* as a container of packages and classifiers that has explicit dependencies. The difference between an EMOF metamodel file and a metamodel module

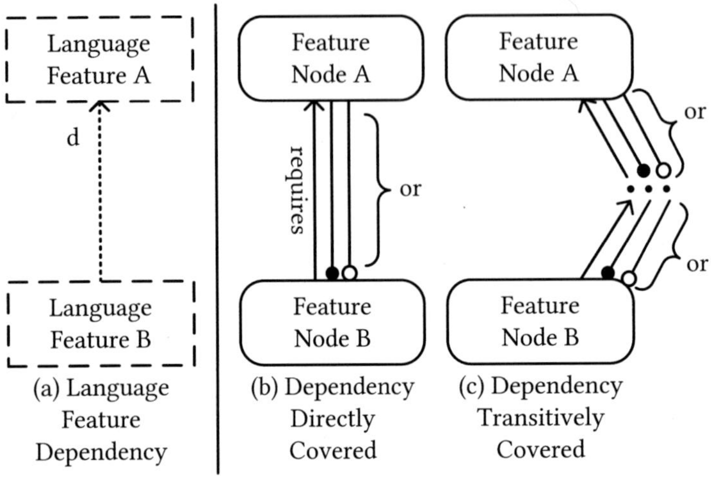

Figure 6.2.: Relation between Language Feature Dependencies and Feature Model Dependencies

is that the dependencies between metamodel modules have to be declared explicitly and follow certain restrictions. This thesis considers a metamodel that was subdivided into multiple metamodel modules still as a metamodel. As a metamodel module is based on a metamodel file, the concept of deployment also applies to metamodel modules.

Classifiers of one metamodel module M may depend on classifiers of another metamodel module N. If this is the case, it is regarded as M being *dependent* on N. Section 2.2 explains the different types of dependencies between classifiers. Additionally, this thesis introduced a new type of dependency between two classes in Chapter 5. For a dependency to exist between two metamodel modules, however, it is irrelevant precisely what types of dependencies there are between both metamodel modules. The emphasis is foremost on the presence and the direction of the dependencies. A dependency from M to N implies that when a tool uses M or when a metamodel extension reuses M, N has to be deployed as well. Together, a set of metamodel modules and their dependencies form a *dependency graph*. Inspired by the acyclic dependencies principle [Mar03], Metamodel module dependencies are not allowed to form cycles. A cycle would mean that if one of the metamodel modules is used, all of the metamodel modules in the cycle have to be deployed, which makes the modularization meaningless.

There is a special case of dependencies between metamodel modules. A *transitive module dependency* is a dependency between two metamodel modules that are otherwise already dependent by a path of dependencies via other metamodel modules. Figure 6.3 shows a simple case of such a constellation where the path is only two dependencies long. M is dependent on O and O is dependent on N. This makes the dependency from M to N a transitive dependency. Transitive dependencies do not contribute new metamodel modules to the dependency graph.

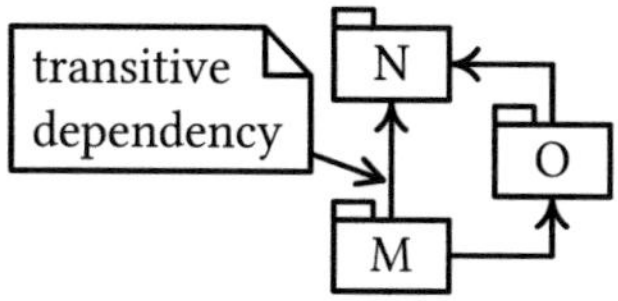

Figure 6.3.: A Transitive Metamodel Module Dependency

There are three special cases of metamodel modules. A *root metamodel module* is a metamodel module that contains a non-abstract root container. Root metamodel modules form the basis for view types.

An *abstract metamodel module* is a metamodel module that cannot be used without other metamodel modules that build on it. Abstract metamodel modules cannot implement a language feature on their own. This means a language feature has to be implemented by at least one non-abstract metamodel module. For a metamodel module M to be abstract, several conditions have to be fulfilled:

- M does not contain a root container, or it contains a root container that only contains abstract classes. The reason behind this condition is the following. A root container can always be instantiated, as it is by definition non-abstract. However, if the root container does not contain any instantiable classes, it cannot be used on its own.
- M does not add any non-abstract subclass to a class that is contained by a root container. The reason behind this condition is

the following. A non-abstract subclass of a class that is contained by a root container is itself contained by the root container (see Section 2.2). A non-abstract class that is contained by a root container can be instantiated in a root container instance. Therefore, M would be usable and not abstract.

- M does not contain a class that extends a concrete class of another metamodel module that is contained by a root container. The reason behind this condition is the following. If M would extend a class that is instantiable in a root container, the extending class can also be instantiated. Therefore, M would be usable and, thus, not abstract.

It is possible but unusual for an abstract metamodel module M to depend on a non-abstract metamodel module N. There may be references and containments from classes of M that point into N. There may even be inheritances and extends relations that point from M into N. However, these must adhere to the constraints above, or else M would not be an abstract metamodel module. Such inheritance and extends relations are an indication of a part of M that is abstract and may be better placed in an own metamodel module.

An *extension metamodel module* is a metamodel module that extends one or multiple metamodel modules. A metamodel module extends another metamodel module by having an extends relation to a class of the other metamodel module. An extension is either abstract or non-abstract, depending on whether it extends only abstract metamodel modules or at least one non-abstract metamodel module.

6.3.4. Layers

A *layer* is a logical grouping of language features and metamodel modules that implement a specific semantic. Each language feature and metamodel module is allocated to exactly one layer. There can be an arbitrary number of layers in a modular metamodel. Having just one layer is equivalent to having no layering at all. The layers are ordered concerning the dependencies of their language features and metamodel modules; similar to the layered software architecture pattern [Bus+96], module dependencies, feature required relations and parent relations may only point into the same or more basic layers (basic concerning its level of abstraction). Here, more basic means that they depend on fewer other layers. Cross-layer dependency cycles are avoided as a basic layer is not allowed to depend on a more specific layer. In this thesis, basic layers are graphically represented at the top. This is analogous to class diagrams, where more abstract classes are shown a the top and inheritance arrows point upwards.

6.3.5. Layers, Feature Models, and Modules

Figure 6.4 shows how layers, feature nodes, and metamodel modules relate to each other. Each feature node knows the metamodel modules by which it is implemented. These *implemented-by relations* may only point into the same or more basic layers.

A non-abstract metamodel module should only implement one feature. If a non-abstract metamodel module implements multiple features, this indicates that it lacks in separation of concerns. A feature may be implemented by multiple metamodel modules. This usually happens if it is a cross-cutting feature.

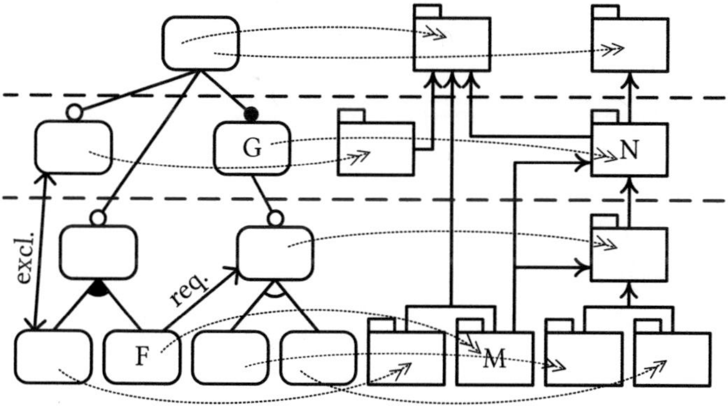

Figure 6.4.: Illustrative Example for the Relation Between the Modularization Concepts (based on [HSR19])

The module dependencies have to be supported by the feature model dependencies for the module dependency graph to be valid. A module dependency from metamodel module M to metamodel module N is considered as *supported* if by following dependencies from the feature that is implemented by M (i.e., feature F) the feature that is implemented by N (i.e., feature G) can be reached. If every module dependency is supported by feature relations, this is addressed as the module dependencies being *conform* to the feature model. Child/parent are followed from the child to the parent feature. Considering the example in Figure 6.4, metamodel module M implements the language feature F, and metamodel module N implements the language feature G. As one can reach G from F, by first following the requires relation and then following the parent relation, the dependency from M to N is supported.

6.3.6. Special Roles in the Scope of this Thesis

In addition to the general roles, which Section 2.2.10 introduced, this chapter introduces two new roles, which execute the application of this approach. The metamodel developer role is further subdivided into metamodel architect and module developer. The *module developer* is responsible for the internals of metamodel modules. S/he creates and modifies classes and their properties. The *metamodel architect* is responsible for allowing module dependencies, creating and evolving the feature model, linking features to metamodel modules, and creating and evolving the layering of metamodel modules and features. Both roles cooperate when creating or modifying module dependencies, as these are determined by the classes within a metamodel module. One or multiple persons may perform a role. It is possible for someone to personify both roles.

6.3.7. Discussing the Research Questions and Challenges

This section explains the rationale behind the metamodel modularization concepts. It explains how the rationale ties into the research questions and challenges of this contribution (see Section 6.2). Note that several of the metamodel modularization concepts can address the same research question or challenge. It is not intended to evaluate the research questions here but in Chapter 10.

By proposing *metamodel modules* with *explicit dependencies* and by *forbidding dependency cycles*, this contribution tackles several research questions and challenges.

The taming of dependencies on the metamodel module level aims to make the decision of metamodel architects to introduce a dependency to a metamodel module to which thus far no dependency existed yet more deliberate. By having less conceptually incorrect or redundant dependencies on the metamodel module level, unnecessary coupling could be prevented or reduced. Therefore, **RQ IIIa** (Improve Evolvability) is addressed.

The taming of dependencies further aims to improve the understandability of metamodels. When developers navigate a modular metamodel, the complexity they face is reduced, compared to a large entangled metamodel. This is because they are merely confronted with the content of the metamodel module of interest and possibly with the content of metamodel modules to which dependencies exist. Together with a more fine-grained modularization in self-contained metamodel modules instead of large metamodel files, this addresses **RQ IIIb** (Understandability).

The division of a metamodel into metamodel modules further enables to depend on parts of the modular metamodel according to the needs of the metamodel-based tool or metamodel extension. Only the metamodel module that are needed and their dependencies have to be deployed. Technically this is achieved by implementing metamodel modules as Eclipse plugins (see Appendix B). This addresses **RQ IIIc** (Need-specific Dependence). Further, it enables metamodel-based tools like editors to implement support for individual metamodel modules. By doing so, the tools may tailor the extent of features that they offer the tool users. Models of modular metamodels only instantiate the metamodel modules that are really needed for instantiation. Therefore, the concept of metamodel modules also addresses **RQ IIId** (Selective Use).

Decomposing a metamodel into metamodel modules, intends to foster reuse between DSMLs. Metamodel modules can also be reused in other contexts if they have a proper separation of concerns, which is addressed below. This may even go as far as two DSMLs sharing a common core of metamodel modules. Instances of this common core will then be compatible with tools of both DSMLs if the parts of the languages that extend the core are implemented using extension mechanisms that fulfill the criterion of

Model Level Unintrusiveness (see Section 5.6.3). This addresses Problem 4 (Commonalities in Related Languages).

The use of *feature models* and the enforcement of module dependencies to conform to feature dependencies addresses several goals.

The intent to provide an explicit structure is to mitigate the loss of knowledge of the overall structure of the metamodel. This addresses Problem 2 (Loss of Knowledge).

By using the feature model, metamodel developers are guided when they extend the metamodel. The hierarchical structure should help them to introduce new language features more consistently. Thereby hardening the metamodel against the degradation of its overall structure.

By forcing module dependencies to conform to feature dependencies, aims to achieve two things. Firstly, module dependencies should become more conceptually correct. This should increase the understandability and evolvability of the metamodel, as inter-module dependencies are more meaningful . This addresses **RQ IIIb** (Understandability). Secondly, it should increase the potential of the metamodel to be dependent and used according to the needs of the tool, extension or tool users. This addresses **RQ IIIc** (Need-specific Dependence) and **RQ IIId** (Selective Use).

Having a feature model for a DSML can serve as an interface for tool users to select the language features that they are interested in when they use metamodel-based tools.

The purpose of *layers* is to group associated metamodel modules and to enforce a dependency direction. Thus, layers prevent dependencies from going into a more specific layer. More basic layers are therefore decoupled from the more specific layers regarding their decencies but also the complexity that the developer faces. A further benefit is, that specific layers can be exchanged or omitted to reuse more basic layers. As it is another modularization concept, it addresses the goals in a similar way as the concept of metamodel modules. Therefore, these shared goals are only mentioned briefly. Layers tackle erosion and uncontrolled dependencies, thereby increasing a metamodel's understandability and evolvability. As layers provide a more explicit structuring, they provide guidance for developers and decrease the loss of knowledge.

6.4. Layers in Metamodels for Quality Modeling and Analysis

The metamodel modularization concepts from the previous subsection apply to metamodels in general and can be used with an arbitrary number of layers. Based on the metamodel modularization concepts, this section gives more specific guidance by proposing a reference structure for metamodels for quality modeling and analysis. To recap, a layer groups several metamodel modules, which in turn contain classifiers and their relations. The remainder of this section briefly explains the rationale behind this concrete layering, followed by the presentation of the individual layers.

When investigating metamodels that are used for quality modeling and analysis as well as their extensions, it was identified that they reflect in most cases language features from three categories: structure, behavior, and quality. Features that fall into these categories can be found in metamodels like UML MARTE [Obj11], UMLSec [Jür02], the Descartes Metamodel [KBH14], the PCM [Reu+16], AutomationML [Dra+08], ROBOCOP [GL03], and BPMN2 [Obj14]. Not all of these metamodels cover all categories. For a more detailed listing consider Table 9.1.

To analyze a model, further information is needed in addition to structure, behavior, and quality that is produced by analyzers and simulators. Examples are input and output states and configurations like simulation length or the number of measurements taken during evaluation. Based on this observation, parts of the metamodel that deal with structure and behavior, quality, and analysis should be separated into different layers in the reference structure. Structure and behavior are further divided into paradigm and domain. This is beneficial, as paradigm contains domain-independent concepts, which can be reused in other domains.

In conclusion, the above consideration results in four layers. The number of layers is, however, not fixed. The layers can be further split to separate different abstraction levels within the layers. Even fewer layers can be used. The paradigm and domain layers can be used to model structural information. By adding the quality layer, quality information can also be modeled. The analysis layer is only necessary if analyses should be conducted. The paradigm, domain, and analysis layers are needed for structural analyses. All four are needed for quality analyses.

6.4.1. Paradigm

The *paradigm* (π) is the most basic and most abstract layer. It defines abstract classes for reoccurring patterns of structure and behavior but without dynamic semantic. For example, in the automotive domain, components, their interfaces, and connections may be specified in π without specifying whether these are software, electronic, mechanical, or other types of components. As it carries no semantics, a π layer is not intended to be used without any additional layer. The advantage of having a π layer is that π metamodel modules that originate from the development of other languages can be reused if they fit the concepts to be modeled. This would not be possible if domain-specific semantics were located on this layer. Thus, the abstractions of the paradigm layer have to be domain-independent and carry the potential to be reused for other domains. First-class concepts that are defined by π should be abstract. This means they are implemented by only abstract classes. If there are non-abstract first-class concepts, they could be instantiated as is, which is not always meaningful. Exceptions can be made for first-class concepts, for which it is meaningful to be instantiated in another layer without adding further class properties. It is not recommended to provide root containers in π to avoid instantiation of concrete first-class abstractions in π. Second-class abstractions of π can be concrete (i.e., non-abstract) but do not have to be.

6.4.2. Domain

The *domain* (Δ) layer builds upon the π layer and assigns domain-specific semantics to its abstract first-class concepts. Δ builds on structural as well as on behavioral abstractions. For example, by creating subclasses of the component class (e.g., for the domains of software, mechanics, and electrics), the abstract component class can be enriched by domain-specific properties (attributes, references, ...). This will result in a metamodel module for software components, a module for mechanical components and one for electric components. If a developer is only interested in software, the Δ

layer merely includes metamodel module with the software components. It is also possible to have metamodel modules of multiple domains in the Δ layer (e.g., mechanics and electrics). A language that consists only of a π and Δ layer can already be applied, e.g., for quality-agnostic design and documentation of a system. If abstract first-class concepts are defined in π, these have to be inherited by classes of Δ to be usable. Δ abstractions can also reuse (by containment) second-class abstractions of π and reference other first-class abstractions of π. If new concepts are introduced on Δ (without inheritance into π), it should be considered if they contain an underlying pattern that can be modeled in π. Abstractions for modeling or analyzing quality properties, however, are not located on the Δ layer but are part of the layers mentioned hereafter.

6.4.3. Quality

The *quality* (Ω) layer defines quality properties for the abstractions of Δ. For example, reliability, performance or security properties could be added to the component concept. To be more specific, resource demands can be extended to the single processing steps of the services of a component, to be able to evaluate the performance of a service. A Ω layer is not always needed. To document the structure and behavior of a system merely the layers π and Δ are required. Analyzes can be conducted for structure and behavior, and do not always need explicit quality information. The Ω layer contains second-class abstractions that enrich the first-class abstractions of Δ. Abstractions that define quality properties that are contained in a root container of Ω must not change during an analysis. If they change, they model state information and have to be contained by a container from the Σ layer. Ω does also model derived quality properties. They must not be reachable from a root container in Ω by following containment relations. They will instead be contained by containers from the Σ layer.

6.4.4. Analysis

The analysis layer (Σ) comprises abstractions used by specific analysis approaches. Σ builds upon the previous layers by providing configuration data, run-time state, output data, and input data that does not belong to the more general Δ abstractions. Analyses may be either design time or runtime analyses. This is orthogonal to this layering, as it may at the most influence the content of metamodel modules of Σ. Σ can also be used to model data that is needed by other tools (e.g., monitoring approaches). For example, a sensitivity analysis needs a reference to a variable as input. The sensitivity analysis modifies this variable over several analysis runs. The reference and the value range are stored in modules of the Σ layer. In general, the features of the more basic layers can be used in several analyses. Several analyses may share modules from Σ. E.g., a performability analysis may reuse the output module of a performance analysis. Analyses may also have their own metamodel modules. On the Σ layer, new root containers, first-class abstractions, and second-class abstractions can be created as required by an analysis. Abstractions of the other layers should be reused when possible, but analysis-specific abstractions should not be specializations of more basic abstractions. This would mean, that Σ is not adequately separated from the other layers. The only constraint that holds is the avoidance of metamodel module dependency cycles.

6.4.5. Discussing the Research Questions and Challenges

This section explains the rationale behind the *specific layering* for metamodels for quality modeling and analysis.

The clear separation of the four layers enables decoupling and exchange of these layers. Thus, the layers π, Δ and Ω can be reused for different analyzers. π and Δ can be reused for different quality properties. π can be reused for different domains. The specific layering therefore tackles Problem 4 (Commonalities in Related Languages). By separating tool-specific metamodel content, Problem 5 (Tool-specific Metamodel Content) is addressed. By separating abstract concepts from domain and even more specific concepts, Problem 6 (Generality Compromise) is addressed. The concrete layering further answers the question of how to prioritize orthogonal decomposition dimensions in the specific case of metamodels for quality modeling.

6.5. Refactorings

This section describes class, metamodel module, and feature model refactorings. These refactorings are helpful or even necessary for applying the processes that are presented in Section 6.6. The class refactorings are essential in the application of the reference structure to separate concerns in classes and fix dependency directions. The metamodel module refactorings are essential when modularizing a legacy metamodel, but may also be used in refining and correcting a modular metamodel that has been implemented from scratch in a modular way. The metamodel module refactorings either split or merge metamodel module. The feature model refactorings are optional refactorings that can be used to clean up feature models after they have been completely specified.

The refactorings were assembled as they were used in applying the reference structure and from general experience. The list is not necessarily complete, as there may be more refactorings that can also be useful. This section does not feature trivial refactorings (like renamings or reordering) nor elemental modifications. For example, moving a class is even made trivial by the Modular Designer (see Appendix B.2).

The refactorings are formalized by a graph transformation system. The individual graph transformation rules are specified by diagrams, which show the left- and right-hand side of the rules. If an element is shown on the left-hand side but not on the right-hand side, the element is deleted. Conversely, if an element is not present in the left-hand side but appears on the right-hand side, the element is created. Labels track the identity of elements. E.g., if the left-hand side shows a class that is labeled C1 and the right-hand side shows a class with the label C1, both sides refer to the same class. Elements that appear on both sides remain all of their properties, even if they are not illustrated. E.g., if C1 has attributes and references, it keeps them unless it is illustrated otherwise. Elements that in addition to their existence, carry no further information, are not labeled. This is not necessary, as it is irrelevant whether they are preserved during the transformation or merely deleted and recreated. Examples for such elements are the implement relation between features and metamodel modules, and unambiguous feature relations (e.g., requires, optional child). The module dependencies that Section 6.5.2 shows are not transformed and, therefore, also not labeled, as they are determined by the classifiers inside the metamodel modules. They are merely illustrated to help to understand a module refactoring.

Some of the refactorings are supported by the Modular EMF Designer (Modular Designer). The Modular Designer is the tool support for the reference structure approach. Metamodel architects can use it to visualize and modify the layers and module structure of a metamodel. For in-depth information about the Modular Designer, consult Appendix B.2.

6.5.1. Class Refactorings

To apply this approach, several refactorings are necessary to split classes, break dependency cycles and reverse the direction of dependencies. These make use of the class extension relation that Chapter 5 introduced. The class refactorings are executed by a module developer.

6.5.1.1. Class Split

The class split refactoring is used to separate concerns in a class. It is shown in Figure 6.5 (1). Class properties of C are factored out into the new class E, which extends the remainder of C, which is labeled C'. Incoming dependencies remain on C'. Attributes, references, and containments can be factored out without complications. Inheritance can also be factored out; however, in EMOF it is not possible to substitute E for C'. Thus, factoring out inheritances is only appropriate in cases where substitutability is not required. These cases can be identified by analyzing incoming references onto the superclass. If it is not referenced, the inheritance is only used to inherit the class properties of the superclass and can be factored out.

The class split refactoring can be used to break dependency cycles. This is shown in (2). C1 is split, and the outgoing dependency of C1 that contributed to the cycle is factored out into E. As C1' does not depend on E, the cycle is broken.

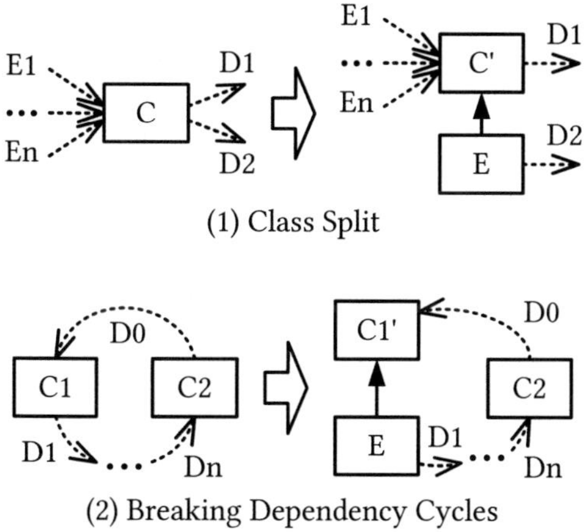

Figure 6.5.: The Class Split Refactoring (based on [HSR19])

6.5.1.2. Dependency Inversion

Figure 6.6 (1) illustrates dependency inversion refactorings. They are used by module developers to enforce the Dependency Inversion Principle [Mar03]. The principle states that abstractions (class A in the figure) must not depend on specifics (S), but specifics should depend on abstractions. Depending on the type of the dependency that should be inverted, multiple refactorings are possible.

A reference (1a) can be inverted by using a class split (1ai). The reference D is factored out into the new class E. This option should be chosen if S implements a first-class abstraction (i.e., the existence of an instance of S is not dependent on an instance of A). An indicator for this is when an instance of S is referenced by multiple other objects.

The reference can also be inverted into an extends relation (1aii). This should be done if S implements a second-class abstraction and is not referenced by any other class. If S is referenced by multiple classes, a common superclass N can be introduced for these classes, which is then extended by S (1aiii).

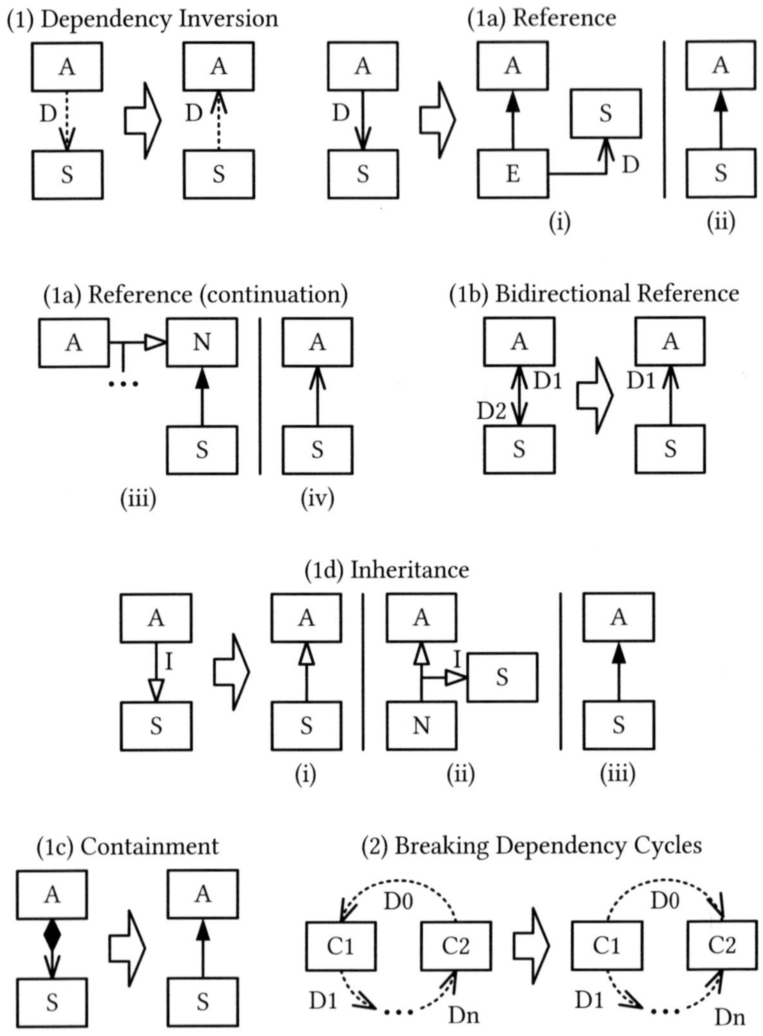

Figure 6.6.: The Dependency Inversion Refactoring (based on [HSR19])

Sometimes, the reference can be correctly owned by both A and S. In such cases, the reference can just be reversed (1aiv).

A bidirectional reference between A and S (1b) is a special case of (1a). In EMOF, a bidirectional reference consists of two standard references that have each other set as opposites. This is indicated by the two labels D1 and D2 that are next to the bidirectional reference. As explained in Section 4.4.4.1, bidirectional references are unnecessary and should be avoided. In such cases, the reference from A to S should be removed (only the reference from S to A remains). If the relations between A and S are simple references, a helper method can be provided that provides navigation from A to S. If A and S are located in different metamodel modules, the helper method should be placed with code that works on the metamodel module of S. It should not be placed together with code that works on the metamodel module of A, as this would violate the separation of concerns on the code level. In the special case that the reference from S to A is a containment, the reference from A to S is a container reference and can be deleted without replacement (see Section 4.4.4.2).

A containment (1c) can be inverted by replacing it by an opposing extends relation.

In 1a and 1c, also the multiplicity of the original dependency from A to S has to be modeled correctly after the refactoring. If the multiplicity has no lower and upper bounds (i.e., "0..*"), no further modeling is necessary, as an arbitrary number of instances of the extension class can be applied to an instance of A. If there is at least an upper or lower bound, a constraint has to be defined that enforces the multiplicity.

There are multiple ways to invert an inheritance from A to S (1d). If S is a specialization of A, the inheritance was specified in the wrong direction. Instances of A are sometimes erroneously typed with S, and the class properties from S are not needed. In this case, the inheritance can be simply reversed (1di). Some incoming dependencies may have to be redirected from A to S depending on their meaning.

If A and S implement different abstractions, the inheritance is removed and N, a new subclass of A and S, introduced (1dii). Incoming dependencies of A and S must be redirected to the correct class (either A, S or N).

If S is only used to add class properties to A and not for typing, the inheritance can be replaced by an opposite extends relation. For this to be feasible, there must not exist any incoming dependencies (except inheritance) to S and its superclasses.

One case is not shown in the figure. If A possesses an attribute that does not conform to A's level of abstraction, the attribute can be factored out using a class split. This is similar to (1ai) except S is not a class but a data type or enumeration.

Dependency inversion can be used to break dependency cycles (2). Reversing one dependency in a cycle is sufficient. In the illustration, the dependency from C2 to C1 is inverted, which breaks the cycle.

6.5.2. Metamodel Module Refactorings

The approach of applying the reference architecture relies on several refactorings that manipulate metamodel modules, their dependencies, and content. Many of these refactorings perform a split of a metamodel module, which is supported by the Modular Designer. To split a metamodel module, a metamodel architect first creates a new metamodel module and then uses the Modular Designer to move classes or whole packages from the original into the new metamodel module. The Modular Designer then automatically updates incoming references on the moved classes. When the metamodel module structure of a metamodel is altered, the respective feature model should always be updated accordingly. Thus, the following metamodel module refactorings also address the updating of the feature model.

The formalization of the module refactorings is different from the other refactorings. The diagrams that are shown for the individual module refactorings are only illustrations. The module refactorings are composite refactorings that are composed of several smaller transformation rules. Figure 6.7 shows these transformation rules. The deletion of a metamodel module or package is shown in (1). In (2), a new metamodel module or package is created. (3) shows a class move from one package into another package. The split and extraction refactorings perform metamodel module creations and then move classifiers into the new metamodel modules. The merge refactoring moves all the classifiers of one metamodel module into the other and then deletes the empty metamodel module.

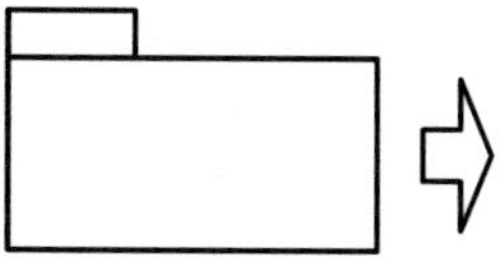

(1) Delete Module

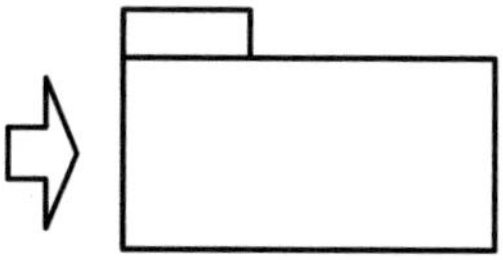

(2) Create Module

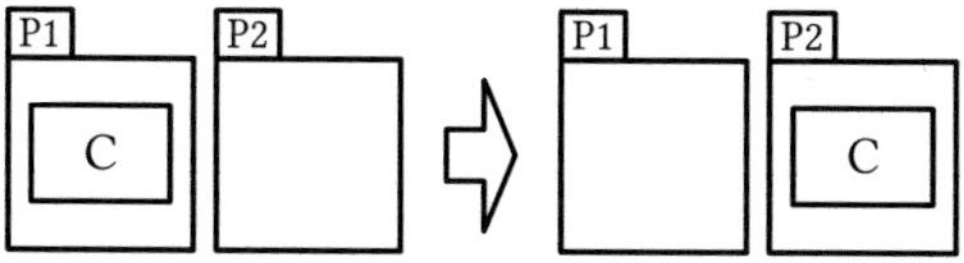

(3) Move Class

Figure 6.7.: Metamodel Module Refactoring Constituents

6.5.2.1. Horizontal Split

If there are parts of a metamodel module for which it should be conceptually possible to use them independently of each other but which are technically intertwined, a metamodel architect must split the metamodel module. Consider the original metamodel module M and two resulting metamodel modules M1 and M2. There may be a part P of M on which M1 and M2 both depend on. In such a case, the metamodel architect factors P out in its own metamodel module. The horizontal split can be easily generalized to a split into an arbitrary number of metamodel modules. For the sake of simplicity, this section presents the horizontal split into two metamodel modules (M1 and M2).

The results of a horizontal split are illustrated in Figure 6.8. Note, this section heavily refers to the subfigures of Figure 6.8. For the sake of brevity, it only refers to the labels of the subfigure and does not explicitly reference the figure. (0) shows the potential worst-case outcome. All resulting metamodel modules could be mutually dependent. Depending on whether the metamodel architect factors out a common part, P is present or not present (illustrated by the large brackets). In subsequent refactoring steps, a module developer has to use dependency inversion to bring the metamodel modules into a state where their dependencies match the illustrations in (1), (2), or (3).

(1) shows the simplest case. Both metamodel modules are entirely unrelated. In the feature model, this results in two unrelated features. In this case, it is unlikely that there are many dependencies between classes of M1 and M2. If there are dependencies, either classes are not placed correctly, the dependencies are conceptually erroneous, or the cases (2) or (3) apply.

(2) represents the case where M1 and M2 are independent of each other, but share a common base that was also contained in M before the refactoring. In the feature model, the result is identical to (1) with the addition that the resulting features have implemented-by relations to their respective metamodel module and P. P does not implement an own feature. If this were the case, the result would be (3) with an additional metamodel module factored out. If there were dependencies from P to M1 and M2, these would have to be reversed by a module developer. For dependencies between M1 and M2, the same applies as in (1): either classes are not placed correctly, the dependencies are conceptually erroneous, or the case (3) applies.

(3) shows the case where one metamodel module depends on the other. This split is similar to two splits that the remainder of this section presents. The difference is that in this split, M1 can be a root metamodel module on the same layer as M2 and no extension has to take place. In the feature model, this results in two features. The feature that is implemented by M1 is dependent on M2 (either via child or requires relation). All dependencies from M2 to M1 had to be reversed by a module developer.

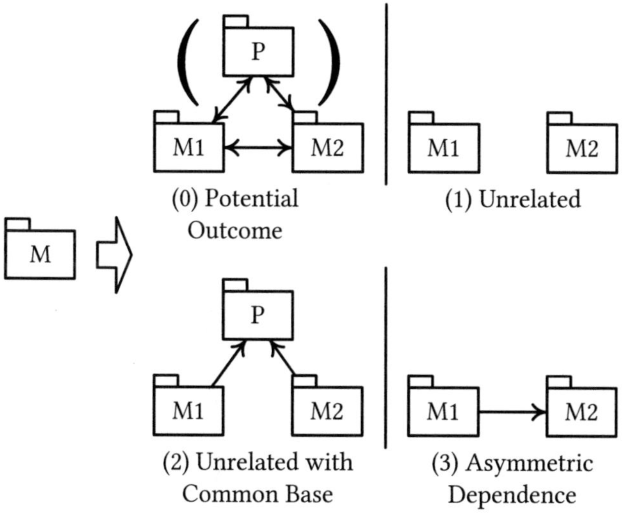

Figure 6.8.: The Horizontal Split Metamodel Module Refactoring (based on [HSR19])

6.5.2.2. Extension Extraction

A metamodel architect uses this refactoring if a metamodel module M has a part P that is optional but cannot be used independently. Figure 6.9 illustrates the extension extraction. The metamodel architect factors out P into a new metamodel module and declares a dependency from P to M. For this split to be an extension extraction, P cannot be a root metamodel module, and an extension relation has to be part of the dependency from P to M. A module developer may have to split classes that are essential to M if they contain optional class properties that belong to P. The module developer further reverses all dependencies from elements of M to P. If there are incoming dependencies onto P from other metamodel modules, they have to be considered for dependency inversion. Whether they should be reversed depends on the conceptually correct feature dependencies of the features they implement. Usually, metamodel modules that implement cross-cutting features that are intrusively implemented have many incoming dependencies that have to be reversed. In the feature model, a new feature is created that is implemented by P. P is then either an optional child of M or has a required relation to M.

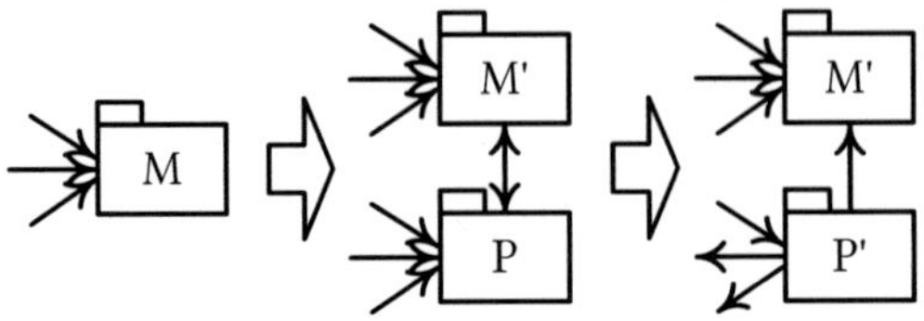

Figure 6.9.: The Extension Extraction Refactoring [HSR19] (©2019 IEEE)

6.5.2.3. Feature Support Extraction

Features support extraction is a special case of the extension extraction. It is illustrated in Figure 6.10. A metamodel architect can perform this refactoring if there is a part P of a metamodel module M1 that is dependent on another metamodel module M2 and it is meaningful to use M1 without P. The metamodel architect creates a new metamodel module P and declares dependencies from P to M1 and M2. If there are class dependencies from M1 to P, a module developer must reverse them. S/he may also conduct class split refactorings to separate the content of both features. For P a new feature is created that is implemented by P and is in most cases a child of F1. It may also be a child of F2. In both cases, a requires relation points to the other feature.

This refactoring can be used to lift a feature up to a more abstract layer. Consider F2 to be a very specific feature, which is therefore located on a more specific (lower) layer. As F1 requires F2, F1 cannot be at a more abstract layer. Else the required relation from F1 to F2 would violate the layering. If F1 provides concepts that are more general than the layer of F2, these concepts should be separated from their application onto F2. This results in M1' (the pure concepts) and P (their application onto F2). M1' and its feature F1' can then be lifted to the appropriate layer.

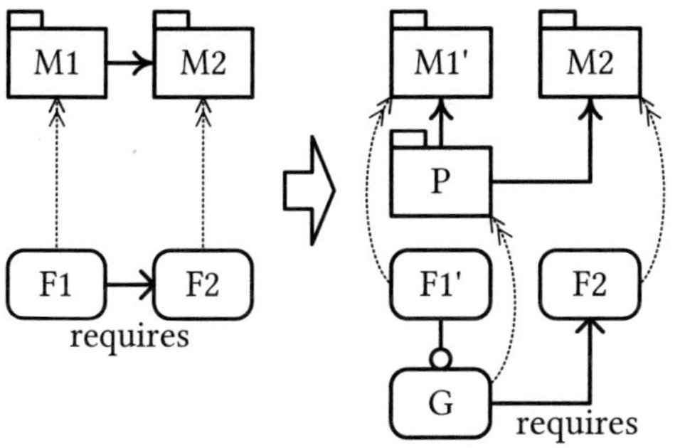

Figure 6.10.: The Feature Support Extraction Refactoring (based on [HSR19])

6.5.2.4. Vertical Split

The metamodel architect performs this refactoring if a metamodel module could be assigned to multiple layers. Figure 6.11 illustrates the refactoring. The metamodel architect divides the metamodel module in a way that each classifier can be assigned to precisely one layer. If necessary, a module developer has to split classes. The metamodel architect assigns the resulting metamodel modules to their respective layers. If there are module dependencies that violate the layering, a module developer has to perform dependency inversion.

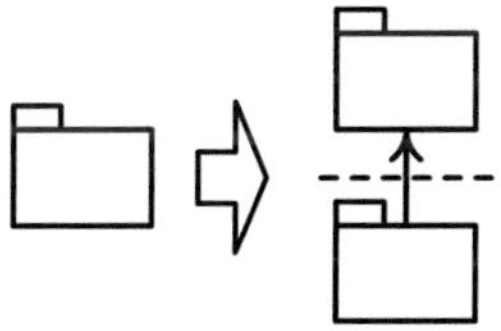

Figure 6.11.: The Vertical Split Refactoring [HSR19] (©2019 IEEE)

The feature model is updated accordingly. With the exception of π metamodel modules, for each new metamodel module that resulted from the split, a new feature is created and is assigned to the layer of the module. If there are module dependencies between more special to more basic layer, conforming feature dependencies are created. Incoming feature relations have to be respecified to reflect incoming module dependencies.

6.5.2.5. Merge

Merging can be used in various circumstances. Especially if there is a mandatory child feature relation between two language features or a dependency cycle between their metamodel modules, the metamodel architect should consider whether it is meaningful to merge those features and their metamodel modules. Figure 6.12 illustrates the refactoring. The figure does not show dependencies between the two metamodel modules that are merged because there may be various dependency constellations amongst them. These constellations are one directional, bidirectional and no dependency. A merge between two metamodel modules that are not dependent occurs, e.g., if abstract classes that function as ubiquitous superclasses are consolidated into one metamodel module even if they are not dependent on each other. A metamodel architect performs a merge using the Modular Designer by moving all classifiers of one metamodel module into the other and then deleting the empty metamodel module. From the feature that was implemented by the deleted module, all incoming and outgoing relations are transferred to the other feature. Finally, the feature is deleted too.

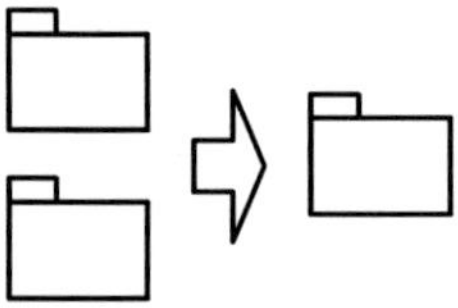

Figure 6.12.: The Module Merge Refactoring [HSR19] (©2019 IEEE)

6.5.3. Feature Model Refactoring

This section presents refactorings that make a feature model more precise in certain situations. A metamodel architect performs these refactorings. The refactorings do not change the module structure of a metamodel. They also do not change the feature selection behavior of a feature model. If they did, they would not be refactorings. Most of the refactorings have preconditions that have to hold for the refactoring to be applicable. If these preconditions are violated after the refactoring has been applied, the selection behavior of the feature model changes. Thus, these refactorings should be applied to clean up the feature model after its completion.

6.5.3.1. Pull Up Relation

The pull up relation refactoring moves feature relations up on the parent/child hierarchy. The refactoring is illustrated in Figure 6.13. The relations that are refactored may either be requires or excludes relations. Because of this, they are illustrated without arrowheads. In the illustrations, only two child features are shown. The refactoring, however, can easily be generalized to more than two child features. There are two cases where this refactoring can be applied.

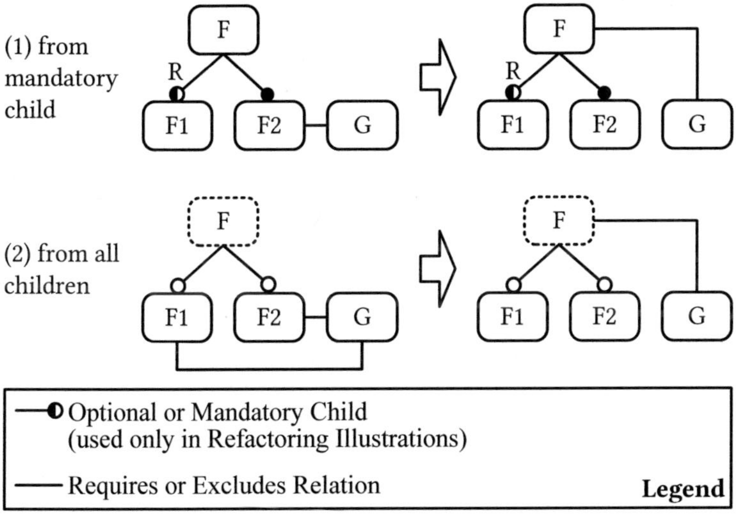

Figure 6.13.: The Pull Up Feature Relation Refactoring

In the first case (1), a relation is pulled up from a mandatory child. Even tough F1 does not own the feature relations, the relation of F2 does also apply to F1. This is the case, as to select F1, F has to be selected, as it is its parent. To select F, F2 has to be select, as it is a mandatory child. Thus, the relation can be pulled up to F. This refactoring increases the clarity of the feature model, as it is immediately apparent that the whole subtree below F is affected by the feature relation to G. This refactoring has to be reversed if F2 is removed as a child of F or changes to an optional child.

If a feature F has several child features (F1 and F2) that all share a relation to the same target G, the relation can be pulled up to F provided that F is an empty feature. The refactoring is shown in (2). It reduces the number of unnecessary elements of a feature model. The refactoring has to be reversed if child features are added to F that do not share the feature relation to G.

6.5.3.2. Transform Required into Mandatory Child

Figure 6.14 shows the refactoring. It is used to remove common required relations to a sibling feature (G) by turning the required feature into a mandatory child. It is necessary that the parent F is an empty feature. If not, this refactoring changes the selection behavior of F as G is always selected. Another prerequisite is that all child features (F1 to Fn) are dependent on G. This refactoring increases the clarity of a feature model by reducing the number of required relations.

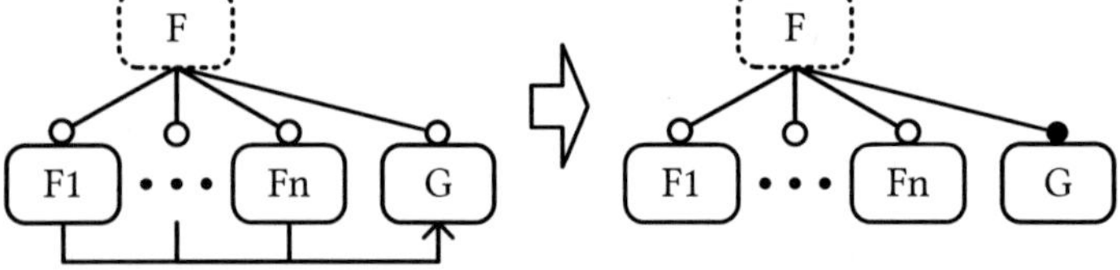

Figure 6.14.: The Transform Required Relation into Mandatory Child Refactoring

6.5.3.3. Merge Mandatory Child into Parent

This refactoring fuses a mandatory child with their parent. For example, an empty root feature can be eliminated this way. Figure 6.15 (1) illustrates the refactoring. The mandatory child feature G is merged into the parent F. All implemented-by relations to metamodel modules from G are moved to F. This refactoring can be used after the transform required relation into mandatory child refactoring. If a language has precisely one mandatory language feature, this refactoring should be used to make this language feature the root feature. This refactoring can also be used to get rid of grouping features that are no longer needed.

There is a special case of the merge mandatory child into parent refactoring that can be used to ungroup features. The reversed refactoring can be used to group features. It is illustrated in (2). To remove an empty grouping feature G, it has to be a mandatory child. The children of G are made direct children of the parent of G (F). The reversed refactoring takes some children of a feature F and puts a mandatory empty grouping feature between them.

6.5.3.4. Transform Mutual Exclusion

Using this refactoring, a set of mutually exclusive features is transformed into an alternative feature set or an alternative feature set can be dispersed. Figure 6.16 shows the refactoring. It is illustrated with three child features but can be generalized for an arbitrary number of features.

To form an alternative feature set, a common parent is needed. If F, G, and H are children of the same parent, this is already fulfilled. If not, the new empty parent feature P is created. It also has to be considered if required relations have to be specified to the former parent. This is the case if an antecedent is a non-empty feature. In both cases, the excludes relations are simply replaced by an alternative set relation. Especially, if the features have the same parent, this refactoring reduces the complexity of the feature model and improves its hierarchical structure.

To get rid of an alternative feature set, P has to be empty so that it can be deleted. If it is not empty, it is not deleted but requires relations have to be specified from its child features to P. This increases, however, the complexity

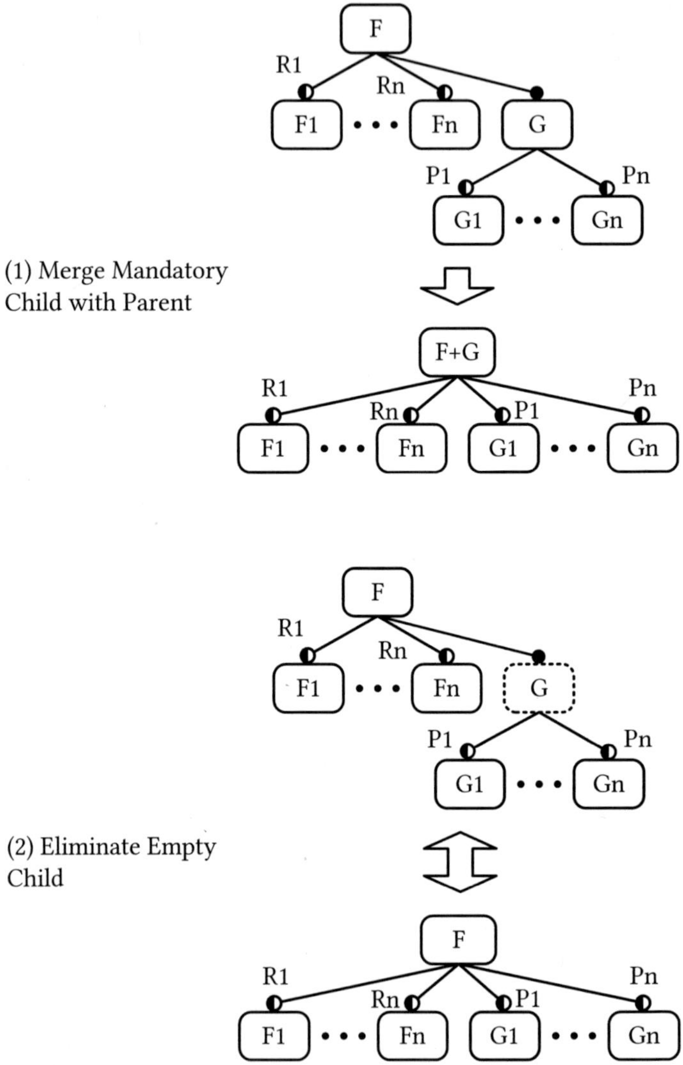

Figure 6.15.: The Pull Up Mandatory Child Refactoring

of the feature model. In any case, the alternative set relation is replaced by excludes relations between all features. Although this refactoring usually increases complexity, it can be used to get rid of an alternative set that turned out to be inadequate.

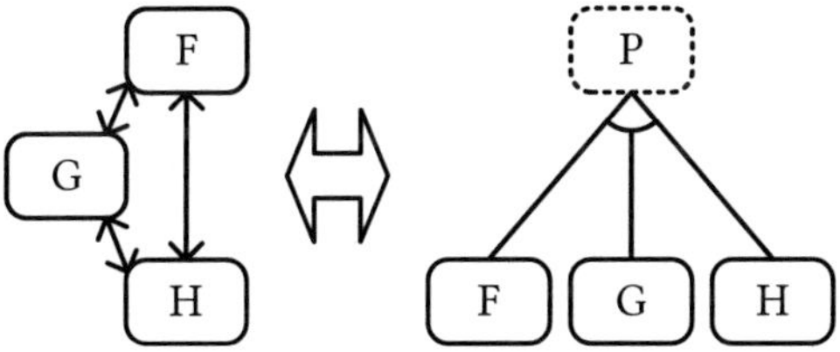

Figure 6.16.: Transform Mutual Exclusion Refactoring

6.5.3.5. Omit Transitive Relations

To clean up feature models, redundant relations can be omitted. Several cases are displayed in Figure 6.17 and Figure 6.18.

1. Transitive required relations can simply be omitted. In general, the path of required relations from F to H via G may contain features and required relations than just G.
2. The required relation from F to a feature H that is a mandatory child of a feature G that is already required can be omitted. There may be even further features and child relations between G and H as long as there is a path of mandatory child relations between the two features.
3. Required relations to features that are already required by the parent should be omitted.
4. Required relations to descendant features are bad modeling. They should be replaced by making the branch which connects the parent with the descendant completely mandatory.
5. Required relations to a mandatory sibling can simply be omitted.

6. Required relations to an optional sibling can be transformed into an optional child relation.

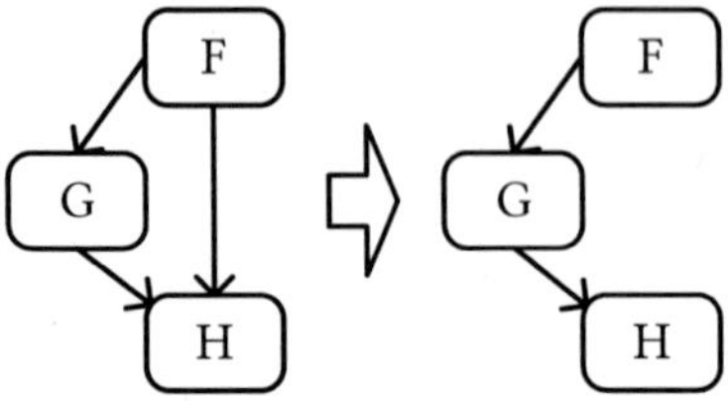

(1) Transitive Required Relation

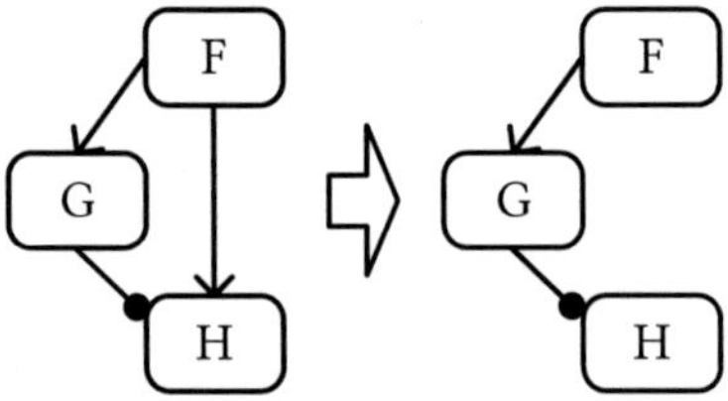

(2) Require Mandatory Child of Required Feature

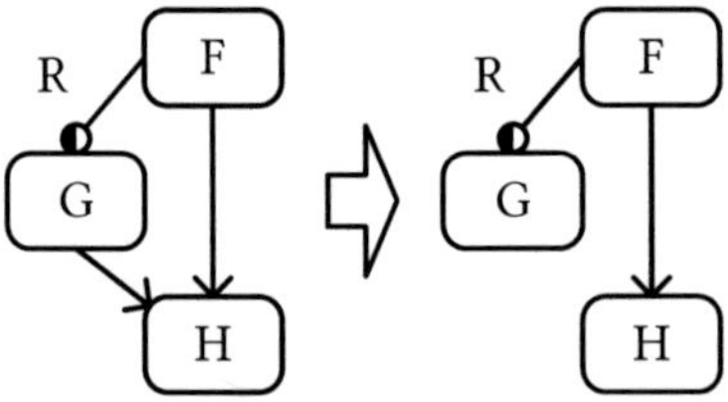

(3) Required Relation to Feature Required by Parent

Figure 6.17.: Feature Relation Refactorings (Part 1/2)

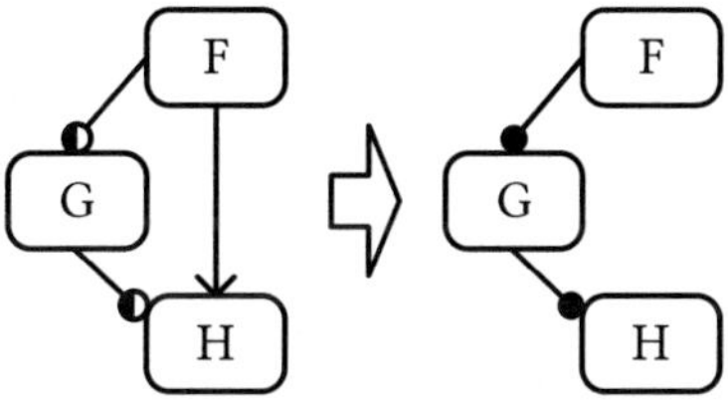

(4) Required Descendant

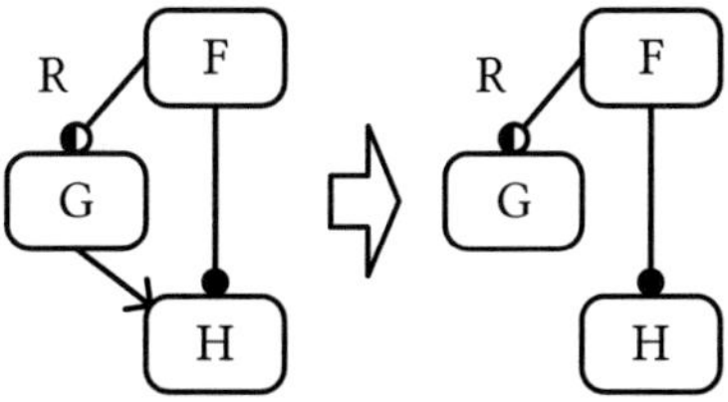

(5) Required Relation to
Mandatory Sibling

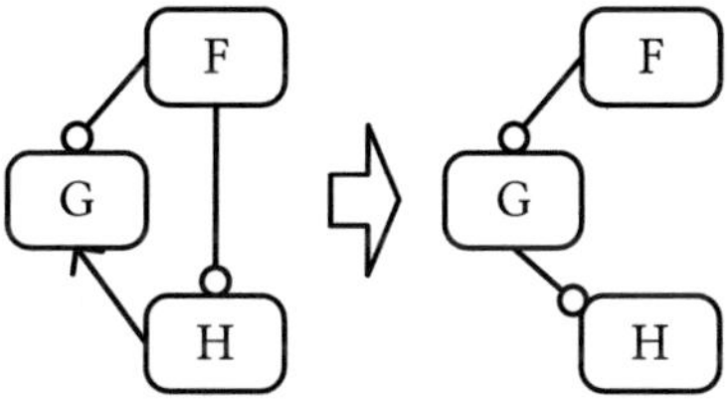

(6) Required Sibling to Parent

Figure 6.18.: Feature Relation Refactorings (Part 2/2)

6.6. Application Process

This section presents application processes for three scenarios: (1) the creation of a new metamodel, (2) refactoring of an already existing metamodel to fit the reference structure, (3) extending an existing metamodel that was implemented or refactored according to the reference structure approach (i.e., it is modular, layered and has a feature model representation). The main difference between the processes is: in 1, the feature model is constructed before the metamodel modules are implemented; in 2, the metamodel modules already exist and are modularized hand-in-hand with an evolving version of the feature model; in 3, the modular metamodel and its feature model already exist and are merely extended.

Metamodeling is a creative design process with many degrees of freedom. The same is true for the process of refactoring and modularization. It is the goal of the Modular Designer to support the developers as much as possible and to automate as much as possible. However, most activities in metamodeling are manual tasks that cannot be automated like: how to implement the concepts of a language, how to group classes into metamodel modules, where to use extensions, where to split existing classes and metamodel modules, and so on.

When applying the reference structure approach, feature models are used to express the variability of the language (in analogy to related approaches [AKM13; Sch+15]). In the first and second process, a feature graph is used as a predecessor stage of a proper feature model. It consists of features and their relations. In contrast to a feature model, its parent-child relations do not have to form a tree because there can be multiple roots (features with no outgoing dependencies).

6.6.1. Creating a New Metamodel

Figure 6.19 illustrates the process of creating a new metamodel using the reference structure approach. The individual process steps are not meant to be performed in a strict iterative manner. Some steps may be skipped, which is explained in the descriptions of the respective steps. It can be beneficial to backtrack to a prior step (e.g., when it is discovered that a feature was forgotten or a feature can be split).

If there is no reuse of metamodel modules, this is a pure top-down design process. If there is reuse, it is a mixture of top-down (decomposing the features of the language) and bottom-up (assembling the existing metamodel modules). The following presents the individual steps of the process.

1) **Language Feature Identification** At first, as with any software project, the metamodel architects identify the requirements of the language. This step does not differ from the usual design of metamodels (see Section 2.2.5). The concerns of the tool users have to be identified. Each language concern results in a language feature. Note that this is the requirements identification phase; no technical artifacts are implemented. The result of this process step is a collection of language features.

2) **Reuse** Readily available metamodel modules may exist in organization-internal or even public online repositories. This step is skipped if no reuse takes place. The metamodel architect assigns metamodel modules that can be reused to implement language features to the respective language features. Metamodel modules on which reused metamodel modules depend on, have to also be incorporated. Dependencies of reused metamodel modules that implement an own language feature that was not yet identified in the first process step are assigned to that new language feature. Such metamodel modules are usually root metamodel modules. Dependencies of reused metamodel modules that do not implement a new language feature are assigned to the language feature of the reused metamodel module. The result of this process step is a collection of language features of which some are already implemented by reused metamodel modules.

3) **Creating the Feature Graph** By creating an empty root feature node and labeling it with the name of the language, a metamodel architect starts the feature model. For each of the identified language features, the metamodel architect creates a feature node that is named after the language feature. As a reminder, a feature node and its language feature are simply refereed to as a feature if both are addressed simultaneously (see Section 6.3.2). A metamodel architect has to

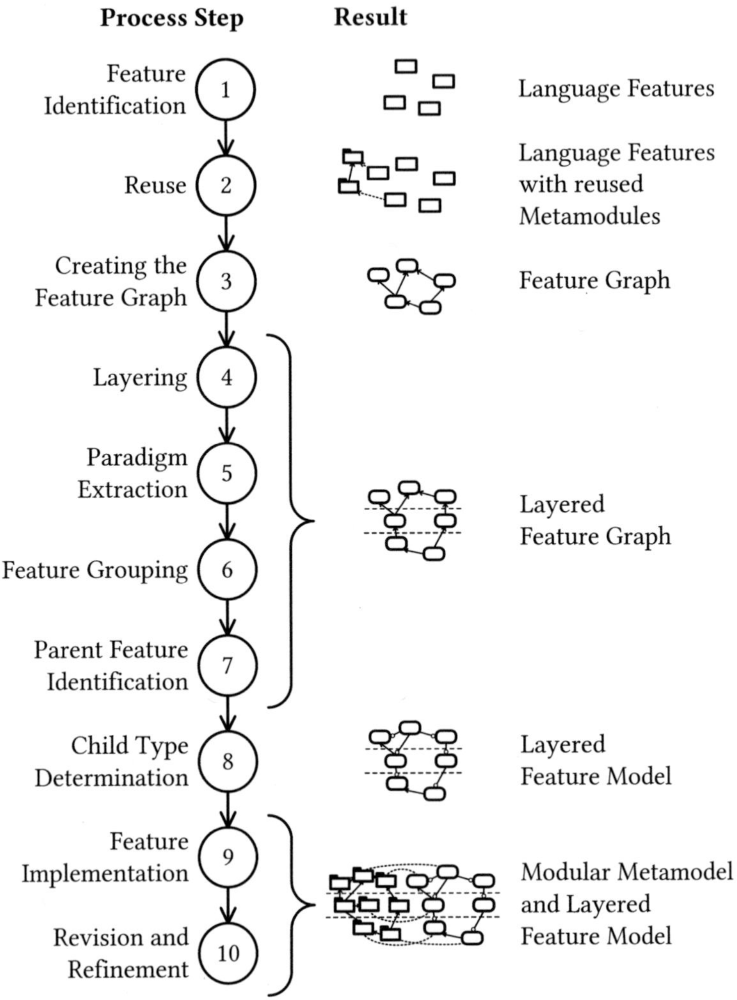

Figure 6.19.: Process Overview: Creating a new Metamodel

declare a relation from a feature F to another feature G according to the following rules:

- A **requires relation** is declared if a reused module that implements F has a dependency to a reused feature that implements G.
- A **requires relation** is declared if feature F is an extension of feature G.
- A **requires relation** is declared if feature F is dependent on concepts of feature G.
- A **excludes relation** is declared if feature F prohibits the use of feature G or vice versa.

Cycles of requires relations are forbidden. A metamodel architect has to solve cycles by reversing requires relations. The direction of the requires relations has to be based on what is conceptually correct. If a cycle seems to be unbreakable, probably one feature has to be split as it covers too many concerns. Between two features that do not rely on reused metamodel modules, a required relation can be reversed instantly. If metamodel modules are involved, the module dependencies that are not supported by the feature dependencies have to be reversed in step 9 (feature implementation).

The result of this process step is a feature graph.

4) **Layering** In this step, features are vertically split and assigned to layers following the guidelines in Section 6.4. A metamodel architect assigns features that contain language features only relevant to a single layer to that layer. S/he performs the following steps for each layer except for π, starting from the next basic layer.

   a) If an unassigned feature contains features relevant to the current layer alongside with other features, s/he creates a new feature to hold the concepts that are irrelevant to the current layer. S/he assigns the original feature to the current layer; the new feature remains unassigned (and will be handled further when the next layer is modularized). S/he declares a requires relation from the new feature to the original feature.

Feature relations that pointed to the original feature are either left unchanged, redirected or duplicated to the new feature.

b) S/he reverses all feature relations coming from features of more basic layers to features of this layer.

After these points have been completed, some feature relations may point from more basic into more advanced layers. This is the result of a feature F extending a feature that is more specific. This can be resolved by performing a feature support split on F (see Section 6.5.2.3).

The result of this step is a feature graph in which each feature is assigned to exactly one layer, all feature dependencies are non-cyclic and do not violate the layering.

5) **Paradigm Extraction** In this step, concepts that could be reused in other domains are extracted into their own layer. The root feature is always part of the π layer. To form the remaining π, a metamodel architect considers for each language feature whether it contains any fundamental concepts or patterns. For these fundamental concepts and patterns, s/he creates new features in π and creates requires relations pointing to them from the dependent Δ language features.

6) **Feature Grouping** The grouping of language features is either used to achieve a logical structuring (without effect on feature selection) or to form feature sets (with effects on features selection, see Section 2.4). Groups of features can only be formed from features of the same layer. For each group, a metamodel architect creates a new feature within the same layer and makes it the parent of each feature of the group. Grouping can be done according to multiple reasons. Multiple features could share a commonality (e.g., they are all structural abstractions, view types, or of the same type). In some cases, groups are used to form feature sets (i.e., alternative sets or OR sets). If two or more features are fully interconnected with excludes relations, a metamodel architect has to use an alternative feature set. The alternative feature set then replaces all excludes relations. If no feature grouping is necessary, this step is skipped.

7) **Parent Feature Identification** In this step, the parents of each feature that does not yet have one from the grouping step are identified. First, a metamodel architect identifies all features that are direct

children of the root amongst the π and Δ features. These are the standalone features of the language. They represent view types and usually have no outgoing feature dependencies. If they have outgoing feature dependencies, then only to π features.

Next, the metamodel architect identifies the parents of the remaining features, which do not have a parent yet. One of the features to which a requires relation exists is usually the parent. If a feature is an extension of another feature, the metamodel architect declares a parent relation from the extending to the extended feature. In all cases, the parent relation replaces an existing dependency relation between the two features. Like the requires relations, a parent relation cannot point into a more specific layer.

The result of this step is a layered feature graph where every non-root feature has a parent declared.

8) **Child Feature Type Determination** Some features already got their child type in step (5). These features are either part of alternative sets or OR sets and remain this way. For the other features, which do not yet have a parent, a metamodel architect specifies the child features types as follows.

   a) The root feature has no parent but is always mandatory.

   b) Child relations that cross the π layer boundary are always OR sets, even if the parent has only one child. This enforces that π features cannot be selected on their own, but always together with at least one child.

   c) Grouping features and parents of feature sets are mandatory if the child relation does not cross a layer border.

   d) Child relations that cross the other layer boundaries are optional. If this were not the case, there would be hard coupling between the layers.

   e) The remaining features, which do not yet have a type assigned to their child relation, are optional.

The result of this process step is a proper feature model that is layered and conforms to the dependency constraints of the reference structure approach.

9) **Feature Implementation** In this process step, module developers implement each feature by metamodel modules. Exceptions are empty features and features that are already entirely implemented by reused metamodel modules. Empty features are the root feature and the parents of feature sets and feature groups. If the module developers introduce new module dependencies that are not conforming to the feature model, a metamodel architect and a module developer carry out the following steps. Together, they consider the new feature dependency d from the feature F that is implemented by metamodel module M to the feature G that is implemented by metamodel module N.

    a) If the information that is modeled by d is already present in the implementation of N and is only used to ease backward navigation, the metamodel architect forbids the dependency.

    b) If there is no opposing dependency (i.e., G is not dependent on F) and the new dependency that will be introduced by d is meaningful in this specific context, s/he allows the new feature dependency d.

    c) If there is an opposing feature dependency, the metamodel architect considers dependency inversion of d (see Section 6.5.1).

    d) If none of the above options are feasible, the metamodel architect allows the new feature dependency d. This will result in a dependency cycle between F and G, which has to be resolved in the next step.

    The result of this process step is a modular metamodel with a feature model, which may still contain some flaws regarding the conformance of the module dependency graph to the feature model.

10) **Revision and Refinement** Using the module refactorings described in Section 6.5.2, metamodel architects in cooperation with module developers can revise and refine the feature model to resolve issues

like dependency cycles, features that could belong to multiple layers and features that fulfill multiple responsibilities. This step is skipped, if no refinement is necessary. After each refactoring, a metamodel architect updates the feature model accordingly. Finally, a metamodel architect can use the feature model refactorings from Section 6.5.3 to clean up and clarify the feature model. The result of this process step is the final layered modular metamodel with feature model which both fulfill the dependency constraints of the reference structure approach.

6.6.2. Refactor an Existing Metamodel

This section specifies the process to refactor an existing metamodel to fit the proposed reference structure. Figure 6.20 gives an overview. Like the previous process, the single steps of the process are not intended to be executed in a strictly sequential manner. Especially, when refactoring a legacy metamodel with which the metamodel developers are not entirely familiar with, the developers' knowledge increases during the refactoring process. Thus, dependencies and unmodularized language features become apparent, and the modularization must be revised iteratively.

1) **Horizontal Decomposition** The metamodel architects subdivide existing metamodel modules according to the horizontal decomposition refactoring until they only implement a single responsibility. A good starting point is given by the package structure and the outline of the documentation if they exist. The dependencies are not yet adjusted, this is done in a later step in the process.

   In case a large number of models of the original metamodel is accessible, the parts of the metamodel that are used for instantiating the models give hints for decomposition. If a metamodel module is commonly instantiated only in parts, this indicates the metamodel module must be further subdivided.

   Sometimes, already implemented metamodel modules may be available from other metamodels that cover a similar subject matter. If some of these metamodel modules offer abstractions that are sufficiently similar to the ones of the current metamodel, these metamodel

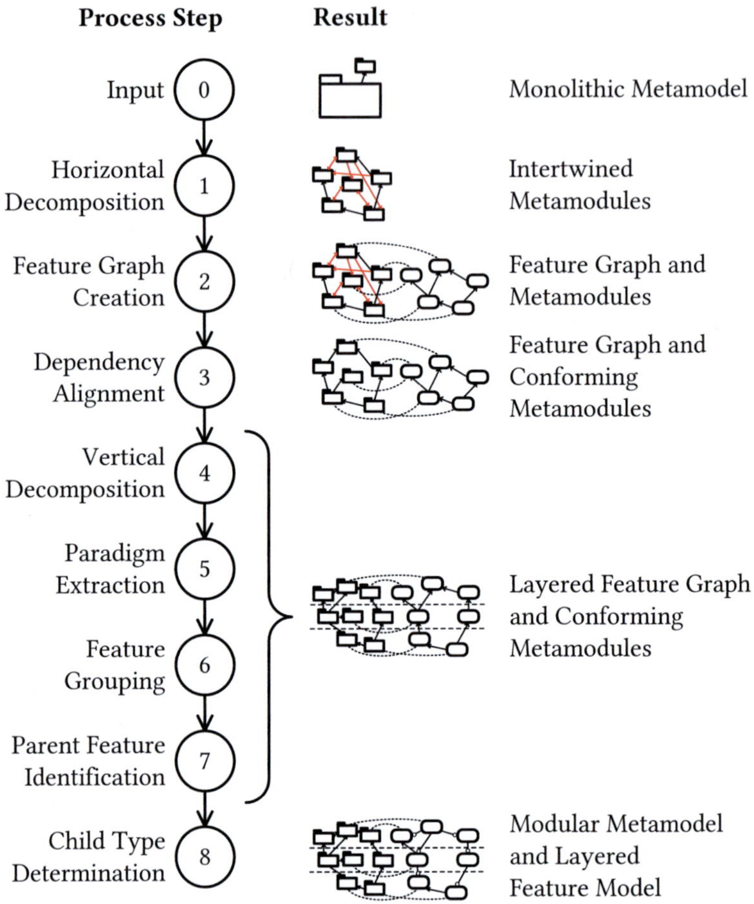

Figure 6.20.: Process Overview: Refactoring a Legacy Metamodel

modules can be used to replace the respective parts of the metamodel. In such a case, incoming classifier dependencies have to be redirected to the reused metamodel modules. Depending on the extent of the reuse, this enables to consolidate the common parts of two or even more metamodels. This has the advantage that instances of common language features have to be modeled only once. Language-specific extensions can then be applied on these instances.

The result of this step is a set of metamodel modules that may be strongly interconnected and possibly contain dependency cycles. These shortcomings have to be refactored in the following steps.

2) **Feature Graph Creation** In this process step, a feature graph is created that represents the language features of the metamodel. First, a metamodel architect has to consider for each metamodel module whether it represents a language feature. Abstract metamodel modules do not represent language features. Abstract metamodel modules define abstractions that are needed by multiple metamodel modules. Usually, all metamodel modules without incoming dependencies represent language features. The exception are abstract metamodel modules that merely implement extension points that are currently not used. Metamodel modules that have incoming dependencies either represent standalone features or extension features. If the metamodel module can be used on its own, it implements a standalone feature. If the metamodel module cannot be used on its own but extends other metamodel modules, it implements an extension feature.

   Second, the metamodel architect creates a feature node for each language feature that s/he identified. Third, regardless of the module dependencies, the metamodel architect declares feature required relations according to the conceptual dependencies of the language features and the guidelines and constraints of the reference structure.

   The result of this step is a set of metamodel modules and a feature graph that represents the conceptual feature dependencies. The module dependency graph does not yet conform to the feature dependency graph.

3) **Dependency Alignment** In this step, a metamodel architect inspects module dependencies that are not in line with the feature graph. S/he starts with the most specific modules. These are usually the ones with the least incoming dependencies. For each incoming and outgoing dependency d on the classifier level that is not reflected in

the feature graph, s/he executes the following steps. d points from metamodel module M to N.

a) S/he checks whether the affected classifiers in both metamodel modules are correctly placed. If not, s/he moves the respective classifier into the other metamodel module.

b) If a classifier is encountered that does not fit M nor N, s/he considers whether it either belongs to another metamodel module or whether it (and possibly further classifiers) can be factored out into a new metamodel module.

c) If there is a feature dependency from N to M, s/he considers dependency inversion of d.

d) If there is no feature dependency from N to M, s/he considers introducing a feature dependency from M to N.

e) If there is a feature dependency from N to M, s/he considers reversing it. If it is meaningful to do so, s/he reverses all inter-module dependencies that go from N to M as well.

S/he updates the feature graph accordingly. The result of this step is a modular metamodel that is free of dependency cycles, and all module dependencies conform to a feature dependency.

4) **Vertical Decomposition** Metamodels in the focus of this thesis can be reused at least in parts for modeling and analyzing different quality properties or even different domains. This optional step can be performed to improve the reusability of the metamodel. First, metamodel architects assign metamodel modules that only implement language features relevant to a specific layer to that layer. On each metamodel module M that implements language features belonging to multiple layers, metamodel architects and module developers perform the vertical split refactoring. A metamodel architect updates the feature graph accordingly. The result of this step is a layered modular metamodel that conforms to a layered feature graph.

5) **Paradigm Extraction** In this step, metamodel architects inspect Δ for abstractions and patterns that are fundamental to the language and can be reused in other domains. Suitable candidates are often amongst the packages that contain mostly abstract classes. If there

is an abstraction or pattern to be factored out whose classes are not abstract, a module developer can factor it out into abstract classes from which the concrete classes then inherit. A module developer moves properties that belong to the abstractions or pattern into the abstract classes, while domain-specific properties stay in the concrete classes. Incoming dependencies remain on the concrete classes. After each refactoring, a metamodel architect updates the feature graph accordingly.

6-8) Feature Model Forming In these steps, the metamodel architects transform the feature graph into a feature model. First, a metamodel architect creates a root feature. Then the metamodel architects perform the steps Feature Grouping, Parent Identification, and Child Feature Types Determination from Section 6.6.1. The result of these steps is a feature model and a modular metamodel of which all module dependencies conform to the feature model.

6.6.3. Extending a Modular Metamodel

This section presents the process of how an existing language is extended. Figure 6.21 illustrates the process. This process applies to the extension of a layered modular metamodel for which a conforming feature model exists. The process of extending a metamodel that is not layered, not divided into modules, and has no feature model is much simpler as it is much more unstructured. For such a plain metamodel extension, please refer to Section 8.2.2.

1) Feature Identification In this process step, the metamodel architects make a requirements assessment of which new which new concepts should be introduced. An important question that the metamodel architects have to ask about the new concepts is whether they (1) represent an intrusive addition to existing language features or whether they (2) are optional extensions. They must only choose the first case if the new concepts are essential to the language feature to which they should be added. This means they are always used if the language feature is used. For all concepts that fall under the first case, the process ends here, as no metamodel extension takes place.

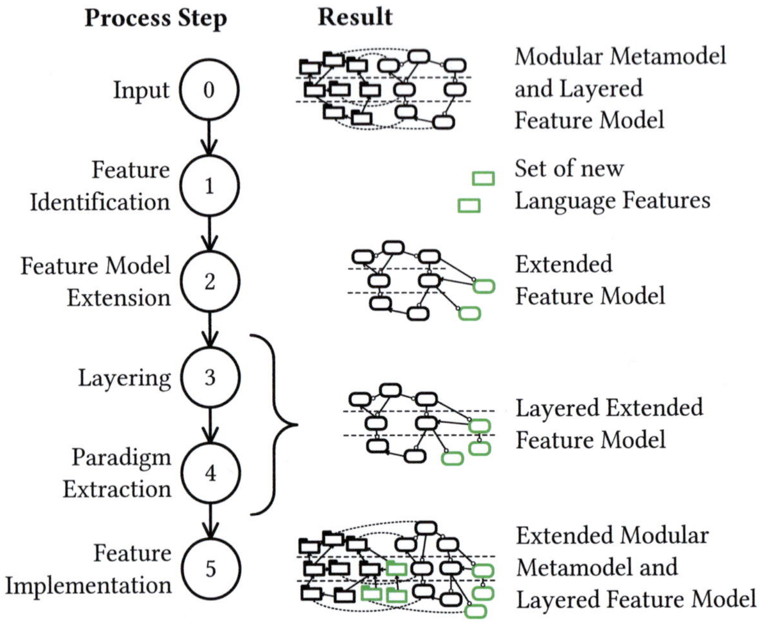

Figure 6.21.: Process Overview: Extending a Modular Metamodel

The module developers implement them in the existing metamodel modules to which they belong.

If there are any new concepts left that fall under the second case (optional extension), the metamodel architects proceed as follows. They group the concepts into language features. A language feature is a unit of reuse. Thus, the metamodel architects should consider whether a language feature is always used as a whole. If there are parts of a language feature that could be used independently, they have to be moved into an own language feature. The result of this step is a set of new language features.

2) **Feature Model Extension** In this process step, the metamodel architects integrate the new language features into the feature model. For each language feature, the metamodel architects create a new

feature node. Next, they note down feature dependencies amongst the new features. They then review the feature model to determine which features the new language features depend on. They note down these dependencies. For each new feature, they identify the parent amongst its dependencies. If this is non-trivial, they use the guidelines in step 6 (Feature Grouping) and 7 (Parent Feature Identification) of Section 6.6.1. New extension features are always optional child features. For the remaining feature dependencies, a metamodel architect creates required relations. The result of this process step is an addition of new features to the feature model of the language that is extended.

3-4) Layering and Paradigm Extraction In this process step, a metamodel architect places the new feature in the proper layer. The layering must not be violated by the new feature dependencies. This means a feature is at least as specific as the most specific feature it depends on. If this is too specific, a metamodel architect performs a feature support extraction (see Section 6.5.2.3). If a new feature does not fit exactly one layer, a metamodel architect splits it as described in step 4 (Layering) of Section 6.6.1. At last, the metamodel architects perform paradigm extraction (see step 5 of Section 6.6.1). The result of this process step is an extended feature model, which is properly layered.

5) Feature Implementation In this final step, the module developers implement the new language features by metamodel modules. If class extensions have to be implemented, the process in Section 8.2.2 has to be followed. The module dependencies must conform to the feature dependencies. If the feature dependencies seem insufficient, they consult with the metamodel architects according to the decision support in process step 9 (Feature Implementation) of Section 6.6.1. The result of this process step is the finished extension of the modular metamodel and its feature model.

Part III.

Validation

7. Bad Smell Detection and Correction Evaluation

This chapter presents the explorative study which was conducted to evaluate smells, their detection implementation, and their corrections. Only the implemented smell detections were evaluated. This evaluation was conducted as an explorative study, as during the evaluation, this allowed gained insights to improve this contribution's concepts and implementation. Examples of insights include improvements of smell definitions, their effect, detection, correction, and the interplay between smells.

This chapter is structured as follows. Section 7.1 states the goals of this evaluation. Section 7.2 presents the evaluation process. Section 7.3 briefly presents the metamodel that is analyzed for smells. Section 7.4 explains how the thresholds for the metric-based smells were chosen and lists the thresholds. Section 7.5 gives an overview of the detection results by presenting counts of smell occurrences. Section 7.6 presents a list of details about the individual occurrences that were corrected. Appendix A shows the full list, which contains all occurrences. Section 7.7 presents the corrections that were performed. Section 7.8 gives an overview of the results. Section 7.9 presents threats to the validity of this evaluation. Section 7.10 interprets the results.

7.1. Evaluation Goals

This evaluation refers to the research questions that were specified in Section 4.1. From these research questions, the evaluation goals are derived as follows.

G1) Bad Smell Meaningfulness Research question **RQ Ia** (Bad Smells) asks which bad smells exist and what their effects are. Therefore, this goal is concerned with whether the types of bad smells that are presented in Section 4.4 can be indicators for problems. Some smells are always harmful where they appear. For most bad smells, however, an occurrence is not necessarily a bad thing. For other smells, the harmfulness of their occurrence depends on the subject matter that is modeled. Some concepts have an inherently high complexity or necessitate specific modeling strategies that might be considered inadequate in other situations. To demonstrate that a bad smell definition is meaningful, situations have to be identified where the occurrence of a smell indicates improvement potential.

G2) Detection Appropriateness The research question **RQ Ib** (Smell Identification) asks how the smells can be detected and which detections can be performed automatically. For the smell detections that have been implemented, it should be evaluated whether they work like described in Section 4.4. This includes two aspects. First, it includes, whether the reported occurrences fit the definition of the smell. Second, it includes, whether all occurrences are reported that should be reported according to the definition of the smell. This evaluation focuses on the first aspect.

G3) Correction Appropriateness The research question **RQ Ic** (Smell Resolution) asks how the bad smells can be corrected. Therefore, it should be evaluated if the corrections that are specified in Section 4.4 resolve the smells and whether they are beneficial to the metamodel.

This evaluation does not focus on whether the detection tool is beneficial in detecting the bad smell occurrences. This was already done by Arendt [Are14] in a user study with students. Two groups had to perform several tasks. One group used EMF Refactor. The other group used the basic tools that are provided EMF. Arendt was able to show that the group that used EMF Refactor performed the tasks quicker and made fewer mistakes.

7.2. Evaluation Approach

As a course overview, this evaluation can be divided into the following steps: detection, inspection, correction, and redetection. In the inspection phase, the smell occurrences are investigated whether they adhere to their respective smell definition in Section 4.4 and whether they are harmful. In the correction phase, occurrences are corrected that have been discovered in the detection phase. In the redetection phase, it is investigated, whether the corrected occurrences disappear from the detection results.

These phases relate to the goals of the evaluation as follows. G1 (Bad Smell Meaningfulness) is targeted, as the harmfulness of occurrences is discovered in the inspection phase. The inspection phase also targets G2 (Detection Appropriateness), as the occurrences are investigated whether they adhere to the detection definitions. G3 (Correction Appropriateness) is targeted, as the effectiveness of the corrections that are performed is evaluated in the redetection phase. The redetection phase also targets G2 (Detection Appropriateness), as it is inspected whether corrected smells are no longer detected.

Figure 7.1 shows the evaluation approach in detail. The following list explains the single process steps.

1) **Detection** As the first process step, all implemented smell detections are performed on the metamodel.

2) **Confirm Correctness** Each smell occurrence is inspected whether it is a correct occurrence according to the definition of the smells. If in this step it is immediately apparent that an occurrence is harmful or benign, this fact is documented.

3) **Occurrence Selection** In this process step, for each smell, two occurrences are selected that will be corrected later. This process step is divided into several substeps. It is performed for each smell, as indicated by the fork in front of process step 3.1. If there are no occurrences of a smell, the smell is skipped.

   3.1) **Ignore Already Fixed** Smell occurrences that are already fixed as a side effect of a correction that targets an occurrence of another smell are ignored. It is already demonstrated, that such occurrences can be corrected and that the detection recognizes this. If the occurrence is already fixed, the process continues with 3.5, otherwise with 3.2.

3.2) Inspect Occurrence The occurrence is inspected regarding its harmfulness and whether it is caused by an occurrence of another smell.

3.3) Put Aside Benign In practice, a benign occurrence should not be fixed, as there is no meaningful correction. Although it does not affect the goals of this evaluation, benign occurrences are put aside to focus on the correction of harmful smells. Later, they are only resorted to if there are no harmful occurrences left that could be corrected. If the occurrence is harmful, the process continues at 3.4. Otherwise, it continues at 3.5.

3.4) Put Aside Caused by other Smell An occurrence that is caused by the occurrence of another smell is corrected according to the description of the other smell. Although the correction of the other smell is also a legitimate correction for the current smell, this evaluation focuses on occurrences that are not caused by other smells. This is done to evaluate the corrections of the current smell. If the occurrence is caused by the occurrence of another smell, the process continues at step 3.5. Otherwise, it continues at 3.8.

3.5) Uninspected Occurrences Remain If an occurrence is ignored or put aside, this decision gate is reached. The purpose of this decision is to iterate the occurrences of the smell until enough have been selected for a correction. If there are still occurrences left that have not yet been considered for a correction, the selection subprocess restarts at 3.1 to consider a new occurrence. If all occurrences were examined, the process continues at 3.6 to consider occurrences that have been put aside before.

3.6) Occurrence Caused by other Smell Available The occurrences that were put aside earlier include benign ones and occurrences that are caused by another smell's occurrence. At this point, no other occurrences remain, and, thus, these have to be considered for selection. This evaluation prefers occurrences that are caused by the occurrence of other smells over benign occurrences. This is done, as a correction of such an occurrence is meaningful, in contrast to a correction of a benign occurrence. If an occurrence that is caused by the occurrence of another smell is still available, the process continues at 3.8. Otherwise, it continues at 3.7.

3.7) Is Benign Occurrence Available If there are only benign occurrences of the current smell available, such an occurrence is selected in step 3.8. Otherwise, less than two occurrences are chosen for the correction of this smell and the process continues with step 4. If the smell is metric-based, an adjustment of the metric threshold has to be considered.

3.8) Select Occurrence The occurrence that is currently under consideration is selected for the correction. This may either be an ideal occurrence from step 3.4, a harmful occurrence that is caused by another smell from step 3.6, or a benign occurrence from step 3.7.

3.9) Two Occurrences Selected If two occurrences of the current smell were selected for the correction, the process continues at step 4. Otherwise, the process continues at step 3.5.

4) Correct This process step is executed for each occurrence that was selected. This is indicated by the fork that is in front of this process step. In this step, the occurrences are corrected. Each correction is performed in a new copy of the PCM in order to be able to investigate the effect of the correction individually.

5) Redetection In this process step, for each correction, a new detection of all smells is performed to determine the effect of the correction. The differences to the initial result from step 1 are then documented.

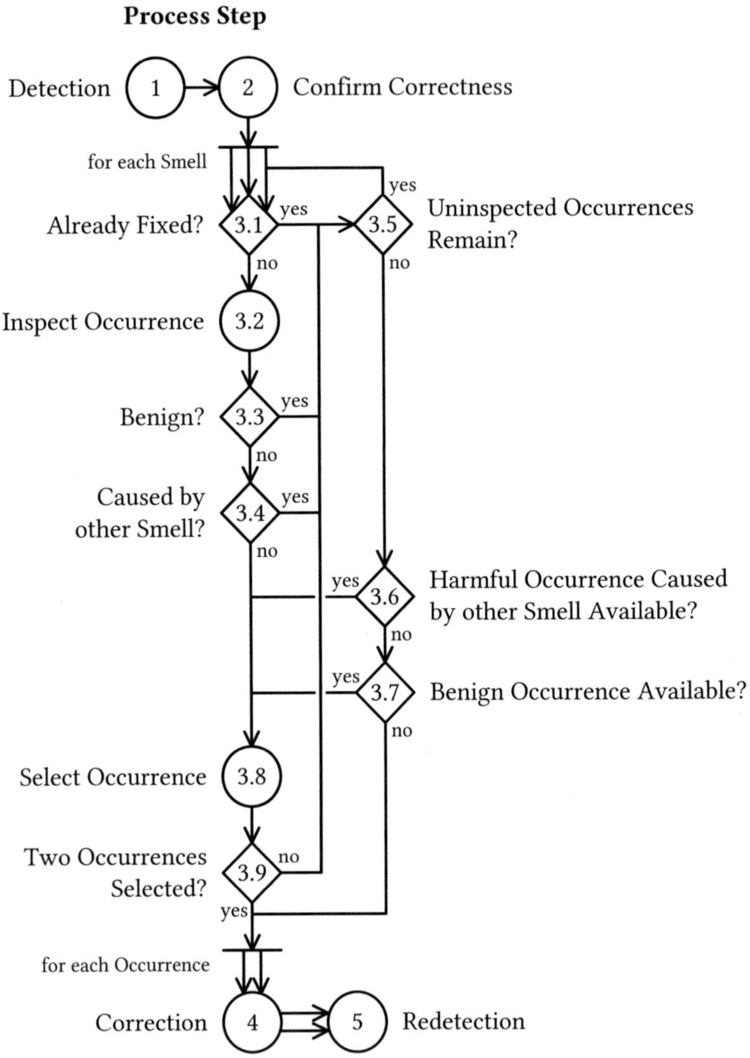

Figure 7.1.: Evaluation Approach

7.3. Subject Metamodel

The subject of this evaluation is the Palladio Component Model (PCM) [Reu+16] version 4.1[1]. It is used for the modeling of component-based software architectures. On such software architectures, analyses for several quality properties can be performed. The most prominent analyses of the PCM cover performance and reliability. The PCM consists of five metamodel files, all of which were analyzed for bad smells in this evaluation. The identifier metamodel file provides a superclass for all classes that need an identifier attribute. The units metamodel file defines units and provides a superclass that keeps track of a unit. The stoex metamodel file defines arithmetic on random variables. The probfunction metamodel file defines abstractions to model probability functions, which can be used in stochastic expressions. The pcm metamodel file defines the concepts for the component-based architecture and its quality properties.

7.4. Metric Thresholds

To determine the occurrences of metric-based smells, their metric thresholds have to be defined. Section 7.4.1 presents the criteria after which the thresholds were determined. Section 7.4.2 explains the determination process and the final value of the threshold for every metric-based bad smell.

7.4.1. Metric Thresholds Determination Approach

In the scope of this evaluation, it was not a goal to find the optimal thresholds that are suited for all metamodels. On the one hand, metrics have the advantage that they are easy to compute. On the other hand, the interpretation of their results is not straightforward. Absolute benchmark values that indicate optimal results do not exist in metamodeling. Even in other fields, they are rare. The reason for this is that such absolute benchmark values are only feasible if the evaluation of the metrics value is not dependent on the subject that is investigated. This means for some metrics, whether a metric

[1] `https://sdqweb.ipd.kit.edu/wiki/PCM_4.1` (last visited 23.08.2019)

value is considered good or bad depends upon the inherent complexity of the domain. In such cases, the values have to be interpreted by a developer.

In the best case, when detecting a metric-based smell, all harmful occurrences and no false positives are detected. In general, however, this is unachievable. For the analysis of the PCM, the thresholds were chosen so that a satisfactory tradeoff could be achieved regarding the number of occurrences. On the one hand, the detections should report enough occurrences. On the other hand, not too many benign occurrences should be detected. Setting the threshold very high reduces the overall number of reported occurrences but increases the ratio of harmful occurrences. Lowering the threshold results in more occurrences. At some point, however, no harmful occurrences can be found anymore.

To achieve the goals of this evaluation, the metrics were adjusted to fulfill the following criteria:

C1) Occurrence Count This criterion states that for a smell, at least two occurrences should be detected. The occurrences are inspected to ensure that they really are occurrences of the smell according to the smells detection description. The two occurrences are then corrected to evaluate the effectiveness of the correction. Thus, for metric-based smells, this criterion is needed to evaluate G2 and G3.

C2) Harmfulness This criterion states that for a smell, at least one harmful occurrence should be detected. This is needed to demonstrate that a smell can have adverse effects (i.e., G1).

If there is further tolerance in the specification of the threshold, it may be adjusted to improve the following two optional criteria:

O1) Many True Positives As many harmful should be reported as possible. This increases the significance of G1.

O2) Few False Positives The number of benign occurrences should be as low as possible. All occurrences have to be reviewed for correctness. They also have to be inspected for their harmfulness. This can be time-consuming, as a meaningful correction has to be found in order to declare an occurrence to be harmful.

The threshold specification approach of this evaluation is not intended to be applied for real applications of the smell detections. The disadvantage is that it does not focus on finding as much of the harmful occurrences as possible. In practice, in the tradeoff between O1 and O2, O1 should be prioritized a little more. A lower threshold leads to more detected occurrences and has the potential to increase the total number of detected harmful occurrences. The larger quantity of occurrences should then be reviewed less thoroughly compared with the review approach of this evaluation. The intention in practice should be to cover as many occurrences as possible and to fix the occurrences that are obviously harmful, as they tend to be the most harmful.

7.4.2. Smell Metric Thresholds

Table 7.1 shows the thresholds that were chosen for the analysis of the PCM. The first five smell detections are metric-based.

Bad Smell	Metric Threshold	Occurrences
Missing Class: Primitive Obsession	3	1
Missing Class: Shared Properties	2	4
God Class	8	10
Wide Hierarchy	10	2
Deep Hierarchy	8	15
Dead Classifier: Dead Class		9
Dead Classifier: Dead Enum		0
Multipath Hierarchy		10
Concrete Abstract Class		2
Container Relation		41
Obligatory Container Relation		44
Specialized Relation		6
Speculative Hierarchy		5
Dependency Cycle		13
Dependency Cycle (with Cont. Ref.)		(959)
		Sum: 162

Table 7.1.: Metric Thresholds and Smell Occurrences in the PCM

The threshold of the Missing Class (Primitive Obsession) detection is set to three. It specifies how many attribute with primitive types a class has to own to be detected as an occurrence. With a threshold of three, one occurrence is reported. C1 is, therefore, not fulfilled. For the PCM this is, however, a meaningful value. Higher thresholds report zero occurrences. This prohibits the evaluation of G2 and G3. A lower threshold is in general not meaningful, as two properties do not have to be factored out into a new class necessarily. This would not produce any further harmful occurrences. Therefore, O1 cannot be improved any more. Further, a lower threshold at two reports an excessive number of occurrences. It would, therefore, worsen O2. As the one reported occurrence is harmful, C2 is fulfilled.

The threshold for the Missing Class (Shared Properties) smell specifies the number of identical class properties that two classes have to share to be reported as an occurrence. For the analysis of the PCM, the threshold is set to two. This results in four occurrences, which is sufficient to fulfill C1. A higher threshold produces no occurrences at all. Therefore, O2 cannot be improved any more. All four occurrences are harmful, which fulfills C2. A lower value results in too many occurrences, and, thus, would go against O2. Further, it is not meaningful as it is expected not to produce many new harmful occurrences. In general, one shared class property cannot be factored out without producing a new shared property (e.g., a containment to the class that holds the extracted property). A lower value would, therefore, not work towards O1.

The threshold of the God Class smell specifies how many class properties a class has to own in order to be reported as a god class. For this evaluation, the threshold is set to eight. This produces ten occurrences, which also include seven harmful occurrences. Therefore, C1 and C2 are fulfilled for God Class. O1 could be improved by lowering the threshold, as it can be assumed that there are further classes with less than eight properties that are not adequately modularized. The lowering of the threshold would, however, produce many new occurrences and would, therefore, go against O2.

For the Wide Hierarchy smell, the threshold specifies how many or more subclasses a class has to have to be reported as an occurrence. The threshold is set to ten, which reports two occurrences. This is sufficient to fulfill C1. None of the occurrences is harmful. This does not fulfill C2. Lowering the threshold, however, is unlikely to produce harmful occurrences. It would result in more benign occurrences and would go against O2. In the PCM, there is currently no known improvement potential that would allow reducing Wide Hierarchies meaningfully. Therefore, new harmful occurrences, are unlikely. A threshold of ten at least works towards O2.

The threshold of the Deep Hierarchy smell, specifies the number of classes that have to be at least contained in a chain of inheritances. In this evaluation, a threshold of eight results in 15 occurrences, all of which are harmful. This fulfills C1 and C2. A lower threshold could improve O1 but would go against O2. As 15 is already a relatively high value compared with the other smells, the threshold was not further lowered.

7.5. Detection Result Overview

Table 7.1 shows the results of the bad smell detection on the PCM. The first five bad smells are metric-based and therefore their threshold is also shown. The lower bad smells are anti-pattern based, and therefore do not require a metric threshold.

The number of dependency cycles is shown twice. The first number shows the count of cycles that are detected after all container references were removed from the PCM. A container reference leads to either a container relation or an obligatory container relation occurrence. Together with its opposite containment reference, a container reference causes a dependency cycle between the two involved classes. The second count represents the number of cycles as reported by EMF Refactor when applied onto the unmodified PCM. The number is much higher as the sum of cycles and container references, as the detection for dependency cycles also detects combinations of cycles. Due to the many container references, a multitude of combinations of cycles was detected. The number of Dependency Cycles without container references does only contain separate cycles. There are no connected cycles that lead to an increase in the number due to cycle combinations. The total sum of smell occurrences does not include the number of Dependency Cycles with container references. This would bloat the sum and diminish the counts of the other occurrences. This is why the number is shown in brackets. When reporting the results of the smell occurrence corrections, the consequences are reported regarding the number of Dependency Cycles with container references. This is done to show the effect of the correction onto the unmodified PCM.

7.6. Bad Smell Occurrences

Table 7.2 shows an excerpt of the details of the smell occurrences. It lists only smell occurrences that have been directly targeted by corrections. A full listing of the smell occurrences is shown in Appendix A. Both tables have the same structure, which is explained in the following.

Involved Classes	Correction No.	Harmful	Fixed	Consequence
Missing Class: Primitive Obsession (1)				
ProcessingResourceSpecification	1	✓	✓	none
Missing Class: Shared Properties (4)				
CollectionDataType, CompositeDataType	2	✓	✓	none
InfrastructureCall, ResourceCall	3	✓	✓	−47 Dependency Cycles, −1 Container Relation, −2 God Classes
God Class (10)				
EntryLevelSystemCall	4	✓	✓	−58 Dependency Cycles, −2 Container Relations, +1 Multipath Hierarchy
ScenarioBehaviour	5	✓	✓	−3 Container Relations, −241 Cycles
Wide Hierarchy (2)				
Entity	6	×	✓	+16 Deep Hierarchies
AbstractInternalControlFlowAction	7	×	✓	none

continues on next page

Table 7.2.: Metric Occurrences in the PCM and Corrections

Involved Classes	Correction No.	Harmful	Fixed	Consequence
Deep Hierarchy (15)				
BasicComponent, ImplementationComponentType, RepositoryComponent, InterfaceProvidingRequiringEntity, InterfaceRequiringEntity, ResourceInterfaceRequiring-Entity, Entity, Identifier	8	✓	✓∗4	−1 Multipath Hierarchy, +8 Dependency Cycles, −1 Concrete Abstract Class
BasicComponent, ImplementationComponentType, RepositoryComponent, InterfaceProvidingRequiringEntity, InterfaceRequiringEntity, ResourceInterfaceRequiring-Entity, Entity, Entity, NamedElement	8	✓		
CompositeComponent, ImplementationComponent-Type, RepositoryComponent, InterfaceProvidingRequiringEntity, InterfaceRequiringEntity, ResourceInterfaceRequiring-Entity, Entity, Identifier	8	✓		

continues on next page

Table 7.2.: Metric Occurrences in the PCM and Corrections

Involved Classes	Correction No.	Harmful	Fixed	Consequence
CompositeComponent, ImplementationComponent-Type, RepositoryComponent, InterfaceProvidingRequir-ingEntity, InterfaceRequiringEntity, ResourceInterfaceRequiring-Entity, Entity, NamedElement	8	✓		
PowerExpression, Power, Product, Term, Comparison, BooleanExpression, IfElse, Expression	9	✓	✓	−1 Speculative Hierarchy
DeadClass (9)				
DummyClass	10	✓	✓	none
ResourceInterfaceProviding-RequiringEntity	11	✓	✓	−1 Multipath Hierarchy
Multipath Hierarchy (10)				
System, ComposedProvid-ingRequiringEntity, ComposedStructure, InterfaceProvidingRequir-ingEntity, InterfaceRequiringEntity, ResourceInterfaceRequiring-Entity, InterfaceProvidingEntity, Entity	12	✓	✓	none

continues on next page

Table 7.2.: Metric Occurrences in the PCM and Corrections

Involved Classes	Correction No.	Harmful	Fixed	Consequence
ResourceType, ResourceInterfaceProvidingEntity, Entity	13	✓	✓	none
Concrete Abstract Class (2)				
ResourceInterfaceRequiring-Entity, InterfaceRequiringEntity	14	✓	✓	none
ResourceInterfaceProviding-Entity, ResourceType	15	✓	✓	none
Container Relation (41)				
PCMRandomVariable, ClosedWorkload	16	✓	✓*17	−830 Dependency Cycles, −17 Container Relations, −1 God Class
PCMRandomVariable, PassiveResource	16	✓		
PCMRandomVariable, VariableCharacterisation	16	✓		
PCMRandomVariable, InfrastructureCall	16, 3	✓		
PCMRandomVariable, ResourceCall	16, 3	✓		
PCMRandomVariable, ParametricResourceDemand	16	✓		
PCMRandomVariable, LoopAction	16	✓		
PCMRandomVariable, GuardedBranchTransition	16	✓		
PCMRandomVariable, SpecifiedExecutionTime	16	✓		

continues on next page

Table 7.2.: Metric Occurrences in the PCM and Corrections

Involved Classes	Correction No.	Harmful	Fixed	Consequence
PCMRandomVariable, EventChannelSinkConnector	16	✓		
PCMRandomVariable, AssemblyEventConnector	16	✓		
PCMRandomVariable, Loop	16	✓		
PCMRandomVariable, OpenWorkload	16	✓		
PCMRandomVariable, Delay	16	✓		
PCMRandomVariable, CommunicationLinkResourceSpecification	16	✓		
PCMRandomVariable, ProcessingResourceSpecification	16	✓		
PCMRandomVariable, CommunicationLinkResourceSpecification	16	✓		
VariableUsage, UserData	17	✓	✓*9	−762 Dependency Cycles, −9 Container Relations, −1 God Class
VariableUsage, CallAction	17	✓		
VariableUsage, SynchronisationPoint	17	✓		
VariableUsage, CallReturnAction	17	✓		
VariableUsage, SetVariableAction	17	✓		
VariableUsage, SpecifiedOutputParameterAbstraction	17	✓		

continues on next page

Table 7.2.: Metric Occurrences in the PCM and Corrections

Involved Classes	Correction No.	Harmful	Fixed	Consequence
VariableUsage, AssemblyContext	17	✓		
VariableUsage, EntryLevelSystemCall	17, 4	✓		
VariableUsage, EntryLevelSystemCall	17, 4	✓		
Obligatory Container Relation (44)				
Workload, UsageScenario	18	✓	✓	−3 Dependency Cycles
InfrastructureCall, Abstract-InternalControlFlowAction	19	✓	✓	−1 God Class, −10 Dependency Cycles
Specialized Relation (6)				
ForkAction, ForkedBehaviour	20	✓	✓∗5	−2 Container Relations, −89 Dependency Cycles
ForkedBehaviour, ForkAction	20	✓		
InternalCallAction, ResourceDemandingInter-nalBehaviour	20	✓		
RecoveryActionBehaviour, RecoveryAction	21	✓	✓	−1 Obl. Container Relation, −1 Dependency Cycle
RecoveryAction, RecoveryActionBehaviour	20	✓		
RecoveryAction, RecoveryActionBehaviour	20	✓		
Speculative Hierarchy (5)				
ServiceEffectSpecification, ResourceDemandingSEFF	22	×	✓	+68 Dependency Cycles

continues on next page

Table 7.2.: Metric Occurrences in the PCM and Corrections

Involved Classes	Correction No.	Harmful	Fixed	Consequence
ComposedStructure, ComposedProvidingRequiringEntity	23	×	✓	+1 God Class
Dependency Cycles without Container (13)				
EventChannelSourceConnector, EventChannel	24	✓	✓∗2	none
EventChannelSinkConnector, EventChannel	24	✓		
ResourceTimeoutFailureType, PassiveResource	25	✓	✓	none

Table 7.2.: Metric Occurrences in the PCM and Corrections

The occurrences are grouped after their smells. Each group of occurrences is proceeded by a row that declares the bad smell and the size of the group in brackets. These rows can be recognized as they are printed in bold. For a smell occurrence, the first column lists the involved classes as reported by EMF Refactor. The second column specifies which correction addresses the occurrence. Some corrections have the side effect that they also fix other smell occurrences. In these cases, the Correction No. column shows the numbers of these corrections. As Appendix A shows, much more smell occurrences were fixed compared with the number of corrections. Some occurrences are even fixed by multiple corrections. The column with the label Harmful specifies whether the smell occurrence is considered harmful. A check mark denotes a harmful occurrence. A cross implies a benign occurrence. The last two columns present the effect of the correction. The Fixed column reports whether the correction eliminated the smell occurrence. The Consequence column lists the effect on other smell occurrences. A minus indicates that further occurrences of another smell were fixed.

A plus states that new occurrences of another smell were detected. If a correction fixes multiple occurrences of the smell that it initially addresses, this is indicated by a multiplicator besides the check mark in the Fixed column. In such cases, the Fixed and Consequence cells are only specified for the first smell occurrence. They are also valid for the other fixed occurrences of the same smell. They can be found by looking for the same number in the Correction No. column.

7.7. Correction and Revaluation

In this section, the correction and revaluation of the smells are presented.

For each smell at most two corrections were performed. If a smell occurs less than two times, as much corrections were performed as possible. This is only the case for the Missing Class (Primitive Obsession) smell, which features one occurrence in the PCM. The Dead Classifier (Dead Enum) smell does not occur in the PCM and therefore could not be fixed.

Each correction was performed separately. This way the effect of each correction can be measured in isolation. If multiple corrections are performed at once, the effects cannot be attributed to the proper corrections.

The corrections are presented as follows. First, the smell occurrence is explained, and it is discussed if the occurrence is harmful or benign. Second, the correction is presented. Third, the effect of the correction is reported and discussed: was the occurrence fixed, what was the benefit of the correction, and how other smells were affected.

7.7.1. Missing Class Primitive Obsession

This smell detection only reported one occurrence. Therefore, this one occurrence was fixed.

Occurrence 1: ProcessingResourceSpecification

Description The class ProcessingResourceSpecification contains four attributes with primitive types. Two of them are related. They model reliability relevant properties. This occurrence is not considered to be harmful. It is a matter of taste in modeling style, whether a new class should be introduced to factor out two attributes. As this is the only occurrence of this smell detection, it was nevertheless fixed to evaluate its detection and correction.

Correction (1) The new class ProcessingResourceReliabilitySpecification was created. A new containment was created from ProcessingResourceSpecification to ProcessingResourceReliabilitySpecification. The two attributes were moved to the new class.

Result A detection run on the modified metamodel showed that the occurrence was fixed. The refactoring causes the complexity of the affected class to be factored out. No other smell occurrences were affected.

7.7.2. Missing Class Shared Properties

With a threshold at two shared properties, this smell detection reported four hits. Two of them are in the pcm metamodel file. The other two of them are in the dependencies of the PCM: one in stoex, one in probfunction. To focus on the PCM, the two occurrences in the PCM were chosen to be corrected.

Occurrence 1: DataTypes

Description The classes CollectionDataType and CompositeDataType share two class properties: inheritances to DataType and Entity. DataType has one further subclass: PrimitiveDataType. It does not inherit from Entity. These shared properties, however, can easily be consolidated, as Entity is a very general superclass that also fits PrimitiveDataType. That both classes are siblings is another indicator that this smell should be fixed. Thus, this occurrence is considered to be harmful.

Correction (2) There are two ways to meaningfully fix this occurrence. First, a new intermediate class is introduced between the two data types and their superclass DataType. Second, the inheritance to Entity is pulled up into DataType. The first solution does not affect the PrimitiveDataType class but increases complexity as it adds a new class. The second solution makes PrimitiveDataType an Entity, but keeps the complexity low. The second solution was performed, as PrimitiveDataType may as well be an entity. It gains the name and id attributes, which are suited for a PrimitiveDataType.

Result The correction fixed the occurrence and did not affect any other smells. By reducing the total number of inheritances and organizing them meaningfully into the class hierarchy, the complexity of the metamodel is reduced.

Occurrence 2: UniqueCalls

Description The InfrastructureCall and ResourceCall share their inheritance to CallAction, a constraint, and a containment to PCMRandomVariable that specifies a call count. This occurrence is considered harmful. Three shared properties should be consolidated, especially amongst sibling classes.

Correction (3) This occurrence was addressed by introducing a new superclass for both classes (UniqueCallAction). Its theme was given to it by the constraint that ensures that the call is unique within the containing action. The inheritance from both call classes to the new superclass replaces the inheritance to CallAction. The three shared properties were pulled up to UniqueCallAction. Initially, the duplicated references to PCMRandomVariable both had opposite container references. During the pull-up, one opposite reference had to be removed. The other was assigned as an opposite to the reference from UniqueCallAction to PCMRandomVariable. This container reference should have been removed to fix the resulting Container Relation smell. However, to not muddle the effect of the correction, only the occurrence of the Missing Class (Shared Properties) was addressed.

Result The correction removed the smell occurrence. By eliminating three duplicated properties, one container reference and introducing just one new class and one inheritance, the complexity of the metamodel was reduced. As further consequences, the correction removed one Container Relation occurrence, two God Class occurrences, and 47 Dependency Cycle occurrences. Both of the involved call classes were God Classes before the correction. They are no longer God Classes because the properties were factored out. By removing one container reference and splitting the classes and therefore also their dependencies, many cycles were fixed.

7.7.3. God Class

At a threshold of eight properties, the God Class detection reported ten occurrences. Of these, seven are harmful. All of them are located in the PCM. Of these seven harmful occurrences, four were already fixed by the corrections of other smells. One was even fixed by two independent corrections. This indicates that God Classes also favor the occurrence of other smells. Of the three remaining smells, two are caused by other smell occurrences. In conclusion, the one remaining occurrence that is independent of other smells was corrected together with one harmful occurrence that is caused by other smells.

Occurrence 1: EntryLevelSystemCall

Description EntryLevelSystemCall owns eight class properties. This includes two containments to VariableUsage as input and output parameters. It does not inherit from the CallReturnAction class, which also features these two properties. This occurrence is therefore considered to be harmful, as EntryLevelSystemCall contains unnecessarily many properties because of this missing inheritance.

Correction (4) To address this occurrence, an inheritance is defined from EntryLevelSystemCall to CallReturnAction. Both containments including their opposite container references to VariableUsage are deleted.

CallReturnAction is currently contained in the seff package. After the correction, however, it has seff and usage model specific subclasses. Thus, in a real development scenario, CallReturnAction should also be moved to a more general package. This was not done in the scope of this correction to not skew the results of the second detection.

Result The correction removed the occurrence. By reducing the number of relations by four and introducing just one inheritance, the complexity of the metamodel is reduced. As further consequences, the removal of the two containments with their opposite references solved many dependency cycles. The new inheritance, however, introduced a new Diamond Multipath. By its new superclass, EntryLevelSystemCall now has two paths to Entity. As this is only a Diamond and not a Direct Multipath and both paths to Entity are meaningful, this fix is also considered to be meaningful even though it introduces a new Multipath occurrence.

Occurrence 2: ScenarioBehaviour

Description The ScenarioBehaviour class owns eight properties. Three of them are container references, which are unnecessary. Thus, this occurrence is considered to be harmful.

Correction (5) The smell was addressed by deleting the redundant container references.

Result After the correction, the occurrence was no longer reported by EMF Refactor. As the container references are irrelevant for understanding ScenarioBehaviour, the correction makes the class easier to understand. The three Container Relation occurrences were also fixed, as well as the Dependency Cycles they were involved in (241 in total).

7.7.4. Wide Hierarchy

With a threshold of ten, the detection reports two occurrences. Both of them are benign and located in the pcm metamodel file. To evaluate the detection and correction of this smell, they were nevertheless corrected.

Occurrence 1: Entity

Description The Entity class is one of the three most abstract and widely used classes in the PCM. With its 34 direct subclasses, it exceeds the threshold by a factor of three. Through its inheritances to NamedElement and Identifier, it provides its subclasses with a name and ID attribute. This is its sole function. There are no incoming references. Under its subclasses, there are no classes that do not need the attributes that Entity provides. Nor can groups of classes be identified that could benefit from a new intermediate superclass. Therefore, this occurrence is considered to be benign.

Correction (6) As this is a benign occurrence, there is no meaningful fix. Three new intermediate classes were introduced between Entity and its subclasses. The intermediate classes inherit from Entity. Each intermediate class was declared as the new superclass of nine of the subclasses. The inheritance to the intermediate class replaced the inheritance to Entity.

Result The correction fixed the occurrence. This correction introduced 16 new deep hierarchy smells. The intermediate classes increase the depth of the inheritance hierarchies. When new intermediate classes are introduced that high in the inheritance hierarchy, many classes down in the inheritance chains were affected. As this was not supposed to be a meaningful correction in the first place, the introduction of more smells is irrelevant.

Occurrence 2: AbstractInternalControlFlowAction

Description The AbstractInternalControlFlowAction has eleven direct subclasses and is, therefore, an occurrence of the Wide Hierarchy smell. Like with the last occurrence, there are no meaningful intermediate classes that could be introduced between AbstractInternalControlFlowAction and its subclasses. Therefore, this is also considered to be a benign occurrence.

Correction (7) Analogously to the Entity occurrence, one new intermediate class was introduced. Analogously to the Entity occurrence, this is also not a meaningful correction.

Result The correction eliminated the occurrence. It had no further consequences, as the correction took place further down in the inheritance hierarchy compared with the Entity occurrence.

7.7.5. Deep Hierarchy

Fifteen inheritance chains are at least eight classes long. Four of them are located in the PCM. All eleven other occurrences end with the Expression class of the stoex metamodel file. All occurrences are considered to be harmful, as it was possible to identify meaningful ways to shorten them. To focus on the PCM, its four occurrences were prioritized in the scope of the correction. From the other occurrences, one was short enough to be cut below the threshold. This occurrence was therefore chosen to test the redetection after the correction.

Occurrences 1: BasicComponent and CompositeComponent

Description The most specific classes in the four chains of the PCM are BasicComponent and CompositeComponent. These two classes are the start for two deep hierarchies each. The classes Identifier and NamedElement are the ends of two Deep Hierarchies each. This duplication results from Entity being an indirect superclass of BasicComponent and CompositeComponent. As Entity has NamedElement and Identifier as superclasses, the occurrences are doubled. These four inheritance chains of the PCM can meaningfully be shortened and are therefore considered harmful.

Correction (8) The class ResourceInterfaceRequiringEntity provides optional abstractions. To fix the four Deep Hierarchies, an extension extraction (Section 6.5.2.2) on ResourceInterfaceRequiringEntity can be performed by using dependency inversion (Section 6.5.1.2). This procedure is explained in the following. ResourceInterfaceRequiringEntity has to be removed from the inheritance chain. Incoming inheritances are redirected to its superclass. The inheritance to its superclass is deleted. To be able to still use its class properties when necessary, a reference was created from ResourceInterfaceRequiringEntity to InterfaceRequiringEntity. As ResourceInterfaceRequiringEntity is no longer part of the inheritance chain, it needs a container. Thus, a new containment was created from Repository to ResourceInterfaceRequiringEntity.

Result The correction resolved the four Deep Hierarchies in the PCM. They all included ResourceInterfaceRequiringEntity. As it was removed from the hierarchies, they were shortened enough to drop below the threshold. The performed refactoring is beneficial for the metamodel, as an abstraction that is not essential to the inheritance chains is factored out. Through the reduced complexity, the classes below the removed superclass become better understandable. The correction has further consequences on other smells. One Multipath Hierarchy and one Concrete Abstract Class were fixed. The correction caused eight new Dependency Cycle occurrences. Removing ResourceInterfaceRequiringEntity from the inheritance chain fixed a Multipath Hierarchy, as it provided an additional inheritance path from ResourceInterfaceProvidingRequiringEntity to Entity. ResourceInterfaceRequiringEntity was also a concrete class in an inheritance chain that should have been abstract. It remains concrete and can be instantiated to annotate InterfaceRequiringEntity instances. The new containment from Repository to ResourceInterfaceRequiringEntity causes the Dependency Cycles. Repository is already involved in many cycles, adding the new containment introduced even more. The creation of new cycles could have been avoided in two ways. First, a new root container could have been created. Such a new container does not cause any dependency cycles as long as no inadequate containments are added to it. A new root container, however, brings an additional model file when instantiated. Second, an inheritance to an abstract class that is already contained could have been created. If the superclass does not depend on more specific classes, new Dependency Cycles are avoided. Such a suitable contained superclass class, however, could not be found. In such cases, a superclass and a containment to it can be created.

Occurrence 2: PowerExpression

Description In the stoex metamodel file, there is an inheritance chain of 8 classes that starts from PowerExpression and ends at Expression. It is considered harmful, as there are meaningful ways to shorten the chain.

Correction (9) The subclass of Expression in the chain is the IfElse class. It has no properties and no incoming references. Expression has no other subclasses. IfElse can, therefore, be merged into its superclass Expression. Two incoming inheritances of IfElse are redirected to Expression. IfElse can then be deleted.

Result The correction shortened the inheritance chain by one class. As it is now seven classes long, it does no longer reach the threshold. The separation between Expressions and IfElse was unnecessary because of two reasons. Firstly, there are only IfElse expressions. Secondly, there is no separation of class properties between Expression and IfElse, as none exist. By eliminating the unnecessary IfElse subclass, the complexity of the inheritance chain is reduced. As a further consequence, a Speculative

Hierarchy occurrence was resolved. Expression had only IfElse as a subclass. Now it has the two classes that formerly were subclasses of IfElse as its own subclasses. This resolved the Speculative Hierarchy occurrence.

7.7.6. Dead Class

Nine dead classes were found. Seven of which are root containers and therefore benign occurrences. The remaining two are harmful. The following corrections address these two occurrences.

Occurrence 1: DummyClass

Description DummyClass has no incoming containments and is, therefore, a Dead Class. It has no class properties and no incoming dependencies. It was used as a workaround to be able to use the QVT-R transformation engine, as it needed a class in the root package of a metamodel. It is also not used as a root container and therefore a harmful occurrence of the Dead Classifier (Dead Class) smell.

Correction (10) To correct this Dead Class occurrence, DummyClass is simply deleted. In the scope of this evaluation, it is assumed that the class is no longer needed. Either the problem was fixed in the transformation engine or another transformation engine could be used. Under these assumptions, this is a meaningful correction.

Result The correction fixed the occurrence. It no longer appeared in a detection run on the corrected metamodel. As the correction removed an unneeded class, the complexity of the metamodel was reduced. As DummyClass had no relations to other classes, this correction did not affect other smell occurrences.

Occurrence 2: ResourceInterfaceProvidingRequiringEntity

Description ResourceInterfaceProvidingRequiringEntity has no incoming inheritances or containments. Its superclasses also have no incoming containments. As it is not used as a root container, it is a harmful Dead Class occurrence. This can also be explained on the semantic level. In the PCM, some Entities provide ResourceInterfaces (i.e., ResourceTypes). There are also Entities that require ResourceInterfaces (i.e., Components and Systems). However, no single Entity provides and requires ResourceInterfaces.

Correction (11) To correct this smell occurrence, the Dead Class merely is deleted. As there are no incoming dependencies, no further action is necessary. In the scope of this evaluation it is assumed that in the future, no ResourceInterfaceProvidingRequiringEntity will be introduced.

Result After the correction, the smell occurrence was no longer detected. By deleting the Dead Class, the complexity of the metamodel was reduced. The class will no longer distract developers that stumble upon it. The correction also resolved a Multipath Hierarchy occurrence. ResourceInterfaceProvidingRequiringEntity was the source of this occurrence, which was a Diamond Multipath via its direct superclasses to Entity.

7.7.7. Multipath Hierarchy

For the Multipath Hierarchy, ten occurrences have been detected. All of which are located in the PCM. Five of these occurrences have been identified as harmful. Two other corrections also resolve the ResourceInterfaceProvidingRequiringEntity Multipath Hierarchy occurrence. Therefore, it is not addressed by a correction, although it is a harmful occurrence. Two of the remaining harmful smells were addressed by corrections.

Occurrence 1: System

Description System has two direct superclasses, ComposedProvidingRequiringEntity and Entity. Entity is also an indirect superclass of ComposedProvidingRequiringEntity. This is, thus, a Direct Multipath Hierarchy occurrence. It is considered harmful, as all direct multipath are harmful per definition (see Section 4.4.3.7).

Correction (12) This occurrence can be addressed by removing the inheritance to Entity from System. System is still an Entity, as it inherits from ComposedProvidingRequiringEntity.

Result After the correction was performed, System is no longer the root of a Multipath Hierarchy. Its remaining superclass ComposedProviding-RequiringEntity still has a Diamond Multipath Hierarchy to Entity. It is, however, included in the multipath that starts from CompositeComponent. Therefore, it does not appear as a new Multipath Hierarchy occurrence. By removing the unnecessary inheritance to Entity, the complexity of the metamodel is reduced. The inheritance relation no longer shows up in diagrams. System can still be identified as an Entity, because of its superclass ComposedProvidingRequiringEntity. In the Contextual Explorer, Entity is still listed as an indirect superclass. Therefore, also the understandability of the metamodel increases. This correction has no consequences for the occurrences of other smells.

Occurrence 2: ResourceType

Description ResourceType has two direct superclasses: ResourceInterface-ProvidingEntity and Entity. ResourceInterfaceProvidingEntity already inherits from Entity. ResourceType is, therefore, the root of a Direct Multipath Hierarchy. The inheritance is therefore redundant, and this occurrence is considered harmful.

Correction (13) To address this occurrence, the inheritance from Resource-Type to Entity is removed.

Result The correction resolved the occurrence. Analogous to the previous occurrence, the complexity and understandability of the metamodel were improved through the elimination of redundancy. The correction had no further consequences on the occurrences of other smells.

7.7.8. Concrete Abstract Class

Of this smell, two occurrences were detected in the PCM. Both of them are considered harmful and are addressed by a correction each.

Occurrence 1: ResourceInterfaceRequiringEntity

Description The concrete class ResourceInterfaceRequiringEntity has the abstract subclass InterfaceRequiringEntity. It is therefore detected as a Concrete Abstract Class occurrence. It is harmful, as ResourceInterfaceRequiringEntity should be an abstract class. It makes no sense to instantiate a class with such a high abstraction level.

Correction (14) To address this occurrence, ResourceInterfaceRequiringEntity is declared abstract.

Result After the correction, the occurrence was no longer detected in the PCM. The benefit of this correction is, that the metamodel gets correcter, as a class is no longer instantiable that should not have been instantiable in the first place. The metamodel is also better understandable. ResourceInterfaceRequiringEntity being concrete may no longer confuse developers. In the corrected metamodel version, it is immediately apparent that the class is not meant for instantiation but only for inheritance. The correction had no further effect on the occurrences of other bad smells.

Occurrence 2: ResourceInterfaceProvidingEntity

Description This occurrence indicates that the concrete class ResourceInterfaceProvidingEntity has the abstract class ResourceType as a subclass. The occurrence is harmful. ResourceInterfaceProvidingEntity is not meant to be instantiated. The class is too abstract.

Correction (15) To address this occurrence, ResourceInterfaceProvidingEntity is made an abstract class.

Result After the correction, the occurrence was no longer detected in the PCM. The benefit of this correction is analogous to the correction of the previous occurrence. The metamodel is made correcter and better understandable. The correction did not affect the occurrences of other smells.

7.7.9. Container Relation

Forty-one occurrences of the Container Relation smell were detected in nine classes. All occurrences are located in the pcm metamodel file. All occurrences are harmful, as all container relations are redundant and therefore harmful. Several occurrences are also fixed by corrections of other smells. Appendix A provides a detailed listing. The correction of the Container Relation smell focuses on the two classes with the most occurrences: PCMRandomVariable and VariableUsage. PCMRandomVariable has 17 Container Relation occurrence. Two of which are also fixed by a correction of another smell. VariableUsage has nine occurrences. Two of which are also fixed by a correction of another smell.

Occurrence 1: PCMRandomVariable

Description PCMRandomVariable has 17 container references and therefore produces 17 Container Relation occurrences. All of them are considered harmful by definition of the smell. Container relations are redundant regarding the functionality they provide. They only clutter the classes that own them. Container references are irrelevant for understanding a class. If incoming containments really have to be considered to understand a class, the metamodel editors provide various ways to explain them. EMF provides, for example, the Contextual Explorer view and the References view.

Correction (16) To address the occurrences of PCMRandomVariable, all container references are just deleted. Every Ecore editor automatically unsets the opposite value of the containment reference that points to the container reference.

Result After the correction, the 17 occurrences of PCMRandomVariable are no longer detected. The correction reduced the number of references of PCMRandomVariable to zero. Its only class properties that are left are the inheritance to RandomVariable and a constraint. PCMRandomVariable is, thus, much less complex and easier to understand, as the container references are irrelevant to understanding it. The correction also fixed 830 Dependency Cycles. As a container reference is always involved in a Dependency Cycle with its containment reference, the 17 container references contributed significantly to Dependency Cycle combinations. The correction also fixed a God Class occurrence. With its 17 container references alone, PCMRandomVariable was already a God Class. After the deletion, its class count dropped to two, which is below the God Class metric threshold.

Occurrence 2: VariableUsage

Description VariableUsage owns nine container references and, thus, produces one Container Relation occurrence each. As container references are redundant, the resulting occurrences are considered harmful.

Correction (17) To address the occurrences of VariableUsage, the container references are deleted.

Result The correction fixed all nine occurrences. The benefit and further consequences of the correction are analogous to the previous correction. The complexity of the class is reduced and thus its understandability increases. Regarding further consequences, 762 Dependency Cycles were fixed, and VariableUsage is no longer a God Class.

7.7.10. Obligatory Container Relation

There are 44 Obligatory Container Relation occurrences in the PCM. All occurrences are harmful because all Obligatory Container Relation occurrences are harmful in general. The argumentation can be found in the smell definition Section 4.4.4.3. To summarize, an Obligatory Container Relation is redundant regarding its functionality, is detrimental to understandability, and hinders reuse. The following corrections address two occurrences that were not fixed by the corrections of other smells.

Occurrence 1: Workload

Description The Workload class has a container reference to UsageScenario with the lower bound of 1. Therefore it produces an Obligatory Container Relation occurrence. The occurrence is harmful per definition.

Correction (18) To address the occurrence, the container reference is deleted. The opposite attribute of the containment reference is automatically unset.

Result The correction fixed the smell occurrence. The correction has the benefits that were described above. Complexity is reduced. Understandability and reuse are improved. As further consequences, three Dependency Cycles were fixed in which the container reference was involved.

Occurrence 2: InfrastructureCall

Description InfrastructureCall has a container reference to AbstractInternalControlFlowAction with a lower bound of 1. It, therefore, produces an Obligatory Container Relation occurrence. As an Obligatory Container Relation occurrence, it is harmful per definition.

Correction (19) The occurrence is addressed by removing the container reference. The opposite attribute of the containment reference is automatically unset.

Result The correction fixes the occurrence. The benefit of the correction is analogous to the previous correction. This correction affects the occurrences of other smells as follows. One God Class occurrence disappeared at the InfrastructureCall class. With one class property less, its property count fell below the threshold. Ten Dependency Cycles were fixed in which the container reference was involved.

7.7.11. Specialized Relation

Six Specialized Relation occurrences were detected. All six occurrences are harmful, as they are caused by unnecessary container references. All are located in the pcm metamodel file.

Occurrence 1: ForkAction

Description ForkAction has a containment reference to ForkedBehaviour, which features an opposing container reference. The containment reference specializes a container reference from a superclass of ForkAction (i.e., AbstractAction) to a superclass of ForkedBehaviour (i.e., ResourceDemandingBehaviour). The container reference has an opposing containment reference. The container references from ForkedBehaviour to ForkedAction specializes the containment between their two superclasses. This constellation of classes and references, therefore, results in two Specialized Relation occurrences. The occurrences are harmful, as the specialized container reference and the specializing container reference are unnecessary.

Correction (20) The occurrences can be addressed by removing both container references.

Result After the correction was performed, the occurrences were no longer detected. The container reference between the superclasses was also involved in three other occurrences which were also fixed. In total, five Specialized Relation occurrences were resolved. As container references were removed, the benefit of this correction is analogous to the Container Relation corrections. Complexity is reduced, and understandability is improved. The correction affected the occurrences of other smells by removing two Container Relations and 89 Dependency Cycles in which the container references were involved.

Occurrence 2: RecoveryActionBehaviour

Description RecoveryActionBehaviour has a container reference to RecoveryAction that specializes a relation between superclasses of the two classes. As the reference is unnecessary, the occurrence is harmful.

Correction (21) The occurrence can simply be addressed by deleting the container reference of RecoveryActionBehaviour.

Result The correction resolved the smell occurrence. As a container reference was removed, the benefit of this correction is analogous to the Container Relation corrections. As a further consequence, the removal of the container reference resolved one Obligatory Container and one Dependency Cycle occurrence.

7.7.12. Speculative Hierarchy

There were five Speculative Hierarchy occurrences detected in the PCM. One occurrence is considered to be harmful. The harmful occurrence is located in the stoex metamodel file. It is fixed by a Deep Hierarchy correction. The other occurrences are in the pcm metamodel file. Two of these occurrences are targeted by the corrections below.

Occurrence 1: ServiceEffectSpecification

Description The abstract class ServiceEffectSpecification has only one subclass, which is ResourceDemandingSEFF. Both classes have class properties and incoming references. Because of this, the separation between the two classes is meaningful for the purpose of modularization and separation of concerns. This occurrence is, therefore, considered to be benign. As no other harmful occurrence is left, this occurrence is corrected to evaluate the correction and redetection.

Correction (22) This occurrence can be addressed by merging the ServiceEffectSpecification into ResourceDemandingSEFF. To achieve this, several steps have to be performed. All class properties of ServiceEffectSpecification are moved to ResourceDemandingSEFF. The incoming reference to ServiceEffectSpecification is redirected to ResourceDemandingSEFF. ServiceEffectSpecification can then be deleted.

Result After the correction was performed, the occurrence was no longer detected. As the occurrence is benign, this correction is not meaningful. It has the benefit that a class is eliminated. This benefit is however overshadowed by the fact that the remaining class now has unnecessarily many class properties. The class properties also belong to different language features. This reduces the understandability of the class. As a further negative consequence, 68 new Dependency Cycles were detected. Through the merging of the two classes incoming references were directed to only the remaining class. This caused the additional Dependency Cycles.

Occurrence 2: ComposedStructure

Description The abstract class ComposedStructure has ComposedProvidingRequiringEntity at its only subclass. It is, therefore, an occurrence of the Speculative Hierarchy smell. Both classes have class properties, incoming dependencies and express separate concepts. A consolidation is therefore not meaningful. This means the occurrence is benign. As no other harmful occurrence is left, this occurrence is corrected to evaluate the correction and redetection.

Correction (23) This occurrence can be addressed by merging the classes. The class properties of ComposedProvidingRequiringEntity are moved to ComposedStructure. All incoming inheritances are redirected from ComposedProvidingRequiringEntity to ComposedStructure. ComposedProvidingRequiringEntity is then deleted.

Result The correction fixes the occurrence. The effect of the correction is analogous to the previous correction. Although on class is eliminated, the effect of the correction is mainly adverse. Modularity is reduced and, therefore, also understandability. As a further consequence, the correction causes a new God Class occurrence. As two classes were merged, the resulting class now contains more class properties than the God Class threshold.

7.7.13. Dependency Cycle

To get a better overview of the Dependency Cycles in the PCM, all container references were removed before the cycle detection. Container references always cause at least one Dependency Cycle with their opposing containment reference. More Dependency Cycles may arise from one container reference due to combinations with other Dependency Cycles. As container references are already covered by the Container Reference smell evaluation, this evaluation focuses on non-container cycles.

In the modified PCM, 13 Dependency Cycles are detected. All reside in the pcm metamodel file. Of these, seven are considered to be harmful. Two of the harmful occurrences are addressed by the following corrections.

Occurrence 1: EventChannel

Description The EventChannel class is involved in two Dependency Cycles, one with EventChannelSourceConnector and another with EventChannelSinkConnector. Each is caused by a bidirectional reference. This occurrence is harmful, as the bidirectional references are not necessary.

Correction (24) This occurrence is addressed by deleting the two opposite references going from EventChannel to the connectors. This is meaningful. Connectors have to know where they connect. An EventChannel must not necessarily know, who is connected to it.

Result The correction fixed both occurrences. The benefit is a lower complexity, which makes the EventChannel class more precise and better to understand. This correction did not affect any occurrences of other smells.

Occurrence 2: ResourceTimeoutFailureType

Description ResourceTimeoutFailureType and PassiveResource form a Dependency Cycle with the length of two because of their bidirectional reference. This occurrence is harmful, as bidirectional references are not meaningful in general and should be avoided.

Correction (25) This occurrence is addressed by removing the reference that points from ResourceTimeoutFailureType to PassiveResource. A PassiveResource does not need to know any FailureTypes that exist based on it.

Result The correction resolved the occurrence. As a result, the PassiveResource class now has one pointless reference less and is, therefore, less complex and easier to understand. The correction had no further consequences on other smells.

7.8. Result Overview

The correction and redetection results are summarized in Table 7.3. All 162 detected occurrences were correct according to the definition of their respective smell. The Dead Classifier (Dead Enum) detection did not find any occurrences. Although the Wide Hierarchy smell has to occurrences in the PCM, they are both benign. Each of the 25 corrections was successful in the sense that the occurrence that it targeted was no longer detected after the correction was applied. Twenty-three corrections are meaningful, as they target harmful smell occurrences. The 25 corrections fixed 69 occurrences in total.

Bad Smell	Total Occurrences	Correct Occurrences	Harmful	Benign	Corrections Performed	Corrections Successful
Primitive Obsession	1	1	1	0	1	1
Shared Properties	4	4	4	0	2	2
God Class	10	10	7	3	2	2
Wide Hierarchy	2	2	0	2	2	2
Deep Hierarchy	15	15	15	0	2	2
Dead Class	9	9	2	7	2	2
Dead Enum	0	0	0	0	0	0
Multipath Hierarchy	10	10	5	0	2	2
Concrete Abstract Class	2	2	2	0	2	2
Container Relation	41	41	41	0	2	2
Obligatory Container	44	44	44	0	2	2
Specialized Relation	6	6	6	0	2	2
Speculative Hierarchy	5	5	1	2	2	2
Dependency Cycle[2]	13	13	7	6	2	2
Sum	162	162	135	20	25	25
Ratio (%)		100.0	83.3	12.3		100.0

Table 7.3.: Metric Occurrences and Corrections in the PCM

[2] The detection was performed on a metamodel from which all container references were removed.

7.9. Threats to Validity

This section refers to the types of validity that were presented in Section 2.5.2.

Two threats to the internal validity of this evaluation are imposed by errors in the judgment of an occurrences correctness or harmfulness. These are, however, considered to be minor threats, as they only affect individual occurrences. To seriously threaten the internal validity of the overall evaluation, many misjudgments had to occur, which is unlikely. Regarding the harmfulness judgment, all harmful occurrences of a smell would have to be misjudged in order to threaten G1 (Bad Smell Meaningfulness) for this one smell. For most smells, several harmful occurrences were detected, which increases the margin for error. To further mitigate the threat for the correctness judgment, the smell detections were thoroughly tested.

Another threat to the internal validity is the improper specification of a threshold. In the worst case, this may lead a smell detection to either produce no occurrences or no harmful occurrences. Within this evaluation, all metric-based smell detection produced occurrences. Regarding harmfulness, the only metric-based smell detection that did not produce any harmful occurrences is the detection for Wide Hierarchies. For this smell, there can be no conclusions drawn concerning G1 (Bad Smell Meaningfulness). However, this only affects this one smell. The validity of the other metric-based smells is unaffected. This is, further, considered a minor threat, as it does not take effect unnoticed but obviously. This can be seen in the case of Wide Hierarchies. No other metric-based smell is affected.

7.10. Result Interpretation

This section interprets the results from Section 7.8 regarding the evaluation goals from Section 7.1.

G1) Bad Smell Meaningfulness This goal is concerned with whether a smell indicates improvement potential. For a smell, this can be demonstrated when at least one harmful is identified. From the 14 detections that have been evaluated, 12 delivered harmful occurrences (see Table 7.3). For these smells, G1 was evaluated positively. For the Wide Hierarchy and Dead Classifier (Dead Enum) detections, G1 was not validated in this evaluation.

G2) Detection Appropriateness This evaluation goal is concerned with the correctness of the bad smell detections. This means whether the reported occurrences are correct according to the definitions of their respective smells. All 162 occurrences were investigated, each positively. For 13 detections, the correctness of their reported occurrences was confirmed. For these detections, G2 is evaluated positively. The Dead Classifier (Dead Enum) detection did not report any occurrence. Therefore, G2 was not evaluated for Dead Classifier (Dead Enum).

As already mentioned, this does not guarantee a correct implementation. Just because every reported occurrence is correct, does not necessarily mean that every occurrence which will ever be reported by the detection is correct. In addition, a detection could also miss correct occurrences (i.e., produce false negatives), which was not evaluated in the scope of this study. These shortcomings can be addressed in future work.

G3) Correction Appropriateness This evaluation goal is concerned with whether the corrections for the smells fix their occurrences. This means whether an occurrence that has been corrected is no longer reported by its smell detection. All 25 corrections that were performed were successful in this regard. For 13 smell detections, G3 is, therefore, evaluated positively. This means there is at least one correction that successfully fixes the smell. For Dead Classifier (Dead Enum) no correction could be performed, as no occurrences were reported. For this smell variation, G3 was not evaluated.

For some smells, there are several ways how to correct their occurrences. This study can only claim an evaluation of G3 for the corrections that were performed.

8. Metamodel Extension Mechanism Evaluation and Comparison

This chapter[1] presents the evaluation of the metamodel extension mechanisms that Chapter 5 presented. The mechanisms are evaluated according to the comparison criteria of Section 5.6. This enables a comparison of the extension mechanisms.

This chapter is structured as follows. Section 8.1 presents the evaluation of the extension mechanisms according to the comparison criteria. Section 8.2 interprets the results of the evaluation and presents the metamodel extension process. At the end of this thesis, Section 12.2 concludes the metamodel extension contribution.

8.1. Extension Mechanism Evaluation

This section presents the evaluation of the extension mechanisms. It, first, gives an overview of the results followed by the evaluation of the individual extension mechanisms.

As stated by Section 5.6 the catalog of comparison criteria could also be expressed as a QGM plan. The goal, however, which is derived from **RQ II** (Extension Mechanism Comparison), is too broad. The **goal** is to find the advantages and disadvantages of the extension mechanisms. This does not really fit the QGM approach. If applied regardless, the criteria can be

---

[1] This chapter is in parts based on a bachelor's thesis [Her17], which I supervised.

seen as evaluation questions, which have only one metric. This metric is the metric that is presented for each criterion.

Table 8.1 presents an overview of the results of the evaluation. The first column gives the names of the extension mechanism. The remaining columns deliver the result of the evaluation of the comparison criteria. The fourth column specifies the complexity class of the content retrieval operation of the extension mechanism (i.e., $O(...)$). The other columns feature the following values. A ✓means the extension mechanism fulfills the criterion. A × means the extension mechanism does not fulfill the criterion. A ~ means the extension mechanism does not quite fulfill the criterion, but it also does not fail the criterion. If a cell is empty, this means that the criterion cannot be evaluated for the mechanism. This is, however, the case only once for Intrusive Addition. Intrusive Addition is not an external extension mechanism. It is shown here simply as a baseline for comparisons.

8.1.1. Intrusive Addition

Metalanguage Support Intrusive Additions are performed by adding and altering metamodel elements. It is therefore supported by standard EMOF. This means it has Metalanguage Support.

Applicable without Preparation Intrusive Addition does not need any preparation. However, it is completely intrusive. As Intrusive Addition is not a proper external extension mechanism, this criterion cannot be appropriately assessed. This is indicated by the empty cell.

Model Level Unintrusiveness Intrusive Addition adds new class properties to the base metamodel. The extension content is therefore located in the base model files.

Direct Extension Content Retrieval Intrusive Addition adds new class properties intrusively to the base classes in the base metamodel. The base objects carry the extension content. Thus, the extension content can be accessed directly from the base objects in constant time.

Applies to Subclasses Intrusive Addition adds new class properties intrusively to the base class B. Therefore, these properties are also available to all subclasses of B.

Extension Mechanism	Metalanguage Support	Applicable without Preparation	Model Unintrusiveness	Content Retrieval Computational Complexity	Applies to Subclasses	Orthogonality	Multiplicity	Containment Tree Integrity	Model File Integrity	Extension Object Deletion	Adds a Type
Intrusive Addition	✓		×	1	✓	✓	×	✓	✓	✓	
Direct Inheritance	✓	✓	×	1	×	×	×	✓	✓	✓	✓
Referencing (External Cont.)	✓	✓	✓	n	✓	✓	✓	×	×	×	×
Referencing (Reused Cont.)	✓	×	×	m	✓	✓	✓	×	✓	×	×
EMF Profiles	×	✓	×	n	✓	✓	✓*	×	~	×	×
Extension Point Inheritance	✓	×	×	k	✓	✓	✓	✓	✓	✓	×
Decorator (Predefined)	✓	×	×	k	✓	✓	✓	✓	✓	~	~
Decorator (External, Specific)	✓	✓	×	k	✓	✓	✓	✓	✓	~	~

Table 8.1.: Extension Mechanisms: Evaluation of the Comparison Criteria

Orthogonality Multiple Intrusive Additions can be performed on a class. The base class grows in size regarding its class properties. The only limitation is that the names of class properties have to be unique. This, however, can easily be circumvented by choosing new names for new class properties. Intrusive Addition, therefore, supports Orthogonality.

Multiplicity There is no such thing as an instantiation of an Intrusive Addition. A base object merely carries the values of the added class properties. This is only the case once and is bound by the multiplicity bounds that were specified for the class properties. Multiplicity is, therefore, not supported by Intrusive Addition.

Model File Integrity Intrusive Addition adds new class properties intrusively to existing classes. This means that also the extension content (the values of the class properties) is located in the base model file. Intrusive Addition, therefore, does not produce any new model files and preserves Model File Integrity.

Containment Tree Integrity Intrusive Addition adds class properties directly to the base class. Therefore, the containment tree is kept intact. Intrusive Addition is the ideal benchmark to judge the maximal integrity of the containment tree.

Extension Object Deletion The class properties that are added by Intrusive Addition are located directly in the base classes. The extension content is, thus, contained in the base objects. If a base object is deleted, the extension content is too. The problem that tools delete extension content because they are unaware of the extension, however, does not exist with Intrusive Addition. Such tools are not able to handle a model file to with unknown extension content has been added.

Adds a Type In a strict sense, Intrusive Addition cannot be evaluated according to the Adds a Type criterion. There is no Extension class which could be applied as a type to instances of B. The addition of new types, however, can be easily implemented using Intrusive Addition. This is done by creating a new inheritance to the desired superclass.

8.1.2. Direct Inheritance

Metalanguage Support Direct Inheritance uses an inheritance relation that crosses the boundary of metamodel files. Inheritance relations are a standard feature of EMOF, and so are metamodel file boundary crossing relations. Thus, Direct Inheritance has Metalanguage Support.

Applicable without Preparation To establish an extension by using Direct Inheritance merely an inheritance relation is created from the extension class to the base class. No preparation is required. Thus, this extension mechanism is entirely unintrusive.

Model Level Unintrusiveness As Figure 5.5 (2) shows, Direct Inheritance creates a subclass E to add extension content to the base class B. When instantiated, the instance of E takes the place of the B instance. It is contained by the container that would also contain the B instance, which is located in the base model file. Therefore, Direct Inheritance is intrusive on the model level.

Direct Extension Content Retrieval Direct Inheritance adds class properties to a base class B by subtyping B. On instantiation, the subtype E is instantiated instead of B. The instance of E carries the values of the extension content. Thus, they can be retrieved in constant time.

Applies to Subclasses An extension that has been implemented with Direct Inheritance cannot be instantiated on other subclasses of the base class B. An object can only be instantiated from precisely one class. Direct Inheritance adds its class properties to B by supplying a new subclass E. If there are more subclasses of B besides E, only one of them can be instantiated.

A workaround can be established by supplying extension classes explicitly for all subtypes. This, however, results in increased extension metamodel complexity and is only applicable to known subclasses. Subclasses that have been externally added and are unknown are not supported.

Orthogonality Direct Inheritance does not support Orthogonality. The reason is analogous to the evaluation of the Applies to Subclasses criterion. Multiple class extensions that are implemented using Direct Inheritance result in multiple subclasses of the base class B. Of these subclasses, only one can be instantiated. Therefore, only one of the class extensions can be used at a time.

A workaround is possible to establish orthogonality for specific class extensions. Consider two extension classes that extend the same base class. By creating a new class that inherits from both extension classes, they can both be instantiated by creating an object of the common subclass. If there are more than two class extensions that ought to be used together, every combination has to be subtyped. This approach, however, brings a considerable increase in complexity and is, therefore, not practical.

Multiplicity Direct Inheritance does not support multiplicity. A class extension that uses direct inheritance is instantiated by instantiating the subclass E. This can only be done once, which means that all class properties of E are also available only once.

Model File Integrity Direct Inheritance preserves the integrity of model files. As this extension mechanism uses subtyping, an instance of the extension class E is used instead of an instance of the base class B. This implies that the model files are not fragmented, as the extension content is deposited in the base model files.

Containment Tree Integrity Direct Inheritance preserves Containment Tree Integrity. The reason is analogous to the evaluation of the Model File Integrity criterion. When instantiating an extension that uses direct inheritance, an extension object is used instead of the base object. It resides in the same containment as the base object would. Therefore, the containment tree is not fragmented by instantiating a Direct Inheritance extension.

Extension Object Deletion Direct Inheritance uses a subtype to add class properties to the base class. When instantiated, an extension object is used instead of a base object. On deletion, the extension object is removed with all its extension content. This means that Direct Inheritance features Extension Object Deletion.

Adds a Type Direct Inheritance uses an inheritance relation from E to B to implement the extension. On instantiation, the base object is created as an instance of E instead of B. The base object is, therefore, an instance of the extension class. Therefore, Direct Inheritance adds a type.

8.1.3. Referencing with External Container

Metalanguage Support Referencing with External Container uses a reference that crosses metamodel file boundaries to establish the extension dependency. In addition, it needs a class and a containment relation in the extension metamodel file. These are all supported by EMOF. Thus, Referencing with External Container is supported by the metalanguage.

Applicable without Preparation Referencing with External Container does not require any preparation. A new container is used that is placed in a metamodel file of the extension. Thus, this extension mechanism does not rely on containment in the base metamodel. The only interaction between the metamodel extension and the base metamodel is the reference that points to the base class. Therefore, this extension mechanism is entirely unintrusive.

Model Level Unintrusiveness Referencing with external is unintrusive on the model level. The extension class E is contained by the external container Ct, which is located in the extension metamodel. On instantiation, an E instance resides in the extension model file.

Direct Extension Content Retrieval When instantiated, the extension objects are located in the instance of the external container. The extension objects reference their base objects. From a base object, however, direct navigation to its extension objects is not possible with this extension mechanism. To find all extension objects of a base object, all instances in the external container of the metamodel extension have to be iterated and tested if they point to extension object in question. This means the computational complexity of the extension content retrieval is in $O(n)$ for this extension mechanism. n is the number of extension objects of the metamodel extension.

Applies to Subclasses This extension mechanism uses a reference to point from the extension class E to the base class B. This reference can also be set to point to an object of any subclass of B. Referencing with External Container, therefore, also applies to subclasses.

Orthogonality This extension mechanism uses a reference to implement the extends relation. There may be any number of extensions that are implemented this way referring to the same base class B. An arbitrary number of such extensions can be instantiated on a base object at the same time. Referencing with External Container, therefore, enables Orthogonality.

Multiplicity To apply a class extension that is implemented with this extension mechanism multiple times on the same base object, multiple extension objects have to be created. Each of the extension objects is placed in the Ct object and refers to the base object via the reference. Thus, Referencing with External Container supports Multiplicity.

Model File Integrity Referencing with External Container brings its own root container Ct to store its extension objects. When instantiated, the root container object is stored in its own model file. Thus, Referencing with External Container causes model file fragmentation and, therefore, does not preserve Model File Integrity.

Containment Tree Integrity Referencing with External Container does not store its extension objects in the base objects. The extension objects are stored in new root container objects that are located in separate extension model files. Therefore, the containment tree is fragmented, and Containment Tree Integrity is not supported.

Extension Object Deletion If a base object is deleted, all its extension objects remain in the Ct instance. The reference r is then void. Therefore, Referencing with External Container does not provide automatic Extension Object Deletion. This has the advantage that extension content is not lost. However, if these residue extension objects remain, they accumulate over time.

Adds a Type Referencing with External Container does not add a type. As the extension object only references the base object, the base object is not affected by this extension mechanism.

8.1.4. Referencing with Reused Container

Metalanguage Support Referencing with Reused Container uses a reference to establish the extension dependency and an inheritance to contain the extension class. Both relations cross the metamodel file boundary. As both relations are standard features of EMOF, Referencing with Reused Container has Metalanguage Support.

Applicable without Preparation This extension mechanism requires preparation, as it requires a suitable superclass in the base metamodel. If such a superclass is not available, the extension mechanism is not applicable unless a suitable superclass is created in the base metamodel. In such cases, the extension mechanism is not completely unintrusive on the metamodel level.

Model Level Unintrusiveness Referencing with Reused Container is intrusive on the model level. The extension class E is contained by Ct which is located in the base metamodel. When instantiated, an E object is contained in a Ct object, which is located in a base model file. Thus, Referencing with Reused Container is intrusive regarding model files.

Direct Extension Content Retrieval This extension mechanism does not support direct navigation from a base object to the instances of its extension. The extension objects are contained in the containment c. All A instances that are stored in c have to be iterated until the one is found that points to the B object in question. Thus, the computational complexity is in $O(k)$. k is the number of elements in c. As c is part of the base metamodel, k could be constituted from objects of the same extension, of other extensions, and of the base model itself.

Applies to Subclasses Referencing with Reused Container uses a reference (r) to link extension objects to their base object. Instances of subclasses of B can be substituted for B. This means instances of subclasses of B can be referred to by r. Therefore, this extension mechanism applies to subclasses.

Orthogonality An arbitrary number of extension classes can be created, each of which owns a reference that points to the same base class. From these extension classes, multiple can be instantiated on the same base object. This means, Referencing with Reused Container supports Orthogonality.

Multiplicity The evaluation of this criterion is analogous to Orthogonality. Multiple extension objects can be created that refer to one base object. This is also the case if the extension objects are all instances of the same extension class. This means a class extension that uses Referencing with Reused Container can be instantiated multiple times on a base object. Therefore, this extension mechanism supports Multiplicity.

Model File Integrity Referencing with Reused Container preserves Model File Integrity. As it reuses the existing container Ct in the base metamodel, the extension objects are stored in a base model file. No further model files are created.

Containment Tree Integrity This extension mechanism reuses the container Ct that is not contained by B. If it were contained by B, it would be an application of the Extension Point Inheritance mechanism (see Section 5.4.6). Therefore, this extension mechanism does not deposit its extension objects in their base objects and does not preserve Containment Tree Integrity.

Extension Object Deletion When a base object is deleted, the extension objects that refer to it are not deleted. Their reference is merely set to void. Referencing with Reused Container, therefore, does not provide automatic Extension Object Deletion.

Adds a Type Referencing with Reused Container does not add a type. The explanation is analogous to Referencing with External Container. The extension class uses a reference to establish the extension. The type of a base object is not affected.

8.1.5. EMF Profiles

Metalanguage Support EMF Profiles is not part of EMOF. To implement and to instantiate stereotypes, an extension to the metametamodel and an extension to the metamodeling framework is required. It is, therefore, not supported by the metalanguage.

Applicable without Preparation EMF Profiles can be applied to any class in any metamodel without prior preparation. There are no requirements a metamodel has to fulfill to be extendable with EMF Profiles.

Model Level Unintrusiveness As EMF Profiles adds instances of stereotypes to the base model, it is intrusive on the model level. In a model file, EMF Profiles creates another root object, in which the stereotype instances are deposited. EMF Profiles, thus, requires the EMF Profile plugin and the extension metamodel to be installed to load and modify models that contain stereotype applications.

Direct Extension Content Retrieval EMF Profiles does not support constant time retrieval of stereotype instances, which are the extension objects of this extension mechanism. EMF Profiles supports an API with helper methods which support this navigation. In the background, however, all stereotype applications of a profile are iterated.

Applies to Subclasses A stereotype E can also be instantiated on an instance of a subclass of B. Therefore, EMF Profiles fulfills the Applies to Subclasses criterion.

Orthogonality EMF Profiles supports Orthogonality. There may be several independent stereotype definitions that point to the same base class. They may be instantiated on one base object at once.

Multiplicity At the time of writing this thesis, the current implementation of EMF Profiles does not properly support Multiplicity. The definition of stereotypes features an attribute that specifies the upper bound of stereotype applications on one base object. Manually, by using the basic tree editor, multiple stereotype instances can be created that point to the same base object. If the number of stereotype instances that point to one base object succeeds the upper bound, an error is reported on validation. If the number of stereotype instances adheres to the upper bound, the model file is validated successfully. Therefore, by setting the upper bound to be unlimited or greater than 1, multiple instances of the same stereotype can be legitimately created on one base object. Thus, by using this mechanism to instantiate a stereotype, EMF Profiles supports Multiplicity.

This procedure, however, is not the intended way to use EMF Profiles. Usually, a user would either use the add stereotype function from a tree editors context menu or use a custom editor that hides the fact that EMF Profiles is used. Such a custom editor uses the API to create stereotype instances programmatically. The respective API function, however, throws errors on an attempt to instantiate a stereotype multiple times on one base object. This happens even if the upper bound is adhered to. I assume this to be an error, as there is even an API method that provides the functionality to read multiple Stereotype applications of the same stereotype from one base object. The tree editor support for EMF Profiles only enables to apply a stereotype once to a base object. I assume, however, that this is a technical limitation that is easy to fix, as the underlying metametamodel supports Multiplicity. In conclusion, EMF Profiles supports Multiplicity, even though there are currently some issues.

Model File Integrity If a stereotype only supplies attributes (i.e., tagged values), there is no model file fragmentation. The stereotype applications are deposited in the base model file in their profile container object, which is an additional root object in the base model file. No further model files have to be created. If the stereotype, however, should supply complex data structures that have to be modeled by additional classes and references, tagged values are not sufficient. In the current implementation, a stereotype may not own containments. Therefore, either a new container has to be created, or an existing one has to be reused to store the instances of the new classes. New containers lead to model file fragmentation; reuse does not. Whether EMF Profiles abides Model File Integrity, therefore, depends on the circumstances.

Containment Tree Integrity Stereotype instances are stored in the base model file, but they are not contained by their base objects. Every profile container object is an additional root container in its base model file. This fragments the containment tree. EMF Profiles, therefore, does not preserve Containment Tree Integrity. If a stereotype refers to new classes that are contained in external containers, the containment is fragmented even more. Each external container results in a new model file with its own containment tree.

Extension Object Deletion In the current implementation of EMF Profiles, stereotype applications are not automatically deleted on the deletion of the base object onto which they were applied. EMF Profiles, therefore, does not provide Extension Object Deletion.

Adds a Type The application of a stereotype does not add a type.

8.1.6. Extension Point Inheritance

Metalanguage Support Both variants of Extension Point Inheritance use an inheritance relation to establish the extension. As inheritance is a standard EMOF feature, this extension mechanism is supported by the metalanguage.

Applicable without Preparation Both variants of this extension mechanism require preparation of the base metamodel. In both cases, the extension point subclass has to exist, or the extension mechanism is not applicable. The extension point superclass and a containment to it can still be created in the base metamodel. In this case, however, this extension mechanism is not completely unintrusive on the metamodel level.

Model Level Unintrusiveness Both variants of the Extension Point Inheritance extension mechanism are intrusive on the model level. For local extension points, E is contained by B. For global extension points, E is contained by S, which is the superclass of B. Both, B and S are contained in the base metamodel. Their instances and, therefore, also the instances of E are contained in the base model files. Thus, this extension mechanism is intrusive regarding models.

Direct Extension Content Retrieval In both variants of this extension mechanism, the base class contains the extension class. Therefore, a base object contains its extension objects. The search for the correct extension object is limited to extension objects of the base object instead of all extension objects of one metamodel extension. The extension point class A can, however, also be used by other extensions. The computational complexity of the retrieval is, therefore, in $O(m)$.

Applies to Subclasses Both variants of Extension Point Inheritance can also be applied to instances of subclasses. A subclass of B inherits the containment to A. Therefore, extension objects can also be contained in instances of B subclasses. This establishes their extension.

Orthogonality Both variants of Extension Point Inheritance support Orthogonality. There can be an arbitrary number of independent extension classes that inherit from A. On instantiation, their extension objects are all stored in the base object via its containment to A.

Multiplicity Both variants of Extension Point Inheritance support Multiplicity. Of an extension class, any number of instances can be created for the same base object. They are all stored by the containment to A.

Model File Integrity Both variants of Extension Point Inheritance preserve Model File Integrity. This is the case, as extension objects are stored in their respective base objects. No further model files are necessary.

Containment Tree Integrity Both variants of Extension Point Inheritance keep the containment tree intact. This is the case, as extension objects are stored in their respective base objects. No new root objects are created.

Extension Object Deletion As extension objects are stored in their respective base objects, both variants of Extension Point Inheritance exhibit Extension Object Deletion. If an object is deleted, all objects it contains are also deleted. This is also the case for a base object and the extension objects it contains.

Adds a Type Neither variant of Extension Point Inheritance adds a type. Storing an extension object in a base object does not alter its type.

8.1.7. Decorator Pattern

Metalanguage Support The Decorator Pattern uses inheritance and containment to establish the extension. As both relations are standard EMOF functionality, this extension mechanism is supported by the metalanguage.

Applicable without Preparation The predefined decorator variant (a) requires preparation, as the superclass for the decorators (AD) has to be present in the base metamodel. The other variants (b and c) do not require preparation concerning AD, as they do not specify it in the base metamodel. One could argue that the variants (1) require preparation, as they require a superclass of the base class. Such a class could be added intrusively. However, if this is not possible, the variants (2) can be used as they do not require a superclass.

Model Level Unintrusiveness All variant combinations of the Decorator pattern are intrusive regarding models. The extension class E is contained by the containment c. The owning class of c is located in the base metamodel. Therefore, all instances of E are contained in the base model file.

Direct Extension Content Retrieval For all variant combinations of the Decorator pattern, direct retrieval of extension content is not possible. The search for the right extension object, however, is limited to the number of decorator instances of the base object. In general, the base object is located at the end of a chain of nested decorators. These decorators might be from the same extension or from other metamodel extensions. Therefore, the computational complexity for the extension content retrieval is within $O(m)$ for all variant combinations.

Applies to Subclasses For all variant combinations of the Decorator pattern also apply to subclasses of B. A decorator instance can contain another object as long as it is a subclass of S, which is the case for subclasses of B. As the Decorator pattern uses this containment to establish the extension, the Applies to Subclasses criterion is fulfilled.

Orthogonality All variant combinations of the Decorator pattern support Orthogonality. No matter where AD is located, as it is a subclass of S and all decorators can contain an arbitrary subclass of S, even Decorators with different AD classes can be used in conjunction.

Multiplicity All variant combinations of the Decorator pattern support Multiplicity. To instantiate a decorator multiple times on a base object, it is simply nested as many times as desired.

Model File Integrity All variant combinations of the Decorator pattern preserve Model File Integrity. All decorator instances are contained in the base model file as they are directly or indirectly contained by c. No further model files are produced.

Containment Tree Integrity All variant combinations of the Decorator pattern preserve Containment Tree Integrity. The instantiations of the Decorator pattern cause nested cascades of decorators a the locations where they are applied in the model file. No new root objects are produced.

Extension Object Deletion Extension Object Deletion cannot be evaluated across-the-board for the Decorator pattern. It depends on the code that manipulates the model file. One would expect that such code will delete a whole chain of decorators together with the base object. This is, however, not the only alternative. It is also possible to just delete the base object and leave the remaining decorator chain intact.

Adds a Type The Decorator pattern does not reliably add a type. From the perspective of the containment c, the type of the outer decorator instance is in effect. It is, however, not the case that every decorator class (i.e., extension class) that is instantiated adds its type to the base object. This would be necessary for the Decorator pattern to fulfill the Adds a Type criterion.

8.2. Result Interpretation

This section interprets the results of the mechanism evaluation (see Section 8.1). It is subdivided into a summary of the extension mechanisms (Section 8.2.1), a recommendation of how to proceed when implementing extensions (Section 8.2.2), and an analysis of the causal relations of the comparison criteria (Section 8.2.3).

8.2.1. Extension Mechanism Appraisal

Direct Inheritance is the ad-hoc approach to external extension. It is intuitive, quick, and effortless to implement. It is applicable without preparation, provides immediate content retrieval and keeps the containment tree intact. It has, however, the big drawback of not supporting orthogonality. Independent development of extensions leads to incompatible extensions if the same classes are extended. Therefore, Direct Inheritance is only recommended for the development of prototypical extensions.

Referencing with a reused container requires some preparation. A suitable superclass that is contained in the base metamodel has to be available. It has the slowest content retrieval performance. Extension objects of this metamodel extension and possibly of other extensions that use the container have to be iterated. This is no problem if the size of the model and the number of extension objects is small. If large models are expected, a hash table should be used to speed up the retrieval. Referencing with a reused container causes no model file fragmentation. It is intrusive on the model level. If all tools are either robust regarding unknown subclasses or can be modified to handle such cases, this poses no problem. In conclusion, Referencing with a reused container should be preferred over referencing with an external container, as it does not cause any additional model files. Provided the tools can handle unknown subclasses.

Referencing with an external container is the most flexible extension mechanism. It is applicable without preparation and is least intrusive, as it does not alter base models. It, therefore, fragments containment trees and causes one more model file. Content retrieval is rather slow, as all extension objects of the metamodel extension have to be crawled. This can be tackled analogous to referencing with a reused container. Whenever no adequate contained superclass is available in the base metamodel and the base metamodel cannot be altered, referencing with an external container should be used.

EMF Profiles requires an EMOF extension and is, therefore, the only extension mechanism that was investigated that is not supported by the metalanguage. It has similar characteristics to the referencing extension mechanisms. It requires no preparation, causes tree fragmentation and possibly model file fragmentation, depending on the situation. EMF Profiles provides an API for reading and modifying stereotype applications. It is model level intrusive and should, therefore, be handled in this regard analogously to referencing with a reused container. The presence of the API gives it an edge over Referencing with External Container.

Extension Point Inheritance requires preparation: either a global or local extension point. A global extension point causes the least intrusion and does not clutter the base metamodel. Extension Point Inheritance is model level intrusive, which should be handled analogously to the previously mentioned extension mechanisms that are model level intrusive. If an extension point is present or a global extension point can be added, and the tools can handle the model level intrusiveness, Extension Point Inheritance should be preferred over other extension mechanisms. It features quick content retrieval, and no model nor containment tree fragmentation. It, therefore, causes minimal code complexity overhead in tools. Developers should be aware of the automatic Extension Object Deletion. The automatic deletion can also be an advantage, as extension objects do not accumulate after their base object is deleted.

The Decorator pattern is model level intrusive. It either requires preparation (variants 1) or suffers from unused class properties (variants 2). It adds more complexity (considering the metamodel and tools) compared with the other extension mechanisms. For some variants, existing tools cannot handle decoration (1b, 1c). They have to be modified to support it. The handling and deletion of cascading decorator chains have to be implemented in editors. Therefore, this solution is considered less practical compared with the other extension mechanisms.

8.2.2. Metamodel Extension Process

From the insights of Section 8.2.1, the following process was devised to support the implementation of external additions. The process is illustrated in Figure 8.1.

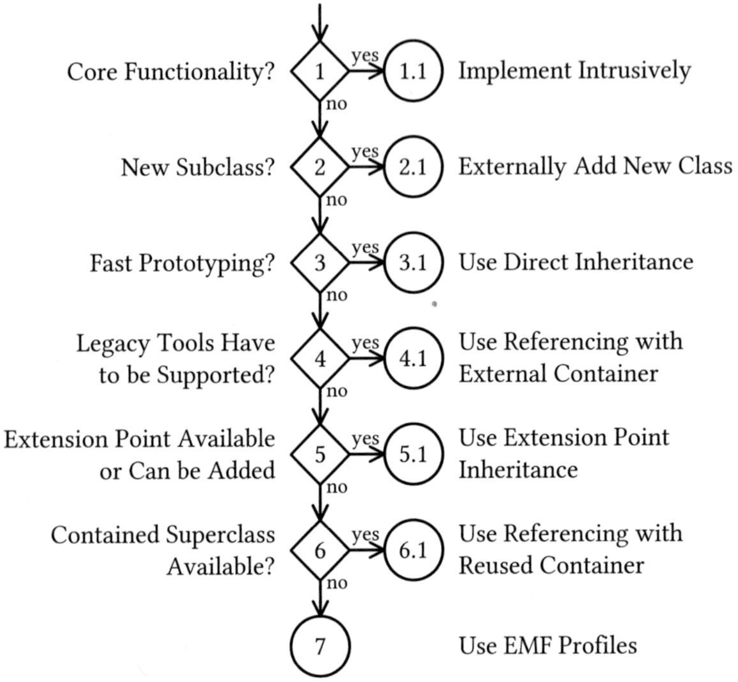

Figure 8.1.: Metamodel Extension Process

1) **Intrusive vs. External** First, the nature of the features that ought to be implemented has to be considered. It has to be decided if they are core functionality of the language. Core features of a language are always used if the language is used. Core features should be implemented intrusively, and the process ends here. A non-core feature is an optional feature. It should be implemented externally. To do so, the process continues at step 2.

2) **Extension Type** If a new subclass ought to be added, inheritance must be used. In this case, the process ends here. If class properties should be added to an existing class, the process continues at step 3.

3) **Prototyping** If the goal of the extension is to quickly establish a throwaway prototype, Direct Inheritance should be used. Otherwise, the process continues at the next step.

4) **External Container** If legacy tools have to be supported that cannot be altered to cope with model intrusion, Referencing with External Container has to be used. Otherwise, the process continues at the next step.

5) **Extension Point** If extension points are available, they should be utilized through Extension Point Inheritance. If no extension points are available and the metamodel can be modified, a global extension point should be added and used. If the metamodel cannot be modified and no extension points exist, the process continues at the next step.

6) **Container Reuse** If an adequate superclass that is contained in the base metamodel is available, referencing with a reused container should be used.

7) **Stereotyping** EMF Profiles can be used in all other cases. All tools must be ensured to be able to support model files with multiple root objects.

8.2.3. Causal Relations

This section presents and explains the causal relations that were discovered in the scope of the evaluation. The propositional logic notation is used to express the relations. The meaning of a criterion is negated by the $\neg$ operator. The binary implication operator ($\implies$) expresses that if the left operand is true, the right operand must also be true. The binary equality operator ($\iff$) expresses that the truth value of both operands must be equal. If negations are used, two versions of the logical expressions are given: the original version and a simplified in which the negations are eliminated. The elimination happens by negating the meaning of the criterion.

The remainder of this section presents the causal relations. For every causal relation, first, the logical formula is given. Then the formula is explained and substantiated. At first, the universally valid causal relations are given.

Second, causal relations are given that are valid for the inspected extension mechanisms, but which are not necessarily universal.

$$\begin{aligned}\text{Model Unintrusiveness} &\implies \neg\,\text{Model File Integrity}\\ \text{Model Unintrusiveness} &\implies \text{Model File Fragmentation}\end{aligned} \tag{8.1}$$

The causal Relation of Equation (8.1) describes that extension mechanisms that are unintrusive on the model level cause model fragmentation. This can be explained as follows. If an extension mechanism is unintrusive regarding model files, its extension objects have to be contained somewhere else. This is then either another model or another kind of file. As argued above, this causal relation describes an effect between the two criteria. It is, therefore, universally valid. It holds even if new extension mechanisms are discovered or implemented.

$$\text{Containment Tree Integrity} \implies \text{Model File Integrity} \tag{8.2}$$

Causal Relation 8.2 states that an extension mechanism that preserves Containment Tree Integrity also preserves Model File Integrity. Containment tree integrity means that no further root objects are introduced. Model file fragmentation is only possible with new root objects. Each new model file has to have its own root object. Therefore, model file integrity is always given if containment tree integrity is preserved. As argued above, this causal relation describes an effect between the two criteria. It is, therefore, universally valid. It holds even if new extension mechanisms are discovered or implemented.

$$\begin{aligned}\neg\,\text{Model File Integrity} &\implies \neg\,\text{Containment Tree Integrity}\\ \text{Model File Fragmentation} &\implies \text{Containment Tree Fragmentation}\end{aligned} \tag{8.3}$$

This causal relation (Equation (8.3)) is the negation of the previous causation. The simplified version states that if an extension mechanism causes model file fragmentation, it also causes containment tree fragmentation. Each model file needs its own root object. This means that the containment tree must be fragmented. As argued above, this causal relation describes an effect between the two criteria. It is, therefore, universally valid. It holds even if new extension mechanisms are discovered or implemented.

$$\begin{aligned}\text{Containment Tree Integrity} \implies & \mathit{Compl}(\mathit{Retrieval}() \in \mathcal{O}(1)) \vee \\ & \mathit{Compl}(\mathit{Retrieval}() \in \mathcal{O}(k))\end{aligned} \tag{8.4}$$

Containment tree integrity implies a faster extension content retrieval compared with a fragmented containment tree. In an intact containment tree, the extension content or the extension objects are contained by the base objects. In the worst case, all extension objects of a base object have to be iterated to find the extension object in question. Extension objects of other base classes do not have to be considered as they are contained by their respective base class. The computation complexity of such an operation is $\mathcal{O}(k)$. As argued above, the Causal Relation 8.4 describes an effect between the two criteria. It is, therefore, universally valid. It holds even if new extension mechanisms are discovered or implemented.

$$\begin{aligned}\neg\ \text{Containment Tree Integrity} \implies & \mathit{Compl}(\mathit{Retrieval}() \in \mathcal{O}(n)) \vee \\ & \mathit{Compl}(\mathit{Retrieval}() \in \mathcal{O}(m)) \\ \text{Containment Tree Fragmentation} \implies & \mathit{Compl}(\mathit{Retrieval}() \in \mathcal{O}(n)) \vee \\ & \mathit{Compl}(\mathit{Retrieval}() \in \mathcal{O}(m))\end{aligned} \tag{8.5}$$

In a fragmented containment tree, more effort has to be spent to find extension content. As the extension content is not contained by the base classes, it has to be stored jointly somewhere else. This extension content has to be iterated when searching for a specific extension content. As argued above, the Causal Relation 8.5 describes an effect between the two criteria. It is, therefore, universally valid. It holds even if new extension mechanisms are discovered or implemented.

$$\begin{aligned}\neg\ \text{Applicable without Preparation} \implies & \neg\ \text{Model Unintrusiveness} \\ \text{Requires Preparation} \implies & \text{Model Intrusiveness}\end{aligned} \tag{8.6}$$

The simplified version of Causal Relation 8.6 states that an extension mechanism that requires preparation of the base metamodel is also intrusive on the model level. This can be explained as follows. For all extension mechanisms that require preparation, the preparation is an abstract class (A) in the base metamodel that also is contained by a container (C) that is located in the base metamodel. The extension mechanisms then use A as a superclass for their extension classes. This causes the extension objects to be contained by a C instance in a base model. This means the extension mechanism is intrusive on the model level. As long as no other kind of preparation is discovered, this causal relation holds.

$$\begin{aligned} \neg\,\text{Containment Tree Integrity} &\implies \neg\,\text{Extension Object Deletion} \\ \text{Containment Tree Fragmentation} &\implies \text{Extension Objects Remain} \end{aligned} \tag{8.7}$$

The simplified version of Causal Relation 8.7 states that an extension mechanism that causes containment tree fragmentation does not provide automatic Extension Object Deletion. The rationale behind this relation is that in a fragmented containment tree, references are used to establish an extension. This means base objects do not contain their extension objects. If they contained their extension objects directly, their extension objects would be deleted. A referencing extension object, however, is not automatically deleted. This relation is, however, only valid for the inspected extension mechanisms. An extension mechanism could provide automatic Extension Object Deletion by extending the modeling framework runtime.

$$\begin{aligned} \neg\,\text{Model File Integrity} &\implies \neg\,\text{Extension Object Deletion} \\ \text{Model File Fragmentation} &\implies \text{Extension Objects Remain} \end{aligned} \tag{8.8}$$

This causal relation (Equation (8.8)) is a less strict version of the previous relation. Model file fragmentation causes containment tree fragmentation, which does not provide automated Extension Object Deletion. Like the previous relation, this relation is only valid for the investigated extension mechanisms. An extension mechanism could provide automatic Extension Object Deletion by extending the modeling framework runtime.

9. Case Studies of the Reference Structure Approach

This chapter[1] is concerned with the four case studies that were conducted in the scope of this thesis. A case study is a metamodel and its modularization according to the reference structure approach from the previous chapter (Chapter 6). Later in this thesis (Chapter 10), the case studies are used for the validation of the reference structure approach. The raw metamodel files of the original and modularized versions of the case studies are publicly available online[2].

This chapter is structured as follows. Section 9.1 presents the approach of selecting the case study metamodels. Section 9.2 explains which extension mechanisms were used to modularize the case studies. Section 9.3 proposes the stopping criteria for the modularization of the case study metamodels. Section 9.4 shows results of counting metrics as a first overview of the case study metamodels. Section 9.5 presents the case study metamodels in detail. Section 9.6 proposes the concept of metamodel module repositories and presents patterns for reusable modules.

9.1. Case Study Selection

This section presents the initial set of case study candidates (Section 9.1.1), the criteria to select the final case studies from the initial set (Section 9.1.2), and the selection results (Section 9.1.3).

[1] This chapter is in some parts based on [HSR19] (©2019 IEEE).

[2] `https://sdqweb.ipd.kit.edu/wiki/Metamodel_Reference_Architecture_Validation` (last visited 23.08.2019)

9.1.1. Initial Set

The following gives a brief overview of the initial set of case study candidate metamodels. The list is a compilation of metamodels that I encountered during my study, which are related to quality modeling and analysis. It was not a goal to perform an exhaustive survey of metamodels for quality modeling and analysis, but to find a set that sufficiently fulfills the selection criteria. This is, therefore, not a complete list.

Palladio Component Model The Palladio Component Model[3] (PCM) is a DSML for modeling of component-based software architectures [Reu+16; BKR09; Reu+11]. Initially, the focus of the PCM was on performance prediction. With time, extensions have been developed to support further quality dimensions and analyses like reliability and security. Chapter 3 already gave a brief introduction of the PCM.

Descartes Modeling Language The Descartes Modeling Language[4] (DML) [KBH14; Hub+17] is a DSML for the architecture modeling and run-time performance analysis and adaptation of self-aware distributed software systems.

ROBOCOP ROBOCOP [GL03; BC06] is an approach & metamodel for component-based software that targets mainly embedded real-time systems and provides analysis capabilities for several quality dimensions.

SOFA2 SOFA2[5] [Her11a; Čer+09; BHP06] is a component framework and metamodel that also provides capabilities for the modeling of structure, behavior and non-functional aspects.

Smart Grid Topology This metamodel[6] is used for impact and resilience analysis for smart grid topologies [Ras+15]. I was involved in the development of the metamodel. For reasons of space, this thesis has to sometimes refer to it as SmartGrid.

[3] https://www.palladio-simulator.com/ (last visited 26.08.2019)

[4] http://descartes.tools/dml (last visited 26.08.2019)

[5] https://sofa.ow2.org/ (last visited 26.08.2019)

[6] https://sdqweb.ipd.kit.edu/wiki/Smart_Grid_Model (last visited 26.08.2019)

Structured Metrics Metamodel The Structured Metrics Metamodel[7] (SMM) [Obj18] defines software metrics.

AutomationML The Automation Markup Language[8] [Dra+08] provides modeling capabilities for the engineering of automation systems.

KAMP4aPS KAMP4aPS[9] [Hei+18; Koc17] is used to model automated production systems and predict the impacts of changes in these systems.

BPMN2 The Business Process Model and Notation[10] 2 (BPMN2) [Obj14] is a DSML that is used for the modeling of business processes.

Capella Capella[11] [Roq16] is a metamodel-based embedded systems engineering tool.

AUTOSAR The AUTomotive Open System ARchitecture [Für+09] metamodel is used for the development of embedded systems in the automotive domain. AUTOSAR covers a wide abstraction range from coarser units of the system down to the implementation level.

EAST-ADL EAST-ADL[12] [EAS13; Cue+10] is an architecture description language (ADL) for embedded systems in the automotive domain. It complements AUTOSAR by providing the architecture level.

9.1.2. Selection Criteria

I assembled two sets of selection criteria to find appropriate case study metamodels: mandatory criteria and prioritization criteria. These criteria are applied to the initial set of case study candidates in Section 9.1.3.

A metamodel has to fulfill all *mandatory criteria* to be feasible for modularization as a case study. If it does not fulfill one mandatory criterion, it is unfit as a case study and, therefore, is no longer a case study candidate. The set of mandatory criteria is complete in the sense that, during the work

7 `http://www.omg.org/spec/SMM/` (last visited 26.08.2019)
8 `https://www.automationml.org/` (last visited 26.08.2019)
9 `https://github.com/KAMP-Research/KAMP4APS` (last visited 26.08.2019)
10 `http://www.omg.org/spec/BPMN/` (last visited 26.08.2019)
11 `https://www.polarsys.org/projects/polarsys.capella` (last visited 26.08.2019)
12 `http://www.east-adl.info/Specification.html` (last visited 26.08.2019)

with the case study metamodels, there were no other reasons encountered that prevented the modularization of metamodels.

The *prioritization criteria* aim to increase the internal and external validity of the evaluations that are presented later in this thesis. From the case study candidates, the subset that fulfills the prioritization criteria the best is chosen as case study metamodels. There are two kinds of prioritization criteria: simple prioritization criteria and heterogeneity criteria. Simple prioritization criteria are evaluated on each candidate separately. They either improve the internal or external validity of the validation. Which type of validity is improved, is stated in the explanation of the criteria below. Heterogeneity criteria are not evaluated on single case study candidates but sets of candidates. Heterogeneity criteria are concerned with ensuring the diversity of the case study candidates. They, therefore, improve the external validity of the validation.

9.1.2.1. Mandatory Criteria

Public Availability The metamodel files that constitute a metamodel must be publicly available. Without access to the metamodel files, the metamodel files cannot be modularized and the reference structure approach is not applicable.

Scope This thesis concentrates on quality modeling. Although the application of the reference structure approach is broader, this is not investigated here. Thus, the case study candidates are restricted to those that are concerned with quality modeling and analysis.

Upper Size Limit The metamodels cannot be too excessive in size, as the effort for understanding the metamodel, acquiring the domain knowledge about how the metamodel is used and performing the refactoring significantly increases with the size of the metamodel. In the first iteration of the modularization, the PCM was refactored. With its over 203 classes and 567 dependencies, the PCM is considered a large metamodel. The effort to obtain the necessary knowledge and to modularize the metamodel was considerable. To keep the modularization effort within a reasonable limit, the size of further case studies cannot exceed the size of the PCM by much.

Lower Size Limit If a metamodel is so small that there is no modularization potential, the application of the reference structure approach is limited. At most, a paradigm extraction could be conducted if the metamodel contains domain information. However, that would only cover a small portion of the reference structure approach and would not evaluate the overall benefit. Thus, the case study candidates are restricted to metamodels that have at least minimal modularization potential. To be specific, there must be at least one possible split or extraction that is not a paradigm extraction.

9.1.2.2. Prioritization Criteria

Heterogeneity: Size To be able to evaluate if the reference structure approach has benefits for metamodels of different sizes, the set of candidates should contain metamodels of various sizes. As the structure of a metamodel (package structure as well as dependencies) gets more convoluted as larger they get, it is to be expected that the reference structure approach brings more benefits for larger metamodels. Thus, it is important to also evaluate small metamodels.

Heterogeneity: Age The older a metamodel is, the more changes it has witnessed due to maintenance. To be able to evaluate if the reference structure approach has benefits for metamodels of different age, the set of candidates should contain metamodels of various ages. The argumentation here is analogous to the size criteria. As a metamodel is changed over time, it tends to degrade structurally. It can be expected that the reference structure approach brings more benefits on metamodels that have more structural deficiencies. Thus, it is important to also evaluate young metamodels.

Heterogeneity: Maturity The stage of maturity of a metamodel is determined by how much it changed recently and how much it potentially changes in the near future. There are different stages of maturity. These stages cannot be clearly separated. In the design stage, a metamodel changes and grows rapidly as all of its features are implemented. In the testing stage, the rate of modifications slows down. Most of the features are implemented by now, but some errors are still fixed, and improvements and additions conducted. In the post-release stage, there are still some changes made as tool users detect errors and need to model further information.

Maturity is related to but not identical to age. For example, a young metamodel might be very stable, or an old metamodel might be frequently changed.

To be able to evaluate if the reference structure approach can be applied to and has benefits for metamodels in different evolution stages, the set of candidates should contain metamodels in various stages of maturity.

Heterogeneity: Layers The reference structure approach is designed to be used with any number of layers. Of course, the number of layers should fit the metamodel to be meaningful. To be able to evaluate if the reference structure approach is beneficial no matter how many layers are produced, the set of candidates should contain metamodels that carry information that can be classified into various combinations of layers of the reference structure.

Heterogeneity: Domains and Analyses The reference structure approach is meant for metamodels that are used in arbitrary domains for arbitrary analyses. To be able to confirm this, the set of candidates should cover various domains and should be used for various analyses.

Heterogeneity: Package Structure Depth Many metamodels consist only of one package that contains a high number of classifiers (e.g., in the AtlantEcore Zoo[13] [Vép+06]). It is to be expected that the reference structure approach performs better in such flat metamodels, as they tend to have more modularization potential. On the other side, the evaluation should show that the reference structure approach brings benefits for metamodels with package structures of various depths. Thus, various package structure depths should be represented in the set of candidates.

Meta-Language Metamodels can be specified in various meta-languages. As the reference structure approach aims at Ecore-based metamodels,

[13] `http://web.imt-atlantique.fr/x-info/atlanmod/index.php?title=Zoos` (last visited 23.08.2019)

the inputs for the approach have to be Ecore files. In this respect, the origins of metamodel files can be classified into three categories:

1. The metamodel is implemented in Ecore.
2. The metamodel is implemented in another meta-language and is then transformed into Ecore.
3. The original metamodel is not accessible but has been reengineered in Ecore.

Metamodels from origin 2 may lack meta-language features that Ecore provides. For example, metamodels that are transformed from XSD (XML Schema Definition) into Ecore have a completely flat package structure. Missing meta-language features are significant drawbacks of such meta-languages, and it can be argued that it is also a shortcoming of the metamodels that are defined in such meta-languages.

Metamodels from origin 3 may be of a different quality compared with the original, depending on the aspects that were important the metamodel developer who reengineered the metamodel. For example, if it was the primary goal of the metamodel developer to reconstruct the entities and their relationships, s/he may neglect the package structure.

In summary, metamodels that were transformed or reengineered in Ecore may have artificial flaws. Depending on the types of flaws, affected metamodels should get lower priority to improve the internal validity of the validation.

Availability of Knowledge To be able to evolve a metamodel, sufficient knowledge of the metamodel is required. Additionally, when modularizing a metamodel according to its language features, knowledge of the domain is required to be able to cut the metamodel properly. The process of acquiring the necessary knowledge outweighs the effort to perform the refactorings. Thus, concerning efficiency and regarding the fact that knowledge is also needed in metamodel evolution, it is advantageous to have as much knowledge about the case study metamodels as possible. However, it should be possible to apply approach with and without prior knowledge of the domain and the metamodel. Thus, to ensure external validity, for at least one of the case study metamodels there should be no in-depth a priori knowledge available.

Instance Availability An evaluation in this thesis needs models to evaluate the ratio of usage of the metamodels. The more models are available, the stronger is the external validity of the evaluation. Thus, metamodels that have more instances available are prioritized.

Changelog Availability An evaluation in this thesis needs modification scenarios to evaluate the evolvability of a metamodel. Such modification scenarios can be extracted from changelogs. These modification scenarios were actually conducted and are, therefore, more credible than hypothetical ones.

Another source for evolution scenarios are commit histories in version control systems. Compared to explicit changelogs, evolution scenarios cannot be extracted as easily. An evolution scenario may be executed in several commits, or multiple evolution scenarios can be performed in one commit. Sometimes, two separate evolution scenarios are even entangled in the commit history, as they were executed by multiple people concurrently.

If metamodel developers did not properly state the changes they performed in the commit messages, the changes have to be extracted from the differences between the commits. This is challenging, as some changes alter the source of a metamodel in multiple locations. E.g., depending on the used editor, the deletion of an element also removes dependencies that point to the deleted element. To relate these source changes to its respective change on the metamodel level is challenging, especially, if the commit mixes multiple changes.

Thus, metamodels that have a public changelog are prioritized to ensure internal validity.

9.1.3. Selection Result

The following explains why metamodels from the initial set of case study candidates were selected or excluded. Table 9.1 gives an overview of the criteria evaluation. The left column lists the metamodels. The final case study selection is shown in bold. The next four columns show the mandatory criteria. A cell shows a "×" if the metamodel does not fulfill the criterion. The next six rows show represent the heterogeneity prioritization criteria. A "↑" represents a high value. A "~" represents a medium value. A "↓" represents a low value. The layers column features the symbols of layers if the metamodel defines concepts that belong into the layer. The π is not shown, as π can be formed from any metamodel. Some layers are put into parentheses, which means that the metamodel does not cover the layers, but there are metamodel extensions that do. If a layer is marked with a small question mark, I suspect that the metamodel covers the layer. The domains and analyses criterion is rated with the following symbols. A "×" means the metamodel is too similar to a metamodel that was has a superior prioritization from other criteria (i.e., it is already set as a case study). A "✓" means the metamodel features domains and analyses that are unique compared to the other case study candidates. The remaining four columns show prioritization criteria that do not target heterogeneity. Criteria that lead to discarding a metamodel are shown in bold in the row of the discarded metamodel.

The following explains the evaluation of the criteria starting with metamodels that did not fulfill the mandatory criteria. Next, the final selection on the basis of the prioritization criteria is discussed.

9.1.3.1. Candidates Discarded due to Mandatory Criteria

The following candidates did not fulfill at least one of the mandatory criteria.

SMM The SMM does not fulfill the scope criterion, as it only defines metrics. Where the measurements are taken from is left open. Therefore, the SMM does not fit into what is investigated in the scope of this thesis. If the requirements for the scope of the candidates were less strict, the SMM would be a good candidate, as amongst all candidates it covers a unique domain (software metrics) and a unique layer combination ($\pi\Omega$). The SMM metamodel is available in CMOF[14]. If the metamodel

[14] `https://www.omg.org/spec/SMM/` (last visited 26.08.2019)

	Mand. Criteria				Heterogeneity Prio. Criteria						Prio. Criteria			
Metamodel	Public Availability	Scope	Upper Size	Lower Size	Size	Age	Maturity	Layers	Domains & Analyses	Package Structure	Meta-Language	Knowledge	Instances	Changelog
PCM					↑	↑	~	$\Delta\Omega(\Sigma)$		↑	✓	~	✓	✓
DML								$\Delta\Omega\Sigma^?$	×		✓	~		
ROBOCOP								$\Delta\Omega\Sigma^?$		↓	×	×		
SOFA2								$\Delta\Omega\Sigma^?$	×		✓	×		
SmartGrid					↓	~	↑	$\Delta\Sigma$	✓	~	✓	✓	~	~
SMM		×					↑	Ω	✓		~	×		
AutomationML				×	↓		↑	Δ	✓	↓	~	×		
KAMP4aPS					↑	↓	↓	$\Delta\Omega$	✓	~	✓	~	~	~
BPMN2					↑	~	↑	$\Delta(\Omega\Sigma)$	✓	↓	~	×	✓	×
Capella			×		↑			$\Delta\Omega^?\Sigma^?$			✓	×		
AUTOSAR	×		×		↑		↑	$\Delta\Omega^?\Sigma^?$	✓			×		
EAST-ADL							↑	$\Delta\Omega^?\Sigma^?$	×		~	×		

Table 9.1.: Case Study Candidates: Criteria Evaluation

does not contain any features that are unsupported by EMOF, the metamodel could be transformed from CMOF into Ecore.

AutomationML AutomationML does not fulfill the lower size limit criterion, as the following elaborates. The core of AutomationML, which is named CAEX (Computer Aided Engineering Exchange) [Com16; FD05], defines concepts for the modeling of the hierarchical structure of plants. This hierarchical structure also establishes links to two other languages (COLLADA and PLCopen). COLLADA (COLLAborative Design Activity) [Sta12] is used to model geometry and kinematics. PLCopen [Com13], which defines the programming language for PLCs (programmable logic controllers), is used to model behavior. This link, however, is implemented by string references. Such loose coupling comes with the loss of type safety, as arbitrary objects may be referenced. On the other hand, the CAEX metamodel is not coupled to COLLADA and PLCopen. This means for AutomationML as a case study there is no need to factor these aspects out. The remaining CAEX does not contain language features that could be separated. Thus, AutomationML does not fulfill the lower size limit criterion.

Compared with the other candidates, CAEX is a rather small metamodel with its 37 classes. As it is a standard, it is of stable maturity. It features a unique layer combination ($\pi\Delta$). It covers a domain that is similar to KAMP4aPS but without the maintainability prediction focus. It is available in Ecore[15] and XSD[16]. It has a flat package structure. This is most likely the result of a transformation from XSD into Ecore.

Capella With its 413 classes, the Capella metamodel exceeds the upper size limit criterion. It is available in Ecore[17]. With systems engineering for embedded systems, its domain is quite similar to other languages like ROBOCOP.

AUTOSAR The AUTOSAR metamodel is not publicly available. It also exceeds the upper size limit. Durisic et al. [Dur+14] report that version

[15] `https://github.com/kit-sdq/AutomationML-CAEX-Metamodel` (last visited 26.08.2019)

[16] `http://www.plt.rwth-aachen.de/cms/PLT/Forschung/Projekte2/~ejwy/CAEX-IEC-62424/` (last visited 26.08.2019)

[17] `http://git.polarsys.org/c/capella/capella.git/` (last visited 26.08.2019)

4.1.2 of the metamodel contains over 6000 elements. This makes it a magnitude larger than the next largest metamodel. As it is a standard, it can be considered to be of stable maturity. It also covers a unique domain (embedded systems down to the implementation level).

9.1.3.2. Candidates Discarded due to Prioritization

The following candidates were discarded, as there were candidates that fulfilled more prioritization criteria.

DML The DML is used to model component-based software architecture with a focus on runtime performance prediction. In this aspect, it is too similar to the PCM, which fulfills more prioritization criteria. DML is available in Ecore. In-depth knowledge about the metamodel is indirectly available to me, as a research contact is familiar with the metamodel.

ROBOCOP The domain of ROBOCOP is quite similar to Capella, as it targets embedded systems. On the other hand, it is also similar to the PCM and DML as it covers performance analysis of component-based systems. However, a more deciding factor is, that there is no metamodel based version available. A version that was reengineered from the specification and grammars is available [Koz11a]. This reengineered version does not consider a package structure.

SOFA2 SOFA2 is used in the domain of component-based software architecture. It is therefore too similar to the PCM, which fulfills more prioritization criteria. Its metamodel is available in Ecore.

EAST-ADL As it is a standard, it can be considered to be of stable maturity. It covers the domain of embedded systems architecture. Therefore it domain is very similar to Capella, ROBOCOP and the PCM, which fulfills more prioritization criteria. Its metamodel is available as XSD on request[18].

[18] `www.east-adl.info/Specification.html` (last visited 26.08.2019)

9.1.3.3. Selected Candidates

This section presents the metamodels have been selected to be modularized in the case studies. First, this section states the result of the prioritization criteria for each metamodel without comparing them. Afterward, it explains why the selection of metamodels is suited according to the prioritization criteria.

Palladio Component Model With its 203 classes, the PCM is quite large. As the development of the Ecore metamodel started in August 2006, and the first version was made publicly available in October, it is the oldest of the case study metamodels. In consequence, its structure is historically grown (see my papers [SH16b; SL14]), as new features were added to the metamodel and no refactorings were executed to restore its structure. It is quite mature, as it has been relatively stable. The PCM covers the π, Δ and Ω layers. There are extensions that feature Σ content, which are not subject of this case study but will be used in the evaluation. The PCM has a deeply nested package structure. However, its module structure is quite monolithic (one metamodel module contains 73 % of all classes). It is available in Ecore, and many instances are available to me. A changelog is also available[19].

Before my modularization work on the PCM, I knew the PCM as a user and the development of a second level analysis tool [Str11; SH12; Str13]. However, I had no in-depth knowledge of the class structures of the metamodel. This knowledge grew as I worked with the PCM [Str+13a; SL14; BSK15; Str+16a; Str+16b].

Smart Grid Topology With 30 classes, the Smart Grid Topology metamodel is small compared to the other candidates. Its development started in January 2014. Thus, I consider it of medium age. It has not changed much in the last years. So it can be considered to be stable. It covers the π, Δ and Σ layers. It does not need a Ω layer, as the analyses operate solely on the structural parts of the topology that are defined in Δ. Its domain, the resilience of smart grid topologies, is unique amongst case study candidates. It is quite modular, as its 30 classes

[19] `https://sdqweb.ipd.kit.edu/wiki/PCM_Changelog` (last visited 26.08.2019)

are divided into three metamodel modules. The package structure of the metamodel modules is flat, which is adequate considering their size. The metamodel is available in Ecore. I have in-depth knowledge about the metamodel, as I was involved in its development. There are some models publicly available. A proper changelog is not available, only the history in the version control.

KAMP4aPS With its 185 classes, the KAMP4aPS metamodel is rather large. It has been under development since 2016 [Koc17], so it is comparatively young. At the time it was considered as a case study, it just recently completed its initial development. So, it has a low maturity. It occupies the Δ and Ω layers. As it is used for maintainability prediction of automated production systems, it covers a unique domain/analysis combination. It is already quite evenly modularized. The package structure of the metamodel modules is mostly flat but adequate. KAMP4aPS is available directly in Ecore. I was able to request expert knowledge about the metamodel from its initial developer. The instances that were used to evaluate the metamodel are available [Koc17]. A proper changelog is not available, only the history in the version control.

BPMN2 BPMN2 only covers the π and Δ layer. It nevertheless fulfills the mandatory scope criterion, as there exist approaches to quality analyses for BPMN2. Literature research conducted by Heinrich [Hei14] yielded several such approaches. For example, Saeedi et al. [SZS10] enable modeling of time, cost, and reliability. Gulla [Gul07] introduces modeling capabilities for performance information. The modularization case study, however, focuses on the BPMN2 metamodel, which occupies the π and Δ layer.

With 161 classes, BPMN2 is in the upper range regarding range. Its predecessor specification (BPMN) was first released in March 2007. At first, no metamodel was available. It was released with the BPMN2 specification in January 2011. So, the BPMN2 metamodel is of medium age. As it is a standard, it has a stable maturity. With the domain of business processes, it covers a unique domain amongst the case study candidates. The metamodel is officially available in CMOF and XSD. There are open source tools that feature an Ecore version. Even though CMOF supports deep package structures, the package structure of the BPMN2 is entirely flat. I had no prior knowledge of BPMN2. There are many instances publicly available, as there is an online repository for BPMN2 models. There is no changelog publicly available that I am aware of. Changes from version 1.2 to 2.0 are reported in the specification [Obj14]; however, they are too coarse-grained to extract evolution scenarios.

The PCM was already set as a case study, as it was a pilot project for metamodel modularization. In the process of modularizing the PCM, a significant part of the reference structure approach was developed. In retrospect, however, the PCM performs well when evaluated according to the prioritization criteria.

The final candidates perform well regarding the (non-heterogeneity) prioritization criteria. All metamodels are available in Ecore. There are many instances available for the PCM and BPMN2, and at least some for Smart Grid Topology and KAMP4aPS. A plus factor for the PCM is the availability of a changelog. In-depth knowledge is available to me for Smart Grid Topology and KAMP4aPS. However, not all metamodels were well known to me, as I had no in-depth knowledge about the BPMN2 metamodel. Another plus factor for the BPMN2 is its status as a standard.

The heterogeneity of the final selection is good, as the following will now elaborate. Concerning size, the selection covers small metamodels (Smart Grid Topology) and large metamodels (PCM). With the PCM as an old metamodel and KAMP4aPS as a young metamodel, the selection is diverse concerning age. Regarding maturity, the selection is heterogeneous. KAMP4aPS was still in an early stage; Smart Grid Topology and BPMN2 are stable. On the one hand, the PCM is historically grown with all detriments that come with it. On the other hand, Smart Grid Topology and KAMP4aPS had a rather short history of maintenance. The selection covers a diverse range of layer combinations: $\pi\Delta$ by BPMN2, $\pi\Delta\Omega$ by PCM and KAMP4aPS, $\pi\Delta\Sigma$ by Smart Grid Topology. Each metamodel of the final selection covers a unique domain. The depth of package structures is diverse, as the PCM has a very deep and the BPMN2 has a very flat package structure. Further, the selection contains modular metamodels (KAMP4aPS and Smart Grid Topology) as well as monolithic ones (PCM and BPMN2).

9.2. Applied Extension Mechanisms

The implementation of the case studies uses the Extension Point extension mechanism (see Section 5.4.6) and Referencing with Reused Container (see Section 5.4.4) where possible, as they introduce the least number of new classes. Where these extension mechanisms could not be used, Referencing with External Container (see Section 5.4.3) was used. The applicability of EMF Profiles (see Section 5.4.5) is identical to the applicability of Referencing with External Container, as the use of both mechanisms does not depend on the presence of predefined containers. The number of new classifiers (if a stereotype is considered a classifier) introduced by both extension mechanisms is equal if the extension references further classes. If only attributes are added, EMF Profiles requires one classifier less than Referencing with External Container, as the stereotype can directly contain the attributes. These are named tagged values. On the other hand, Referencing uses the standard Ecore modeling concepts. This simplifies gathering evaluation results, as the standard EMF API and tools can be used to process metamodels and models. Referencing with External Container was chosen because of this reason. If EMF Profiles had been used, the modularized versions of the metamodels would be even less complex.

9.3. Modularization Stopping Criteria

All four case studies were refactored until they satisfied the following criteria: (1) full vertical decomposition (each metamodel module can be assigned to exactly one layer), (2) no feature dependencies and no module dependencies violate the layering, (3) full horizontal decomposition (each metamodel module is at most as extensive as a language feature), (4) no dependency cycles. The PCM, Smart Grid Topology, and KAMP4aPS case studies fulfill an additional criterion: (5) dependency inversion was applied to decouple all metamodel modules from all other metamodel modules that represent extensions. In BPMN2 as many extensions were decoupled until a point was reached where further dependency inversion would merely decrease coupling and, thus, further increase the observed benefit.

9.4. Counting Metrics Results

To give an overview of the case studies, several basic counting metrics were applied to all metamodels. Table 9.2 shows the results. The first row shows the names of the metamodels. They are grouped after the four case studies. Within a group, the left metamodel is the original version; the right metamodel is the modularized version. The metamodel elements that were counted are listed in the first column. Although a containment is a special case of reference, the number of containments is not included in the number of references. The dependencies row shows the sum of all dependencies (attributes, inheritances, references, containments).

Metamodel	PCM	mPCM	SmartGrid	mSmartGrid	KAMP4aPS	mKAMP4aPS	BPMN2	mBPMN2
Metamodel modules	5	27	3	6	5	9	4	28
Packages	24	42	3	7	12	23	4	31
Classes	203	229	30	34	185	185	157	163
Attributes	56	54	9	9	14	14	135	135
Inheritances	193	194	25	25	163	163	157	162
References	198	174	15	18	117	115	134	151
Containments	120	131	11	14	101	92	103	79
Dependencies (Σ)	567	553	60	66	395	384	529	527

Table 9.2.: Case Studies: Counting Metric Results

9.5. Case Study Metamodels

This section presents all case study metamodels: the PCM (Section 9.5.1), Smart Grid Topology (Section 9.5.2), KAMP4aPS (Section 9.5.3), and BPMN2 (Section 9.5.4). For each metamodel, this section presents the original metamodel, describes the modularization and presents the resulting modular metamodel. The description of the modular metamodels does not go into detail about transitive dependencies, as they do not influence the dependency graph (see Section 6.3.3).

It is important to note that the modular versions of the case study metamodels were created for the validation (see Chapter 10). They were refactored solely according to the rules of the reference structure. Bad smells that the reference structure does not address were not fixed, as this would damage the internal validity of the validation.

This section provides several diagrams that were exported from the Modular Designer. The Modular Designer is the tool support for the reference structure approach. Metamodel architects can use it to visualize and modify the layers and module structure of a metamodel. For in-depth information about the Modular Designer, consult Appendix B.2.

9.5.1. Palladio Component Model

The starting point for the modularization is version 4.1[20] of the PCM.

9.5.1.1. Original Metamodel

The PCM features six view types. These view types are good indicators for the topmost decomposition. these view types are now briefly explained. For more in-depth information, please consult the respective literature [Bus+16; Reu+11]. The *Repository* view type is used to define components and interfaces. Components provide and require Interfaces, which results in *Provided Roles* and *Required Roles.* The definitions of the Components is independent of the software systems in which they are used. The *SEFF* (Service EFFect Specification) view type enables the modeling of the behavior of the services of the components and their resource demands. It resembles a flowchart and an activity diagram. There is an abstract SEFF class that allows for the extension of SEFFs of arbitrary type (e.g., data flow). For the sake of simplicity, however, behavior describing SEFFs are simply addressed as SEFF. Systems and Composed Components can be described using the *Assembly* view type. There, Components can be instantiated

[20] `https://sdqweb.ipd.kit.edu/wiki/PCM_4.1` (last visited 26.08.2019)

(by so-called *Assembly Contexts*), and their Roles can be connected. In the *Resource Environment*, *Resource Containers*, which represent servers and workstations, their connections, and resources are modeled. In the *Allocation* view type, the Assembly Contexts of a system can then be deployed to Resource Containers of a Resource Environment. The *Usage Model* enables the modeling of behavior of the users of the system.

The module structure of the PCM is shown in Figure 9.1. It consists of five metamodel modules. *Identifier* provides a superclass for all classes that need an identifier attribute. *Units* defines units and provides a superclass that keeps track of a unit. *StoEx*, which is short for stochastic expression, defines arithmetic on random variables, which are used in the PCM to define and modify parameter values. *ProbFunction* defines abstractions to model probability functions, which can be used in stochastic expressions.

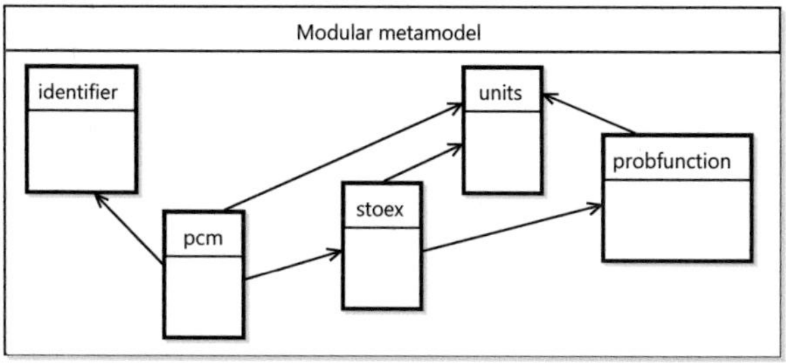

Figure 9.1.: PCM Module Structure (Modular EMF Designer Diagram)

Around 73 % of the classes of the PCM metamodel reside in the *PCM metamodel module*. This metamodel module defines all main concepts of the PCM like components, interfaces, composition, assembly, resource environments, deployment, and usage models. Figure 9.2 shows the package structure of the PCM metamodel module. If a package is located within another package, it means the outer package contains the inner package. The arrows between the packages represent dependencies between the classes of the packages. The figure makes several simplifications to ensure clarity. Dependencies to and from the packages on the third nesting level (e.g., composition) count towards the dependencies of their parent packages (e.g., core in the case of composition). The figure omits transitive dependencies

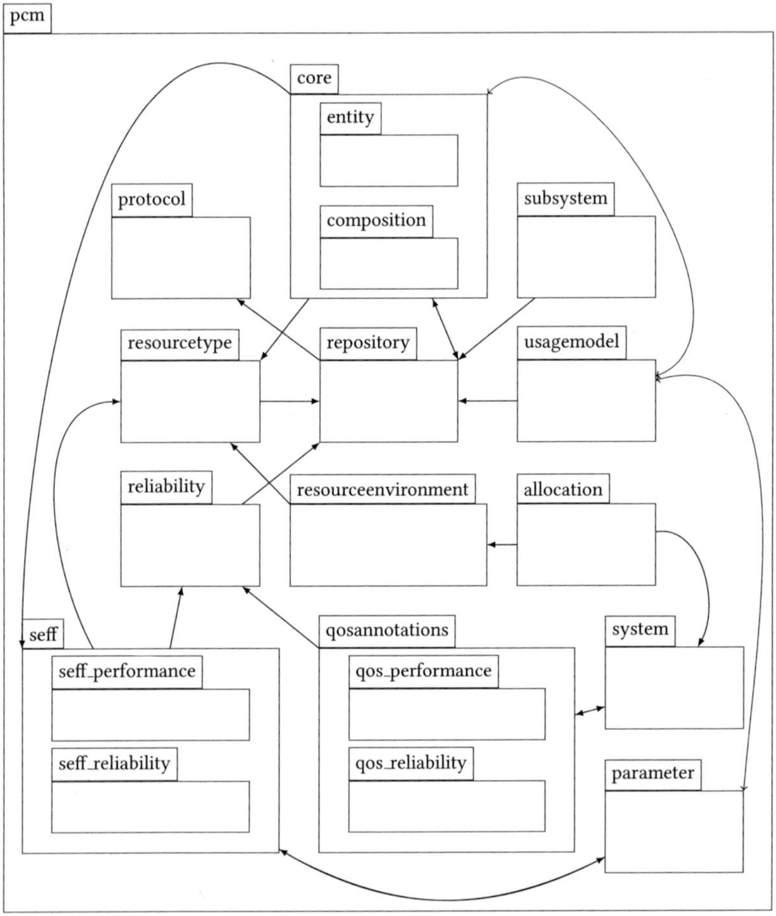

Figure 9.2.: Package Structure of the PCM [SL14]

and dependencies to the entity package as these are numerous. All view types of the PCM are reflected in the package structure. The Assembly view type is implemented in the Composition package.

The *PCM package* is the root package of the PCM metamodel module. It merely contains the other packages. The *Core* package contains the entity and composition package, as well as a class that implements random variables. *Entity* provides several abstract superclasses. *Composition, Repository, UsageModel, ResourceEnvironment, Allocation*, and *SEFF* contain mostly classes that implement their respective view types. However, they also contain classes of cross-cutting features and extensions. These are considered to be bad smells. The *System* and *Subsystem* packages contain one class each, which represents a software system and a software subsystem respectively. *ResourceType* contains classes that specify Resource Types, which are used by the Resource Containers. *Protocol* provides one single abstract class, which can be used as an extension point to define protocols [Reu01]. It is currently unused. *Parameter* implements abstractions for the specification and manipulation of variable values. *Reliability* provides modeling of failure types and their occurrences. The *SEFF Performance* subpackage provides resource related calls as well as resource demands. This may suggest, that its parent package *SEFF* is free from resource-dependent abstractions. However, it is not. *SEFF Reliability* provides abstractions to handle recovery from failures. It has the same problem as the SEFF Performance package, as the classes in SEFF still contain reliability related properties. *QoS Annotations* stands for quality of service annotations and implements an extension point for Systems. This extension point can be utilized by performance and reliability abstractions that are defined in its subpackages *QoS_Reliability* and *QoS_Performance.*

9.5.1.2. Modularization

The refactoring of the PCM, split the PCM metamodel module into 23 smaller metamodel modules to separate its language features (see my paper [SL14]) properly[21]. The modularization of the PCM metamodel module was driven by the effort to separate the view types and to extract their advanced features to make them extensions. By doing so, the basic view type metamodel modules would be decoupled from their advanced features. The other four metamodel modules were already sufficiently modular and fitted well into the π layer. The number of classes in the modular PCM (mPCM) grew from 203 to 229. This is due to splitting classes during refactoring and the creation of new containers for extensions. The number of references dropped from

[21] The mPCM feature model was further influenced by a diploma thesis [Kan17].

198 to 174, as redundant dependencies that violated the reference structure were removed or remodeled. The number of containments increased from 120 to 131, as new extending classes needed to be contained.

The next section presents the metamodel modules of the mPCM and explains the PCM was refactored to achieve the modularization. During the refactoring, the refactorings and modifications of the following types were performed many times. Concrete modifications and refactorings will only be mentioned if they are of particular interest.

- Moving of classifiers between packages (possibly packages of different metamodel modules)
- Moving packages into another package (possible into another metamodel module)
- Creating, deleting, renaming packages and modules
- The deletion of redundant relations that violated the constraints of the reference structure
- The reversion of dependencies that violated the constraints of the reference structure
- The creation of a new root container for a metamodel module
- The creation of containments from root containers
- Renaming of classes (e.g., after factoring out properties belonging to another concern)

9.5.1.3. Modular Metamodel

Figure 9.3 shows the module structure of the mPCM. For the sake of simplicity, transitive dependencies are hidden. This section presents the resulting metamodel modules. For each metamodel module it explains its purpose, its dependencies, and how it was created in the refactoring process.

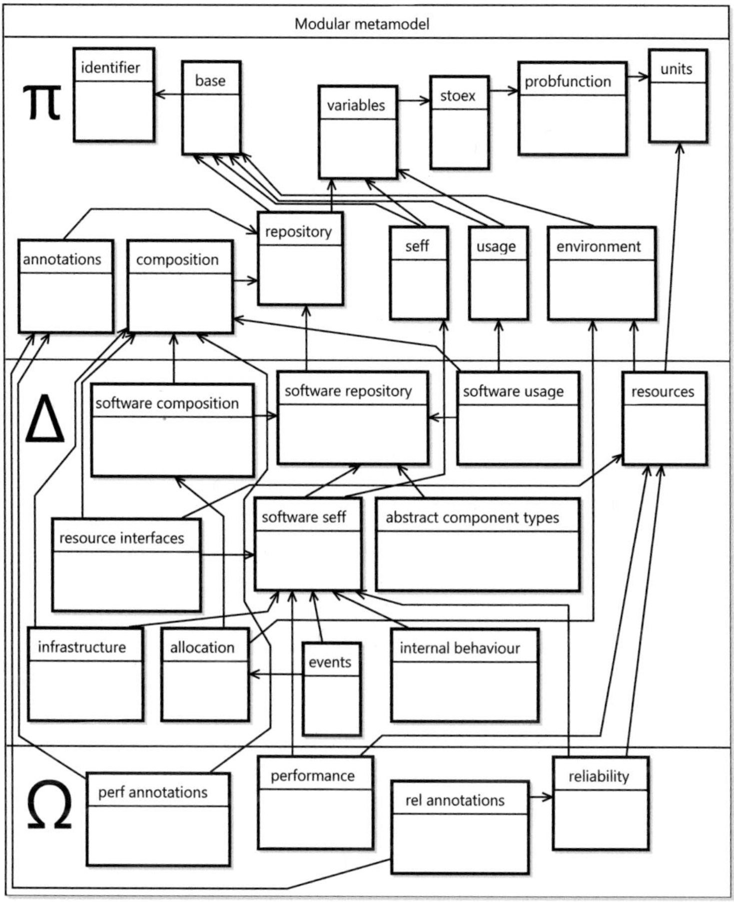

Figure 9.3.: mPCM Module Structure (Modular EMF Designer Diagram)

Paradigm The π layer contains the unaltered metamodel modules Identifier, Units, Probfunction and StoEx. It also contains the two basic metamodel modules Base and Variables that are used by many other metamodel modules. π further contains 5 metamodel modules that define view types.

Base The Base metamodel module provides two superclasses that are commonly inherited from. The NamedElement class provides a name attribute. Entity inherits from NamedElement and the Identifier class (from the Identifier metamodel module) to combine the name and ID attributes. As almost all other metamodel modules use these superclasses, dependencies to Base are not explicitly mentioned. The Base module does also contain a dummy class, which is not used and was only introduced to the PCM as a technical workaround. The execution engine of the transformation language QVT-R was not able to handle a root package without any classes. The class was not removed, as it does not violate the constraints of the reference structure. Thus, by removing it, it would have harmed the internal validity of the evaluation. The large initial horizontal split created Base. It originates from the Entity package. It was not split as a language feature, but as a featureless metamodel module that is used by other language features.

Variables This metamodel module enables to model properties of variables. It does that on the basis of the arithmetic of random variables and thus depends on the StoEx metamodel module. Variables originated from the Parameter package. It was factored out due to a horizontal split to separate its language feature. The class PCMRandomVariable, which is now part of the Variables metamodel module, had many outgoing container relations, which were redundant. As Variables is a π metamodel module, many of the referenced containers are located in more specific layers. Container relations to such classes violated the constraints of the reference structure and had to be removed. The other container relations remained, except if they caused a dependency cycle, to not harm the internal validity of the evaluation.

Repository The Repository now contains the most basic versions of the abstractions of the former repository view type. All extensions (e.g., infrastructure, events) and content of more specific layers (e.g., software, performance, reliability) was factored out. What remains are Components, Interfaces and their relations (Roles). Repository was formed in the scope of the big initial horizontal split and the subsequent paradigm extraction from its Δ counterpart.

Composition This metamodel module lays the abstract superclass ComposedStructure for all structures in the PCM that contain instances of components and their connectors. Composition provides the new superclass Containable. From this superclass, all classes that can be contained in a ComposedStructure must inherit. This metamodel module defines AssemblyContexts and Connectors as containable. Composition depends on Repository, as an AssemblyContext references a Component. In addition, some ComposedStructures need Interfaces. So, a further superclass in Composition inherits from a superclass in Repository that provides Roles. Composition is transitively dependent on Variables, as a ComposedStructures may feature parameters. Composition originated from the initial horizontal split and the subsequent paradigm extraction from its Δ counterpart.

Usage, SEFF The metamodel modules Usage and SEFF implement the domain-independent portion of their respective view types Usage Model and SEFF. Both metamodel modules are dependent on Variables, as they use random variables. Both originate from the initial horizontal split and the subsequent paradigm extraction from their Δ counterpart.

Environment The environment resulted from the resource environment view type. All resource-dependent content was factored out into Δ metamodel modules. ResourceContainers are now Containers, LinkingResources, which connect Containers, are now Links.

Annotations Annotations contains the quality independent part of the QoS Annotations package. It establishes an extension for services of Signatures and is, therefore, dependent on the Repository metamodel module. It originated from the initial horizontal split and the subsequent paradigm extraction from its Δ counterpart.

Domain The Δ layer of the mPCM provides abstractions for the domain of software components. Therefore, the Δ layer extends the view type implementing metamodel modules of Repository, Composition, Environment, SEFF, and Usage by respective Δ modules.

Software Repository This metamodel module extends its counterpart in π by domain-specific content: exceptions and interfaces that provide operations. It also defines an atomic component that has an abstract class as a generic extension point to specify the effects of services. Although the behavior describing SEFF metamodel module uses this extension point, it is not behavior-specific and can, therefore, be used for other kinds service effect specifications. Therefore, this metamodel module is free from content of the behavior features. On its own, the Software Repository can be used to define software components their interfaces and operations. It is, however, mostly used together with composition and SEFF. Software Repository is transitively dependent on Variables, as it enables component-wide parameters for their operations. Software Repository originated from the initial horizontal split. It implements a standalone feature and therefore needs to be separated from metamodel modules it is not dependent on.

Abstract Component Types This is a small metamodel module, which defines two abstract component types. They can be used as blueprints in the component architecture of a system, as components with full service effect specifications are not yet available. As soon as they are available, they can replace the abstract components. This metamodel module distinguishes implemented components from unimplemented components. Thus, it is Δ content and depends on the Software Repository instead of only depending on the Repository metamodel module. It is transitively dependent on Repository. This metamodel module resulted from an extension extraction from Software Repository. It is not essential for the modeling of Software Repositories; therefore it is an extension.

Resources This metamodel module extends the Environment metamodel module's containers and links by hardware resource specifications. These can either be used just for documentation or to simulate performance, as these resources process the resource demands that can be extended into SEFFs. In addition to its dependency to Environment, Resources also depends on Units, as for a ResourceTypes a Unit can be assigned. An extension extraction separated the Resources language feature from Environment. To achieve this, several classes were split and a new root container created.

Software Composition The Software Composition metamodel module extends its counterpart from the π layer by domain-specific abstractions. It provides several concrete classes that inherit from the abstract Composition concepts. These classes are System, CompositeComponent, SubSystem, and several Connectors. They are specific to the domain of component-based Software. Therefore, this metamodel module is necessary in this context. This metamodel module can only be used together with Software Repository to describe how ComposedStructures (e.g., Systems and CompositeComponents) are internally structured. In addition to Composition, this metamodel module is dependent on Software Repository and transitively on Repository, as in Composition Components are instantiated into AssemblyContexts. This metamodel module originated from the initial horizontal split.

Allocation The Allocation metamodel module implements the Allocation view type. It provides the concepts that are necessary to deploy AssemblyContexts on Containers. Therefore it is dependent on Software Composition and Environment. It is transitively dependent on Composition. This metamodel module originated from the initial horizontal split.

Software SEFF This metamodel module provides many concrete classes that represent domain-specific Activities that it adds to SEFF. It further extends the Software Repository by behavior as it provides a new subclass of the generic extension point that was mentioned earlier. Therefore, this metamodel module depends on SEFF and Software Repository. It depends transitively on Variables and Repository. This metamodel module originated from the initial horizontal split.

Internal Behavior This metamodel module is an extension of Software SEFF and enables to model SEFFs that are not called through the interfaces of a component, but internally from other SEFFs. They are analogous to private methods in object-oriented programming. This metamodel module is dependent on Software SEFF, as it is an extension. It is transitively dependent on SEFF and Software

Repository. An extension extraction removed these concepts from Software SEFF.

Software Usage This metamodel module extends its π counterpart by domain-specific concepts. It adds the description of workloads and user-specific data. It enables the modeling of activities that call into the software system (so-called EntryLevelSystemCalls). It is therefore dependent on the Software Repository, as it references Operations; and Composition, as it references the provided role of a ComposedStructure. It is transitively dependent on Variables. This metamodel module originated from the initial horizontal split.

Infrastructure This metamodel module is an extension of the SEFF, Repository, and Composition view types. It introduces a new type of component, interfaces, roles, connectors, and calls. These new abstractions are named infrastructure and are used to model middleware. Besides the dependencies to the view type implementing metamodel modules it extends (SEFF, Software SEFF, Repository, Software Repository, and Composition), it is transitively dependent on Variables. Like the following cross-cutting extensions (Events and Resource Interfaces), an extension extraction created this metamodel module. As it is a cross-cutting extension, it had to be extracted from the packages of the respective view types.

Events This metamodel module is an extension of the SEFF, Repository, Composition, and Allocation view types. It introduces abstractions to model event-based communication. It provides event interfaces, roles, emit actions, connectors and also event channels that can be assembled and allocated. Besides the dependencies to the view type implementing metamodel modules it extends (SEFF, Software SEFF, Repository, Allocation, and Composition), it is transitively dependent on Variables.

Resource Interfaces This metamodel module is an extension of the SEFF, Repository, Composition, and Environment view types. It provides modeling concepts to place resource demands on specific resources from within SEFFs. Besides the dependencies to the view type implementing metamodel modules it extends (SEFF, Software SEFF, Repository, and Composition), it extends Resources and is transitively dependent on Variables.

Quality The quality layer contains two metamodel modules that implement abstractions to model Performance and Reliability. Further, two extension metamodel modules provide advanced concepts for Performance and Reliability respectively.

Performance The *Performance* metamodel module enables the modeling of performance determining properties. This is achieved by adding resource demands to the activities within SEFFs and processing rates to Resources. This metamodel module is therefore dependent on SEFF, Software SEFF and Resources. As well as transitively dependent on Variables. An extension extraction created Performance, to rid the quality-independent language features SEFF and Resources from performance abstractions.

Performance Annotations The *Performance Annotations* metamodel module allows to add unparametrized performance specifications to the operations of required roles of systems and to provided roles of components. Usually, the performance of an operation is determined by the resource demands of its SEFF and the processing rate and the contention on the required resources. However, it is not always possible to specify such detailed descriptions of the behavior and demand of an operation. Therefore, Performance Annotations can be used as a coarse performance abstraction. An extension extraction created Performance Annotations.

Reliability In short, the *Reliability* metamodel module provides several failure types and modeling constructs to apply failure rates to Activities of SEFFs and to Resources. It also enables the modeling of recovery behavior after a failure. An extension extraction created Reliability, to rid the quality-independent language features SEFF, Repository and Resources from reliability-specific abstractions.

Reliability Annotations This metamodel module allows to specify the reliability of Operations that are required by a System. It is dependent on Annotations and Reliability. An extension extraction created this metamodel module.

9.5.1.4. Uncorrected Bad Smells and Modeling Errors

As already mentioned, only bad smells and modeling errors were refactored that violated the constraints the reference structure approach imposes. This section briefly elaborates on the bad smells and modeling errors that were not fixed as well as on general improvements that were not implemented.

By using the extension mechanisms (see Section 5.4), a large portion of the QoS Annotations metamodel modules could be dropped. The two π metamodel modules SEFF and Usage have a large overlap and should be consolidated. The class ResourceTimeoutFailureType has a reference to PassiveResource, which breaks modeling levels. Either ResourceTimeout-FailureType is not a FailureType but a failure occurrence, or the reference is nonsensical. HDDProcessingResourceSpecification has redundant relations to ResourceContainer. The modules identifier and base could be merged, as they are both concerned with identity. They were not merged, as it was the goal not to modify the five metamodel modules the original PCM metamodel module is dependent on. ExceptionType is not a first-class concept, as it is not contained in a root container but in the Signature class. This conflicts with ExceptionType being a type, as it should be possible to use instances of types from multiple places.

The following bad smells that were manually detected. For the full results of the automatic bad smell detection on the PCM, refer to Appendix A. ResourceInterfaceProvidingRequiringEntity is a Dead Class, as it is not referenced by any other class. Even if it were, it should not be abstract. Either RequiredResourceDelegationConnector or ResourceRequiredDelegationConnector is a Dead Class. There is a possible dead reference from Signature to FailureType. CharacterisedVariable may be a Dead Class. Before resolving possible dead properties and classes, they should be confirmed by searching dependent code for references. If no references are found, the class or property should be deleted, assuming there are no plans to use it in the future. There are still many redundant references that did not cause Dependency Cycles between metamodel modules and did not violate the layering. These include redundant opposite relations and all container references. ExceptionType might be a Dead Class.

9.5.1.5. Feature Model

Figure 9.4 shows the feature model of the mPCM. All relations are required relations. Therefore, it omits the explicit required labels. Quality, View Types, Behavior, Structure, and Cross-cutting Extensions are grouping features and are therefore mandatory. The view types are subdivided into structural and behavioral features. Only the direct child features of the grouping features are classified by the grouping feature. For example, SEFF is a view type; its child feature Internal Behavior is not a view type. It is placed as a child of SEFF to demonstrate that it is an extension of SEFF and nothing else (in contrast to the Cross-cutting Extensions). Resources and Abstract Component Types are also extensions and no view types. The Cross-cutting Extensions are advanced features and have no incoming requires relations from the rest of Δ. This means they could even be put in a sub-layer between Δ and Ω to enforce this decoupling. The small arrow that marks a required relation indicates that the relation was pulled up from all child features. For example, the requires relation from Quality to Resources was initially present in the Reliability and Performance feature.

Due to space constraints, the figure does not show the feature model together with the metamodel module structure. This would have visualized the relations between the features and metamodel modules. Therefore, this paragraph explains these relations. The grouping features do not have implementing metamodel modules. Neither has the mPCM root feature. The remaining feature nodes represent language features, are implemented by exactly one metamodel module and are named like this feature. The π metamodel modules have no counterparts in the feature model, as they cannot be used without domain modules. Therefore they do not implement language features.

9.5.1.6. Further Decoupling Potential

By looking at the feature model (Figure 9.4), more decoupling potential becomes apparent. This decoupling is not mandated by the guidelines of the reference structure, as the respective language features are intended to be used together. Such decouplings, however, increase the degree of indirection and complexity.

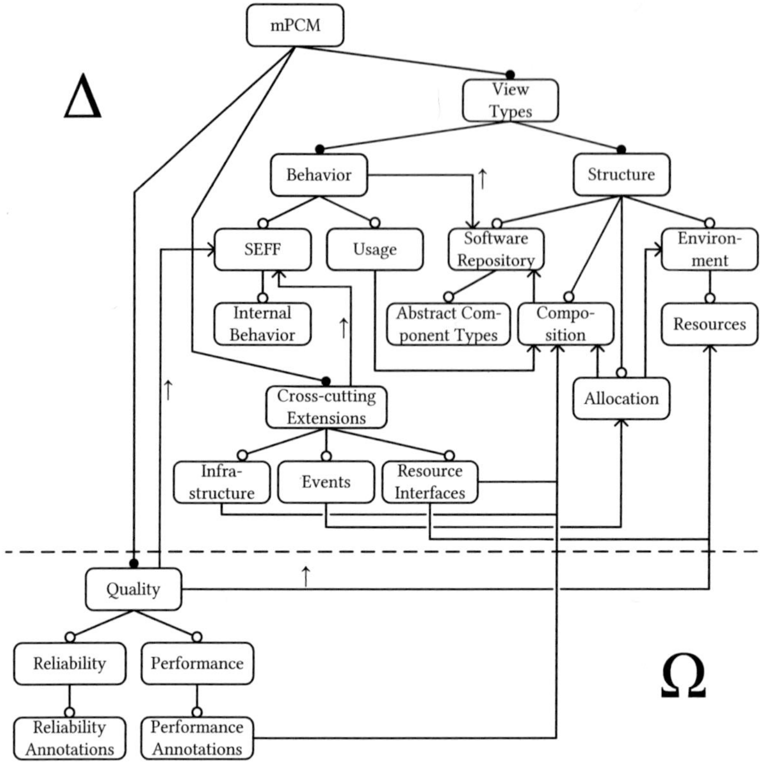

Figure 9.4.: mPCM Feature Model

SEFF and Usage are dependent on Software Repository. By performing feature support extractions, the two features could be decoupled from Software Repository. This would enable the creation of system-independent Usage and SEFF Models without the need to install and load the Software Repository metamodel module. For example, Usage could be decoupled quite easily by moving the EntryLevelSystemCall class into a new metamodel module. As EntryLevelSystemCall has no incoming dependencies within the Δ Usage metamodel module, this would decouple Δ Usage from Software Repository.

The cross-cutting extensions are dependent on several view types like the name suggests. If one of the extension features is selected, all required view type features are also selected. If it is desired to use only a subset of the view types with a specific extension, feature support extractions have to be performed to separate the parts of the respective extension that depend on the individual view types.

Both quality features are dependent on the SEFF and Resources features. By feature support extractions the parts that are dependent on these two features could be split. For example, this enables to model the performance of resources without being dependent on SEFF.

9.5.1.7. Predefined Metamodel Module Selections

The modularization of the PCM enables a selection of language features according to the needs of the tool user. Based on the feature model in Figure 9.4, this section presents selections that fulfill the needs of specific user groups of the PCM. Of course, any selection is possible that fulfills to the constraints of a feature selection. However, these predefined selections will cover the needs of most tool users. For two selections, two variants are given: a basic one and an advanced, which is indicated by the plus after its name. The basic version is the minimal selection, which is suited, for example, for novices. The advance version contains all optional features for the concern.

ADL ADL stands for architecture description language. In the context of the PCM, this means the description of the component architecture without any quality information. This selection is usually used in early design stages or when reengineering the architecture of a legacy software system It consists of all structural view types: Software Repository, Composition, Allocation, Environment, and Resources. Optionally, if the description of behavior is also needed, SEFF, Usage or both can also be selected.

ADL+ This selection contains all selected features from the ADL selection with the addition of advanced features for expert tool users. It includes Abstract Component Types and all cross-cutting extensions. Optionally, if behavior is included in the ADL selection, Internal Behavior is also selected.

Performance Prediction This selection includes all view types as well as the Performance feature. As Quality is the parent feature of Performance, its required relations have to also be satisfied. Therefore, Resources is also selected. SEFF is already selected, as it is a view type.

Performance Prediction+ This is the advanced version of the Performance Prediction selection. It includes the same additional features as the ADL+ selection with the addition of Performance Annotations.

Reliability This selection is used for reliability analysis. It includes all view types, Resources, and the Reliability feature. Optionally, the advanced Δ features can be included as well as the Reliability Annotations feature.

9.5.2. Smart Grid Topology

9.5.2.1. Original Metamodel

The Smart Grid Topology metamodel features four view types: the topology, types of devices in the topology, input state and output state. Input and output state are used by the analysis that is performed on the metamodel. It predicts the impact of the current power supply onto the smart devices in the topology.

Figure 9.5 shows the module structure of the Smart Grid Topology metamodel. It consists of three metamodel modules. The Input and Output state view types are implemented in their own metamodel modules. The Topo metamodel module implements the device type and topology view types.

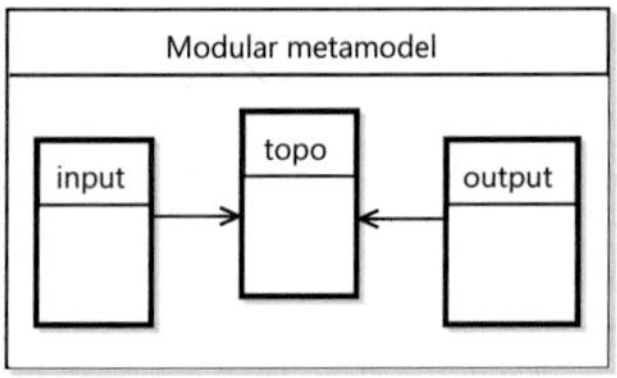

Figure 9.5.: Smart Grid Topology Module Structure (Modular EMF Designer Diagram)

9.5.2.2. Modularization

During the modularization, the input and output metamodel modules remained unmodified. The main metamodel module was split in several ways to separate the two view types and also to extract π metamodel modules. The number of classes increased from 30 to 34. The number of dependencies increased from 60 to 66.

9.5.2.3. Modular Metamodel

Figure 9.6 shows the module structure of the modular metamodel. It populates the layers π, Δ, and Σ. The following presents the resulting metamodel modules. For each metamodel module, this section explains its purpose, its dependencies, and how it was created in the refactoring process.

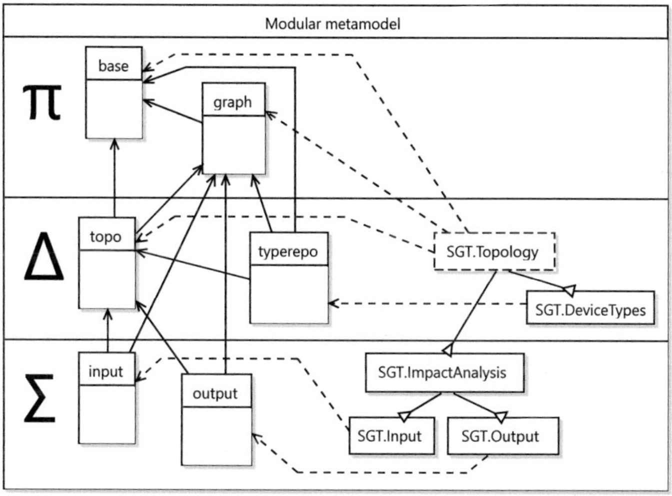

Figure 9.6.: Modular Smart Grid Topology Module Structure and Feature Model (Modular EMF Designer Diagram)

Paradigm This layer contains the domain-independent metamodel modules Base and Graph.

Base This metamodel module defines abstract superclasses that are used by all other metamodel modules. They provide name and ID attributes. As almost all other metamodel modules depend on Base, incoming dependencies will not be mentioned. This metamodel modules has no dependencies. Base originated from the horizontal split of Topo. It is not a language feature. It was factored out, as it is used by several metamodel modules.

Graph This abstract metamodel module defines a simple network graph structure. Nodes are connected by logical and physical connections and can be connected to power supply. Graph originated from the horizontal split of Topo.

Domain The Δ layer provides abstractions that are specific to the domain of smart grids. It contains the Topo and TypeRepo metamodel modules.

Topo This metamodel module provides several smart-grid-specific types of devices and extends them into the graph structure by means of subtyping. It, therefore, depends on Graph. This metamodel module originated from the horizontal split of the original Topo metamodel module.

TypeRepo TypeRepo extends SmartMeters, NetworkNodes, and PhysicalConnections by Types that are stored in a Repository that is independent of concrete smart grid topologies. The base classes lie in Topo and Graph. The horizontal split of the original Topo metamodel module factored TypeRepo out. Originally the devices and connections knew their types. Thus, a horizontal splits were performed to remove the type-dependent properties from the devices and connections. As this type information does not belong in the type definitions either, a new root container that now holds the three kinds of type applications was created.

Analysis The Σ layer contains the Input and Output metamodel modules. They were not modified, as they were already sufficiently modular and fit the Σ layer well.

9.5.2.4. Feature Model

The feature model for the modular Smart Grid Topology metamodel is shown directly in the layered module diagram (Figure 9.6). The root node represents the Topology language feature. As the Topology language feature is always used, its feature was pulled up and merged with the formal root feature. Thus, it is implemented by the Topo metamodel module and its dependencies. As the TypeRepo is an extension metamodel module, it is reflected by the optional child feature DeviceTypes. ImpactAnalysis is a grouping feature node. Usually, grouping features are mandatory child features. However, it is best located on the Σ layer. Therefore it is optional, as its parent relation crosses a layer boundary. From a functional feature selection perspective, it is equivalent if the feature is placed on Δ or Σ. It is also equivalent if it is mandatory or optional as long as its children are all optional. The optional child features of ImpactAnalysis are implemented by their respective metamodel module.

9.5.3. KAMP4aPS

9.5.3.1. Original Metamodel

The KAMP4aPS metamodel features three view types. The Automated Production System (APS) view type is used to model the structure of such a system. The Field of Activity view type adds information about artifacts that are relevant for the evolution of the system. This includes information about the staff, tests, documentation, specifications, and further documents and files. The Modification Marks view type describes how the system is modified. Based on the information of the three view types, the KAMP4aPS analysis predicts the extent of maintenance of the automated production system.

Figure 9.7 shows the module structure of the original KAMP4aPS metamodel. The APS, Field of Activity and APS Modification Marks metamodel modules implement their view type. The Modification Marks metamodel module is a generalized part from the KAMP metamodel that is reused by the APS Modification Marks metamodel module. Basic contains superclasses that contribute name and ID attributes.

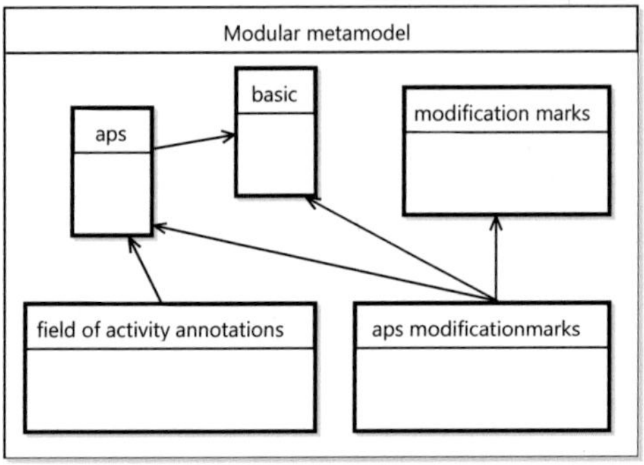

Figure 9.7.: KAMP4aPS Module Structure (Modular EMF Designer Diagram)

9.5.3.2. Modularization

During the modularization, the APS metamodel module was split into parts of different specificity: Automation Systems (AS), automated production systems, and a specialization for a specific kind of automated production system named a pick and place unit (PPU). The same kind of modularization was performed on the module that describes modifications. In the scope of these two modularizations, several dependency inversions were performed to direct the module dependencies to go from the most specific to the most abstract metamodel modules.

The refactoring increased the number of metamodel modules from 5 to 9. The number of classes stayed constant at 185 as existing containers could be well utilized. The number of dependencies dropped from 395 to 390, as some redundant opposite references were removed that violated the reference structure.

9.5.3.3. Modular Metamodel

Figure 9.8 shows the module structure of the modular metamodel. It populates the layers π, Δ, and Ω. This section presents metamodel modules that resulted from the modularization or were modified. For each metamodel module it explains its purpose, its dependencies, and it was created in the refactoring process.

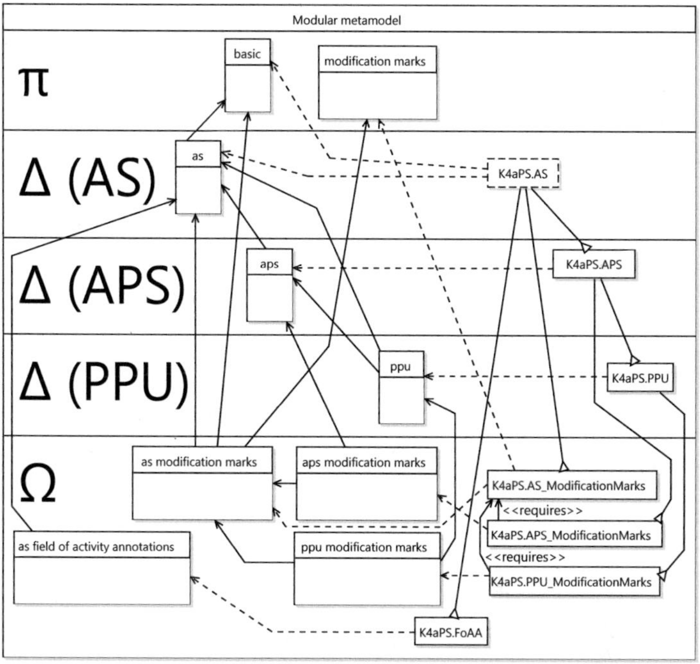

Figure 9.8.: mKAMP4aPS Module Structure and Feature Model (Modular EMF Designer Diagram)

Paradigm The π layer contains the Basic and Modification Marks metamodel modules. They were not changed, as they are already sufficiently modular and domain-independent.

Domain The Δ layer contains the metamodel modules that originated from the horizontal split of the APS metamodel module. The more specific of these metamodel modules depend on the more abstract ones, as new subclasses are introduced and existing classes are referenced.

The Δ layer is subdivided into three sublayers to enforce the proper direction of the dependencies. This subdivision is optional. It, however, demonstrates nicely that the number of layers is not fixed to the ones that the reference structure suggests.

AS The AS metamodel module contains quite general abstractions that can be used to model a wide range of automation systems. Such general modeling comes, however, with the loss of specificity.

APS The APS metamodel module introduces more specific abstractions that are concerned with automated production systems.

PPU The PPU metamodel module provides abstractions for pick and place units.

Quality The Ω layer contains the Field of Activity Annotations metamodel module, which was not altered, as it is already sufficiently modular and only references the most abstract concepts from the AS metamodel module. All metamodel modules of the Ω layer, are located here as they define abstractions that are needed to determine the maintainability of an automation (or more specific) system.

Modification Marks The Ω layer further contains the three metamodel modules that resulted from the split of the APS Modification Marks metamodel module. It was split in a way to mirror the structure of the Δ layer: one metamodel module for the Modification Marks of the AP metamodel module, one for APS, and one for PPU. These metamodel modules reference their respective Δ counterpart as well as the AS Modification Marks module, as it provides superclasses.

9.5.3.4. Feature Model

The feature model for mKAMP4aPS is shown directly in the layered module diagram (Figure 9.8). The root node represents the AS language feature.

As the AS language feature is always used, its feature was pulled up and merged it with the formal root feature. Thus, it is implemented by the AS metamodel module and its dependency Basic. The structure of the feature model pretty much mirrors the module structure. PPU is an optional child of APS. APS is an optional child of AS. AP, APS, and PPU have their respective ModificationMarks as optional children. AS, APS and PPU, their ModificationMarks and FoAA are implemented by their respective metamodel modules. Additionally, AS ModificationMarks is implemented by the abstract π ModificationMarks metamodel module. As the APS and PPU ModificationMarks features are dependent on the AS ModificationMarks feature, they have required relation pointing towards it.

9.5.4. BPMN2

9.5.4.1. Original Metamodel

Figure 9.9 shows the internal structure of the BPMN2 concepts that is conveyed by the standard [Obj14]. It suggests a layered and modular structure. However, a look at the classes that implement these concepts shows that they are often mutually or cyclically coupled by dependencies. Starting from the basic concepts in the middle, this section gives a brief overview of the concepts shown in the figure. For a more detailed explanation, please consult the standard [Obj14]. Some of these concepts were introduced by in BPMN2 (choreography, conversation, event sub-processes, ...); these are good candidates to be modularized out, as they are optional concepts.

Infrastructure Infrastructure contains the most basic classes of BPMN2: Definitions, the root container of all BPMN2 models, and Import, which is used to reference external resources.

Foundation Foundation, which is not shown in the figure, provides classes that are fundamental to an abstract syntax and are needed by the three other core packages.

Commons Commons (Common Elements in the figure) provides classes that are needed by the advanced concepts Process, Choreography, and Collaboration.

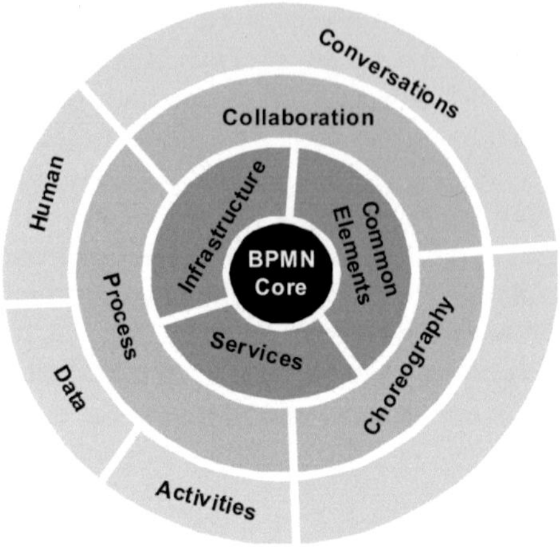

Figure 9.9.: BPMN2 Concept Structure [Obj14]

Services Services provides fundamental abstractions that are needed to model services, interfaces, and operations.

Process A Process is a sequence of activities. It is related to flowcharts and activity diagrams. It consists of tasks, interactions with events, branching, loops, and many more. These elements can be partitioned into pools and lanes. A pool represents the actor who performs the process.

Collaboration Collaborations are used to model the interactions between processes and their message exchanges.

Choreography A Choreography is used to express the interaction between processes in a sequential way.

Data Data can be required by activities. It can represent information or physical objects and is used in messages.

Activities Activities are the main elements of a process. The most important activities are tasks, calls, and sub-processes. Tasks are atomic activities that can be performed. Calls invoke a global process or task. Sub-processes contain a flow of activities and can be used for hierarchical decomposition.

Human Human is needed to express the involvement of persons in business processes. E.g., there are several types of tasks that have to be performed by a person.

Conversations A Conversation diagram is used to provide an overview of which pools interact with each other, but not how they interact in detail. The details of processes are usually not shown in the pools.

Figure 9.10 shows the module structure of the BPMN2 version 2.0.2. It consists of 4 metamodel modules. The metamodel source was retrieved from the BPMN2 Modeler Eclipse plugin[22] version 1.4.2. The main metamodel module is BPMN2, which contains classes for all BPMN2 concepts. The three other metamodel modules are only used to express diagram information. One is BPMN specific. The others are more general and could be reused by other languages to express diagrams. There is a dependency cycle between BPMN2 and BPMN Diagram Interchange. This dependency hardly couples BPMN2 models with their diagram representation, which is undesirable.

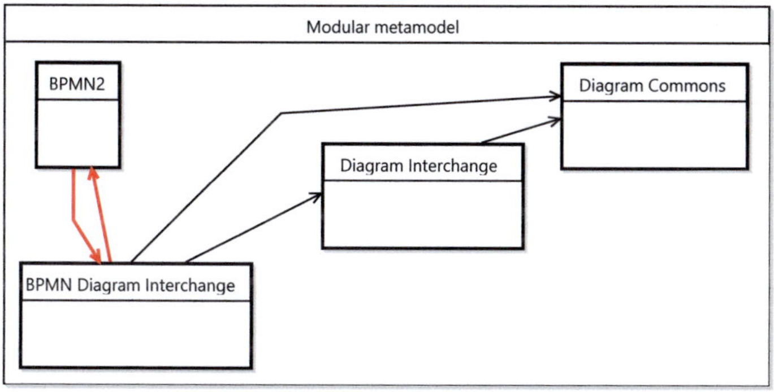

Figure 9.10.: BPMN2 Module Structure (Modular EMF Designer Diagram)

[22] `https://www.eclipse.org/bpmn2-modeler/` (last visited 23.08.2019)

9.5.4.2. Modularization

The only metamodel module that was refactored is the BPMN2 metamodel module. As it implemented all concepts of BPMN2, there was great modularization potential. As a starting point, the metamodel module was modularized into the groups of concepts that are proposed by the specification (as presented earlier).

Figure 9.11 reconstructs the result of the initial horizontal split. The diagram does not represent an exact state of the metamodel module structure in the refactoring of the BPMN2, as in the modularization process other refactorings (e.g., dependency inversion) were performed in between the steps of the big horizontal split. The purpose of this figure is to illustrate the level of entanglement between the parts that the layering in Figure 9.9 suggests.

The final metamodel modules span two layers: π and Δ. The main metamodel module was modularized into 25 metamodel modules according to its language features, which resulted in 28 metamodel modules in total. 16 of these metamodel modules are on the π layer; 9 are on the Δ layer. The number of classes grew only slightly from 157 to 163, as it was possible to often inherit from the abstract class RootElement. RootElement is contained in the root container Definitions and therefore provides a convenient generic extension point. The number of dependencies slightly reduced from 529 to 527 (mainly because of redundant relations that violated the reference structure).

The dependency from the original BPMN2 metamodel module to the BPMN Diagram Interchange metamodel module was not refactored. Removing or inverting the dependency would have decoupled the BPMN2 metamodel module entirely from the diagram-related metamodel modules. In the evaluation, this would have improved the results for the modular metamodel significantly. However, it was important to show the benefits of this approach regarding the more subtle and difficult modularization of metamodel modules. Although the dependency in question violates the constraints of the reference structure, these benefits should not be overshadowed by the results of such an easy refactoring.

The metamodel that was obtained contained one peculiarity that had to be resolved. It contained the class DocumentRoot, which is not covered in

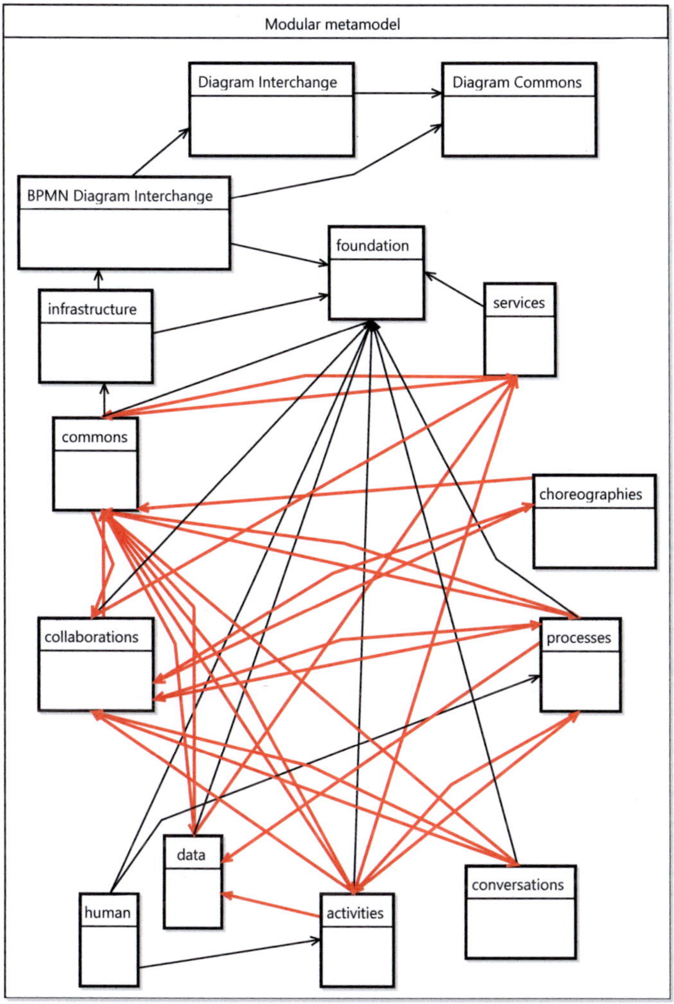

Figure 9.11.: BPMN2 Module Structure after Horizontal Split According to the Structure in the Specification (Reconstructed, Modular EMF Designer Diagram)

the standard. DocumentRoot holds a containment reference to every other class in the metamodel. This is strange, as these classes already form a proper containment hierarchy. This is a grave design flaw, as it completely breaks the modularity of the metamodel. It had to be removed in both metamodels (the original and the modularized version) to get comparable results. Table 9.2 does not include the DocumentRoot and its properties.

9.5.4.3. Modular Metamodel

Figure 9.12 shows the module structure of mBPMN2. For the sake of simplicity, the figure does not show transitive dependencies (e.g., the dependency between BPMN Diagram Interchange and Diagram Commons).

The following presents the resulting metamodel modules. For each metamodel module its purpose, its dependencies, further modularization potential where applicable, and how it was created in the refactoring process is explained. The names of the new metamodel modules relate strongly to concepts of the BPMN2 specification [Obj14]. Thus, here, their internals will only be referred to where necessary.

Paradigm Many BPMN2 concepts are not limited to the use of modeling business processes (e.g., many concepts are shared with or could extend flowcharts); thus, many metamodel modules are located at the paradigm layer. It was seldom the case that a general concept contained domain information and a paradigm extraction had to be performed. Thus, many of the paradigm metamodel modules contain concrete classes. This is, however, justifiable for a refactored legacy metamodel.

Core This metamodel module implements the most basic concepts: Definitions, which is the root container of all BPMN2 models; RootElement, the superclass for all first-class concepts; Documentation; and BaseElement, which provides an ID and a reference to documentation. Core has only one outgoing dependency, a containment to BPMN Diagram Interchange. Almost all other metamodel modules depend on Core. The core metamodel module was not explicitly factored out of another metamodel module. It was the remainder of the modularization.

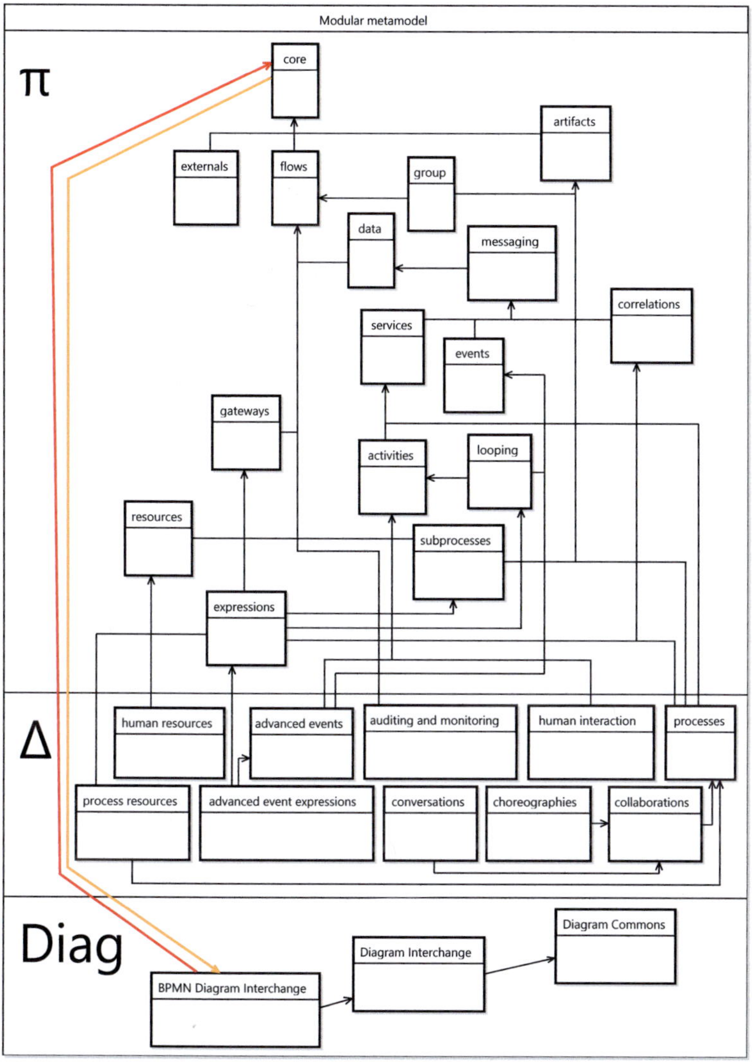

Figure 9.12.: mBPMN2 Module Structure (Modular EMF Designer Diagram)

Artifacts This metamodel module provides all BPMN2 Artifacts except Groups (i.e., Association and TextAnnotation). This metamodel module is domain-independent and is, therefore, paradigm content. Artifacts is only dependent on Core. Five metamodel modules reference the Artifact metamodel module. Here may be further refactoring potential in reversing these references to decouple the dependent metamodel modules from Artifacts. This would make Artifacts an extension metamodel module. Artifacts was factored out of Core due to a horizontal split to separate language features. To make Core independent of Artifacts, Relationship now inherits from RootElement and the explicit containment from Definitions was removed.

Groups This metamodel module defines Groups and the Category concept. A Group is an Artifact that groups values of a Category (i.e., FlowElements). It, therefore, has dependencies to Flows and Artifacts and a transitive dependency to Core. It has no incoming dependencies and, thus, is a pure extension. Groups was factored out due to a feature support extraction from Artifacts (dependencies to Flow were factored out). To decouple Flows from Groups, the reference from FlowElement to CategoryValue was removed. The opposing reference, which was derived and transient, was made a proper persistent reference.

Externals Externals provides capabilities to link external data and extend arbitrary data into BPMN2 models. These are usually used by Tools (mostly diagram editors) to store their tool-specific data, which the BPMN2 metamodel does not cover. Core is the only dependency of the Externals metamodel module. With no incoming dependencies, this metamodel module is a pure optional extension. Externals is the result of an extension extraction from Core. The incoming references from the BaseElement and Definitions classes of Core were reversed and a new container for the now containerless classes was introduced. A redundant derived reference from ItemDefinition, which is now located in the Data metamodel module, was removed to decouple the class from Externals.

Flows Flows is a basic metamodel module that defines flow sequences and abstract classes for their elements. The only dependency of Flows is to Core. This metamodel module was extracted with a horizontal split to extract the respective concern. To decouple Flows from the much more specific concern of Processes and to resolve the dependencies layer violation, the redundant derived reference from FlowNode to Lane was removed.

Data This metamodel module defines data, abstractions for data in- and outputs, and many more data related abstractions. The notion of data that the metamodel module defines is general enough to be considered a part of π. As three classes can be part of a flow, it has inheritances on FlowElement and is dependent on the Flows metamodel module. It further has a transitive dependency on Core. A horizontal split was performed to separate this metamodel module.

Messaging Messaging defines abstractions for messages and their flows in a domain-independent way. It depends on the Data metamodel module, as a Message can hold data. It has a transitive dependency on Core. It is possible that there is more modularization potential in this metamodel module. The dependency to data could be inverted, to make data an extension of messaging. This would make data a pure extension without incoming dependencies. However, due to missing domain knowledge, it could not be decided which dependency direction is better. Messaging was separated in the scope of horizontal splitting.

Gateways This metamodel module introduces gateways, which can be used to fork flows. The gateways do not contain domain information and are therefore located in the paradigm layer. It is only dependent on Flows. An abstract superclass inherits from FlowElement and has several subclasses that define concrete gateways. Gateways was factored out with an extension extraction. However, it could be that flows are always used together with gateways. In this case, the modularization is unnecessary, and the two metamodel modules should be merged.

Correlations In the BPMN2 specification [Obj14], it is written that "Correlation is used to associate a particular Message to an ongoing Conversation between two particular Process instances.". However, correlations are also used by FormalExpressions, which are paradigm concepts. This and the abstract nature of the concept contributed to the decision to assign the Correlations metamodel module to the paradigm. The metamodel module only depends on the Message class. It further has transitive dependencies to Data and Core. If Correlations is only rarely used by Processes and FormalExpression, there is more modularization potential here. To perform a feature support split would decouple both metamodel modules from Correlations. Correlations was factored out from Messaging in the scope of an extension extraction.

Services Although there is no explicit service class in BPMN2, the content of this metamodel module follows the BPMN2 specification that proposes a Services package. It defines Interfaces, which contain Operations, and service endpoints that can be externally extended. These abstractions are general enough to fit the paradigm layer. This metamodel module depends on Messaging and transitively on Data, as an Operation may have Messages and Data as input and output. It has a further transitive dependency to Core. Services was created due to horizontal decomposition.

Events The paradigm metamodel module for events defines the basis on which the domain metamodel module builds upon. It defines the abstract superclass and concrete classes like Start- and StopEvents. It depends on messaging, as Events can be the source and target of MessageFlows. Thus, the Events superclass inherits from InteractionNode. Transitive dependencies exist to Core, Data, and Flows. The Events metamodel module was created due to a paradigm extraction, which separated it from its domain counterpart.

Activities This metamodel module defines the activities within a flow. It is strongly coupled to the Services module, as Activities contains several classes that reference Operations and CallableElements as the represent or use services. Activities depends transitively on Data, Flows, and Messaging. Here is, again, potential modularization potential. If service-oriented activities are not always used, they can be factored out. The Activities metamodel module was extracted with a horizontal split. To resolve a dependency cycle and a layer violation, a redundant derived reference was removed from Activity to BoundaryEvent.

Resources A Process may be performed by a Resource. This metamodel module contains the domain-independent parts of the Resource concept. The metamodel module depends on Activities, as a ResourceRole, which connects a Resource and a Process, references further activities that may be performed by a Resource. Resources also depends transitively on Data and Core. Resources was made an extension, as it is not essential to define Processes and Activities. It was separated from Commons and incoming dependencies from Activities was inverted.

Subprocesses Subprocesses are activities that contain an inner Process. This is achieved by inheriting from FlowElementsContainer of the Flow metamodel module. Subprocesses also has transitive dependencies to Activities, Artifacts, and Messaging. A horizontal split factored it out from Activities.

Looping The Looping metamodel module enables loops in flows. This module depends on activities, as the Activities superclass can be extended by LoopCharacteristics. It is also dependent on Events, as certain loops can throw multiple events. Looping has transitive dependencies to Data and Core. Looping was extracted to make it an extension of Activities, as it is a rather specific feature. As loops are specific activities, Activities were decoupled from Looping using dependency inversion. The containment from the Activity superclass to the LoopCharacteristics superclass was removed. As LoopCharacteristics was no longer contained anywhere, a new container class was created. The container class was made a subclass of RootElement (i.e., using variant b of the referencing extension mechanism) to prevent model fragmentation. LoopCharacteristics could have also been made a subclass of RootElement, which would have reduced complexity, as no new container class would have been needed. As this has the potential to severely clutter the set of RootElements in a Definition, it was decided against it.

Expressions This metamodel module implements informal and formal Expressions. FormalExpressions may be executed by a simulator or interpreted by an analyzer. Many concepts like Gateways, Subprocesses, Loops, Correlations, and Resources use Expressions to express conditions. Thus, this metamodel module depends on Gateways, Subprocesses, Loops, Correlations, and Resources. It is further transitively dependent on Data and Flows. As Expressions depends on so many advanced features, there is more modularization potential. A drawback of the current state of Expressions is by using or reusing it, all its dependencies are required, even if they are not needed by the user or reuser. It could be beneficial, to perform several feature support refactorings, to decouple the general concept of expressions from all the extended metamodel modules. The metamodel module was first created, when during the big vertical split of the Commons. Expressions is a cross-cutting feature, and many metamodel modules depended on it. However, as it is not essential for defining BPMN2 models, a dependency inversion was conducted to make it a cross-cutting extension. The Expressions superclass was also made a RootElement.

Domain The Δ layer provides modeling abstractions for the domain of business processes. It contains the view type implementing metamodel modules Processes, Collaborations, Choreographies, and Conversations. It further extends π metamodel modules by business process specific content like events, auditing, monitoring, and human interactions.

Process Resources This metamodel module contains the domain-specific part of the original Resource concept. Its only purpose is to extend the Processes metamodel module. As the Processes module is Δ content, this metamodel module also belongs in Δ. Thus, it depends on the Process metamodel module and on the Resources metamodel module of π. A dependency inversion was performed to decouple Process from Process Resources. The resulting dependency was extracted into Process Resources. A class split refactoring separated this dependency from the ResourceRole class in order to achieve a paradigm extraction.

Human Resources Human Resources contributes human-specific resource concepts. Its only dependency is to the Resources metamodel module of π, as it uses Performer as a superclass. A horizontal split created this metamodel module from the Process Resources metamodel module in order to separate the human-specific content.

Advanced Event Expressions This metamodel module implements a feature support of the π Expressions metamodel module for Advanced

Events of Δ. It extends two events with Expression support. As the supported feature is part of Δ, this metamodel module is also in Δ. It is, only dependent on Expressions of π and Advanced Events. At first, the dependencies from Events to Expressions were revised to make it an extension and to decouple Events from Expressions. To decouple Expressions from Events, the Advanced Event Expressions metamodel module was extracted as feature support. This was done by splitting the Expressions superclass, which was carrying the reversed dependencies.

Advanced Events This metamodel module holds Events that are too BPMN specific for the π layer. It is, of course, dependent on the Events of π. It also depends on Activities, as Boundary- and CompensateEvents reference the Activity superclass. It has transitive dependencies to Core, Data, Services, and Messaging. It was factored out of Events with a paradigm extraction.

Processes This metamodel module defines the Process concept, which contains LaneSets, which in turn contain Lanes. Processes is part of Δ, as it contains properties that are domain-specific. However, if a concept that is similar to Processes should be defined for another domain, all the classes of π that Processes uses can be reused. It depends on Artifacts and Correlations, as a Process contains the Artifacts superclass and CorrelationSubscriptions. As mentioned earlier, here is further modularization potential. This metamodel module further depends on Services, as a Process is a CallableElement. This metamodel module is transitively dependent on Core, Data, and Flows. Processes was separated due to horizontal decomposition. A reference from Process to Collaboration was reversed, as Collaboration builds on the Process concept but not vice versa.

FlowElementsContainer from Flows is a superclass of Process. The FlowElementsContainer had a containment to the LaneSet class of Processes. To decouple Flows from Processes, the containment was pushed down to the Process class. This was possible, as the containment is not used in the other subclasses of FlowElementsContainer (Choreography and SubChoreography) as stated in the standard. Having this containment at this point in the inheritance hierarchy was not only a layer violation but is also a dead inherited property.

Collaborations Collaborations are used to express the interaction between Processes. Thus, the Collaboration class references the Process class. Collaborations has transitive dependencies to Core, Services, Correlations, Messaging, and Artifacts. This metamodel module was created in the initial horizontal decomposition. Further, a redundant reference from Collaboration to Choreography was removed. This reference was used to keep track of Choreographies that exist between the Processes of a Collaboration. As these Choreographies can also be found by iterating over all Choreographies and checking which Processes are involved, this utility reference can be replaced by a helper method. This decoupled Collaboration from Choreographies and broke the dependency cycle.

Choreographies Choreographies are used to define the interaction between Processes in a sequential way. Choreographies depends on Collaborations, as a Choreography is a subclass of Collaboration. Further, the Participants of a Collaboration are referenced by the activities of a Choreography. Choreographies has transitive dependencies to Flows, Correlations, Messaging, and Artifacts. This metamodel module was created in the initial horizontal decomposition.

Conversations Conversations are used to give an overview of which participants (Pools) interact with each other. It is dependent on Collaborations because of several dependencies. A Conversation expresses the interplay between several participants; a participant is a class from Collaborations. A Conversation may refer to Collaborations between participants. Conversations is transitively dependent on Core, Correlations, and Messaging. Conversations was created in the scope of the big horizontal split. Instances of Conversation classifiers were initially contained in Collaborations. To decouple Collaborations from Conversations, dependency inversion was used and ConversationContainer was created as a container for all conversation specific first-class concepts.

Auditing and Monitoring BPMN2 does not define abstractions for the modeling of auditing and monitoring information. This metamodel module encapsulates one specific extension point for each of these two concepts. It is part of Δ, as Auditing and Monitoring are business process concepts. It depends on Flows, as a common superclass for Auditing and Monitoring classes was created there.

The Auditing and Monitoring metamodel module was extracted into an extension, as Auditing and Monitoring are rarely used optional features. As already mentioned, the new superclass FlowAnnotation was introduced in Flows, as a generic extension point for further extension of Flow elements. The containments to the Auditing and Monitoring classes from Process and FlowElement was replaced by containments to FlowAnnotation. This decoupled Processes and Flows from Auditing and Monitoring.

It would have also been possible to simply make Auditing and Monitoring inherit from RootClass. This would have reduced the complexity. However, this would also clutter the RootClass containment in Definitions.

Technically, these two classes are even redundant. Their purpose can also be fulfilled by using the extension mechanism that is defined in Externals. As the existence of Auditing and Monitoring does not violate the reference structure, they were factored out instead of removing. Removing them would have skewed the internal validity of the evaluation.

Human Interaction Human Interaction provides several types of Tasks that are performed by humans. It is therefore dependent on Activities, as the Task and GlobalTask classes are used as superclasses. Human Interaction is transitively dependent on Core. This metamodel module was created in the scope of the initial horizontal split. It was also horizontally split from the Human Resources metamodel module to separate resource and task-specific concepts.

9.5.4.4. Feature Model

Figure 9.13 shows the feature model of mBPMN2. All relations are required relations. Therefore, it omits the explicit required labels. As the mBPMN2 occupies only the π and Δ layer, the feature diagram consists only of the Δ layer. The non-abstract metamodel modules of the π layer resulted in Δ features.

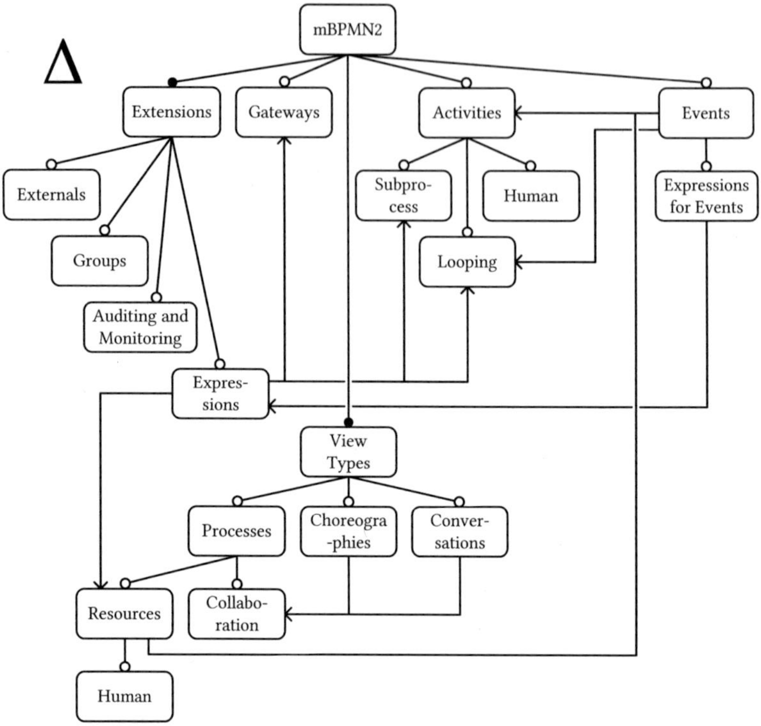

Figure 9.13.: mBPMN2 Feature Model

Extensions and View Types are grouping features and are therefore mandatory. Processes, Choreographies, Conversations, and Collaborations are view types. Resources and Human are no view types but extensions.

Due to space constraints, the figure does not show the feature model together with the metamodel module structure. This would have visualized the relations between the features and metamodel modules. Therefore, this paragraph explains these relations. The two grouping features Extensions and View Types do not have implementing metamodel modules. Neither has the root feature. The remaining feature nodes represent language features, are implemented by exactly one metamodel module and are named like this feature.

Compared with the module diagram (see Figure 9.12), the number of features is less than the number of metamodel modules. This is the case, as many metamodel modules are abstract and many other metamodel modules are strongly coupled to them. The metamodel modules Core, Services, Correlations, Artifacts, Flows, Data, and Messaging are abstract and therefore do not implement language features. As mentioned in Section 9.5.4.3, by using dependency inversion, some of these metamodel modules could be turned into extensions (e.g., artifacts and messaging). This would result in further feature nodes in the feature model.

9.6. Module Repositories and Common Paradigm Modules

By creating modular layered metamodels, their metamodel modules are made reusable. A promising way to foster reuse in metamodeling is to build public repositories for metamodel modules of the π and Δ layers. Feature model, on the other hand, cannot be reused, as they are specific to a variable language.

Besides the reuse of metamodel modules, there is also another important side effect. Sufficient reuse leads to the sharing of metamodel modules between related metamodels. The common core of two or more metamodels is then interoperable. This means that the parts of the models that instantiate the common metamodel modules can be viewed, edited, and used with the tools of the related languages. Metamodel-specific content is then extended on such a common core. Consolidating such a common core from related metamodels has the potential to provide a common platform for language engineering in the respective domain. E.g., by enriching the modular PCM with metamodel modules from related languages, a common platform for component-based software architecture modeling could be created as a base for future extensions of new qualities and analyses.

The π metamodel modules that resulted from the case studies are, however, not necessarily the best choice for a public repository. The reason is that they were altered as little as possible to fulfill the constraints of the reference structure. Each refactoring that is not necessary to achieve this goal could have damaged the internal validity of the validation (see Section 10.5). Therefore, there is still optimization potential in these metamodel modules to make them more general and reusable.

In general, the metamodel modules that suit reuse the best, do not stem from the refactoring of legacy metamodels but from designing modular metamodels from scratch. The problem with refactoring legacy metamodels is that by knowing the current state of the metamodel metamodel architects and module developers might unknowingly impose structures of the concepts of the domain onto the abstract π concepts. For practical reasons, they might even consciously be inclined to preserve a great resemblance of the internals of the modular metamodel to the original version. This reduces the migration effort for existing tools and models. It, however, also results in paradigm metamodel modules that are not optimal for reuse. Metamodel modules from design from scratch are more promising for reuse, as they are not biased from preexisting solutions.

The remainder of this section presents π metamodel modules which have high potential to be reused in other domains. They are not presented as they are in the modularized case study metamodels. Instead, they are generalized to make them more reusable, cleaner, and better to understand. In one instance, it is also demonstrated how to combine multiple patterns in such a way that they still remain sufficiently decoupled and, therefore, reusable.

The PCM features the concepts of components, interfaces, and roles. As components and interfaces are first-class concepts, they are defined independently from each other. By using roles, a component can provide and require interfaces. What further constitutes a component or an interface is left to be defined on the Δ layer.

The pattern of *interfaces and roles* is general enough to be reused in other domains. Figure 9.14 shows a simplified generalization of the pattern. The component concept was generalized to Entity. Via Roles, an Entity can provide and require interfaces. In this simplified version, a connector links the roles of two Entities. Entity, Interface, and Connectors have to be contained by a domain module in order to use the pattern. If they are made abstract, they have to be subclassed in the Δ layer, and their subclasses have to be contained.

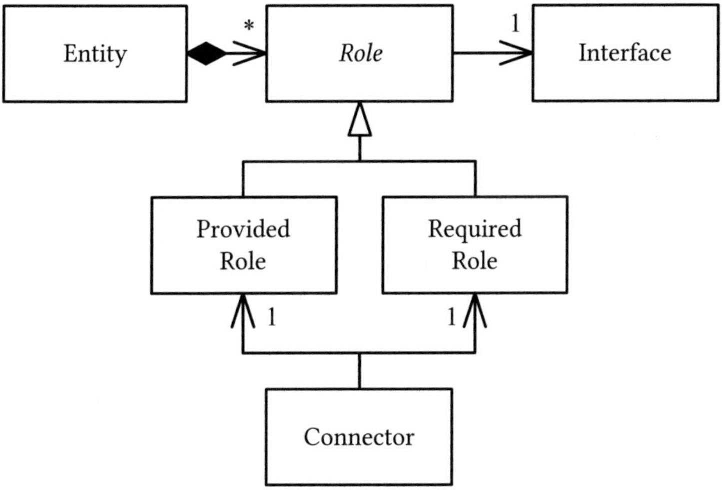

Figure 9.14.: Pattern: Interfaces, Roles, and Connectors

In the PCM, connectors are on another instance level as components. Assemblies are the instances of components, and are connected by assembly connectors. Figure 9.15 shows a generalized version of the pattern. It consists of two metamodel modules. The metamodel module for the type layer contains Entity, the Roles, and Interface. The Instances module contains instances for Entity and Roles. In this version, a Connector links two RoleInstances. The Instances module is coupled to the Types module, but not vice versa. Thus, the Types module can be used without the Instances module if desired. As a side note, with deep modeling, the references that go from the Instances module into the Types module can be replaced by instantiation relations.

Composition is a simple pattern that can be applied to many concepts. In the PCM, composite data types are implemented using the composite pattern [Gam+95]. Figure 9.16 illustrates the pattern. An Entity is either an Atom or composed of other Entities. Cho and Gray present further variants of the pattern [CG11].

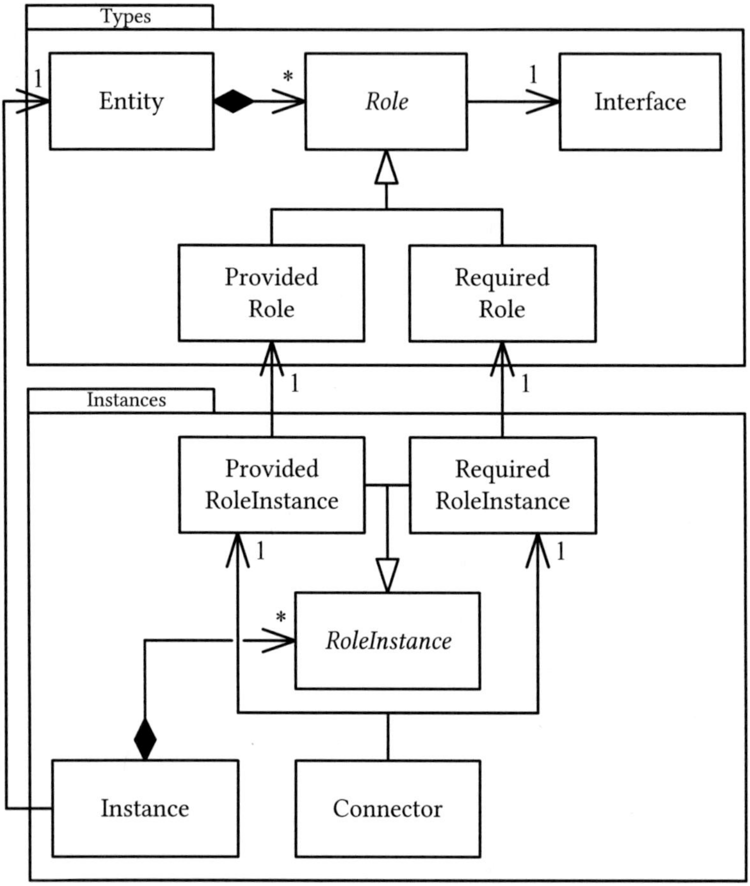

Figure 9.15.: Pattern: Interfaces, Roles, and Connectors on two Instance Levels

In the PCM, another variant of composition is also used. It enables a component to contain instances of components. Figure 9.17 shows the variant of the pattern.

The composition pattern variant with Instances can also be combined with the Interfaces and Roles pattern variant with Instances. This demonstrates

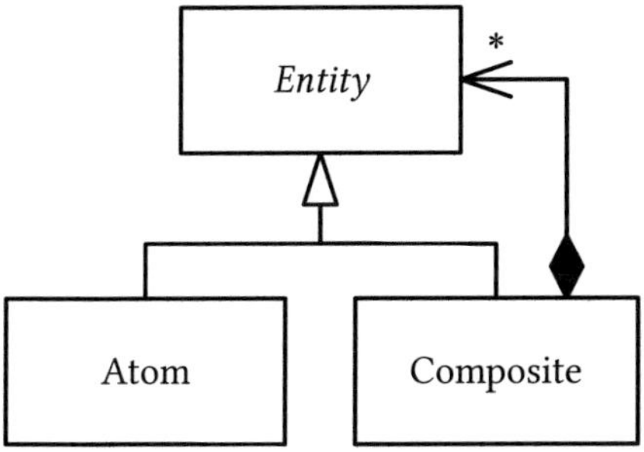

Figure 9.16.: Pattern: Composite [Gam+95]

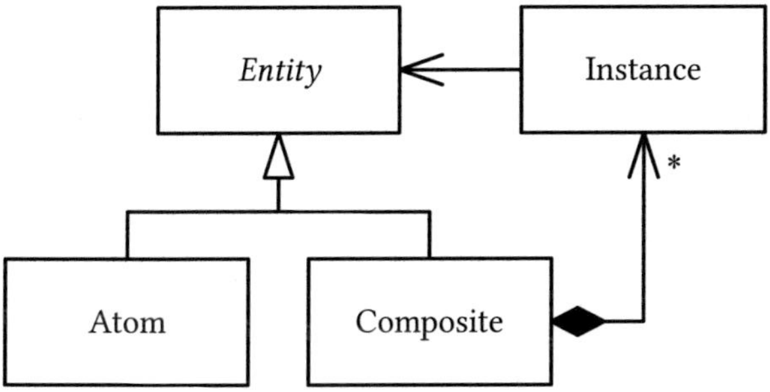

Figure 9.17.: Pattern: Composition of Instances

how to build reusable modules that adhere to the dependency inversion principle and separation of concerns. Figure 9.18 shows a possible implementation. The classes that are needed to model instantiation are placed in their own metamodel module. Composition was separated from Instantiation. Composition, however, contains an abstract superclass for all possible Entities. The Atom class is only one possible concrete exemplar. The extension metamodel module InstantiationWithInterfaces provides Roles to Entities. It also provides RoleInstances to Instances. The extension metamodel module CompositionWithInterfaces provides Connectors to Composites. By doing so, a Composite contains Instances and the Connectors that link the Roles of those instances.

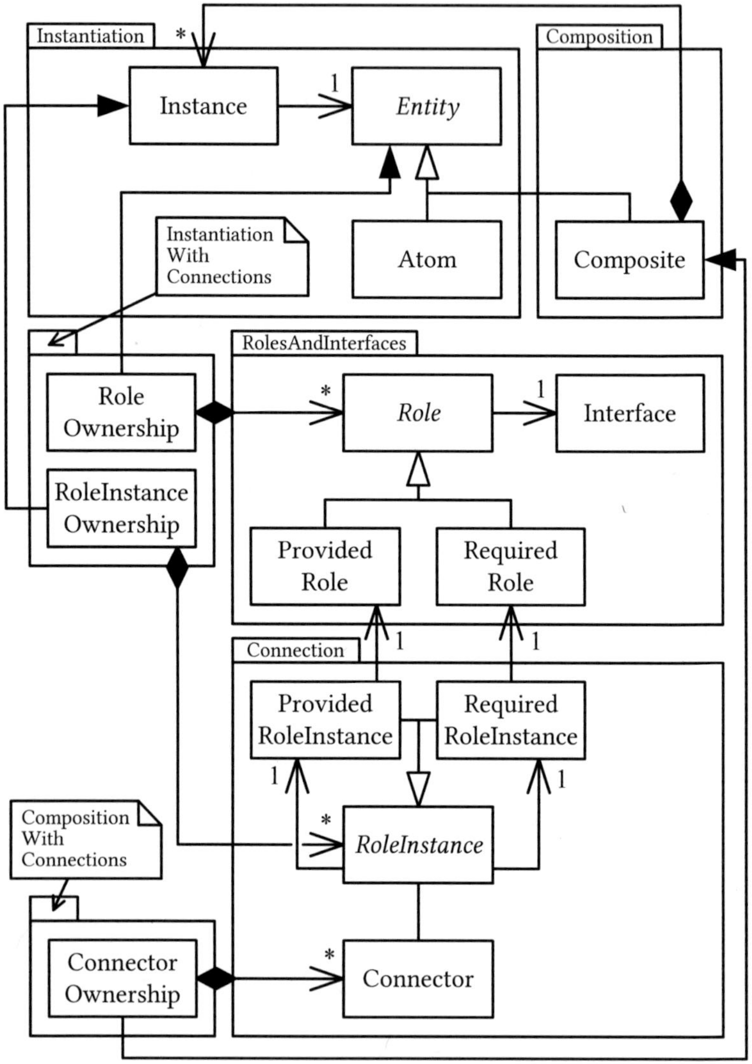

Figure 9.18.: Pattern: Instantiation, Roles and Interfaces, and Composition

To illustrate the module coupling, Figure 9.19 shows the metamodel module view of Figure 9.18. In Figure 9.19, it can be seen how modular the patterns are implemented, which enables fine-grained reuse. For example, in the Δ layer, one could just reuse the Instantiation module. It is also possible to just reuse Instantiation and Composition. InstantiationWithConnections and its dependencies (Instantiation and RolesAndInterfaces), which are automatically reused when InstantiationWithConnections is reused, are a further option. The last option is to reuse all metamodel modules, which adds Connectors to Composites. Even more patterns could be implemented in such a way that they are coupled as little as possible. Because of reasons of limited space of figures, this demonstration stops here. The remaining patterns are presented individually.

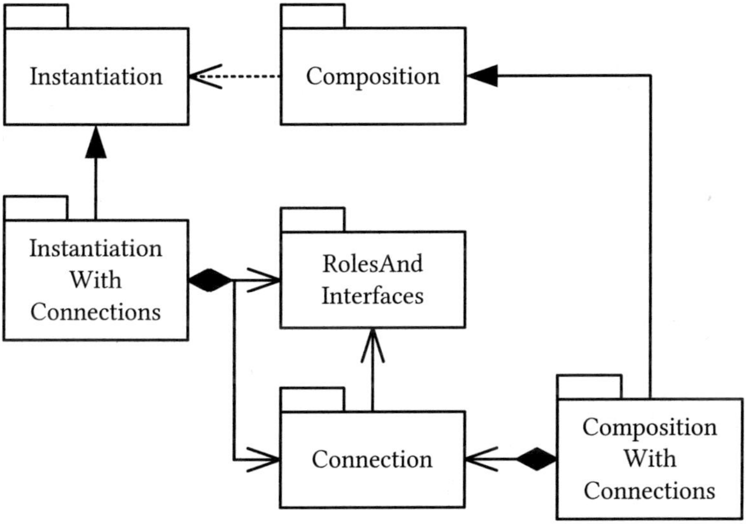

Figure 9.19.: Module Coupling View of the Previous Pattern Composition

In the PCM, a (hardware) Environment consists of containers that are linked and on which other entities can be *allocated.* This pattern is general enough to be used in diverse contexts. On the Δ layer, the containers and links can be enriched by further concepts. In the context of the PCM, these are resources that are associated with the containers and links, as well as the allocation of software components to hardware containers. Figure 9.20 illustrates the generalized version of the pattern. There, Entities are independent of the Environment. A coupling module contains the Allocation class that assigns Entities to Containers.

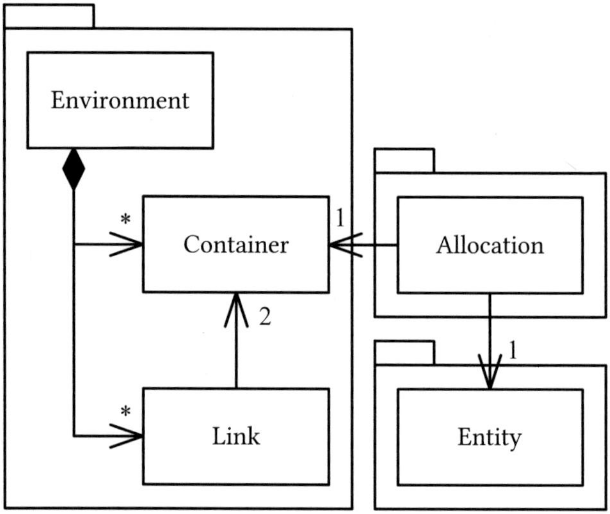

Figure 9.20.: Pattern: Allocation

Language features like *flowcharts* (or activity diagrams) are sufficiently general and already used in several contexts. The PCM uses separate definitions for its SEFFs and UsageModels. A quite similar construct is also used by BPMN2. A common abstract definition in a π metamodel module would be beneficial. The flowchart pattern can be extended by activities that require a resource. Figure 9.21 shows a simple implementation. The FlowChart module should not contain too specific actions to still be general enough. It is better to supply advanced actions through extension metamodel modules. As an example of an advanced action, the figure shows the ResourceRequiringAction that was extended externally. It represents an action that needs a resource.

In the case studies, further patterns were encountered that are general enough to be reused.

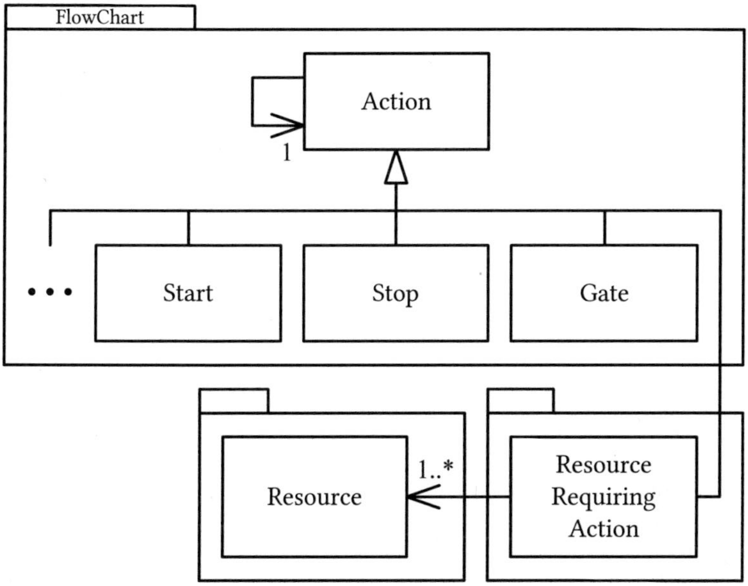

Figure 9.21.: Pattern: Flow Chart and Resource Requiring Actions

Stochastic Expressions is a π metamodel module that can be used if calculations with random variables are needed. This metamodel module was already available before the refactoring of the PCM. It is too complex to be illustrated here.

A common theme when dealing with values is to assign them units. This is also done in the PCM. It is also a good candidate as a reusable π metamodel module.

Directed graphs are a further pattern that is used in many contexts. The Smart Grid Topology metamodel is based on such a graph. In the Δ layer, edges can be extended by properties and nodes can be subtyped and by that also enriched by further properties.

The description of modification is essential to the domain of change impact analysis. For every domain, for which a change impact analysis is implemented, this fundamental pattern is needed. By making it sufficiently general, the pattern can be reused. [Bus+18; HBK18]

Further patterns can be drawn from work that focuses on building DSMLs from patterns [Pes+15; CG11; ES06] and object orientation (e.g., from [Gam+95]). This is, however, not the focus of this thesis, and, thus, remains future work.

10. Validation of the Reference Structure Approach

This chapter[1] describes the validation of the reference structure. It analyzes the case study metamodels from Chapter 9 that were refactored according to the reference structure approach of Chapter 6. Instead of language features, this chapter refers mainly to metamodel modules and their contained packages, as it evaluates the case studies on a technical level.

This chapter is structured as follows. Section 10.1 presents the goal question metric plans (see Section 2.5.1). Section 10.2 explains the evaluation design. Section 10.3 presents and Section 10.4 interprets and discusses the results. These four subsections are subdivided to deal with the two evaluation goals: (1) evolvability and (2) need-specific dependence and use. Section 10.5 discusses threats to validity. Section 10.6 concludes the validation. Appendix C explains the validation tool and the exact setup of the validation environment. At the end of this thesis, Section 12.3 concludes the reference structure contribution.

10.1. Validation Goals and Metrics

This section derives evaluation goals from the research questions that Section 6.2 specified and breaks them down to specific metrics. The first subsection deals with evolvability understandability. The second subsection deals with need-specific dependence and selective use.

[1] This chapter is partly based on [HSR19] (©2019 IEEE).

10.1.1. Evolvability

In the following, the GQM plan for the evolvability evaluation of the reference structure approach is explained. This section further explains why the evaluation is scenario-based and how the parts of a metamodel that are relevant to an evolution scenario are extracted. Lastly, it explains how such a part of a metamodel has to be transformed before the metrics can be evaluated.

10.1.1.1. Goal Question Metric Plan

This evaluation addresses the following research questions.

RQ IIIa (Improve Evolvability) Can concepts from related disciplines be transferred to metamodeling to improve the evolvability of metamodels?

RQ IIIb (Understandability) Can concepts from related disciplines be transferred to metamodeling to improve the understandability of metamodels?

The evolvability of metamodels can be broken down into modifiability, and analyzability (see Section 2.2.6). Modifiability is heavily influenced by the coupling between metamodel modules and the cohesion within metamodel modules. Analyzability and understandability can be approximated by the complexity of a metamodel (see Section 2.2.6). Thus, the goal question metric plan for evolvability is specified as follows.

Goal 1 Evaluate the improvement of the evolvability of metamodels by comparing the original versions to the versions that was modularized according to the reference structure.

Validation Question 1.1 Is the refactored metamodel version more modifiable than the original version?

Metric 1.1.1 Coupling

Metric 1.1.2 Cohesion

Validation Question 1.2 Is the refactored metamodel version more analyzable than the original version?

Metric 1.2.1 Complexity

Goal 2 Evaluate the improvement of the understandability of metamodels by comparing the original versions to the versions that was modularized according to the reference structure.

Validation Question 2.1 Is the refactored metamodel version more understandable than the original version?

Metric 2.1.1 Complexity

Instead of using counting-based metrics to answer the questions of the GQM plan, this validation use metrics by Allen et al. [AGG07; All02]. They are based on measures of information size in bit. In contrast to counting metrics, the metrics of Allen take into consideration that reoccurring patterns in the relations between entities require less effort from a developer to be understood. How the metrics of Allen are calculated, is described in Section 2.5.3.

Evolvability is, however, not an absolute property of a software artifact. It is always to be considered in the context of a specific evolution scenario [Ros+15]. Because of this, Allen's metrics are not applied on metamodels as a whole. Instead, a scenario-based evaluation [Koz11b] is performed by applying the metrics on the part of the metamodel that is relevant to the evolution scenario.

10.1.1.2. Extraction of Relevant Subgraphs

This section explains, how the parts of a metamodel are determined that are relevant to an evolution scenario as well as the rationale behind it. In the following, the part of a metamodel that is relevant to an evolution scenario is addressed as the *relevant subgraph* (or subgraph in short) of the scenario.

Rationale When a developer performs an evolution scenario, s/he needs to sufficiently understand the metamodel or at least the part of the metamodel that is relevant to the current scenario. The initial goal of the developer is to find the metamodel elements that are relevant to the evolution scenario. If a developer's knowledge is not yet sufficient, s/he tries to understand the metamodel by inspecting parts that seem relevant. If there is no documentation, the usual starting point is the package structure (see my paper [Str+16a]), which has to be navigated when searching for specific features of a language. While s/he navigates the package structure, the developer tries to understand the purpose of the packages. This is sometimes accomplished by merely considering the name of the package. If the subject is complex and the name is not sufficient, the developer has to inspect classifiers within the package. To understand the purpose of a classifier, its name and properties are considered. For a class, this may involve following dependencies to other classes, especially to superclasses. For complex subject matters, these other classes may also have to be at least partially understood. Incoming dependencies from outside of a package and especially from another metamodel module or metamodel file are not relevant, as the developer is not aware of them. To evaluate an evolution scenario, a relevant subgraph of a metamodel is extracted that approximates the part of a metamodel that is relevant for this kind of inspection of classes and their packages.

Evolution Scenario Types This scenario-based evaluation inspects different types of evolution scenarios. Figure 10.1 shows the hierarchy of these evolution scenario types. The leaves that are written in bold are concrete scenario types. The other nodes (evolution scenario and modification) are umbrella terms. An *evolution scenario* is either an extension scenario or a modification scenario. *Extension scenarios* represent the implementation of an extension module (i.e., new metamodel modules that depend on existing ones). Extension scenarios do not alter the extended metamodel. In a *modification scenario*, one or multiple classes are modified. A modification changes, creates, or deletes a class property (e.g., attribute, reference, inheritance) of an existing class. The concrete type of modification scenario depends on how the evolution scenario was identified. *Historical modification scenarios* are those that were performed on the metamodel in the past. *Potential modification scenarios* are modifications that might be performed in the future. A *generic modification scenario* merely states that there is a modification of classifiers of a package. These are used to achieve a full coverage of the package structure with evolution scenarios. Section 10.2.1 explains the approach of how these evolution scenarios were collected.

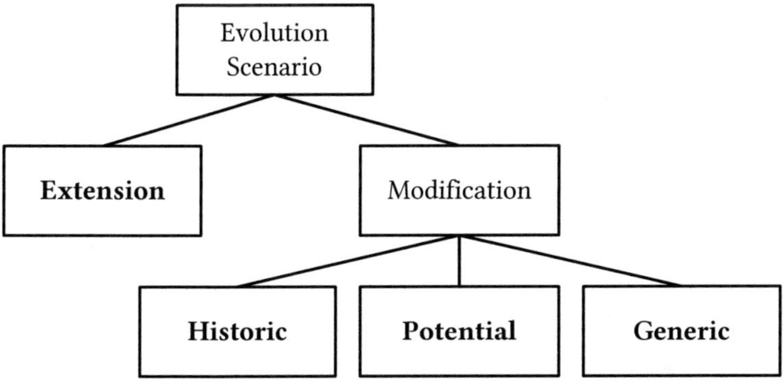

Figure 10.1.: Hierarchy of Evolution Scenario Types

An evolution scenario is defined by its *affected classes*. For modification type scenarios, these are the classes that are affected by the modification. For extension type scenarios, these are the classes on which the classes of the extension depend. The affected classes have to be known and understood by the metamodel developer to be able to perform an evolution scenario. Extension scenarios can be analyzed almost in the same way as modification scenarios. For modification and hypothetical evolution scenarios, the affected classes are simply declared. For an extension scenario, the extension metamodels have first to be analyzed to determine the classes that are extended. The extended classes are then the affected classes.

Extraction Procedure For each evolution scenario, a subgraph was extracted as an approximation of the part of the metamodel to be inspected by the developer when s/he is conducting the evolution scenario. The subgraphs are formed starting with the affected classes of an evolution scenario. From these affected classes, a subgraph is built by following containment references, the superclass hierarchy, dependencies due to generics, mandatory references (i.e., references having a lower multiplicity bound of at least one) and including all classes from the same package.

10.1.1.3. Metamodel Subgraph to Hypergraph Transformation

To be able to apply the metrics to a subgraph, metamodel concepts have to be mapped to modular hypergraph concepts. First, all packages of the subgraph are mapped to hypergraph modules. Second, each class of the subgraph is mapped to a node, and the node is placed in the correct hypergraph module. Third, edges are constructed between the nodes. Non-generic inheritances, references, containments, type bounds and extends relations of classes of the subgraph are transformed into regular edges (hyperedges with only two ends). References and inheritances to generic classes are transformed into a hyperedge with potentially more than two ends due to type arguments. The ends of such a hyperedge are the class which owns the dependency, the class the dependency points at and all classes which appear in type argument if there are any. During the transformation of dependencies to hyperedges, classes might depend on other classes that lie outside of the relevant subgraph. This is only the case if the dependency is a reference with a lower multiplicity of 0. For such classes, nodes are also created and placed into the right hypergraph module. Their outgoing dependencies, however, will not be transformed. Such border classes must be included, as they resemble a dependency to a part outside of the subgraph, which may be considered by the developer. However, the developer does not need to know all the dependencies of the class, as they are outside of her/his scope. It can be seen as an interface to another metamodel module. Attribute types do not play a role in the understanding of the metamodel on the overview level and are thus ignored.

To transform packages to hypergraph modules has some implications. Coupling is measured between packages and cohesion is measured within packages. The alternative to transforming packages to hypergraph modules is to transform metamodel modules to hypergraph modules. This evaluation transform packages, as several case study metamodels are monolithic. They consist of one large metamodel module and few smaller ones. These monolithic metamodels would perform very poorly when transforming metamodel modules. Thus, I decided to calculate the metrics based on packages to allow a more nuanced evaluation.

10.1.2. Need-specific Dependence and Use

This evaluation addresses the following research questions:

RQ IIIc (Need-specific Dependence) Can concepts from related disciplines be transferred to metamodeling to improve the potential to depend only on the desired parts of a metamodel?

RQ IIId (Selective Use) Can concepts from related disciplines be transferred to metamodeling to improve the ability of tool users to selectively use parts of a metamodel according to their needs?

To evaluate both research questions, it has to be shown that a metamodel that has been refactored according to the reference structure enables more targeted dependence and use. Both research questions can be evaluated together if the acts of depending on a metamodel module (as a developer) and using a metamodel module (as a tool user) are sufficiently similar. In the following, this is elaborated.

Reuse is done when a metamodel developer creates a new dependency from a metamodel module to the reused metamodel module. Use is only possible via a tool that has dependencies to the metamodel modules it uses. These requires dependencies are defined by tool developers and used by tool users if they need the language features in question.

Tool users create models and may use tools to process them. Thus, the content of models reflects the needs of the user for features that s/he wants to express and analyze. On the other hand, a model that is meant for processing has to instantiate the concepts that are necessary for the tool that should be applied. To use a metamodel extension, a model is necessary that contains instances of the concepts the extension is based on.

In summary, a good mix of models reflects the needs of usage (of tool users) as well as the needs of dependence (of metamodel extensions and tools). Therefore, it was decided to evaluate dependence and use together through models, as they are readily available and easy to analyze in high numbers. Thus, the GQM plan is specified as follows:

Goal 3 Evaluate the improvement of need-specific dependence and use by comparing the original metamodel to the metamodel that is modularized according to the reference structure.

Validation Question 3.1 Is the ration of the of the refactored metamodel version that is used by its instances larger than the ratio of the original version? This means, does the ratio improve by applying the reference structure approach?

Metric 3.1.1 Metamodel Utilization

To be able to quantify the improvement of need-specific dependence and use, it is necessary to calculate the ratio of how much of a metamodel is used by a model. For this, the *mmUtil* metric, which is short for metamodel utilization, is defined (see Equation 10.1). The utilization metric divides the number of classes that a model M instantiates ($NumInstantiatedClasses(M)$) by the total number of classes ($NumClasses(...)$) of the metamodel modules that are necessary to load the model ($InstantiatedModules(M)$). As the smallest unit of dependence and use is a metamodel module, $InstantiatedModules(M)$ is used. If a model instantiates at least one class from a metamodel module, the whole metamodel module has to be deployed. The more classes (from a constant set of metamodel modules) are used, the higher the utilization gets. A high *mmUtil* is good, as it means that there are less unnecessary metamodel elements in the used metamodel modules. The best value of *mmUtil* is 1. This is the case when M instantiates all classes at least once. A class also counts as instantiated if it has a subclass (it does not have to be a direct subclass) that is instantiated. Each instantiated class is counted only once, regardless of how often it is instantiated.

$$mmUtil(M) = \frac{NumInstantiatedClasses(M)}{NumClasses(InstantiatedModules(M))} \tag{10.1}$$

To compute *mmUtil*, the types (i.e., classes) of the objects in the models are determined. Then all superclasses are collected. This results in *NumInstantiatedClasses*. Then it is determined which metamodel modules have to be deployed to be able to load the model ($InstantiatedModules(M)$). These are the metamodel modules, where the instantiated classes and their superclasses are located and also all metamodel modules these modules depend on. The total count of classes in these metamodel modules is $NumClasses(...)$.

10.2. Evaluation Design

This section explains the rationale behind the evaluation design for the evolvability evaluation (Section 10.2.1) and for the dependence and use evaluation (Section 10.2.2). The selection of metamodels has already been explained in Section 9.1.

10.2.1. Evolvability

This section first explains how the evolution scenarios were collected. Next, it explains why it is justifiable to evaluate a metamodel with historical evolution scenarios that took place before the evaluated metamodel version. It then presents the evolution scenarios for the case studies.

10.2.1.1. Evaluation Metamodel Version

During the design of the evaluation, two alternative approaches had to be considered for case studies that involved historical evolution scenarios. Which version of the metamodel should be modularized: (1) take an old version of the metamodel from before all historical evolution scenarios. (2) take the most up-to-date version of the metamodel. These approaches have some pros and cons. Approach (1) is open to a point of criticism. If it is known how the PCM evolves, it can be shaped in a way that supports the evolution scenarios optimally. A disadvantage of this approach is that the analysis of up-to-date extensions is not possible if they are built on classifiers that were added after the modularized version. Approach (2) has the practical advantage that a modularization might be beneficial to the future development of the metamodel. In conclusion, this validation follows approach (2).

10.2.1.2. Evolution Scenario Collection Approach

First, historical modification scenarios and extension scenarios were gathered, as these are the most realistic evolution scenarios. To collect extension scenarios, the Ecore files of the metamodel extensions had to be accessible in order to determine the affected classes of an extension. The affected classes of an extension scenario are the classes in the extended metamodel that have incoming dependencies from the extension metamodel. The extension also had to be compatible with the current version of the metamodel. To collect historical modification scenarios, available changelogs were searched for modifications. From a modification in a changelog, the modified classes resulted in the affected classes of a historical modification scenario. Next, potential scenarios were collected. This was done by reviewing the metamodel and identifying classes that might be subject of a change or an extension in the future. Indicators were design flaws, semantic errors, and extension potential. If the search for historical and potential scenarios did not yield enough results, so-called generic scenarios were created. A generic scenario has only one affected class. For every package for which no evolution scenario existed that contained only affected classes from the package, a generic evolution scenario was specified by randomly choosing one class from the package as affected class. This was done to increases the variety of the extracted subgraphs. The variety increases if a generic scenario produces a subgraph that includes packages or a combination of packages that was not yet covered by any other scenario's subgraph. As every single package is covered by an evolution scenario, this produces subgraphs that include packages that are unreachable from most other subgraphs. Possible examples of a generic scenario are modifications of names and multiplicities, additions of attributes and dependencies to new classes, and deletions of class properties.

10.2.1.3. Reevaluating Historical Scenarios

As already mentioned, the up-to-date versions of the case study metamodels were modularized. For some case studies, historical modification scenarios were collected. This raises several questions: (1) how can a modification scenario be evaluated on a metamodel on which it was already applied? (2) can a historical modification be evaluated on a metamodel that evolved further in the meantime? (3) what impact does the evolution of the metamodel that took place between the initial application of the evolution scenario and the evaluated metamodel version have? The following three subsections answer these questions. Questions (1) and (2) are concerned with the technical feasibility of reevaluation and are therefore not concerned with the accuracy of the result. The questions consider the metamodel change types (see Section 2.2.5.1). These change types are classified into existence modifications, property changes, as well dependency changes.

Evaluability of Historical Scenarios Considering the procedure in Section 10.1.1, the evaluation of a historical modification scenario is straightforward except for the deletion of classes. For example, if a property change is evaluated on a later version of the metamodel, the class is simply declared as an affected class. For the subgraph extraction procedure, it is irrelevant which property of the element was changed and how it changed. Thus, it is unproblematic if the historical modification scenario was already applied in the past.

As already mentioned, the deletion of classes is an exception. Historical modification scenarios that contain class deletions can, however, still be evaluated. The deleted class has to be removed from the set of affected classes of the scenario, as it is no longer present in the metamodel and would cause errors in the subgraph extraction. The dependencies of the deleted class have to be then added manually to the affected classes according to the rules of the subgraph extraction (see Section 10.1.1.2). This enables the inclusion of all dependencies of the deleted class in the subgraph extraction. Assuming no further evolution took place, it produces the same result as an evaluation of the historical modification scenario on the version of the metamodel on which it was performed.

Evaluability Despite Subsequent Evolution Analogous to the evaluation of deletions in historical scenarios, the type of modifications of subsequent evolution needs the same procedure as aforementioned for scenarios that contain deleted classes. If a class that is contained in the affected classes of a historical modification scenario is deleted after the scenario was performed, all dependencies of the class at the time of its deletion are added to the affected classes, and the deleted class is removed for the affected class set. By doing so, the subgraph of the historical scenario can be recreated, assuming no further evolution took place.

Impact of Subsequent Evolution on the Evaluation This section is concerned with historical modification scenarios and the impact that later evolution of the metamodel has onto the results of the reevaluation. Depending on the types of the modifications that were performed between the initial execution of the scenario and its evaluation, the subgraph that is extracted for the scenario may be altered. The subgraph extraction processes class dependencies. Therefore, a change can only influence the outcome of the evolvability evaluation if it influences class dependencies. The following explains that existence modification and property changes do not alter dependencies; dependency changes alter dependencies and may change the outcome of the subgraph extraction, and how to deal with this issue.

Existence modifications do not alter dependencies between classifiers. They affect the following metamodel elements: packages, classes, data types, enumerations, enumeration literals, attributes, references, operations, and constraints. All element types except classes are irrelevant, as the subgraph extraction does not process them (see Section 10.1.1.2). Even existence modifications cannot influence dependencies between classes, as by definition they have to be unset before a deletion can be performed. The deletion of a class that has no incoming and outgoing dependencies does not change the subgraphs of evolution scenarios. If an evolution scenario has the deleted class as an affected class, the procedure from the preceding paragraph has to be used. In summary, as existence modifications do not alter dependencies, they do not influence the subgraph extraction and therefore do also not influence the evaluation results.

By definition, property changes do not change dependencies between classifiers (see Section 2.2.5.1). For example, changing the name of an attribute or another type of metamodel element is irrelevant for the subgraph extraction.

Dependency changes may or may not influence the subgraph extraction. For example, a class in the subgraph contains a reference with a lower bound of 0. The subgraph extraction will not include the type of the reference in the subgraph. If the reference is changed to a containment or the lower bound is set to 1, however, the target type will be included in the subgraph as soon as the class that owns the containment is included. On the other hand, the declaration or the release of a reference as the opposite of another reference does not affect subgraph extractions. Dependency changes that do not influence the subgraph extraction are unproblematic for the evolvability evaluation.

Considering that some dependency changes influence the results of the evolvability evaluation of a historical modification scenario, raises the question of how valid the results of the evaluation of such scenarios are. This is discussed in the section about threats to validity (see Section 10.5.3).

10.2.1.4. Evolution Scenarios

This section presents all evolution scenarios for the four case study metamodels. The scenarios are marked with their scenario type: extension^{+}, historical modification†, potential modification$^{\times}$, and generic modification$^{\circ}$. The affected classes of generic modification scenarios are not explicitly mentioned, as they consist only of one class after which the scenario is named. In some scenarios, it may seem that affected classes are missing. In these cases, one affected class is strongly coupled (e.g., by containment or inheritance) to the seemingly missing affected classes, so that these classes will be included in the relevant subgraph anyway.

Palladio Component Model For the PCM, two historical extension scenarios, ten historical modification scenarios, one potential evolution scenario and 30 generic evolution scenarios were collected. In total, the evolution scenarios for the PCM amount to a count of 43.

The extension scenarios for the PCM are optional extensions, i.e., they do not implement any core features of Palladio and are therefore not delivered with a standard installation of the PCM. The extension scenarios for the PCM are IntBIIS [Hei+17] and KAMP [Ros+15] (not to be confused with KAMP4aPS, which is a standalone DSML). They were chosen because they are up-to-date and heterogeneous concerning the parts of the PCM they depend on. Figure 10.2 shows the module structure of the PCM and these two extensions.

The first extension is the *Integrated Business IT Impact Simulation* (IntBIIS) [Hei+17] for modeling and analyzing the performance of business processes and information systems. It consists of one metamodel module, 16 classes and has 21 inter-module dependencies that target 11 classes of the PCM. It

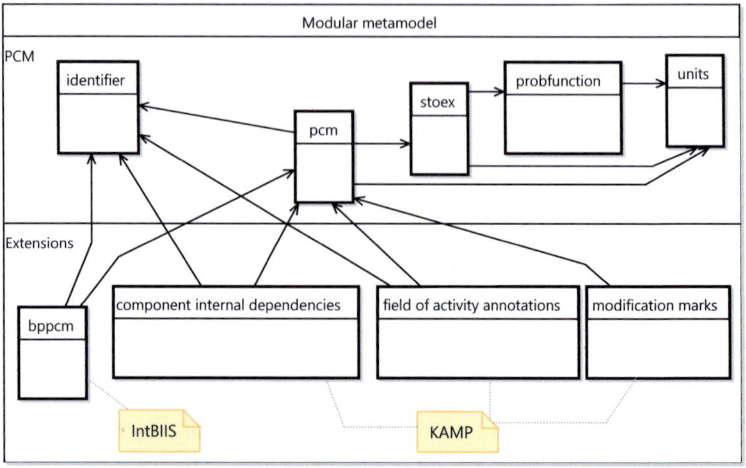

Figure 10.2.: Metamodel modules of PCM extensions (Modular EMF Designer Diagram)

builds mostly on the user behavior defining parts of the PCM. Transferred to the mPCM, it depends on the metamodel modules Identifier, Base, Variables, Repository, Usage, and Software Usage. Its metamodel modules are located at the Δ, and Ω layers.

The second extension is the *Karlsruhe Architecture Maintainability Prediction* (KAMP) [Ros+15] for modeling modifications and analyzing their propagation on the software architecture level. It consists of three metamodel modules, 62 classes and has 42 inter-module dependencies that target 12 classes of the PCM. It builds on the structural parts of the PCM that belong to π and Δ. Transferred to the mPCM it depends on the metamodel modules Identifier, Base, Repository, Software Repository, Composition, and Software Composition. Its metamodel modules are located at the Δ, Ω, and Σ layers.

Eleven historical modification scenarios were collected for the PCM from its changelog[2]. The collection started with the most recent changes and selected the ones that actually changed the structure of the metamodel and

[2] `https://sdqweb.ipd.kit.edu/wiki/PCM_Changelog` (last visited 23.08.2019)

not just the genmodel, version numbers or namespaces. It skipped repeated modifications of the same classes. In addition, there was one proposed modification in the changelog that is considered as a potential evolution scenario. Table 10.2 shows extension, historical and potential evolution scenarios and their respective affected classes. The following presents the evolution scenarios of the PCM.

Scenario Name	Affected Classes
IntBIIS^{+}	ScenarioBehaviour, CollectionDataType, NamedElement, Identifier, Entity, AbstractUserAction, PCMRandomVariable, DataType, OpenWorkload, CompositeDataType
KAMP^{+}	AssemblyConnector, DataType, RequiredRole, ProvidedRole, Entity, RepositoryComponent, Role, OperationProvidedRole, Interface, Signature, Connector, Identifier
AttributeTypes†	NamedElement, Repository, ExternalCallAction, EntryLevelSystemCall
CallAction†	CallAction, AbstractAction, Entity
ComLinkResType†	CommunicationLinkResourceType, ResourceType, ProcessingResourceType
LocalRoleConstraint†	InfrastructureCall, ResourceCall, ExternalCallAction
MultiAllocation$^{\times}$	AssemblyContext, AllocationContext
ProcResSpec†	ProcessingResourceSpecification, Identifier
ResourceDemandingBehaviour†	ResourceDemandingBehaviour, Identifier
ResSign†	ResourceSignature
SchedulingPolicy†	SchedulingPolicy
SyncPoint†	SynchronisationPoint, Entity
UniqueCallTargets†	InfrastructureCall, ResourceCall, ParametricResourceDemand

Table 10.2.: Non-generic Evolution Scenarios of the PCM

The *AttributeTypes*† scenario changed types of attributes of NamedElement, Repository, ExternalCallAction, EntryLevelSystemCall from UML types to Ecore types. In the *CallAction*† modification scenario, the superclass of

CallAction was changed from AbstractAction to Entity, as CallAction is not intended to be used as a stand-alone Action. The CallAction class is located in the behavior metamodel module of Δ. In the *ComLinkResType*[†] scenario, a supertype of CommunicationLinkResourceType (of the Resources metamodel module) was changed to ResourceType (Resources) instead of ProcessingResourceType (Resources). The *LocalRoleConstraint*[†] scenario added OCL constraints, which check if the referenced roles belong to the component in which the calls/action is contained, to the classes InfrastructureCall, ResourceCall, and ExternalCallAction. The *MultiAllocation*[×] scenario aims to enable 1:n mapping of AssemblyContext to AllocationContext by changing the multiplicity of the respective reference. In the *ProcResSpec*[†] scenario, an inheritance relation was introduced from ProcessingResourceSpecification (Resources) to the Identifier class (Identifier). The *ResourceDemandingBehaviour*[†] scenario made the ResourceDemandingBehaviour inherit from Identifier. The *ResSign*[†] scenario changed the multiplicity of the parameter Reference of the ResourceSignature class. The *SchedulingPolicy*[†] scenario removed the SchedulingPolicy Enum and created SchedulingPolicy class. In the *SyncPoint*[†] scenario, a reference was created between the CallAction and the SynchronizationPoint classes. The *UniqueCallTargets*[†] scenario introduced OCL constraints, which check if the requested target is unique within the same action, to the InfrastructureCall, ResourceCall, and ParametricResourceDemand classes.

The scenarios AllocationContext, DelegationConnector, EmitEventAction, EventChannelSinkConnector, ExternalFailureOccurrenceDescription, FailureOccurrenceDescription, ForkedBehaviour, InfrastructureCall, InfrastructureSignature, InternalCallAction, LinkingResource, NetworkInducedFailureType, ParametricResourceDemand, PrimitiveDataType, ProvidesComponentType, RecoveryActionBehaviour, ReleaseAction, Repository, RepositoryComponent, RequiredDelegationConnector, RequiredInfrastructureDelegationConnector, ResourceCall, ResourceEnvironment, ResourceInterfaceProvidingEntity, ResourceRequiredDelegationConnector, ResourceRequiredRole, ScenarioBehaviour, SinkRole, SystemServiceExecutionTime and Workload are generic and therefore not shown in the table.

Smart Grid Topology The Smart Grid Topology metamodel has been quite stable since its initial release. As there is no explicit changelog, only few historical modification scenarios could be collected. In the recent past, two changes were conducted. These result in two historical modification scenarios. Following the remaining scenario collection procedure, which was presented earlier, results in three potential and six generic evolution scenarios. In total, the evolution scenarios for the Smart Grid Topology metamodel amount to a count of 11. Table 10.4 shows the historical and potential scenarios and their respective affected classes.

Scenario Name	Affected Classes
AbstractType$^{\times}$	Repository, NamedIdentifier, SmartMeterType, NetworkNodeType, ConnectionType
AddCoordinates†	NetworkEntity
NewCommEntity$^{\times}$	CommunicatingEntity
NewPhysicalConn$^{\times}$	PhysicalConnection, SmartGridTopology
SmartMeter†	SmartMeter

Table 10.4.: Non-generic Evolution Scenarios of Smart Grid Topology

By the *AbstractType*$^{\times}$ scenario, an abstract superclass is set in place for all types in the TypeRepo. The *AddCoordinates*† scenario adds two attributes that represent geo-coordinates to the NetworkEntity class. The *NewCommEntity*$^{\times}$ scenario introduces a new type of communicating device by adding a subclass to CommunicatingEntity. In the *NewPhysicalConn*$^{\times}$ scenario, an alternative to PhysicalConnection is created. As PhysicalConnection does not have an abstract superclass that would be eligible for inheritance, the root class SmartGridTopology has to also be modified. The *SmartMeter*† scenario modifies the SmartMeter class by removing the aggregation attribute.

The scenarios Cluster, InputEntityState, NetworkNodeType, OutputEntityState, and ScenarioResult are generic and therefore not shown in the table.

KAMP4aPS For the KAMP4aPS case study, 31 evolution scenarios were collected (10 potential and 21 generic). Table 10.6 shows the potential scenarios and their respective affected classes.

The scenario *DocuApplication*$^{\times}$ consists of removing the redundant container reference from all DocumentationFiles classes. In the next scenario,

Scenario Name	Affected Classes
DocuApplication$^{\times}$	ComponentDocumentationFiles, InterfaceDocumentationFiles, StructureDocumentationFiles, ModuleDocumentationFiles
DocumentationFiles$^{\times}$	DocumentationFiles
FoAARepo$^{\times}$	FieldOfActivityAnnotationRepository, Entity
MechanicalAssembly$^{\times}$	MechanicalAssembly
Panel$^{\times}$	Panel, Component, ComponentRepository
ParentEntity$^{\times}$	Module, Interface, Entity
Plant$^{\times}$	Plant
Ramp$^{\times}$	Ramp, Component, MechanicalAssembly
Structure$^{\times}$	Structure, Plant
TurningTable$^{\times}$	TurningTable, Component, Module

Table 10.6.: Non-generic Evolution Scenarios of KAMP4aPS

DocumentationFiles$^{\times}$, the DocumentationFiles class is changed from an interface to an abstract class. The *FoAARepo*$^{\times}$ scenario makes FieldOfActivityAnnotationRepository an Entity. In the *MechanicalAssembly*$^{\times}$ scenario the class MechanicalAssembly is moved into the MechanicalComponents package. The *Panel*$^{\times}$ scenario change the reference from the Panel class to Component to point to ComponentRepository. In the *ParentEntity*$^{\times}$ scenario the redundant or even dead reference to Entity is removed from Module and Interface. The *Plant*$^{\times}$ scenario adds structural features to Plan. For example, the redundant plantName attribute could be removed, as it is already provided by its superclass. The *Ramp*$^{\times}$ scenario consists of moving the Ramp to the Component package and changing the superclass from MechanicalAssembly to Component, as the Ramp is not a mechanical element. In the *Structure*$^{\times}$ scenario, the container reference is removed from the abstract Structure class. In the *TurningTable*$^{\times}$ scenario Component is added to the superclasses of the TurningTable class.

For reasons of space, the names of some generic scenarios had to be shortened. In these cases, the name of the affected class is shown within the parentheses. The generic scenarios are: Arm, BusMaster, ComponentRepository, ControlCabinet, ConveyorBelt, Entity, EtherCATSlave,

HWPropagation (ChangePropagationDueToHardwareChange), InterfaceRepository, ModifyMicroSwitch (ModifyMicroSwitchModule), ModifyModule, ModifySignalinterface, ModuleRepository, MonostableCylinder, PneumaticNetwork, PneumaticSupply, Potentiometer, ReturnSpring, SeedMods (KAMP4aPSSeedModifications), SuspensionRack, and VacuumGripperModule.

BPMN2 The version jump from BPMN to BPMN2 (see [Obj14]) was too big to extract any fine-grained historical modification scenarios. In addition, the maturity and complexity of the metamodel made it hard to identify any potential modification scenarios. Therefore, for the BPMN2 case study, 23 generic evolution scenarios were collected. These are ResAssignExp (ResourceAssignmentExpression), ComplBehDef (ComplexBehaviorDefinition), CorrSubscription (CorrelationSubscription), GlobBRuleTask (GlobalBusinessRuleTask), GlobChoreoTask (GlobalChoreographyTask), ParticipantAssoc (ParticipantAssociation), AdHocSubProc (AdHocSubProcess), ImplThrowEvent (ImplicitThrowEvent), InOutBinding (InputOutputBinding), ItemAwareElem (ItemAwareElement), Artifact, Auditing, BoundaryEvent, CategoryValue, FormalExpression, InteractionNode, LaneSet, ParallelGateway, PotentialOwner, Relationship, Rendering, RootElement, and SequenceFlow.

10.2.2. Need-specific Dependence and Use

To evaluate the *mmUtil* for the PCM, Smart Grid Topology, and KAMP4aPS case studies, all available models that were collected. These are 611 PCM models, 28 Smart Grid Topology models, and 30 KAMP4aPS models.

The *PCM models* include the *Media Store* case study [SK16] and the *Common Component Modeling Example* (CoCoME) [Hei+15], as both are representatives of realistic models. The remaining PCM models stem from internal sources.

The *Smart Grid Topology models* were collected from the project repository[3]. I was involved in creating these models for various purposes. Some were

[3] `https://svnserver.informatik.kit.edu/i43/svn/code/SmartGrid/smartgrid.model.examples/` anonymous/anonymous (last visited 23.08.2019)

created to test the metamodel, the editors and the simulations. Some were created to visualize a topology, others model reference power grids.

The *KAMP4aPS models* were collected from the developer of the metamodel. These models were mainly created for the evaluation of the approach.

The number of *BPMN2 models* is much higher because, in contrast to the other case studies, there is a public online repository with BPMN2 models[4]. For BPMN2, 103 models were collected from internal sources [PSH18; Pil18] and 3739 from the repository. From all these models, 46 models were invalid, could not be loaded and were therefore ignored by the analysis.

To remove potentially sensitive information from the models from internal sources, these models were preprocessed in the following way. The file names were replaced by numbers. Model element names, labels, text annotations and documentation properties were censored. This loss of information is irrelevant to the evaluation, as it is not required. It is relevant, however, which classes are instantiated. This information is still present.

10.3. Evaluation Results

This section presents the results of the evolvability evaluation, followed by the need-specific dependence and use evaluation. The raw data is accessible online[5].

10.3.1. Evolvability

The results of the hypergraph metric analysis are shown in Figure 10.3 (PCM), Figure 10.4 (PCM), Figure 10.5 (Smart Grid Topology), Figure 10.6 (KAMP4aPS), and Figure 10.7 (BPMN2). The results for the PCM are split. The first diagram shows coupling and complexity; the second diagram shows cohesion. The remaining diagrams show the results for the metrics that are labeled on the right side: the upper box contains complexity results,

[4] `https://github.com/camunda/bpmn-for-research/tree/1416f6f2104ae597eafa3097946140ebc2136a53` (last visited 23.08.2019)

[5] `https://sdqweb.ipd.kit.edu/wiki/Metamodel_Reference_Architecture_Validation` (last visited 26.08.2019)

the middle box shows the coupling (between packages), and the lower box presents the cohesion (inside packages). The values of the metric are denoted at the y-axis at the left side. At the x-axis, the names of the evolution scenarios are listed. The scenarios are marked with their scenario type: extension^{+}, historical modification†, potential modification$^{\times}$, and generic modification$^{\circ}$. For each scenario, both versions of the metamodel were evaluated: the original one (black) and the version that was modularized according to the reference structure (gray).

The cohesion results for the PCM (Figure 10.4) are clipped at 0.065 to improve the visibility of the differences between the results of lower value. The result values for the mPCM that are not visible are 1 for FailOccDescription, 0.315 for LinkingResource, and 0.203 for PrimitiveDataType.

If scenarios produce the same subgraph, they result in identical metric results. In these cases, only the name of the alphabetically first scenario is shown. How many scenarios produced the same result, is denoted by the bracketed number beside the name. Such a group of identical results is referred to as a *result group*. Table 10.8 lists the exact content of the result groups. The left column shows the name of the alphabetically first scenario, which is also the name of the group. The right side shows all other scenarios that produced the same result. Only result groups are shown that contain more than one scenario.

The unit for complexity and coupling is bit, as both metrics measure information size as known from information theory. Their value range is unbounded. Low complexity and low coupling values are good. The unit for cohesion is a ratio of bits: the ratio of the current cohesion compared to the cohesion of the maximal cohesive graph. Thus its value range is between zero and one. A high cohesion value is good.

10.3.2. Need-specific Dependence and Use

The results of the metamodel utilization metric are shown in Figure 10.8 (PCM), Figure 10.9 (Smart Grid Topology), Figure 10.10 (KAMP4aPS), and Figure 10.11 (BPMN2). Each case study has its own boxplot. The x-axis shows the name of the metamodel. The left one is always the original version, and the right one is the modularized version. The y-axis shows

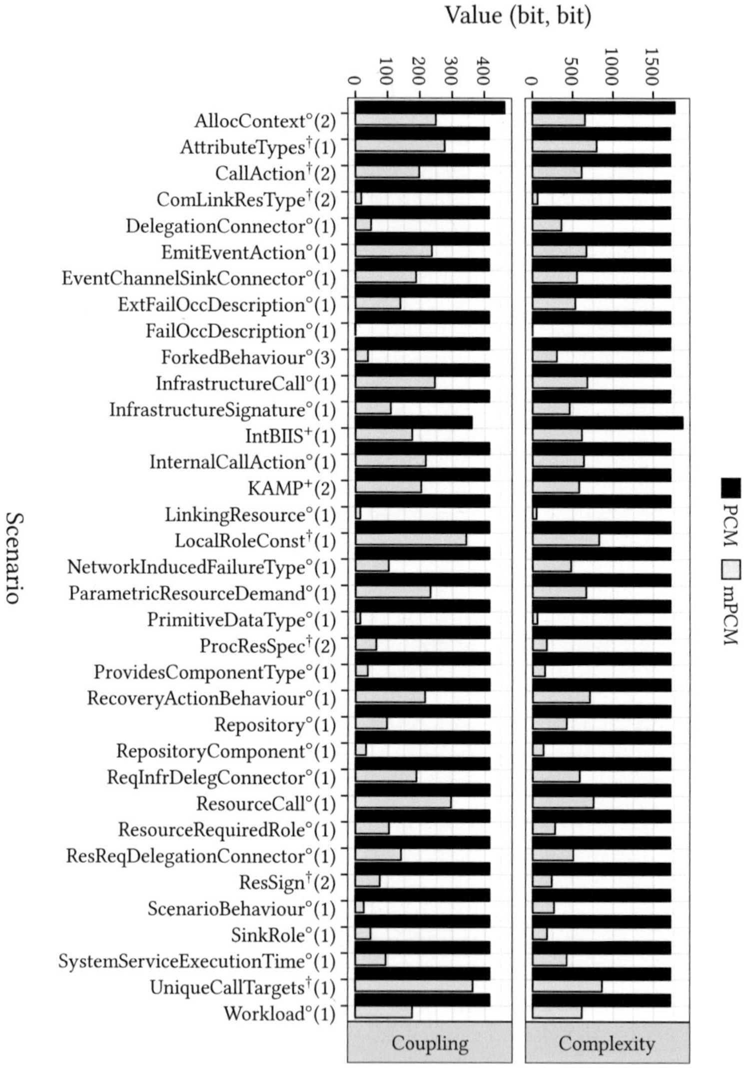

Figure 10.3.: Evolvability Metric Results: PCM (Complexity and Coupling)

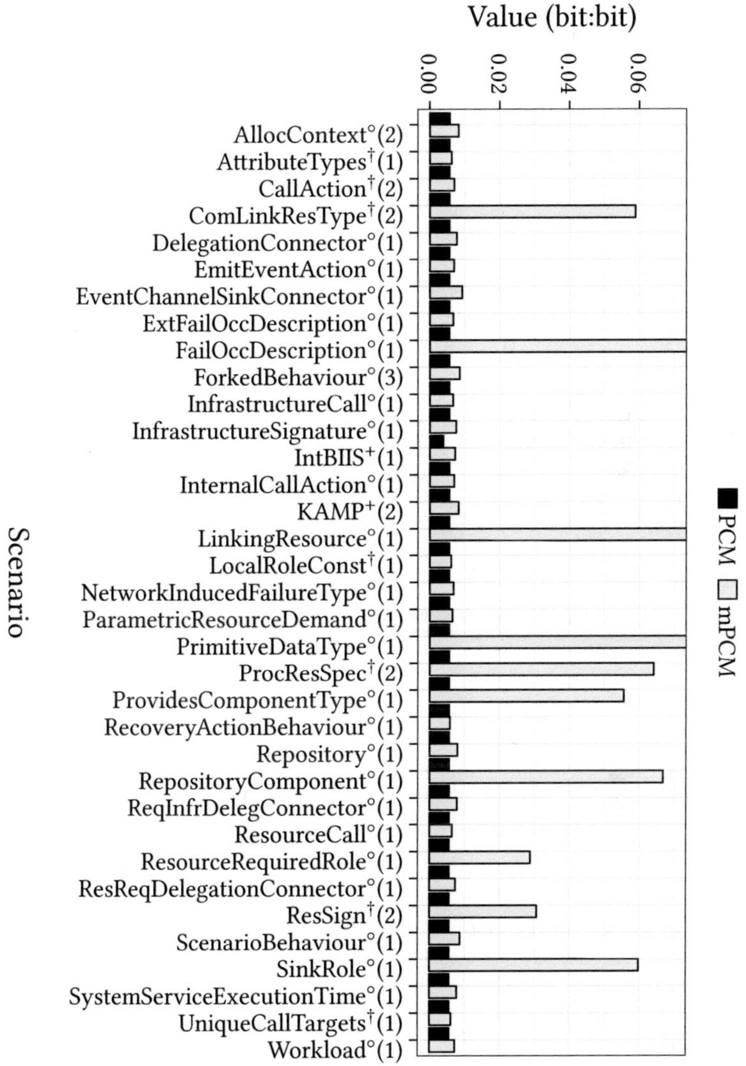

Figure 10.4.: Evolvability Metric Results: PCM (Cohesion)

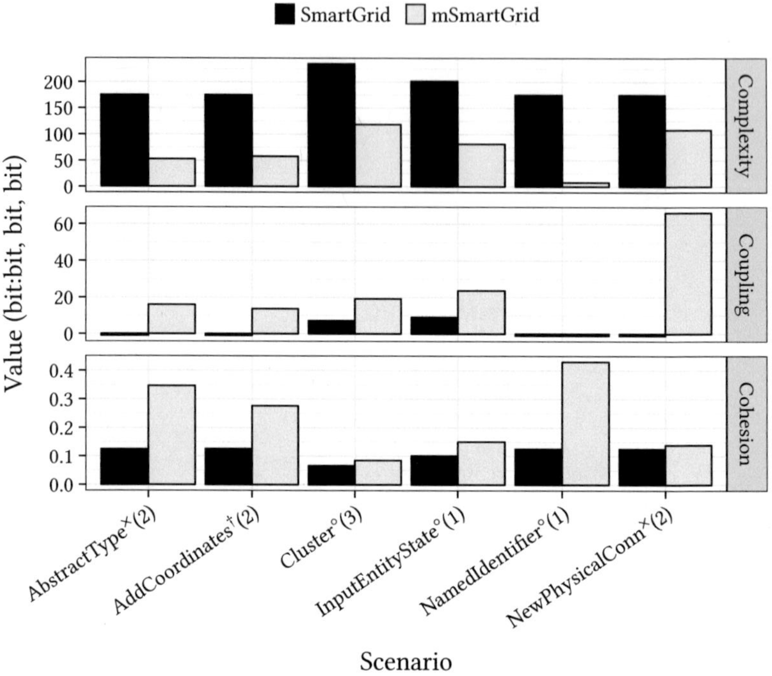

Figure 10.5.: Evolvability Metric Results: Smart Grid Topology

the scale for the *mmUtil* metric. The unit for *mmUtil* is a ratio of classes: the ratio of instantiated classes compared to the total number of classes from all metamodel modules that have to be loaded. Thus, its value range is between zero and one. A high value is good. The lower and upper border of the box represent the first and third quartiles. The bar in the middle of the box shows the median. The whiskers extend from the borders of the box to the last value within 1.5 times the interquartile range. The individual results are represented as points. The results are scattered to prevent overplotting. Thus, within results for one metamodel version, the x-position has no meaning.

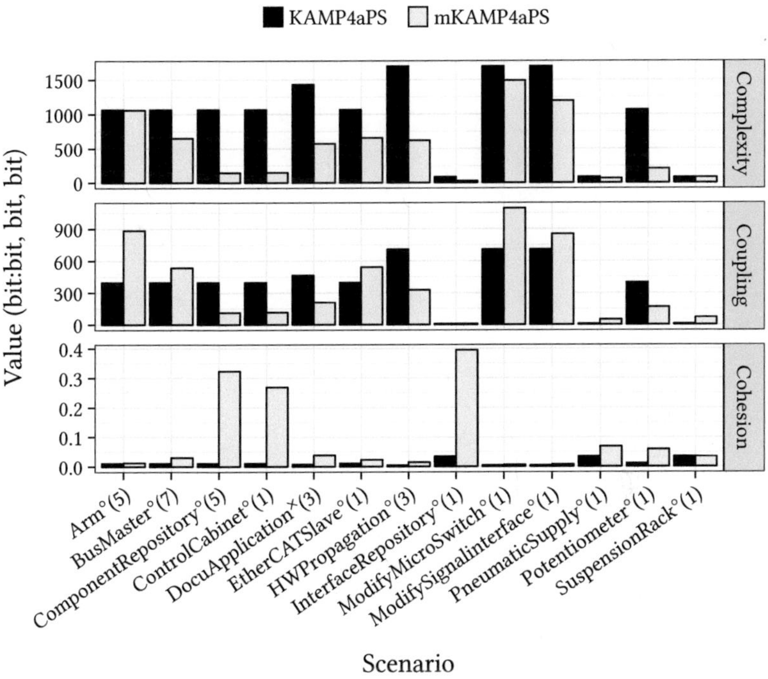

Figure 10.6.: Evolvability Metric Results: KAMP4aPS

10.4. Interpretation and Discussion

This section interprets the results that the previous section presented. It discusses the reasons for differences in the results between the original and the modular versions of the metamodels and their implications.

10.4.1. Evolvability

This section first provides an interpretation for effects that influence all three metrics. Next, it interprets the results for the individual metrics.

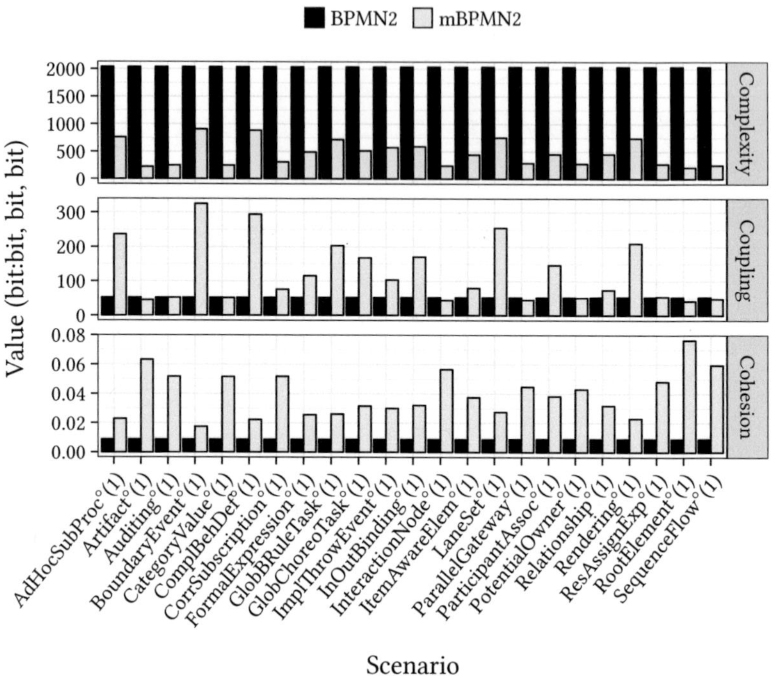

Figure 10.7.: Evolvability Metric Results: BPMN2 (based on [HSR19])

No reliable reference values can be provided for complexity and coupling that would represent good values. This evaluation, however, uses the metrics to compare the original versions of the metamodels to their modularized versions. Thus, the absolute values of the complexity and coupling metrics are of lesser importance.

10.4.1.1. Overall

Before the individual metrics are interpreted, there are some observations that affect all three metrics.

The BPMN2 results of all metrics for the original metamodel are constant over all scenarios. This is the case, as the package of the main metamodel

Result Group Name	Scenarios
PCM	
AllocationContext	MultiAllocation
CallAction	ReleaseAction
ComLinkResType	SchedulingPolicy
ForkedBehaviour	ResourceDemandingBehaviour, SyncPoint
KAMP	RequiredDelegationConnector
ProcResSpec	ResourceEnvironment
ResSign	ResourceInterfaceProvidingEntity
Smart Grid Topology	
AbstractType	NetworkNodeType
AddCoordinates	NewCommEntity
Cluster	OutputEntityState, ScenarioResult
NewPhysicalConn	SmartMeter
KAMP4aPS	
Arm	Entity, MonostableCylinder, PneumaticNetwork, VacuumGripperModule
BusMaster	ConveyorBelt, MechanicalAssembly, Panel, Ramp, ReturnSpring, TurningTable
ComponentRepository	ModuleRepository, ParentEntity, Plant, Structure
DocuApplication	DocumentationFiles, FoAARepo
HWPropagation	ModifyModule, SeedMods

Table 10.8.: Evolvability Evaluation Result Groups

module of the original BPMN2 is very large. As it is dependent on all other metamodel modules, this leads to the whole metamodel to always be included in the subgraph.

There is a similar effect with the results for the PCM. Although it is not as extreme as with the BPMN2, as the AllocContext and IntBIIS scenarios deviate from the majority of the results. In contrast to the BPMN2, the classes of the PCM are distributed over much more packages. It is to be suspected that the many dependency cycles of the PCM cause the subgraph to subsume all classes that are involved in the cycles. All except two scenarios seem to include these big dependency cycles.

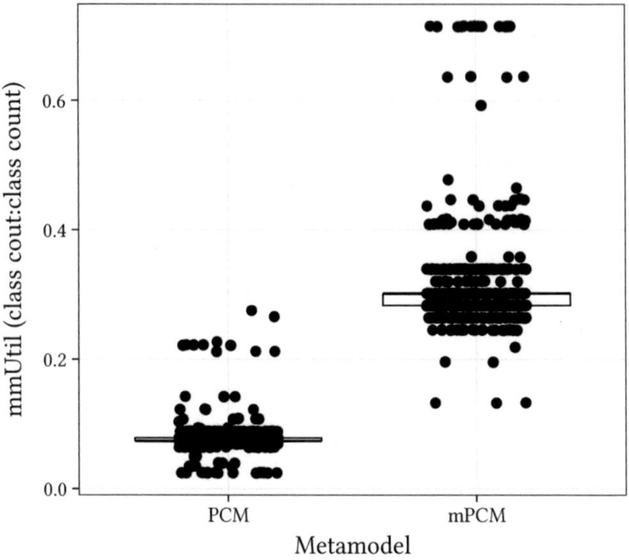

Figure 10.8.: Utilization: PCM (based on [HSR19])

There is one scenario of the PCM that stands out. For the mPCM, complexity and cohesion cannot be evaluated for the FailOccDescription. Cohesion results in a value of one for the mPCM. The reason is that FailOccDescription is the only class in its package and has no outgoing dependencies. The package contains several subpackages, but these do not contribute to the subgraph. Thus, the relevant subgraph for the scenario consists only of this one class.

10.4.1.2. Complexity

Across all case studies and for all evolution scenarios, the complexity for the modular version has decreased in contrast to the complexity for the original version of the metamodels. The only exception is the Suspension-Rack scenario of KAMP4aPS in which the values are identical for both metamodel versions.

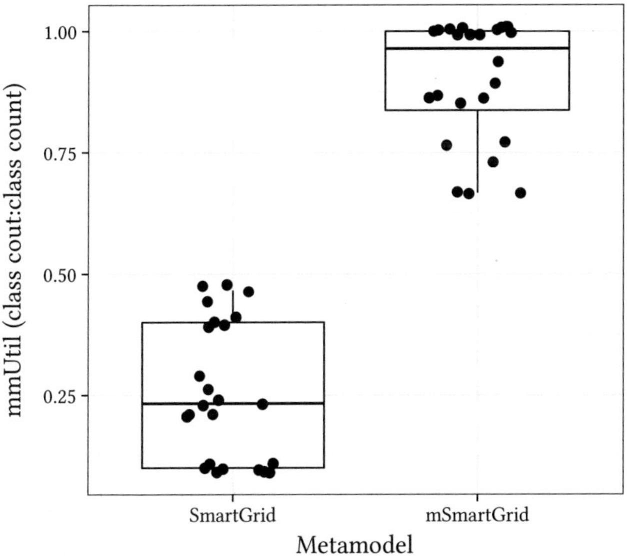

Figure 10.9.: Utilization: Smart Grid Topology (based on [HSR19])

The improvement is attributed to the constrainment of dependencies (layering, no cycles, conformance to language feature dependencies) and to slicing metamodel modules according to language features. Due to these measures, the subgraphs of the modularized metamodels include less unnecessary language features.

By enforcing a directional layering amongst the metamodel modules, meaningless dependencies that point from basic metamodel modules into more advanced ones are prevented. By applying the reference structure, such dependencies are either removed or remodeled by splitting classes and relocating them into more specific metamodel modules. This brings the potential to reduce the subgraphs of the evolution scenarios. For the developer, this indicates a decrease in the complexity of the parts of the metamodel that are relevant to the evolution scenarios. It is not meaningful to follow a dependency to a more advanced abstraction that is not essential to the abstraction that he is currently inspecting.

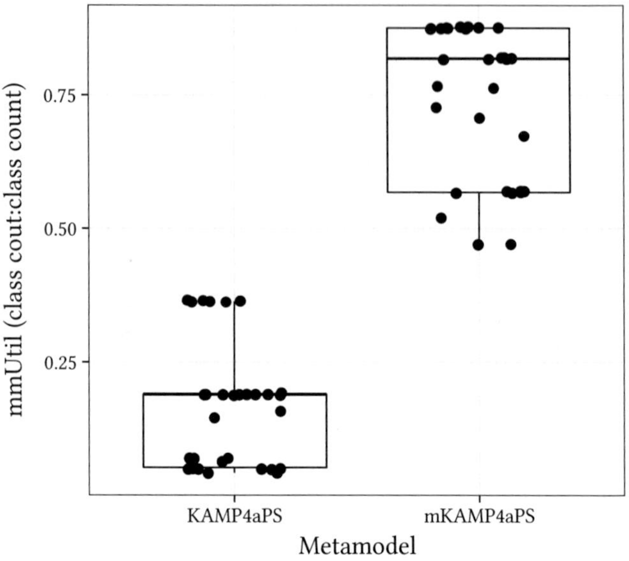

Figure 10.10.: Utilization: KAMP4aPS (based on [HSR19])

The prohibition of dependency cycles between metamodel modules also has the potential to reduce subgraph sizes. If multiple packages of several metamodel modules form a cycle, including one package in a subgraph causes the whole cycle to be included. If such a cycle is broken, the propagation of the subgraph is reduced. Dependency cycles might lead the developer to explore elements of all packages that are involved in the cycle. They usually indicate either a problem with modularization or with dependencies that violate abstraction levels. Breaking the cycle not only improves the modularity of the metamodel, but developers are also kept from exploring the cycle unnecessarily long.

The definition of language features provides necessary and sufficient dependencies as well as their directions. By forcing the metamodel module dependencies to conform to the language feature dependencies, unnecessary and faulty dependencies between metamodel modules are prevented. Subgraphs no longer propagate along such dependencies. For the developer,

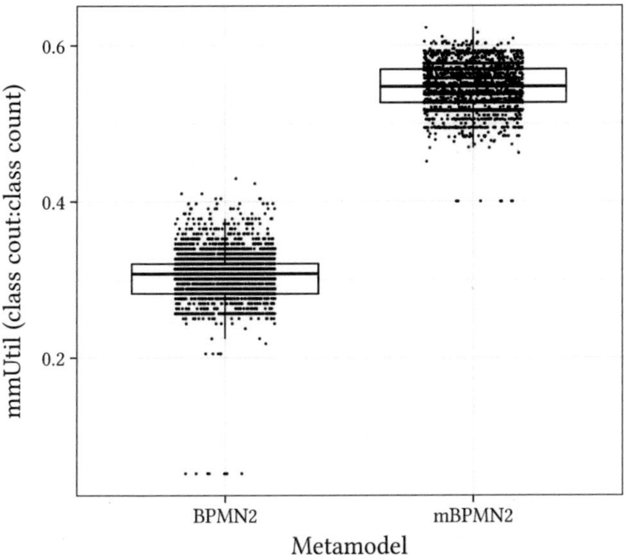

Figure 10.11.: Utilization: BPMN2 (based on [HSR19])

this means that there are less unnecessary and faulty dependencies to consider and that might lead her/him astray.

Slicing metamodel modules according to language features resulted in smaller package sizes, as before too many language features were lumped together. This also reduces the subgraphs. On the one hand, packages contain fewer classifiers. On the other hand, fewer classes mean less outgoing dependencies that might increase subgraphs further. For developers, this indicates that smaller and less complex parts of metamodels are relevant to their evolution scenarios.

The overall complexity of the modularized metamodels was not reduced. Conversely, it grew due to additional indirections and class splits. However, a less complex subgraph of an evolution scenario indicates that the complexity of the part of the metamodel that is relevant to the metamodel developer, who is working on the evolution scenario, is reduced.

10.4.1.3. Coupling

The results for the coupling metric are mixed. For the PCM, the coupling decreased for all scenarios. For the other case studies, however, there are more scenarios where the coupling increased. For Smart Grid Topology, the coupling increased in three result groups. For three result groups (AbstractType, AddCoordinates, and NewPhysicalConn), the coupling value for the original metamodel cannot be computed, as the subgraph for these scenarios consists only of one package. In these result groups, the coupling cannot be compared to the coupling of the modularized version. In the NamedIdentifier scenario, the coupling cannot be computed for both metamodel versions, as only the package of the Base metamodel module is involved in the subgraph. The coupling results for KAMP4aPS increased for seven result groups, remained constant for one result group, and dropped for five result groups. For BPMN2, the results increased in 15 result groups, remained equal in one result group and decreased in seven result groups.

The mixed results for coupling are to be attributed to different factors. Vertical module splits contribute considerably, as they turn parts of cohesion of modules into coupling. Paradigm extraction also contributes, as abstract classes are extracted and placed in another module. The resulting modules in the Δ layer are thus strongly coupled to their modules in the π layer. In some cases, the extraction of cross-cutting features contributed to the coupling, as the metamodel modules of these features contain a package structure that mirrors the structure of metamodel modules that are extended (see my paper [Str+16a]). Such structuring helps developers to navigate. These packages are strongly coupled and tend not to contain many classes and, thus, contribute more to coupling than cohesion.

In the particular case of BPMN2, the coupling for the original metamodel is very low compared to KAMP4aPS and PCM, which have a similar size. This is a result of the main package that contains all language features except the ones that are concerned with graphical diagrams. This coupling, which is rather low, is the only contributor to the overall coupling. When the main package was split, a part of the cohesion of this package was transformed into coupling which caused the growth.

Due to the dependency constraints of the reference structure approach, the effect of a higher coupling is not adverse. To explain this, two cases of package coupling have to be distinguished: coupling of packages within a metamodel module and coupling between packages of different metamodel modules.

In the reference architecture approach, package hierarchies within metamodel modules are only used for the logical structuring of classes to guide developers. Coupling of packages within a module can be viewed as a sort of cohesion within a module, especially as the packages within a module are intended to be always used together. Thus, strong coupling of packages within a module does not harm the evolvability and reusability of the metamodel, even if it is bidirectional or contains cycles. One may suspect that an increase in intra-module package coupling increases complexity and, therefore, damages evolvability. This, however, cannot be observed, as the complexity decreased across all scenarios. An increase in intra-module package coupling accompanied by the complexity remaining constant could also be obscured by a decline in cohesion. This is, however, not the case, as the cohesion increases in all scenarios.

Concerning coupling between metamodel modules, the reference architecture forbids dependency cycles. This especially includes bidirectional coupling, which is the smallest form of a dependency cycle. If in the modularized version, a metamodel module (M) is coupled to another metamodel module (N), N can indeed be used without M, but M is always intended to be used together with N.

Consequently, a strong package coupling is not a problem, if it is either package internal, or unidirectional and has been introduced by intention according to the reference architecture.

10.4.1.4. Cohesion

The values of the cohesion metric increased across all evolution scenarios of all case studies. This is attributed to the modularization according to language features. Classes that implement the same feature tend to be related more strongly. This means they have more dependencies amongst each other and less to classes of other language features. Thus, putting classes of one language feature into the same package and removing classes of other features, tends to increase the cohesion. The increase in cohesion is to be interpreted positively, as it helps developers to better and faster understand language features.

10.4.2. Need-specific Dependence and Use

For all case studies, the utilization has improved. For the Smart Grid Topology and the KAMP4aPS studies, the best utilization for the original metamodel is less than the worst utilization for the modularized metamodel. When comparing the utilization of PCM and BPMN2 for each individual model, the utilization of the modular metamodel is better than the utilization of the original metamodel. In conclusion, the metamodel utilization improved across the board after applying the reference structure approach. This is attributed to the modularization according to language features. Models contain instances of specific language features. If the structure of the metamodel supports the independent use of language features that are not dependent on each other, the metamodel utilization increases, as EMF requires only relevant metamodel modules to load the model. These positive results tell that the reference structure helps to improve the potential for need-specific dependence and use.

10.5. Threats to Validity

Section 2.5.2 presented the four types of validity in case study research according to Runeson [Run+12]: internal validity, external validity, construct validity, and reliability. This section addresses the threats to these types of validity. It refers multiple times to the raw evaluation data and sources for the case studies. These are available online[6].

10.5.1. Internal Validity

In the case studies, the metamodels were refactored according to the guidelines and constraints of the reference structure approach. The refactored

[6] `https://sdqweb.ipd.kit.edu/wiki/Metamodel_Reference_Architecture_Validation` (last visited 26.08.2019)

metamodels were then compared to the original metamodels. Modifications that are conducted during the refactoring that are not mandated by the reference structure approach may have a positive effect on the results of the refactored metamodel version. If this positive effect is then attributed to the application of the reference structure approach, this damages the internal validity of the evaluation. This is why bad smells and other design flaws that are not addressed by the reference structure were not corrected in the modularization to preserve the internal validity of the evaluation. To ensure transparency, the case study metamodels and their revision history, which reflects the refactoring process for each metamodel, are publicly available.

Another threat to validity is posed by optimizing the refactored metamodel version to produce good results concerning the metrics that are evaluated. As there is a degree of freedom in the modularization process, this may even be possible within the bounds of the constraints and guidelines that the reference structure approach imposes. This threat is addressed by conducting two evaluations using metrics that measure opposing aspects. In the evolvability evaluation complexity, coupling and cohesion are measured. It is possible to optimize after these aspects, by grouping classes together that are strongly interconnected and by reducing the degree of interconnectedness between packages. On the other side, the need-specific dependence and use evaluation measures the degree to which a metamodel is utilized by its instances. It is possible to optimize the utilization, by grouping classes together that are always instantiated together by the models. It would even be beneficial to divide a metamodel into tiny packages to increase its utilization values. This would, however, achieve very bad coupling and cohesion values. Contrariwise, optimizing for complexity, coupling and cohesion could produce bad utilization results, as using classes together does not imply a high cohesion between the classes nor low cohesion to other classes. Thus, using these dissimilar metrics addresses the threat of optimizing the refactored metamodel to improve the results of the evaluations. As with the first threat to internal validity, this argumentation is reinforced by the metamodels and their revision history being publicly available.

10.5.2. External Validity

External validity is compromised if the selection of metamodels for the case studies is not representative enough. This would mean that the reference structure approach is not applicable or not beneficial to the target range of metamodels. In the case of this thesis, the target range is metamodels for quality modeling and analysis. To address this threat, metamodels were selected that are as heterogeneous as possible. See Chapter 9 for the details of the case study metamodel selection. Metamodels were selected from different domains (information systems, smart grid, production automation, and business process) to ensure the reference structure approach is not limited to a specific domain. The evaluation results show the metamodels from all the selected domains benefit from applying the reference structure.

External validity is also compromised if merely case studies were chosen for that the reference structure approach works well. The search for case studies encountered metamodels of different degree of modularity. As it was a goal to evaluate metamodels as diverse as possible in the case studies, metamodels of varying degree of modularity were chosen. The benefits of the reference structure approach are less pronounced, the more modular the original metamodel version is and the closer the metamodel modules match the granularity and dependencies of its ideal feature model. This can be observed in the results for the KAMP4aPS and Smart Grid Topology. These metamodels were already quite modular. Thus, they show smaller improvement compared to the other case studies. Nevertheless, the results gathered for KAMP4aPS and Smart Grid Topology show clear improvements when applying the reference structure in comparison to the original metamodels. Consequently, metamodels that already had a quite modular structure also show positive evaluation results. This tackles the threat of investigating only case studies for which the reference structure approach works well.

For the evolvability evaluation, the external validity is also compromised if only evolution scenarios are evaluated, that perform well for the modularized case study metamodels. To address this threat, the evolution scenarios were selected according to a fixed process, which is presented in Section 10.2.1.2. Especially the selection of the generic modification scenarios supports fairness, as it ensures full coverage of the package structure by evolution scenarios.

10.5.3. Construct Validity

The selection of evolution scenarios for the case studies is another threat to validity. For the case studies, different types of scenarios are used as described in Section 10.1.1: historical extension, historical modification, potential modification, and generic modification. Historical evolution scenarios are considered a minor threat as they are derived from changelogs and existing extensions to the metamodels. Thus, the metamodel faced this evolution in the past. Potential modifications were derived by reviewing the metamodel and identifying potential future changes. Generic modifications were specified by randomly choosing packages that did not yet contain an affected class for an evolution scenario. The selection of potential and generic modifications might threaten the construct validity of the evolvability evaluation. However, from the evaluation results, different characteristics for potential and generic modifications could not be identified in comparison to historical evolution scenarios.

Although historical modification scenarios are considered to be more representative than other types of evolution scenarios, they may under certain circumstances pose a risk to construct validity. As explained in Section 10.2.1.3, the evolution of the metamodel from the version on which the scenario was initially performed and the version on which it is reevaluated might alter the outcome of the evolvability evaluation. This concerns the results of the version of the reevaluated version compared to the results of an evaluation on the version on which the scenario was initially performed. Preferably each historical scenario should be evaluated on the version of the metamodel on that it was executed, no earlier nor later. To be able to evaluate the reference structure, however, the metamodels have to be modularized. As such a modularization is very time-consuming, it is not practical to perform it on the metamodel version of each historical scenario. Thus, as Section 10.2.1.1 explains, the current metamodel version was chosen to be modularized. The impact of subsequent evolution is, however, only a minor threat to the evolvability evaluation of historical modification scenarios. As the evaluation of the historical modification scenario is performed on the initial and the modularized version of the metamodel, the impact of subsequent evolution applies to both versions. If subsequent evolution skews the results for one metamodel version, the results for the other metamodel version are skewed in the same direction. A further reason why the impact of subsequent evolution is only a minor threat is that by ignoring the historical background of a historical scenario, merely a generic scenario remains. The benefit of a historical scenario, which is its realism, would then be lost.

Another threat to construct validity is, the subgraphs extracted for evaluation may not be an adequate approximation for the part of the metamodel that is relevant for an evolution scenario. A further threat is that the transformation from subgraphs into hypergraphs may not map metamodel concepts to hypergraph concepts in a way that enables to measure the information size of the metamodel properly. These are minor threats, as the subgraph extraction and transformation is applied by the same mechanism on both metamodel versions. If the results for one metamodel version are skewed, the results for the other metamodel version are skewed in the same direction. Further, these two threats do only apply to the evolvability evaluation. If they turned out to damage the validity of the evolvability evaluation, the need-specific dependence and use evaluation would still be valid.

10.5.4. Reliability

If an evaluation is not reproducible by other researchers, it is not reliable. Several arrangements were met to ensure reproducibility. The evaluation tools, input and sources of the case study metamodels are publicly available. It is further explained how the evaluation tooling has to be set up, used and which exact versions were used. This information is sufficient to ensure the reproducibility of the evaluation results by third parties.

To ensure the reliability of the evaluations, the effects of interpretation by a specific researcher must be eliminated. Therefore, two kinds of metrics are applied in two evaluations (metrics based on information theory as well as the metamodel utilization metric). These metrics give reasonable evidence and reduce the need for interpretation. Due to the experiment design, there is hardly an interpretation that may lead a researcher to another conclusion.

In most cases, the results that are depicted in the diagrams, are unambiguous. Sometimes, however, the results are close enough, that they cannot be easily distinguished by merely looking at the diagram. Section 10.4.1, however, explicitly describes the tendencies of all results. In addition, the raw evaluation data may be consulted to compare the results of the original metamodels against their modularized versions.

10.6. Validation Conclusion

To address the research questions that drive the reference structure approach, Section 10.1 set up a GQM plan. Two evaluations compared the original versions of the case study metamodels to those versions that were modularized according to the reference structure. These case study metamodels are the PCM, Smart Grid Topology, KAMP4aPS, and BPMN2 (see Section 9.5).

The first evaluation is scenario-based. In total, for all case studies, 108 evolution scenarios were collected. The improvement in evolvability was inspected through metrics that take information size into account. These metrics were evaluated for each evolution scenario on the parts of the metamodel that are approximations of the parts that are relevant to the evolution scenario.

The results of the hypergraph analysis show positive results across all scenarios for complexity and cohesion. The results for coupling are mixed. The increase in coupling is justifiable because of several reasons (see Section 10.4.1). The reference structure forbids dependency cycles and bidirectional coupling between metamodel modules. It further enforces coupling based on conceptual dependencies. This means if a metamodel modules is coupled to another metamodel modules, this coupling is intended and inevitable. The increase in cohesion shows that packages group classes that are closely related and may evolve together. Considering the GQM plan of Section 10.1.1.1, it can be concluded that the modifiability of a metamodel is increased by applying the reference structure approach (**Question 1.1**).

The evolvability evaluation reported positive results for the complexity metric across all scenarios. The decrease in complexity helps metamodel developers when they try to understand and navigate a metamodel, therefore the analyzability and understandability increases (**Question 1.2** and **Question 2.1**).

Goal 1 is to evaluate the improvement of evolvability when the reference structure approach is applied. All validations questions of **Goal 1** were positively answered: **Question 1.1**, which asks about modifiability, and **Question 1.2**, which asks about analyzability. Therefore, **Goal 1** is fulfilled and leads to conclude that the research question from which the goal was derived is also fulfilled. This means **RQ IIIa** (Improve Evolvability) is answered positively. The evolvability of metamodel can be improved by transferring concepts from related disciplines to metamodeling.

Goal 2 is to evaluate the improvement of understandability when the reference structure approach is applied. With the positive complexity results, all validations questions of **Goal 2** were positively answered. Therefore, **Goal 2** is fulfilled and leads to conclude that the research question from which the goal was derived is also fulfilled. This means **RQ IIIb** (Understandability) is answered positively. The understandability of metamodel can be improved by transferring concepts from related disciplines to metamodeling.

The second evaluation inspects the ratio of how much of a metamodel is instantiated by its models. This ratio is named metamodel utilization. As Section 10.1.2 argues, the utilization leads to conclude about the ability of metamodels to support need-specific dependence and selective use. Metamodel utilization was analyzed for the original and the refactored metamodel versions.

The evaluation of the metamodel utilization shows very positive results, as the application of the reference structure improved the utilization for each model that was analyzed. This answers **Question 3.1** positively. It further fulfills **Goal 3**, as it is the only question of the goal. The goal is directly derived from the research questions **RQ IIIc** (Need-specific Dependence) and **RQ IIId** (Selective Use). Both research questions are, therefore, answered positively. In conclusion, concepts from related disciplines can be transferred to metamodeling to improve the ability of metamodels to provide need-specific dependence and selective use.

Part IV.

Epilogue

11. Related Work

This chapter[1] presents work that is related to the contributions of this thesis. It is subdivided according to these contributions. Section 11.1 presents related work for the bad smell contribution. Section 11.2 presents related work for the metamodel extension contribution. Section 11.3 presents related work for the metamodel reference structure contribution. Section 11.4 summarizes the related work chapter.

11.1. Bad Smells and Anti-Patterns in Metamodeling

The bad smell contribution of this thesis provides definitions for bad smells and explains how they can be detected and corrected. By correcting bad smells, the quality of metamodels can be improved. Related work to this contribution can be grouped into approaches that deal metamodeling errors and flaws (Section 11.1.1) and approaches that deal with metamodel quality (Section 11.1.2).

11.1.1. Metamodeling Errors and Flaws

Bettini et al. [Bet+19] present an approach to metamodel quality improvement by bad smell treatment. They link bad smells to metamodel quality aspects. This allows goal-driven metamodel improvement regarding the quality aspect on that should be focused. They present automatic detections

[1] This chapter is in parts based on my previous publications [Str+15; SH16a; Str+16a; HSR19; KS18; Com+18].

and corrections for five smells from my past publication [Str+16a]: Duplicate Features in Sibling Classes, Dead Class, Redundant Container Relation, Classification by Enum, and Concrete Abstract Class. The detection and corrections are implemented in the Edelta language [Bet+17]. Edelta is a DSL for the specification of refactorings. The correction of smells is realized by model weaving and Edelta operations. They evaluated their approach on ten metamodels. They first injected a bad smell, corrected it automatically, and observed how several metrics behaved. The observed metrics were maintainability, complexity, understandability, and reusability. If the correction improved the metrics, the correction was judged as a success. In contrast to the work of Bettini et al., this thesis presents new metamodel-based smells.

EMF Refactor [Are14; AT13] is a tool that can be used to automatically detect bad smells and perform refactorings in Ecore-based metamodels and UML models. It is explained in more detail in the foundations (Section 2.2.9). EMF Refactor features several UML class diagram design smells, which were also considered in the literature review to find bad smells that are transferable to EMOF metamodels. For Ecore, EMF Refactor provides only a few automated smell detections (Large EClass, Speculative Generality EClass, Unnamed EClass). Unnamed EClass is not even a proper bad smell, but a simple validity error. Compared to the number of bad smell detections that EMF Refactor features for UML, this number is insufficient. The bad smell contribution of this thesis builds on EMF Refactor by extending it by further bad smell detections for Ecore.

Elaasar [Ela12; EBL11] developed an approach for automated detection of patterns and anti-pattern in MOF-based models. His approach provides a ready to use catalog with patterns specifications but also supports the creation of new pattern specifications by the user. His MOF anti-patterns are grouped in the categories well-formedness, semantic and convention. In contrast to the smells that are presented in this thesis, the anti-patterns mostly resemble validity errors or are too fine-grained to be design-level bad smells.

López et al. [LGL14b] propose a language to specify metamodel properties and the tool metaBest to evaluate such properties on metamodels. In their paper, they provide a catalog of properties. They categorize the properties in: design flaws, best practices, naming conventions and metrics. The properties either detect anti-patterns or breaches of thresholds for the following metrics: number of attributes per class, degree of fan-in and -out, depth of inheritance tree and the number of direct subclasses. The metaBest tool does not operate directly on EMOF but is kept metalanguage-independent to increase its range of application [LGL14a]. Different metalanguages can be supported by providing transformations from the metalanguages to the metamodeling concepts of metaBest. Several of their properties are mere validity errors in Ecore (e.g., no overridden inherited attributes, upper multiplicity bound is not zero). They are not relevant to this thesis.

Three properties that are proposed by López et al. [LGL14b] report constellations that are not harmful in EMOF. As this paragraph elaborates, they should not be reported as problematic. Property D10 states that "No class contains one of its superclasses, with cardinality 1 in the composition end (this is not finitely satisfiable)" [LGL14b]. In general, such constructs are meaningful. They are used, e.g., in the Decorator pattern [Gam+95], where a concrete decorator contains its superclass with a lower and upper multiplicity bound of 1. BP03 states "There is a root class that contains all others" [LGL14b]. In general, multiple root classes may exist in a metamodel (e.g., PCM [Reu+11]). On the contrary, an extension metamodel may not need a root class at all. This is, for example, the case if new subclasses are added to the base metamodel. BP04 states "No class can be contained in two classes" [LGL14b]. This is unproblematic in general, and even best practice for second-class concepts that are used in many places. An example from the PCM is the RandomVariable class. For a second-class concept, the existence of its instances is dependent on the first-class concept which uses it (e.g., a process or a usage model). For this reason, it is not meaningful to deposit them in only one central container and reference them where they are needed. If this were the case, they would exist independently of their container. It is better to contain RandomVariable from every class that needs a random variable. Further counterexamples for BP04 are the Composite pattern [Gam+95] and the Decorator pattern [Gam+95]. In addition to the containment from the metamodel that uses the pattern to the pattern's superclass, a Composite and Decorator both contain the already contained superclass.

As discussed in Section 4.4, metaBest already provides four smells of the bad smell contribution of this thesis. There are further properties that are similar to three smell. Even though their contribution overlaps with this thesis, the bad smell contribution of this thesis features 15 smells that are not covered by metaBest. In contrast to this thesis, they do not give reasons why a property has negative ramifications. This manifests in several properties that are, at least in EMOF, not beneficial to enforce. This was explained in the previous paragraph. This thesis, on the contrary, provides the reasons for the presented bad smells being harmful. It also performs an evaluation, in which the detection results were inspected for their harmfulness, to further affirm their negative effects.

Gómez et al. [GBS12] propose an approach, which aims at evaluating the correctness of a metamodel; i.e., whether it allows invalid instances (preciseness) and whether it can express all instances it is supposed to (expressiveness). Their approach automatically generates a preferably small set of instances to evaluate these two criteria. Ferdjoukh and Mottu [FM18] propose a related approach in which correctness is tested by instantiating models with expected multiplicity counts. Failing to instantiate means there is a semantic error.

The approaches of Gómez and Ferdjoukh are related to the bad smell contribution in the sense that they detect problems in metamodels. As they focus on semantic errors and the bad smell contribution focuses on design flaws, the approaches of Gómez and Ferdjoukh are not in competition with this thesis. They can even be applied in conjunction to improve metamodels.

11.1.2. Metamodel Quality Metrics

A goal of the bad smell contribution of this thesis is to improve the quality of metamodels. Section 2.2.6 presents further information on metamodel quality. The approaches described hereafter propose metamodel metrics to investigate metamodel quality and are, therefore, related. The bad smell contribution of this thesis, on the other hand, pinpoints specific spots in metamodels that should be improved. Therefore, both types of approaches are not in competition. They can be applied cooperatively to analyze and improve the quality of metamodels.

Metrics, in general, do not provide a direct evaluation of the quality of a metamodel. Some metrics can provide indicators for good or bad metamodel quality if they are correctly interpreted. This is done by Vépa et al. [Vép+06]. They present a repository for metamodels, models, and transformations.

They apply metrics that were initially designed for class diagrams onto metamodels of the repository. The applied metrics are: several size metrics (as a basis for other metrics), depth of inheritance tree (DIT), several number of features per class metrics, number of inherited attributes and attribute inheritance factor. For some of the metrics, Vépa et al. provide a rationale of how they relate to metamodel quality.

Di Rocco et al. [Di +14] applied metrics onto a large set of metamodels. Besides the usual size metrics, they also feature the number of isolated classes and the number of concrete immediately featureless classes. Further, they searched for correlations of the metrics among each other. E.g., they found that the number of classes with a superclass is positively correlated with the number of classes without features. Based on the characteristics they draw conclusions about general characteristics of metamodels. Their long-term goal is to draw conclusions from metamodel characteristics concerning the impact onto tools and transformations that are based on the metamodel. Although an assessment of metamodel quality is not their main focus, some metrics they apply can be used to assess the quality of metamodels.

García et al. [GGF09] developed a set of domain-specific metamodel quality metrics for multi-agent systems modeling languages. They propose three metrics: availability, specificity, and expressiveness. These metrics take domain knowledge into account, e.g., the "number of necessary concepts" or the "number of model elements necessary for modeling the system of the problem domain".

There is much work on quality metrics for object-oriented design and UML class diagrams [CK91; Mar98; MGP03; Gen+07]. Further, there are publications that present empirical analyses of object-oriented design metrics [BBM96; SK03]. E.g., Subramanyam found that the correlation between metrics and bug detection varied when applied to different programming languages and observed interactions between metrics. Metamodeling and object-oriented design have many commonalities. On the other hand, the purpose and usage of object-oriented design and class diagrams are very different compared to that metamodels. Thus, their benefit cannot be assumed for metamodels. Section 1.3 elaborates on the differences between metamodeling and object-oriented design.

11.2. Metamodel Extension

This thesis explored metamodel extension mechanisms that are unintrusive, provide instance compatibility, and enable the independent development of extensions. Publications that explore and survey metamodel extension mechanisms are considered as related work to this contribution.

Mechanisms that enable the addition of class properties are not considered to be related work. They are subjects of the evaluation that is presented in Chapter 8. Some mechanisms were not considered in the evaluation, as they do not fulfill the required criteria of Section 5.3. These dismissed mechanisms are presented in Section 5.5. The section also discusses why they are not considered. It also discusses the completeness of the list. The dismissed mechanisms are transformations [CH03; MG06], completions [Hap+14], aspect-oriented modeling (e.g., [KAK09]), language composition approaches for metamodel-based languages (e.g., Melange [Deg+15], metamodel merging [ES06; Léd+01], template instantiation [ES06]), Architectural Templates [Leh18], the Role pattern [Küh17], and Braun's mechanisms [BE15b; Bra17] (Hooking, Aspects, Plugins, and Addons).

There are several frameworks that practice language reuse through different types of language composition. Such approaches are intrusive, do not provide instance compatibility, or even both. They are presented in Section 11.3.1, as they are more closely related to the reference structure contribution of this thesis.

Braun [Bra15] conducted a literature study about the extensibility of enterprise modeling language. In contrast to this thesis, he did not focus on EMOF-based mechanisms. He investigated metalanguages and languages that are related to enterprise modeling. MOF is amongst the metalanguages, but no EMOF-specific mechanisms are mentioned. He mentions the in-built annotation mechanism that allows the addition of unstructured data to the metamodel (EAnnotations). For EMOF, however, this mechanisms does not influence the model level (without the generator being aware of the annotations). He further proposes a classification of extension purposes and extension mechanism types.

Braun wrote his doctoral thesis [Bra17] about the extensibility of enterprise modeling languages. As there was an overlap in the time frames in which his and my thesis were developed, some of the findings overlap. As both theses are closely related, his thesis will be discussed in detail. In the following, first, the commonalities are explained. In these parts, my research confirms his findings. The release of his dissertation, however, opened the possibility to build on his findings and go into detail where he did not. Thus, secondly, it is briefly explained in which aspects this thesis presents novel findings.

Both works overlap in two dimensions: extension mechanisms and comparison criteria. Braun also investigates the extension mechanisms Direct Inheritance, Profiles, and Decorator. As comparison criteria, he also uses Applicable without Preparation, Multiplicity, and Metalanguage Support.

In contrast to Braun, this thesis pursues a different scope. Focusing on EMOF-based languages, allows this thesis to specify comparison criteria that are more tailored to this scope. This thesis also focuses on unintrusive mechanisms, as intrusive mechanisms do not tackle the problems of monolithic metamodels and metamodel erosion. In addition to the extension mechanisms of Braun, this thesis investigates Referencing with External Container, Referencing with Reused Container, Extension Point Inheritance in two variants, and the Decorator pattern in several new variants. Regarding comparison criteria, this thesis adds Model Level Unintrusiveness, Content Retrieval Computational Complexity, Applies to Subclasses, Orthogonality, Containment Tree Integrity, Model File Integrity, Extension Object Deletion, and Adds a Type.

Happe et al. [Hap+14] present their experiences with the extension to performance modeling languages. They discuss model completions, intrusive additions, external extension by dependency, and EMF Profiles. External additions are, however, only presented superficially without going into detail about possible realizations. Model completions do only improve a model. They do not affect the metamodel.

Atkinson et al. [AGF13] investigated modeling language extensibility. Their insights are metalanguage-independent. They provide a classification with two dimensions: extension use-case and extension strategies. The two use cases are as follows. In language enhancement, the language is extended by information from the domain of the language. In language augmentation, the language is extended by information that does not belong to the same domain. The tree extension strategies are orthogonal to the use cases. Metamodel customization corresponds to intrusive addition in the terms of this thesis. Built-in extension mechanisms are supported by the metalanguage. Model annotation is realized by modifying the models (e.g., by weaving). For EMOF, they did not present any built-in extension mechanisms. As stated in Chapter 5 of this thesis, no built-in extension mechanisms are directly supported, but several extension mechanisms can be realized by using the means EMOF provides. Atkinson et al. identified several shortcomings of the extension strategies. They propose Deep Modeling (also named Multi-level Modeling) to be used as a modeling framework to solve these problems. In contrast to the extension mechanisms that are presented in Section 5.4 of this thesis, Deep Modeling in itself, however, does not solve Problem 9 (Incompatible Extensions) and Problem 8 (Instance Incompatibility).

Degueule et al. [Deg+17] propose the concept of model types. Models may conform to one or several model types and can be manipulated and dynamic semantic accessed through these types. Model typing is, however, no option to replace extension mechanisms. The reason for this is that without metamodel extension, there has to be a metamodel that supports all model types. This metamodel (see also VSUMM from Section 11.3.1.1) has all the problems of a monolithic metamodel that erodes over time. Further, it is not clear how existence modifications (see Section 2.2.5) behave when they are performed through model types. Deletions of container that carries data that is not visible in the current model type might lead to data loss. When additions are performed, and a model is valid for the current model type, there may be mandatory features still missing for other model types.

Jiang et al. [Jia+04] present a classification of UML extensions. They present four levels of increasing expressiveness. When transferred from the conceptual view of the paper to a technical realization, their levels of metamodel extension are either intrusive additions of classes and class properties (level 1), and intrusive or external additions of classes and subclasses (level 2 to 4). Similar results can also be achieved with the UML stereotyping extension mechanism, which, however, is not supported by MOF nor EMOF. In contrast, this thesis is focused on EMOF-based extension mechanisms.

11.3. The Reference Structure Approach

Work that is related to the metamodel reference structure contribution of this thesis can be subdivided into several fields. Section 11.3.1 presents related language engineering and language composition approaches. Section 11.3.2 presents the software product line concept and related language product line approaches. Section 11.3.4 presents approaches that structure and dissecting modeling spaces. Section 11.3.3 presents approaches that deal with metamodel modularity. Section 11.3.6 presents metamodel quality assurance approaches. Section 11.3.5 presents works that deal with metamodeling patterns. Section 11.3.7 presents approaches that tackle the coevolution of metamodels and related artifacts. Section 11.3.8 explains the choice of terminology that is used in this thesis.

11.3.1. Language Engineering

The reference structure approach uses the metamodel extension mechanisms to establish modularity and reuse in metamodeling. Approaches from the language engineering community reuse and compose languages and language fragments to create new DSMLs and are therefore related work. These approaches can be subdivided into metamodel- and grammar-based approaches. Metamodel-based approaches are more closely related to the reference structure contribution. In the following, first, the COLD approach is presented, which is a conceptual vision that encompasses grammar- and metamodel-based solutions. Second and third, metamodel-based (Section 11.3.1.1) and grammar-based approaches (Section 11.3.1.2) are presented and discussed. Fourth, Section 11.3.1.3 discusses Deep Modeling approaches. As there are metamodel- and grammar-based Deep Modeling approaches, they are located in a separate section. Language product lines, which are presented in Section 11.3.2, are very closely related to the language engineering approaches that are presented in this section.

The COLD [Com+18] (Concern-Oriented Language Development) initiative, in which I participated, represents a vision to language reuse. It provides concepts and methods to support holistic language reuse. The conceptual part is independent of the approaches that implement it. Its implementations may be metamodel- or grammar-based. In [Com+18], the approaches that are presented to support the COLD approach are the GEMOC Studio [CBW17], MontiCore [HR17], and Neverlang [VC15]. These approaches are further investigated in the remainder of this section. A language concern is a configurable unit of reuse that provides multiple perspectives of a language. A perspective is the definition of a part of a language on the meta-metalevel (e.g., abstract syntax, concrete syntax, static semantics, or apart of a modular tool). A perspective may refer to one or multiple metalanguages (e.g., meta-metamodels) and relate them. A facet is the instance of a perspective and is constituted by one or multiple artifacts depending on how many metalanguages its perspective entails. An artifact is an instance of a metalanguage, e.g., an Ecore metamodel or a grammar. A language concern features three interfaces. The variation interface presents a feature model to select the configure the desired features of the concern. The customization interface provides an extension-point-like to concretize feature of the language. The usage interface provides the means to instantiate the language concern.

The reference structure aims mainly at realizations of the abstract syntax perspective (i.e., abstract syntax facets). COLD is, therefore, much broader. The reference structure approach is, therefore, not in competition with the COLD vision. In addition, this thesis focuses on language-feature-based metamodel decomposition, compatibility-preserving metamodel composition, and domain guidance to metamodel implementation. The reference structure approach may be adjusted to fit into the concepts and processes of the COLD approach. This is, however, out of the scope of this thesis and is, therefore, future work.

11.3.1.1. Metamodel-based

The *GEMOC Studio*[2] [CBW17] provides a language workbench and a modeling workbench for executable models. Relevant to this thesis is the language workbench aspect. It provides several features like capabilities to define animations of executable semantics, generation of execution traces, and support to provide further metamodel-based tooling.

Relevant to this thesis is the *Malange* [Deg+15] approach that is part of the GEMOC language workbench. Melange is an approach to a modular

[2] `http://www.gemoc.org/studio` (last visited 23.08.2019)

and reusable development of DSMLs by combining and subtyping existing DSML artifacts. It handles syntax and semantics. The following only addresses the syntax aspect, as this is the focus of this thesis. Melange provides the following language operators: merge, inherit, and slice. Reuse is mainly established through merge or inherit. Regarding the syntax of a language, the merge operator adds the classes of one metamodel to another. Classes that have identical names are merged. This means after the merge they contain the properties from both classes. The inherit operator functions like the merge operators; it, however, ensures that the sub-language is still compatible with the parent language. This denies some possibilities of a merge. For example, it is not allowed to merge mandatory properties into a class.

Concerning the challenges this thesis addresses, there are some reasons why this thesis cannot build on the Melange approach. By using the language operations, the approach creates new metamodels. It does not ensure instance compatibility. By adding new classifiers or properties to an existing metamodel, the instances of this extended metamodel are no longer compatible with the original tooling. This drawback is somewhat relieved by the fact that Melange provides the same operations for interpreter pattern based tooling. So at least such tooling can be reused. What is even more critical, however, Melange does not provide independent extensibility. If a metamodel is extended by inheritance by two other metamodels, these two extensions cannot be used in conjunction without having to create a third extension that extends the first two extensions. Another hindrance to independent extensibility is the power of the merge operator. E.g., an extension using merging may be incompatible with another extension if they specify classes with the same name which represent different concepts. The resulting collision makes it impossible to use the conflicting extensions together. One workaround is to rename the conflicting class of one extension, which would be against the principle of independent extensibility.

Leduc et al. [LDC18] present an approach for the composition of language concerns that also allows the composition of particular dynamic semantics. The approach is integrated into the Ecore-based ALEX metamodeling framework, which supports the definition of dynamic semantics. By composing language concerns, using their approach, abstract syntax and semantics are composed. This concerns their specification and implementation. Their approach proposes explicit interfaces for the composition of dynamic semantics.

In contrast, the reference structure approach focuses on the abstract syntax of a language. On this level, the reference structure approach does not need implementation level composition, as a metamodel (i.e., abstract syntax) extensions also extend the implementation level. The approach of Leduc is currently not focused on offering any modularization or structuring guidelines regarding the larger structure of a modular language. Nor does it specialized on a specific application domain. Both approaches could, however, be used in conjunction. The reference structure provides guidance on how to modularize and build the larger structure. Metamodel modules could be realized as language concerns. This would enable the composition of semantics within an instance of the reference structure.

CORE (Concern-Oriented REuse) [Sch+16; AKM13] is an approach to software development with a strong focus on reuse. A software program is composed of configurable concerns. A concern from the CORE approach features interfaces that are similar to those of COLD (see Section 11.3.1), as COLD was influenced by CORE. Through the variation interface, the feature of a concern can be selected. The fragments that are associated with the features are then woven together by a model weaver.

Although aimed at software development in general, the CORE approach is metamodel-based. It works similarly to projectional editing in class diagrams. The difference to the reference structure approach is that its focus is on software development in general. Although configurable metamodels can be realized using the CORE approach (see a diploma thesis [Kan17] that was supervised by me), it has some drawbacks that prevent it from being used as a foundation of the reference structure approach. Regarded as an extension mechanism, the core model weaving is intrusive, does not offer instance compatibility, and does not support independent development of extensions (see Section 5.3 and Section 5.6).

Vitruvius [Kra+15; KBL13] is an approach to view-based modeling. It enables to couple several metamodels into a Virtual Single Underlying Metamodel (VSUMM). The metamodel should at least partly describe the same concepts. The instances of the VSUMM metamodels are synchronized by special transformations. They form the Virtual Single Underlying Model (VSUM). The user operates on the VSUM through views [Bur14]. Views are defined by view types, which are technically metamodels with synchronizing transformation into to the VSUM.

The goal of Vitruvius is to construct a holistic virtual metamodel from legacy models. In contrast to the reference structure approach, it does not offer any structuring guidance for a specific domain. The two approaches, however, can complement each other. Once the VSUMM is constructed, the Vitruvius approach has a maintenance problem. If the metamodels of the VSUMM evolve, models, transformations, view-types, and all view-based tool have to evolve in order to stay functional. By applying the reference structure approach, the VSUMM could be evolved into a more modular form. Future additions to the VSUMM should use external extension mechanisms when possible. This could improve the evolvability of the VSUMM.

JetBrains MPS [VS10] is language workbench with a focus on domain-specific programming languages. It enables the extension of languages. Even GPLs like Java or C can be extended. This is handled by transforming the extension into the GPL's code. DSLs can be developed separately or as an internal DSL in a GPL. For DSLs that are developed with MPS, projectional editors are provided. In contrast to a parser-based editor, a projectional editor does in general not allow the user to input arbitrary text. Through autocompletion, only a valid string can be entered which fits the current context in the code. By integrating several existing DSLs in a new DSL or an extension of a DSL, MPS allows the composition of languages.

In contrast to the reference structure approach, MPS has a strong focus on programming languages. It further does not take into consideration the specifics of a possible target domain. Its focus is not on the long-term evolution of languages. The two approaches could, however, be united to bring the benefits of maintainability to the language development style of MPS.

Emerson and Sztipanovits [ES06] present several metamodel composition and reuse techniques. These include the metamodel merging, metamodel interfacing, class refinement, and their own contribution template instantiation. In contrast to the other composition techniques, template instantiation can be performed multiple times within a metamodel. The focus of their contribution is different from the reference structure approach. It provides no structuring guidance considering a specific domain. It does not strive to form a common basis for related languages, that would provide partial instance compatibility. Template instantiation can, however, be used in combination to the reference structure approach to reuse paradigm patterns.

11.3.1.2. Grammar-based

There are language workbenches and language engineering approaches that are grammar-based. For this thesis, their capability of language composition or language extension is relevant.

MontiCore [KRV08; HR17] is a workbench for language-based grammars. It supports the development of language components and modular languages. Amongst others, MontiCore provides support for parser generation, analyses, and transformations. MontiCore supports several language composition methods [Völ11; Hab+15]. Language extension is enabled by language components featuring external nonterminals, which can be seen as extension points. Languages can also reference each other. This enables language inheritance, aggregation, and embedding. Through language inheritance, new nonterminals can be added, and existing nonterminals can be redefined. In language embedding, a language completely reuses one or more already existing languages. This can also be achieved by redefining nonterminals to inject a language into another. Language aggregation is similar to language embedding. It is, however, less thorough, as, for example, the concrete syntax is not automatically composed. MontiCore also supports modularity of the infrastructure of a language. There is support for the compositionality of visitors, symbol management, context conditions, editors [But+18a] and generators [But+18b].

As an additional extension mechanism, tagging languages [Gre+15] can be used. A tagging language is a separate language, which also enables the separation on the instance level (extended instance vs. tagged information). This helps to keep the original language definition and the original models clean. The tagging language is specific to the language that is extended. This means that in contrast to a generic tagging language, a new tagging language has to be developed for each DSL that ought to be extended. The effort can, however, be alleviated by generating as much of the language infrastructure of the tagging language as possible.

Neverlang [VC15] is a grammar-based programming language development framework. It supports modular development of languages. A slice defines a feature of a language. A slice contains several roles (e.g., syntax, type-checking and evaluation). Based on a language's slides, Neverlang composes the infrastructure of the language (e.g., a compiler or interpreter).

In contrast to the reference structure approach, grammar-based language engineering approaches provide no guidance towards structuring or modularizing a language regarding the specifics of its domain. Both types of approaches reside in different technology space (i.e., grammar-based vs. metamodel-based). It is, however, likely that these approaches may benefit from each other. The reference structure approach could benefit from the advantages of the grammar-based world. Examples for such advantages are the ease of language extension and support for programming languages. The reference structure approach may provide incentives on structuring and improving the maintainability of large modular language structures. As both types of approaches are conceptually quite different, this may be an endeavor of considerable effort.

11.3.1.3. Deep Modeling

Deep Modeling approaches [LG10a; AG16; Hin16b] enable the modeling of multiple instance layers by the user as well as the language developer. EMOF, in contrast, does only offer the model layer (M1) to the user. The metamodel or grammar layer (M2) is developed by the language developers (e.g., metamodel developers). This poses some challenges when the user should model more than one instance level. For example, the metamodel developer wants users to be able to model their own data types and also be able to model instances of these data types. The instance relation from the data type instances to their data type has to be modeled by a reference, which is a workaround that does not enable regular type checking.

There are several Deep Modeling approaches. Melanee [AG16] is a metamodel-based approach that is compatible with EMF. When defining a class in Melanee, the graphical syntax of the instances of the class can be specified [AG13]. This makes separate editor generation or development unnecessary. NMF [Hin16b] is a metamodel-based approach for the .Net Framework. In contrast to the other approaches, NMF does not need explicit instance layers [Hin16a]. MetaDepth [LG10a] is a grammar-based approach.

Deep Modeling usually blurs the border between the metamodel or grammar layer (M2) and the model layer (M1). Part of the language should be frozen or hidden in order to be protected from the meddling of users. Some deep modeling approaches feature potencies. For classes, they specify how long an instantiation chain starting from a class can get. On attributes and their values, the potency specifies how many instantiation levels the attribute is carried over and when it can be modified. Some deep modeling approaches feature the refinement or specialization of references. On a lower instance level, the target types of references can be further limited.

In contrast to the reference structure approach, Deep Modeling proposes another way to partition a language: along with the type/instance borders. The reference structure approach does not support multiple instance levels, as a shortcoming of its metalanguage EMOF. This is where the reference structure approach could benefit from Deep Modeling, as it enables the user to model as many instance level as necessary. Deep modeling can be especially beneficial for the definition of paradigm patterns. By refining the references of a paradigm pattern in the domain layer, the classes that are involved in the pattern can be limited to that of a specific domain. The reference structure approach, on the other hand, brings the benefit of language structuring, extensibility, and improved evolvability.

De Lara and Guerra [LG10b] propose the adoption of reuse mechanisms from generic programming for deep modeling. Concepts specify requirements onto dynamic semantics. Templates enable the reuse of patterns that are parametrized with Concepts. Mixin layers are Templates that are applied on the metamodel level. They provide an implementation for the deep modeling framework MetaDepth. Their focus lies strongly on parameterized reuse. The reference structure approach, however, uses reuse by language extension, which assures instance compatibility between the extended and the original language.

11.3.2. Software and Language Product Lines

The reference structure approach of this thesis uses feature models to express the variability of a modular metamodel. A selection of features is instantiated by merely deploying the desired metamodel modules. Software Product Lines (SPLs) [WL99; CN01] are related in the sense that they also provide variability in the functionality of the software. Of particular interest to this thesis are SPL approaches that either work on models or languages.

SPLs are used to handle families of software. In a family, software products have common parts but differ in so-called variation points. If each software product is maintained individually, this multiplies the maintenance effort. The SPL community aims to tackle this problem by consolidating software families, modeling their variability and generating variants. There are approaches that offer automatic extraction of variability models from related software artifacts [Fon+15; Kla14; KKW14; KKK13]. Possible ways to model variability are feature models (see Section 2.4), MontiArc^{HV} [Hab+11] for component-based software, the Common Variability Language (CVL) [Hau+08] for MOF models, and Clafer [BCW11]. The variability models are linked with fragments of software artifacts. The result is sometimes refered to as a 150 percent model [Grö+08], as it contains more functionality than needed for one software product. From such 150 percent models, a software product can be generated by combining the fragments according to the desired selection of the variability specification.

The following approaches are software product lines that either work on models or put forward explicit language product lines (LPLs). Méndez-Acuña et al. [Mén+16b] present a survey such LPLs.

Font et al. [Fon+15] propose an automated extraction of a variability model from a family of models. The variability and model fragments are specified in CVL. The CVL then allows a materialization of a model according to the desired variability selection.

MontiCore [HR17] supports the composition of independently developed modeling languages as well as of language components [But+18b; But+18a]. Syntax, as well as semantics, can be composed. The composition is configured by a language product line. The selection of the product line configures the template-based code generation of the language infrastructure.

On first glance, the concepts of SPLs seems to fit the problem of variability of metamodels, which this thesis addresses. Some SPL approaches even work on MOF models (e.g., [Fon+15]) and can be used to produce a family of metamodels. The variants, however, do not feature partial instance compatibility for the parts the metamodels have in common. Nevertheless, this thesis picks up the useful concept of variability modeling that was made popular by the SPL community.

11.3.3. Modularity, Modularization, and Clustering

The reference structure approach proposes modularization concepts for metamodels. It provides modularization guidelines for the development of new metamodels and the refactoring of legacy metamodels. It also enforces a structuring of a modular metamodel according to its language features. In these aspects, several works are related that are concerned with modularization concepts and metamodel modularization.

Degueule et al. [DCJ17] motivate language interfaces, which abstract the different constituents of a language (abstract and concrete syntax as well as semantics). Similar to model typing, several languages could provide the same language interface. Tools could operate on interfaces and by doing so operate on arbitrary languages that conform to the interface. They are thus no longer bound to a single language. Interfaces could be used for language composition, as required and provided interfaces.

If such interfaces are developed, they have to fulfill some requirements in order to be applicable in the scope of the reference structure approach. These are similar challenges as with model typing. They would have to ensure independent extensibility, instance compatibility, and model manipulation through an interface should not lead to data loss or invalid models. A modular language should also be able to provide several interfaces if it expresses several language features.

Méndez-Acuña et al. [Mén+16a] present Puzzle, which is an approach to treat clones in metamodels. A clone is a part of a metamodel that has been reused by copy and paste. Puzzle features the search for clones and can extraction them into separate metamodels. These can then be reused. The tool refactors the original metamodels by cutting the mutual part out and creating dependencies from the remainders of the original metamodels. Puzzle is related to the reference structure, as it is used to modularize metamodels. It does, however, not guide the modularization or structuring of single metamodels. It may, instead, be used if language families should be consolidated into a single modular metamodel that conforms to the reference structure.

Strüber et al. [SST13] propose to use clustering to modularize large metamodels. The clustering algorithm optimizes cohesion and coupling. High cohesion within a cluster and low coupling between clusters are desired.

The approach also takes the different types of relations into account (reference, containment, inheritance).

In contrast to the clustering approach of Strüber et al., the reference structure approach modularized a metamodel according to its language features. A division according to coupling does not necessarily reflect the parts of a metamodel that are used together (see Section 10.4). Clustering may initially be a good starting point for a modularization or might assist the metamodel developers in modularization decision. It should, however, not be used as the final state of the modularization of a metamodel.

Further work by Strüber et al. involves an approach [Str+14] and tools support [SLT14] for model and metamodel splitting. It uses information retrieval techniques that operate on natural language descriptions of the model or metamodel. Similarly to Strübers clustering approach, information retrieval can provide a good initial proposal for the modularization of a metamodel. It, however, does not achieve a meaningful coupling of the modules. To do so necessitates knowledge about the relations of the language features that the metamodel provides and involves dependency refactorings like, e.g., dependency inversion (see Section 6.5.1.2).

Strüber et al. present a concept [Str+13b] and implementation [Str+16c] for composite models. Composite models are motivated by the needs of distributed modeling and are inspired by component-based software development. It proposes to supply metamodels with export and import interfaces. These interfaces can be used on the model level. An import interface refers to the export interface of another model. An export interface can be referred to by multiple import interfaces. The remainder of the models is encapsulated, which establishes information hiding [Par72] as known from software development.

Although the interfaces of the composite model approach can also be used to split metamodels into metamodel components, it is not the focus of the approach to guide the metamodel developer in the structuring and modularization of a metamodel. In this regard, the reference structure and the composite model approach can be combined. The reference structure provides guidance and improved evolvability on the metamodel level; the composite model approach provides modularity and information hiding on the model level.

EMF Splitter [Gar+14] provides an approach to modularity on the model level. A metamodel is annotated with the modularization concepts Projects, Packages, and Units. These are based on well-known concepts from IDEs like projects, folders or packages, and files. The instances of the annotated metamodel (i.e., models) are persisted according to the annotation of the modularity concepts. This helps to tackle the problem of large models.

Although EMF Splitter could be applied to metamodels (metamodels are models, too), it is not intended for this purpose. Metamodels are usually small compared to models. Thus, the benefit of the approach would be small. Even if used for metamodels, EMF Splitter would merely enforce multiple metamodel files. More important is a meaningful logical structuring, which is not in the scope of the tool. The tool and the reference structure approach, however, can be used in combination. The reference structure improves the evolvability of metamodels. EMF splitter keeps model files small.

The modularity of the semantics of a language is a whole file of research in itself. The reference structure approach focuses on the abstract syntax of a DSML. Approaches for semantic modularity could be integrated or aligned with the reference structure approach. Duran et al. [Dur+17] propose a formalism to compose language modules and their semantics. The mechanism is implemented in the e-Motions DSL, which is used to specify time-dependent behavior [RDV09]. Regarding the abstract syntax of the language, however, the approach is intrusive and does not ensure instance compatibility. They also propose to make the specification of non-functional properties reusable [DZT13]. Moreno-Delgado et al. [Mor+14] reimplemented a part of the PCM and the Palladio Simulator using their approach. Further approaches to modular semantics are presented by Liang [LH96] and Mosses [Mos04]. Liang and Hudak present a monadic approach to modular dynamic semantics of programming languages. Mosses proposes modular structural dynamic semantics for concurrent systems and programming languages.

A further related topic is the modularity and extensibility of metamodel-based tools. This overlaps partly with the research field of modular semantics, if interpreters, simulators, and analyzers are considered. Jung [JHH16; Jun16a] proposes a composition approach for generators. Rentschler developed an approach for modular transformations [Ren15]. Föhrdes [Föh14] presents a modularization of EventSim into simulation components. EventSim [MH11] is a performance simulator, which operates on the PCM. Although the modularity of his solution is not as flexible as the modularity of metamodels that is achieved by the extension mechanisms of Chapter 5, his solution provides improved extensibility compared to the monolithic version of EventSim. These approaches are interesting, as they deal with artifacts which are used in conjunction with metamodels. However, theses modularization approaches cannot be directly transferred onto metamodels.

11.3.4. Approaches for Structuring and Dissecting Modeling Spaces

The reference structure approach provides an explicit structure to the high-level module structure of modular metamodels. It divides the modeling space of a metamodel into levels of different abstraction (paradigm, domain, quality, and analysis). This helps developers to navigate existing modular metamodels, to place their extensions, and to structure new modular metamodels. In this regard, approaches that propose explicit structuring and divisions of modeling spaces are related to the reference structure approach, even if they are not applicable to metamodels.

Atkinson et al. [ASB10] propose the Orthogonal Software Modeling (OSM) approach. A software model is accessed through views that correspond to coordinates in an orthogonal space that is spanned by several dimensions. These dimensions include: abstraction level, encapsulation, projection, and language. Similarly to the reference structure approach, OSM dissects the modeling space for software modeling. By doing so, it provides the software modeler a structure to navigate the software model. It is, however, aimed at software models and not applicable to metamodels.

Coad's UML archetypes [Coa99] for object-oriented design are used to classify classes into things, temporal concepts, roles, and descriptions. The UML archetypes are, therefore, related to the reference structure approach in the sense that they divide the design space of classes into the provided categories. This provides developers information that would not be there otherwise and gives them an aid when designing classes. Although UML archetypes have been devised for classes of object-oriented design, they can be applied to classes in metamodel when they are appropriate. In the scope of the reference structure approach, the classification according to the archetypes takes place within metamodel modules. UML archetypes and the reference structure approach are, therefore, not in competition but complementary.

Siedersleben [Sie04] proposes a reference structure for software architectures, where components are categorized into so-called blood types (technical, domain, and library). Similarly to the previously mentioned approaches, the blood types propose a division of the modeling space. As metamodels do not feature technical or library content, the blood types do not apply to metamodeling.

11.3.5. Metamodeling Patterns

The reference structure approach promotes reuse of parts of DSMLs. The paradigm layer (π) defines domain-independent patterns and constructs. Therefore, works that propose patterns or metamodel construction through pattern instantiation are related to the reference structure approach. Such patterns can be provided in metamodel module repositories to enable their reuse in the scope of the reference structure approach.

Pescador et al. [Pes+15] propose pattern-based development of DSMLs. They propose a taxonomy of patterns into: domain patterns, design patterns, concrete syntax patterns, dynamic semantic patterns, and infrastructure patterns. Patterns are configurable through role cardinalities and feature models. Their approach is supported by a tool, which is named DSL tao. It composes not only the abstract syntax of patterns but also services and graphical syntax. It is, however, not applicable in the scope of the reference structure approach, as they do not focus on providing partial instance compatibility between languages that share the same patterns.

Cho and Gray [CG11] present several metamodel design patterns. These include classifier and relationship, typed relationships, and container. Emerson and Sztipanovits [ES06] propose the metamodel design patterns: compositionality, components and ports, state charts, data flow graphs, the Proxy design pattern.

More patterns can be found in the classic sources for object-oriented design (e.g., Gamma et al. [Gam+95]). Not all of these patterns can be directly transferred to metamodeling. Most will have to be adapted to fit into the containment tree of a metamodel. Others may not apply to metamodels at all.

11.3.6. Metamodel Quality Assurance

The reference structure approach of this thesis provides guidelines and constraints on the modularization and design of metamodels in order to increase their quality. In the metamodeling research community, several approaches deal with metamodel quality assurance. Their goal is also to increase the quality of metamodels. Quality assurance approaches include metamodel quality metrics, error and bad smell detection, and correctness analysis. Quality assurance approaches were already presented in Section 11.1.

In contrast to quality assurance approaches, the reference structure contribution takes a proactive approach. By prescribing structure guidelines, constraints, and modularization concepts, it prevents unfavorable metamodel structures. Quality assurance approaches, on the other hand, detect problems after they manifested. Thus, quality assurance approaches are not in competition to the reference structure from this thesis. They rather complement each other and can, therefore, be employed together during metamodel development and maintenance.

11.3.7. Coevolution

The reference structure approach of this thesis promotes a modularization of legacy metamodels. Considerable research was conducted towards evolving a metamodel together with the artifacts that are based on the metamodel. Artifacts that can be coevolved include models, transformation, generators, and software in general. Coevolution approaches do not offer guidance in metamodel evolution, structuring, or modularization. They are, however, useful when a legacy metamodel is modularized and adjusted according to the reference structure. The effort for migrating the metamodel-based artifacts to the new version of the metamodel is significantly reduced or even entirely automated.

Favre [Fav03] presents an overview of the dimensions of coevolution. Herrmannsdörfer and Wachsmuth [HW14] present a survey of model metamodel coevolution approaches. Burger and Gruschko [BG10] evaluated the metamodel modification types considering whether they break the instances (i.e., models) of a metamodel. Burger and Toshovski [BT14] present an approach to difference-based conformance checking for metamodels. Other approaches are based on the logging of metamodel modifications. Their approach, however, analyzes two arbitrary metamodels and needs no further information. A metamodel M1 conforms to another metamodel M2 if all instances of M1 are also instances of M2. Their approach can be used, e.g., to determine whether coevolution effort is even necessary. Levendovszky et al. [Lev+14] propose the Model Change Language (MCL) [Nar+09] and a tool that performs model modifications according to specifications in MCL. Cicchetti et al. [Cic+08] propose an approach to automatic coevolution that is based on automatic transformation generation. As input, the approach needs a recorded difference model of the evolution that took place in the metamodel. Herrmannsdoerfer also presents COPE [HBJ09; Her11b], which is an approach to the coupled evolution of models and metamodels. In COPE, metamodel modifications are recorded together with their respective model migration operations.

11.3.8. Terminology in Related Approaches

Related language engineering approaches bring forth their terminologies. This section elaborates, why this thesis defines some new terms in Section 6.3 instead of relying on existing terminology.

The language workbench MontiCore [HR17; KRV10] uses the terms *language components*, and *component grammars* to address the abstract syntax definition of language components. This thesis uses the term of modules instead of components, as a metamodel module cannot be instantiated multiple times (in contrast to the component concept from Component-based Software Development [Reu+16]). Of course, it is possible to have multiple other metamodel modules depend on a metamodel module M, but on the type level, M is the same from the perspective of all dependent metamodel modules. In the scope of the Concern-oriented Language Development (COLD) approach [Com+18], a language concern is a configurable unit of reuse that provides multiple perspectives (abstract & concrete semantics, ...) of a language. Thus, in the terminology of COLD, this thesis aims mainly at realizations of the abstract syntax perspective (i.e., abstract syntax facets). This thesis still uses the term metamodel module, as it more strongly conveys that modularization takes place and the individual pieces are only puzzle pieces in the big picture. In addition to explicit dependency control, this is also the case why this thesis does not merely refer to them as metamodels as Degueule does in his approach [Deg+15].

Based on the general meaning of feature in the context of software, this thesis uses the term language feature as a unit of use. The term abstract syntax facet from COLD is not used to emphasize this aspect. By using the term language feature, the separation of the language part, i.e., the abstraction of a thing to be modeled, from its implementation in a metamodel module is emphasized.

11.4. Conclusion

This chapter discussed work that is related to the contributions of this thesis. For the metamodeling bad smells contribution, these are metamodel quality assurance approaches. Works that survey metamodel extension mechanisms are related to the metamodel extension contribution. Related to the reference structure contribution are language engineering, metamodel modularization and modularity, metamodel quality assurance, metamodeling patterns, and coevolution approaches. The remainder of this section summarizes the differentiation of these contributions from their related work.

The bad smell contribution of this thesis is related to other metamodel quality assurance approaches, as they are all concerned with improving the quality of metamodels. Quality assurance approaches can be categorized into approaches that detect bad smells and errors in metamodels, as well as works that investigate metamodel quality using metrics.

Metric-driven quality approaches strive to assess the quality of metamodels in order to assess changes and track the quality throughout evolution. The bad smell contribution of this thesis, on the other hand, detects concrete spots in metamodels that should be improved. Therefore, both approaches have different takes on improving quality. They can, however, be applied in combination during the evolution of a metamodel.

Approaches that detect problems in metamodels are more closely related to the bad smell contribution of this thesis. In the bad smell contribution, a specific subset of metamodeling problems, namely bad smells, is investigated. The contribution presents a catalog of EMOF-based bad smells and examines their consequences. Some related approaches have a different focus. They detect semantic or mere validity errors or do not work for EMOF. Other related approaches only offer implementations of known metamodeling smells. They do not present any evidence nor discussion on why the bad smells that they treat are detrimental.

In the metamodel extension contribution of this thesis, lists of extension mechanisms and comparison criteria were assembled. The extension mechanisms were evaluated regarding the comparison criteria. Works that survey metamodel extension or related mechanisms are, therefore, related.

Such works, however, do either not focus on EMOF, or another kind of focus compared to the metamodel extension contribution. Some include mechanisms that merely modify models and do not enable the modeling of new information. Others provide mechanisms that do not implement external additions as the presented mechanisms are intrusive, do not offer instance compatibility, or independent extensibility. Some only mention mechanisms without any evaluation or in-depth discussion.

The closest related work for the metamodel extension contribution is the dissertation of Braun [Bra17]. It was partly developed in parallel to this thesis. This thesis confirms a part of his findings. It does, however, not focus on EMOF-based unintrusive mechanisms. This allows this thesis to set up more specific comparison criteria. In addition to Braun's findings, four new extension mechanisms with several variants and eight new comparison criteria are presented and evaluated.

The reference structure contribution of this thesis is related to language engineering, and language product line approaches. The commonalities are language reuse, composition, and variability. The related approaches, however, are either not applicable to metamodels, or do not ensure instance compatibility and independent extensibility. In contrast to the reference structure, it is also not their focus to guide modularizations to improve maintainability, and also do not consider domain specifics.

The reference structure approach proposes metamodel modularity concepts, enforces modularity in metamodels, and guides metamodel modularization and design. In these aspects, the reference structure approach is related to metamodel modularization and clustering approaches, and modularization concepts for metamodels and related artifacts. Some metamodel splitting and clustering approaches do not consider the usage of the language. Such modularizations, therefore, do not enable need-specific use and reuse. These approaches also do consider domain specifics. Other approaches do not apply to a single metamodel but extract commonalities from a set of metamodels. This is not the scope of the reference structure approach. It, however, can be used in conjunction if a family of metamodel should be consolidated. Other approaches do not focus on abstract syntax. They, therefore, do not provide independent extensibility, and instance compatibility. Further works provide modularity concepts but do not offer any guidance in modularization. Lastly, there is much work on the modularity of artifacts that are related to or based on metamodels. This is not the scope of the reference structure but should be considered complementary.

The reference structure approach, as well as metamodel quality assurance approaches, strive to improve the quality of metamodels. Quality assurance approaches, on the one hand, support metamodel development reactively. They warn if problems in the metamodel are detected or a quality indicator drops below a threshold. The reference structure approach, on the other hand, enforces modularity and provides guidance to prevent problems in metamodels proactively.

In the paradigm layer of the reference structure, patterns can be defined to be reused in higher layers. There are also other works that propose patterns. The two types of approaches have in common that they endorse reuse and more specifically pattern reuse. Some works simply offer patterns. These can be reused within the scope of the paradigm layer of an instance of the reference structure. Another approach offers intrusive pattern instantiation. It can be used in the scope of the reference structure approach. However, only in the initial design of the paradigm layer, as its goal is not to produce a variable metamodel that offers instance compatibility.

The reference structure approach proposes a process to modularize monolithic legacy metamodels. Coevolution approaches are related, as they investigate the evolution of a metamodel. They also support the automatic or at least semiautomatic evolution of artifacts that are based on the metamodel. They do not offer guidance towards structuring or modularization of metamodels as the reference structure approach does. The automatic coevolution of metamodel-based artifacts is out of the scope of the reference structure approach, which focuses on metamodels. Coevolution approaches can, however, be applied in combination with the modularization of a legacy metamodel.

12. Conclusion

This chapter presents the conclusion of the three main contributions of this thesis. Each contribution is summarized, and it is explained how it addresses the challenges that Chapter 3 presented. Limitations and future work are also presented for each contribution. Section 12.1 contains the conclusion for the metamodel bad smell contribution. Section 12.2 concludes the metamodel extension contribution. Section 12.3 presents the conclusion for the reference structure approach.

12.1. Bad Smells and Anti-Patterns in Metamodeling

This section concludes the metamodel bad smells contribution. Next, Section 12.1.1 summarizes the contribution and addresses its research questions. Section 12.1.2 addresses its limitations. Section 12.1.3 presents future work.

12.1.1. Summary

The chapter of the metamodel bad smell contribution first defined the underlying concepts of metamodel problems: validity error, semantic error, and design flaw. In contrast to these three, a bad smell indicates a potential problem. The indicated problems mostly impair maintainability and are, thus, design flaws. For some bad smells, the cause is a semantic error. A bad smell has an indicator according to which it is identified. According to Arendt [Are14] the indicator of a smell can be a metric violation or an anti-pattern.

RQ Ia (Bad Smells) from Section 4.1 asked what types of problems impair the evolvability of metamodels. In the scope of this contribution, nineteen bad smells for EMOF-based metamodels were collected. These smells were either discovered through a metamodel review of the PCM or found and transferred to metamodeling from a literature review of object-oriented bad smells. None of these sources guarantee an exhaustive discovery of metamodeling bad smells. However, they complement each other. The identified smells mainly concern the appropriateness of abstraction, modularization, inheritance hierarchies, and relations between classes.

Five of the presented smells are exclusive to metamodels. The three modularity smells amongst these five smells, do also pose issues to object orientation. However, as object orientation places another focus on modularity, these smells are minor issues there.

RQ Ia (Bad Smells) also asked for the effects of the bad smells. Thus, for each smell, the effect of a harmful occurrence is discussed. Some smells add unnecessary complexity. Others impair understandability by obfuscating design decisions or the intended structure of the metamodel. Some have negative effects on coupling and cohesion of packages and metamodel files. The causes of these smells are design flaws that have detrimental effects on the maintainability metamodels. Three smells always indicate semantic errors, if an occurrence is not benign. Occurrences of four other smells may include a semantic error as their cause.

RQ Ib (Smell Identification) asked how the smells could be detected and which of them could be detected automatically. For each smell, its detection was explained and whether it can be performed automatically. An automatic detection is possible for 17 smells. For 12 smells, an automatic detection was implemented. For two of these smells, the detections of two variants were implemented, which results in a total of 14 implemented detections. This was done by extending the metamodel quality assurance tool EMF Refactor [Are14].

RQ Ic (Smell Resolution) asked how the smells can be corrected. For each smell, corrections were presented. Two smells can be detected and fixed in a fully automated way. The 15 other automatically detectable smells cannot be automatically resolved. Either the correction cannot be performed automatically, or their detection suffers from false positives, and, thus, the detection results have to be manually reviewed so that no benign occurrences are fixed.

To evaluate the metamodel smell contribution, an explorative study was performed. First, the implemented smell detections were performed on the PCM. The resulting occurrences were inspected for their correctness to evaluate the detection implementations. This, however, does not ensure that the detection does not miss any occurrences. To achieve this remains future work. The reported occurrences were also inspected for their harmfulness to evaluate whether a smell can indicate improvement potential. Harmful smell occurrences were identified and corrected for 12 smell detections. Twenty-five corrections were performed to evaluate the corrections of 13 detections. The benefit of the correction for the metamodel was argued. The positive effect of the correction can be seen as a deficit that is caused by the smell's occurrence. Regarding the harmfulness of the smells, this thesis, however, can only argue for plausibility. The explicit validation of the effect of smells remains future work. After each correction was executed, the smell detections were rerun to investigate whether the correction was successful. All corrections removed the smell occurrence that was targeted. This demonstrates the effectiveness of their correction type in curing the respective smell.

The metamodel smell contribution yields several insights that are valuable for this thesis as well as to metamodeling in general.

First of all, it answers the question of why monolithic metamodels are bad, which addresses Problem 3 (Monolithic Metamodels). Between the packages of a metamodel, new dependencies can be created without limitation. Monolithic metamodels are especially at risk. In monolithic metamodels, it is tempting to generously introduce new dependencies as no constraints have to be considered. They are, thus, prone to smells that include unnecessary or inconsistent dependencies. This includes especially the smells Inconsistent Abstraction and Dependency Cycle.

The second important insight of the metamodel smells contribution is the knowledge about the negative consequences of intrusive addition. This addresses Problem 1 (Package Structure Erosion and Uncontrolled Growth of Dependencies). Through intrusive addition, new abstractions are added to the metamodel. To just add new metamodel elements to the most relevant parts of the metamodel may seem the easy option. With this approach, however, the enforcement of modularity is often not taken into consideration. When concepts are developed iteratively, they are first lumped together with related concepts and then modularized as soon as they have reached a sufficiently large size. In the initial development, the boundaries of the abstractions are often sufficiently present to the developer as s/he is usually working on it in a confined period. Intrusive additions over time, on the other hand, may be performed with longer pauses or by different developers. Thus, it is more likely that it is overlooked that a modularization should be performed.

A further problem of intrusive additions is the following. No matter how good the initial structure of a metamodel may be, if new abstractions are added intrusively, the structure may be either forgotten or misunderstood. If new abstractions are added inconsistently to the existing packages and classifiers regarding the boundaries of concepts and their abstraction, the structure of the metamodel and its understandability suffer. Metamodels that are subject to repeated intrusive additions are, therefore, prone to smells that concern modularity and abstraction levels. This includes the smells Inconsistent Abstraction, Language Feature Scattering, God Classes, and Blob Packages.

The beforehand described problems get even worse in combination. As they do not present a modular structure, monolithic metamodels are prone to intrusive additions. Over time, the problems of unnecessary and inconsistent dependencies and inadequate modularity build up.

The consequences of bad smells are even worse if the metamodel is long living, is evolved and the smells accumulate without being fixed. Metamodels tend to live in metamodel-centric software systems. Many tools, like editors, analyzers, and simulators, are built upon them. If the metamodel is changed, all tools have to be fixed. The effort caused by resolving smells in the metamodel increases over time, as new dependencies pile up. Thus, smells should be fixed as early as possible.

To proactively counter bad smells, several countermeasures are possible. Metamodels should be designed in a more modular way. Monolithic metamodels should be considered for modularization. With standard EMOF, however, it is not always straightforward how to divide abstractions. Therefore, the next contribution (Chapter 5) deals with new ways to couple metamodel files. The insights of Chapter 5 can further be used to counter the adverse effects of intrusive additions by instead performing external extension. A modular metamodel also needs an explicit structuring to be hardened against degradation over time, which is caused by loss of knowledge and ignorance for the structure. This is where Chapter 6 proposes its solution by a layering according to levels of abstraction and using an explicit way to express the module structure and the relations between the modules.

For each smell, this section explained how it might come into being. Some smells are built in by mere carelessness or lack of knowledge. Therefore, knowledge of these metamodel smells is very valuable to metamodel developers. Other smells, however, do only manifest with time, when multiple evolution steps have been performed (some of them in a shortsighted manner). Thus, it is beneficial to include regression testing into continuous integration. With every new change to the metamodel that is committed to the source repository, the smell detection should be executed. If new smells occur, a warning should be generated. In addition, it can be beneficial to generate a report of all smell occurrences. It can also be beneficial to flag persisting smells that are benign as such. This way, they do not have to be considered every time the report is inspected. From time to time, however, it might be worthwhile to consider even the smells that are flagged as benign, as the context of the occurrence might have changed, and the occurrence could have turned into an adverse one.

12.1.2. Limitations

This thesis focuses on EMOF-based metamodels. Section 1.1 gives the rationale behind this decision. Therefore, the metamodel smell contribution also focuses on bad smells of EMOF-based metamodels.

Metamodel developers that work on metamodel to correct bad smells need expertise in metamodeling, and the necessary domain knowledge to understand the metamodel. This expertise and knowledge are necessary to judge whether a smell is harmful and to decide which type of correction is suited. This is, however, not a bigger requirement than what is imposed on metamodel developers in order to do plain metamodeling. The detection, on the contrary, makes them more efficient and reduces their required knowledge about the bad smells.

12.1.3. Future Work

Future work to the contribution of metamodel bad smells includes the discovery of further smells. They may be found in reviews of other metamodel reviews and further transfer from object orientation or other related disciplines. Sometimes, bad smells can be formulated merely from experience, e.g., during metamodeling when a metamodel developer notices that a particular constellation is detrimental.

The effect of smells can be further validated. This could either be done by correlating smell occurrences to metamodel metrics, manual quality assessments, or by conducting user studies. A validation by a correlation to metrics is, however, always only as valid as the metrics that are used. In a user study, for example, metamodel comprehension or how well an evolution scenario is performed could be measured. The results of a metamodel without a smell occurrence could be compared to a version of the metamodel with the occurrence.

Further future work entails the determination of proper thresholds for the metric-based smell detections. By manually inspecting metamodels, sensible thresholds could be determined. This is, however, not scientific. For scientific sound values, the thresholds have to be validated. This validation could be performed analogously to the validation of the negative effect of smells, i.e., correlations to metamodel quality metrics or by user studies.

Future work also entails automation tool support. Detections for the remaining smells that can be automatically detected can be implemented. Fully automated resolutions could be implemented for the smells that allow automatic detection, automatic resolution, and are always beneficial to correct. The current tool support (EMF Refactor) would also benefit from an API that allows headless execution, e.g., for automated regression tests. A more ambitious task is to develop a guidance system that presents possible corrections for smell occurrences that were found to the metamodel developer. By selecting a correction, the system could automatically perform the changes necessary to resolve the occurrence.

In the evaluation, some smells were not completely covered. For the Wide Hierarchy detection, the evaluation goal G1 was not evaluated, as it did not yield any harmful occurrences. Dead Classifier (Dead Enum) did not yield any occurrences, and, thus, G1, G2, and G3 were not evaluated. G1 is concerned with the meaningfulness of the definition of a smell. G2 is concerned with the correctness of the smell's detection. G3 is concerned with the appropriateness of the correction of a smell. By conducting further evaluations on other metamodels, harmful occurrences should be searched for these two smells to evaluate the missing evaluation goals.

The evaluation of the metamodel smell contribution evaluates only the corrections that were performed. In general, there may be several types of corrections for one smell. In future studies, all corrections options can be evaluated.

12.2. Metamodel Extension

This section concludes the extension mechanism contribution. Section 12.2.1 summarizes the contribution and draws conclusions regarding the challenges of Chapter 3. Section 12.2.2 recaps its limitations. Section 12.2.3 presents future work, which builds on the contribution.

12.2.1. Summary

Section 5.1 poses several challenges for metamodel extension. One of them is the clarification of the addition type concept, which is presented in Section 5.2. Additions can be intrusive, branched, or external. An addition can either be a new subclass or a new class property to an existing class. External additions of properties can be implemented in several ways. These are the extension mechanisms that were investigated in the evaluation.

The metamodel extension contribution addresses the following challenges, which were presented in Section 5.1 and Chapter 3. Of course, the contribution addresses Problem 7 (Metamodel Coupling), as it thoroughly investigates ways to compose modular metamodels. All extension mechanisms that were investigated provide the means to couple metamodel files without being intrusive. This is ensured by the selection criterion S1 (Unintrusiveness). They, therefore, enable modularity of metamodels and prevent several problems that were stated by Problem 3 (Monolithic

Metamodels) and Problem 1 (Package Structure Erosion and Uncontrolled Growth of Dependencies). By using the presented mechanisms, it is possible to factor out optional parts of classes and metamodels into optional external extensions. Problem 1 is also addressed by the Applicable without Preparation comparison criterion. Extension mechanisms that require preparation cause minimal erosion, if their prerequisites are not already fulfilled. Extension mechanisms that require no preparation cause no erosion. Problem 8 (Instance Incompatibility) is addressed by the Model Unintrusiveness comparison criterion and by the selection criterion S2 (Instance Compatibility). S2 ensures that the extensions do not cause insurmountable incompatibility of extended models to the original tooling and metamodel. If the Model Unintrusiveness comparison criterion is not fulfilled for an extension mechanism, technical workarounds have to be implemented in order to support the forward compatibility of the original tools and metamodels. Problem 9 (Incompatible Extensions) is addressed by the Orthogonality comparison criterion. All extension mechanisms except Direct Inheritance support the criterion. Metamodel extension enables to form a common base for related languages and to separate abstract and specific metamodel parts. This paves the way for the third contribution (see Chapter 6) of this thesis to address Problem 4 (Commonalities in Related Languages), Problem 5 (Tool-specific Metamodel Content), Problem 6 (Generality Compromise), and Problem 10 (Feature Overload in Metamodel-based Tools).

Section 5.1 specifies the single research question that drives the metamodel extension contribution. **RQ II** (Extension Mechanism Comparison) asks about the advantages and disadvantages of the metamodel extension mechanisms. In this evaluation, six extension mechanisms (11 variants in total) were evaluated according to 11 comparison criteria. No extension mechanism dominates the others in all comparison criteria. They instead have different advantages and shortcomings. These cannot be weighted against each other so that no single score can be computed for the extension mechanisms. They rather are suited for specific circumstances. Some extension mechanisms even complement each other. A decision support of how to select an appropriate extension mechanism can be found in Section 8.2.2.

By using external extensions, some of the metamodeling bad smells that were investigated by Chapter 4 can be corrected. The extends relation enables two important refactorings: Dependency Inversion (Section 6.5.1.2) and Class Split (Section 6.5.1.1). These two refactorings are needed to correct several smells. Inconsistent Abstraction requires Dependency Inversion to redirect the reference that violates abstraction levels. To correct a God Class smell, a Class Split can be performed to separate concerns. To split a Blob Package, classes may need to be split to separate concerns and dependencies might have to be inverted to establish a meaningful dependency direction between the two new packages. Dependency Cycles can be fixed using Dependency Inversion or Class Splits. To split a Metamodel Monolith, Dependency Cycles that will cross the metamodel file bounds have to be fixed. The extends relation is a solution to the problem of orthogonal classification dimensions. It, therefore, helps to correct Missing Hierarchy smells.

12.2.2. Limitations

There are two sources of limitations to the metamodel extension contribution: the focus on EMOF-based mechanisms and the filtering of mechanisms according to the selection criteria (see Section 5.3). These two sources of limitations are explained in the following.

The reference structure approach, which is the main contribution of this thesis, is based on EMOF. Section 1.1 gives the rationale behind this decision. For this reason, the metamodel extension contribution is also focused on EMOF-based mechanisms. This focus, however, brings another advantage. The comparison criteria are applicable to all extension mechanisms, and essential criteria are already specified. Some comparison criteria might not apply to extension mechanisms of other metalanguages. On the other hand, extension mechanisms of other frameworks might need further comparison criteria to be evaluated appropriately. The more similar another framework is to EMOF, however, the more appropriate the comparison criteria that were specified for EMOF become.

The selection criteria of Section 5.3 were specified to tackle several problems (see Chapter 3). These criteria, of course, impose limitations on the scope of the mechanism evaluation of Section 5.4. They include unintrusiveness, instance compatibility, metamodel independence, and novelty.

12.2.3. Future Work

As stated by the limitations section, the investigated extension mechanisms are EMOF-based. Possible future work may entail the investigation of extension mechanisms of other modeling frameworks. Building on that is the strive to either create or find a meta-language that supports perfect extensibility according to the comparison criteria and that can support the reference structure approach.

Other future work aims at the second limitation, which is the focus on mechanisms that fulfill the selection criteria (see Section 5.3). By loosening those criteria, mechanisms are admitted to the evaluation, that were not yet investigated. If one is interested in, for example, intrusive mechanisms, mechanisms that do not preserve instance compatibility, or mechanisms that are specific to a metamodel, these mechanisms could be surveyed and evaluated.

A possible comparison criterion that was not evaluated is coupling (see also modularity by Braun [Bra17, p. 80]). It could still be evaluated in future work. The criterion states how strongly the extension is coupled to the base metamodel. This criterion was not prioritized in this thesis for the following reason. Some extension mechanisms require an extra extension metamodel that is referenced by the extends relation but has no reference to the base metamodel. Others do not need such an explicit extension metamodel but may use one optionally. If none is used, the extension is strongly coupled to the base metamodel. The extension, thus, cannot be used in other contexts. If a separate extension metamodel is used, the extension metamodel is not coupled and thus reusable in other contexts. Thus, an easy workaround exists, that prevents the shortcoming of strong extension coupling.

Several aspects were not in the focus of this thesis, as they are too technical. In future work, they could be investigated. These aspects are the following. The compatibility of different extension mechanisms amongst each other could be investigated. It could be investigated whether an extension mechanism allows the specification of constraints that also restrict the base models and when these constraints apply. It is unclear how compatible the extension mechanisms are with metamodel-based tools and how much additional complexity they cause in those tools. This could be investigated, for example, for transformation and editor frameworks.

12.3. The Reference Structure Approach

This section concludes the reference structure contribution of this thesis. The reference structure approach was presented by Chapter 6. It was applied to case studies in Chapter 9 and validated in Chapter 10. This section is structured as follows. Section 12.3.1 summarizes the contribution and draws conclusions regarding the challenges of Chapter 3. Section 12.3.2 states the limitations of the reference structure contribution. Section 12.3.3 discusses future work.

12.3.1. Summary

The reference structure contribution transfers concepts and best practices from related disciplines to metamodeling. It also proposes a novel approach of modularizing a metamodel according to parts that are used together. This includes restricting the dependencies between these parts to enforce a meaningful coupling. It also uses the extends relation from Chapter 5 to assert the dependency inversion principle. The contribution addresses several of the bad smells that were identified in Chapter 4. The addressed bad smells are mainly those that cause lacking modularity and rampant coupling. The contribution also features the first reference structure for metamodels of the field of quality analysis to improve their compatibility and reuse.

The reference structure approach proposes the concept of language features. A language feature is a unit of use. This means, it is always used as a whole and expresses the smallest possible concern of a user. The language features of a metamodel are captured in a feature model. A feature model serves several purposes. When instantiating models, the tool user can select the language features he wants to use. Developers use it to navigate the metamodel, as it provides a high-level overview. More specific, metamodel developers use it to place new extensions properly. Features are implemented by so-called metamodel modules. This enforces fine-grained modularity and separation of concerns. A metamodel module is quite similar to a metamodel file. The difference is, however, that dependencies to other metamodel modules have to be declared explicitly. With mere metamodel files and packages, new dependencies can be introduced, without any restriction, between packages that were not related before.

In long-living metamodels, this may lead to unnecessary couplings and poor understandability. The need to declare module dependencies explicitly forces metamodel developers to act more consciously when they introduce new dependencies. Module dependencies are constrained through several factors. The feature model defines what dependencies are allowed between metamodel modules. For example, a parent relation allows a module dependency from a module of the child feature to a module of the parent feature. An additional constraint is that no cycles are allowed between metamodel modules. To be able to implement these dependencies as prescribed, it is necessary to use the metamodel extension relation to realize dependency inversion. The reference structure approach also adopts the concept of layers. The features and modules of a metamodel are partitioned into layers, which further restrict module dependencies. Dependencies are only allowed within the same or to more basic layers. This decouples the more abstract layers from the more specific ones. The concepts and constraints of the reference structure approach are supported and enforced by a tool, which is named the Modular EMF Designer. To provide a technical foundation, Appendix B maps the concepts of the reference structure approach onto EMF and presents the Modular EMF Designer.

The concepts and constraints that were mentioned earlier apply to metamodels in general. The reference structure contribution also provides a specific reference structure for metamodels from the field of quality analysis. It is a layering template for creating, reusing, and extending metamodels from that field. To capture reoccurring themes in quality analysis metamodels, the approach proposes four layers: fundamental patterns and concepts (paradigm); domain information, structure, and behavior (domain); quality properties (quality); as well as analysis information and state (analysis). The patterns from the paradigm layer can be reused in other domains. Upon the domain layer, one or more quality characteristics can build. On the quality layer, analysis modules can be based. This decouples the modules according to their specificity. Domain modules should be free of quality information, as there could be multiple quality dimensions. Quality modules should be free of analyzer information, as there may be multiple analyzers.

The reference structure approach also provides three application processes. They guide the design of new modular metamodels, the refactoring of legacy metamodels to conform to the reference structure, and the extension of modular metamodels. Several refactorings that are essential to apply the approach are provided. These fall into three categories: class refactorings, module refactorings, and feature model refactorings.

In conclusion, the reference structure approach addresses several of the challenges that Chapter 3 and Section 6.2 presented. The restriction of dependencies addresses Problem 1 (Package Structure Erosion and Uncontrolled Growth of Dependencies), as it prevents dependency proliferation and, thereby, unwanted coupling. The modularization according to language features addresses Problem 3 (Monolithic Metamodels), as it induces fine-grained modularization. The layered feature model provides an explicit structure, which reduces erosion (Problem 1) and the loss of knowledge (Problem 2: Loss of Knowledge) over time. By utilizing the metamodel extensions, the reference structure approach also addresses the following problems. As it enables to establish common bases for language families, it addresses Problem 4 (Commonalities in Related Languages). This is done by creating extension metamodel modules for language features that are specific to a single language. Common language features result in metamodel modules that are shared. For example, with the specific reference structure for quality analysis, multiple quality modules may share the same domain modules. Problem 5 (Tool-specific Metamodel Content) is also addressed, as tool content can be factored out into optional extensions. E.g., the reference structure places these extension modules in the analysis layer. By doing so, the analysis data does not clutter any quality modules, which makes them more reusable. Problem 6 (Generality Compromise) is solved by enforcing the dependency inversion principle, which decouples abstract from specific modules. For example, the more abstract paradigm modules are not dependent on any other layer. This makes them easy to reuse in multiple domains, as they do not contain any domain-specific concepts. The same is true for the domain and quality layers. As they are not dependent concepts that are beyond their specificity, they can be reused in more specific layers. On the other hand, the domain, quality, and analysis layers are specific enough to be used without any more specific layer. For example, even the domain layer can be used without quality and analysis for the purpose of quality-agnostic design and documentation. By enabling modularity in the metamodel, the reference structure approach enables the development of modular editors. When using such an editor, the tool user is only confronted with the language features, that he selected. Therefore, the reference structure approach also addresses Problem 10 (Feature Overload in Metamodel-based Tools). The selective activation or deactivation of language features may also be provided on top a monolithic metamodel by a monolithic editor that explicitly implements this variability. Such an editor would, however, be less maintainable as a modular implementation.

The reference structure approach was applied in four case studies. In each case study, a metamodel was refactored according to the guidelines and restrictions of the approach. The case study metamodels are: (1) the Palladio Component Model (PCM), which models component-based software architectures with a focus on performance and reliability; (2) a DSML to model smart grid topologies and to analyze their resilience; (3) KAMP4Aps, which is used to analyze the maintainability of automated production systems; and (4) BPMN 2, which is used to model business processes.

The four case study metamodels were inspected in two evaluations. A scenario-based evaluation analyzed whether the application of the reference structure improved the evolvability and understandability of the metamodels. A metamodel utilization evaluation analyzed whether the application of the reference structure improved the ability of the metamodels to support need-specific dependence and selective use.

In the first evaluation, evolvability and understandability were broken down to complexity, coupling, and cohesion. Several evolution scenarios were collected for the case study metamodels. For each scenario, the relevant part of the metamodel was approximated. On these parts, complexity, coupling, cohesion were analyzed using entropy-based metrics. The metrics measure the information size and are better suited than mere counting metrics. The results for coupling are mixed. This is, however, justifiable as after applying the reference structure, the coupling is one-directional, and not all the measured package coupling affects module coupling. Section 10.4.1.3 elaborates in detail why the coupling is benign. For complexity and cohesion, the results report improvements across all evolution scenarios. From these results, it can be concluded that the reference structure improves the evolvability and understandability of metamodels.

In the second evaluation, models were collected for each case study metamodel. Models reflect how the metamodel is used by the tool user and, therefore, also on which parts of the metamodel tools are dependent. For each model, the metamodel utilization was measured. The metamodel utilization is the ratio of which parts of the metamodel need to be deployed and which parts thereof are used to load a model. For all models, the metamodel utilization improved by applying the reference structure to their metamodel. Thus, it can be concluded the reference structure improves the ability of metamodels to provide need-specific dependence for tools and extensions, and selective use for tool users.

12.3.2. Limitations

The reference structure approach has two scopes. One part of the approach can be applied to metamodel-based language with EMOF-based metamodels. Section 1.1 explains the rationale behind this limitation. The concrete layering for metamodels of the field of quality analyses is, of course, only applicable to metamodels of that field.

12.3.3. Future Work

This section discusses future work for the core contribution of this thesis, which is the reference structure approach. Future work for the metamodel bad smell and extension contributions are presented by Section 12.1.3 and Section 12.2.3.

Some future work can be derived from the limitations, which the previous section presented. As the alternative to metamodel-based languages are grammar-based ones, the reference structure approach could be transferred to the technical space of grammars. The approach could also be adapted for other metalanguages. Metalanguages that enable deep modeling are interesting candidates, as they can express multiple levels of instantiation. This can be leveraged, for example, to instantiate patterns from the paradigm layer and to refine the references between the participating classes. The specific four-layered reference structure for metamodels of the field of quality analysis is, of course, only applicable to that field. New reference structure could be provided for other fields, as the remaining modularity concepts of the reference structure contribution apply to metamodels in general.

There is also future work that targets the modularization of legacy metamodels. An initial suggestion for the language features of a metamodel could be identified by analyzing a large set of its models. Classes that are instantiated by groups of models may suggest a cohesive language feature. Such an approach needs to implemented and validated. If sufficient numbers of models are not available, a clustering approach could be used as an initial suggestion for a modularization (e.g., [SST13]). Clustering according to coupling and cohesion could be investigated. It is, however, unclear if it results in a modularization that is sufficiently similar to the language features of a metamodel.

Further future work can be conducted to align the reference structure approach with related approaches. The reference structure approach could be aligned with the concepts and process of the COLD initiative [Com+18]. Work on language interfaces [DCJ17] could be transferred to the reference structure approach. Language interfaces can be used to establish information hiding and to decouple tools from specific metamodels. A deep modeling metalanguage could be used to enable the instantiation of patterns and refinement of their references to constrain their use to the proper domain classes.

The concepts and constraints of the reference structure approach can also be further developed and extended. It should be investigated, whether it makes sense to restrict the types of relations between the layers of the reference structure for metamodel from the field of quality analysis. For example, it may be wrong to specify an extends relation from a class from the domain layer to a class of the paradigm layer.

Regarding the feature model, the introduction of a new relation may be worthwhile: the feature support relation. Some features are cross-cutting. They provide extensions to other features. Such features have several implementing metamodel modules that each extend the metamodel module of another feature. This feature relation has to be implemented in the Modular EMF Designer.

Regarding the application of the reference structure, future work involves the modularization of more metamodels. Metamodels that support related concepts could even be consolidated to share a common base. Such candidates are, for example, the Palladio Component Model and the Descartes Modeling Language. Themed metamodel module repositories may be constructed by identifying reoccurring metamodel modules. The metamodel modules of a repository can then readily be reused when new related languages are created. In the future, instances of the reference structure will also be used to base further quality dimensions and analyses. For example, ongoing research on software security could be based on the modular version of the Palladio Component Model.

Metamodel-related tools, like transformation, simulators, analyses, and editors, are also involved in future work. The modularization and composition of analyses and simulators is a whole field of research by itself. If such tools could support the same modularity as metamodels, tool fragments could be bundled with their metamodel modules. As demonstrated in one of my publications [Str+16b], modular editors are possible. Prototypes for modular editors were implemented for the editor frameworks Sirius and Graphiti in a masters thesis [Jun16b], which I supervised. Future work encompasses an approach that unifies the development of modular metamodels and their modular editors. Such future work further addresses Problem 10 (Feature Overload in Metamodel-based Tools).

The tool support for the reference structure approach can be further improved. A useful new feature would be the loading or identification of metamodel modules that have incoming dependencies into the currently displayed metamodel. Such metamodel modules that were are not present in the current diagram may reside in the workspace or platform. Another new feature would be to inform the user of broken dependencies in a modular metamodel. These can currently be detected by validating the metamodel modules individually. Detection or at least tagging of abstract, root, and extension metamodel modules could also be implemented. A module context view that shows outgoing and incoming dependencies could be beneficial when working with large modular metamodels.

Appendix

A. All Bad Smell Occurrences in the PCM

This table shows all smell occurrences that were detected in the PCM in the scope of the evaluation in Chapter 7. The thresholds that were used for the detection of the metric-based smells can be found in Section 7.4. Section 7.6 explains the structure of the table.

Involved Classes	Correction No.	Harmful	Fixed	Consequence
Missing Class: Primitive Obsession (1)				
ProcessingResourceSpecification	1	✓	✓	none
Missing Class: Shared Properties (4)				
NormalDistribution, LognormalDistribution		✓		
CollectionDataType, CompositeDataType	2	✓	✓	none
InfrastructureCall, ResourceCall	3	✓	✓	−47 Dependency Cycles, −1 Container Relation, −2 God Classes
NotExpression, NegativeExpression		✓		
God Class (10)				
PCMRandomVariable	16	✓		

continues on next page

Table A.1.: Metric Occurrences in the PCM and Corrections

Involved Classes	Correction No.	Harmful	Fixed	Consequence
AssemblyConnector		×		
EntryLevelSystemCall	4	✓	✓	−58 Dependency Cycles, −2 Container Relations, +1 Multipath Hierarchy
ScenarioBehaviour	5	✓	✓	−3 Container Relations, −241 Cycles
ImplementationComponent-Type		×		
VariableUsage	17	✓		
ExternalCallAction		×		
InfrastructureCall	2, 19	✓		
ResourceCall	3	✓		
ProcessingResourceSpecification		✓		
Wide Hierarchy (2)				
Entity	6	×	✓	+16 Deep Hierarchies
AbstractInternalControl-FlowAction	7	×	✓	none
Deep Hierarchy (15)				
BasicComponent, ImplementationComponentType, RepositoryComponent, InterfaceProvidingRequiringEntity, InterfaceRequiringEntity, ResourceInterfaceRequiring-Entity, Entity, Identifier	8	✓	✓*4	−1 Multipath Hierarchy, +8 Dependency Cycles, −1 Concrete Abstract Class

continues on next page

Table A.1.: Metric Occurrences in the PCM and Corrections

Involved Classes	Correction No.	Harmful	Fixed	Consequence
BasicComponent, ImplementationComponentType, RepositoryComponent, InterfaceProvidingRequiringEntity, InterfaceRequiringEntity, ResourceInterfaceRequiringEntity, Entity, NamedElement	8	✓		
CompositeComponent, ImplementationComponentType, RepositoryComponent, InterfaceProvidingRequiringEntity, InterfaceRequiringEntity, ResourceInterfaceRequiringEntity, Entity, Identifier	8	✓		
CompositeComponent, ImplementationComponentType, RepositoryComponent, InterfaceProvidingRequiringEntity, InterfaceRequiringEntity, ResourceInterfaceRequiringEntity, Entity, NamedElement	8	✓		

continues on next page

Table A.1.: Metric Occurrences in the PCM and Corrections

Involved Classes	Correction No.	Harmful	Fixed	Consequence
CharacterisedVariable, Variable, Atom, Unary, Power, Product, Term, Comparison, BooleanExpression, IfElse, Expression		✓		
ProbabilityFunctionLiteral, Atom, Unary, Power, Product, Term, Comparison, BooleanExpression, IfElse, Expression		✓		
Parenthesis, Atom, Unary, Power, Product, Term, Comparison, BooleanExpression, IfElse, Expression		✓		
IntLiteral, NumericLiteral, Atom, Unary, Power, Product, Term, Comparison, BooleanExpression, IfElse, Expression		✓		
DoubleLiteral, NumericLiteral, Atom, Unary, Power, Product, Term, Comparison, BooleanExpression, IfElse, Expression		✓		

continues on next page

Table A.1.: Metric Occurrences in the PCM and Corrections

Involved Classes	Correction No.	Harmful	Fixed	Consequence
BoolLiteral, Atom, Unary, Power, Product, Term, Comparison, BooleanExpression, IfElse, Expression		✓		
StringLiteral, Atom, Unary, Power, Product, Term, Comparison, BooleanExpression, IfElse, Expression		✓		
PowerExpression, Power, Product, Term, Comparison, BooleanExpression, IfElse, Expression	9	✓	✓	−1 Speculative Hierarchy
NotExpression, Unary, Power, Product, Term, Comparison, BooleanExpression, IfElse, Expression		✓		
NegativeExpression, Unary, Power, Product, Term, Comparison, BooleanExpression, IfElse, Expression		✓		
FunctionLiteral, Atom, Unary, Power, Product, Term, Comparison, BooleanExpression, IfElse, Expression		✓		
DeadClass (9)				
UnitRepository		×		

continues on next page

Table A.1.: Metric Occurrences in the PCM and Corrections

Involved Classes	Correction No.	Harmful	Fixed	Consequence
DummyClass	10	✓	✓	none
ResourceInterfaceProviding-RequiringEntity	11	✓	✓	−1 Multipath Hierarchy
UsageModel		×		
Repository		×		
ResourceRepository		×		
System		×		
ResourceEnvironment		×		
Allocation		×		
Multipath Hierarchy (10)				
System, ComposedProvid-ingRequiringEntity, ComposedStructure, InterfaceProvidingRequir-ingEntity, InterfaceRequiringEntity, ResourceInterfaceRequiring-Entity, InterfaceProvidingEntity, Entity	12	✓	✓	none
ExternalCallAction, AbstractAction, CallReturnAction, CallAction, FailureHandlingEntity, Entity				

continues on next page

Table A.1.: Metric Occurrences in the PCM and Corrections

Involved Classes	Correction No.	Harmful	Fixed	Consequence
ResourceInterfaceProviding-RequiringEntity, ResourceInterfaceProviding-Entity, ResourceInterfaceRequiring-Entity, Entity	8, 11	✓		
ResourceType, ResourceIn-terfaceProvidingEntity, Entity	13	✓	✓	none
CompositeComponent, ImplementationComponent-Type, RepositoryComponent, InterfaceProvidingRequir-ingEntity, InterfaceRequiringEntity, ResourceInterfaceRequiring-Entity, InterfaceProvidingEntity, ComposedProvidingRequir-ingEntity, ComposedStructure, Entity		✓		
EmitEventAction, AbstractAction, CallAction, Entity				
RecoveryActionBehaviour, ResourceDemandingBe-haviour, FailureHandlingEntity, Entity, Identifier				

continues on next page

Table A.1.: Metric Occurrences in the PCM and Corrections

Involved Classes	Correction No.	Harmful	Fixed	Consequence
SubSystem, ComposedProvidingRequiringEntity, ComposedStructure, InterfaceProvidingRequiringEntity, InterfaceRequiringEntity, ResourceInterfaceRequiringEntity, InterfaceProvidingEntity, RepositoryComponent, Entity				
ResourceDemandingSEFF, ResourceDemandingBehaviour, Identifier		✓		
InternalCallAction, CallAction, AbstractInternalControlFlowAction, AbstractAction, Entity,				
Concrete Abstract Class (2)				
ResourceInterfaceRequiringEntity, InterfaceRequiringEntity	14	✓	✓	none
ResourceInterfaceProvidingEntity, ResourceType	15	✓	✓	none
Container Relation (41)				
PCMRandomVariable, ClosedWorkload	16	✓	✓*17	−830 Dependency Cycles, −17 Container Relations, −1 God Class

continues on next page

Table A.1.: Metric Occurrences in the PCM and Corrections

Involved Classes	Correction No.	Harmful	Fixed	Consequence
PCMRandomVariable, PassiveResource	16	✓		
PCMRandomVariable, VariableCharacterisation	16	✓		
PCMRandomVariable, InfrastructureCall	16, 3	✓		
PCMRandomVariable, ResourceCall	16, 3	✓		
PCMRandomVariable, ParametricResourceDemand	16	✓		
PCMRandomVariable, LoopAction	16	✓		
PCMRandomVariable, GuardedBranchTransition	16	✓		
PCMRandomVariable, SpecifiedExecutionTime	16	✓		
PCMRandomVariable, EventChannelSinkConnector	16	✓		
PCMRandomVariable, AssemblyEventConnector	16	✓		
PCMRandomVariable, Loop	16	✓		
PCMRandomVariable, OpenWorkload	16	✓		
PCMRandomVariable, Delay	16	✓		
PCMRandomVariable, CommunicationLinkResourceSpecification	16	✓		
PCMRandomVariable, ProcessingResourceSpecification	16	✓		

continues on next page

Table A.1.: Metric Occurrences in the PCM and Corrections

Involved Classes	Correction No.	Harmful	Fixed	Consequence
PCMRandomVariable, CommunicationLinkResourceSpecification	16	✓		
ScenarioBehaviour, UsageScenario	5	✓		
ScenarioBehaviour, BranchTransition	5	✓		
ScenarioBehaviour, Loop	5	✓		
Parameter, InfrastructureSignature		✓		
Parameter, OperationSignature		✓		
Parameter, EventType		✓		
Parameter, ResourceSignature		✓		
VariableUsage, UserData	17	✓	✓*9	−762 Dependency Cycles, −9 Container Relations, −1 God Class
VariableUsage, CallAction	17	✓		
VariableUsage, SynchronisationPoint	17	✓		
VariableUsage, CallReturnAction	17	✓		
VariableUsage, SetVariableAction	17	✓		
VariableUsage, SpecifiedOutputParameterAbstraction	17	✓		
VariableUsage, AssemblyContext	17	✓		

continues on next page

Table A.1.: Metric Occurrences in the PCM and Corrections

Involved Classes	Correction No.	Harmful	Fixed	Consequence
VariableUsage, EntryLevelSystemCall	17, 4	✓		
VariableUsage, EntryLevelSystemCall	17, 4	✓		
VariableCharacterisation, VariableUsage		✓		
AbstractAction, ResourceDemandingBehaviour	20	✓		
ResourceDemandingBehaviour, AbstractLoopAction		✓		
ResourceDemandingBehaviour, AbstractBranchTransition		✓		
ForkedBehaviour, SynchronisationPoint		✓		
ForkedBehaviour, ForkAction	20	✓		
ResourceContainer, ResourceEnvironment		✓		
ResourceContainer, ResourceContainer		✓		
Obligatory Container Relation (44)				
ResourceProvidedRole, ResourceInterfaceProviding-Entity		✓		
ResourceRequiredRole, ResourceInterfaceRequiring-Entity		✓		
Connector, ComposedStructure		✓		

continues on next page

Table A.1.: Metric Occurrences in the PCM and Corrections

Involved Classes	Correction No.	Harmful	Fixed	Consequence
ResourceRequiredDelegationConnector, ComposedStructure		✓		
EventChannel, ComposedStructure		✓		
AssemblyContext, ComposedStructure		✓		
Workload, UsageScenario	18	✓	✓	−3 Dependency Cycles
UsageScenario, UsageModel		✓		
UserData, UsageModel		✓		
AbstractUserAction, ScenarioBehaviour		✓		
BranchTransition, Branch		✓		
PassiveResource, BasicComponent		✓		
RepositoryComponent, Repository		✓		
ProvidedRole, InterfaceProvidingEntity		✓		
DataType, Repository		✓		
Interface, Repository		✓		
RequiredCharacterisation, Interface		✓		
EventType, EventGroup		✓		
InfrastructureSignature, InfrastructureInterface		✓		
RequiredRole, InterfaceRequiringEntity		✓		
OperationSignature, OperationInterface		✓		

continues on next page

Table A.1.: Metric Occurrences in the PCM and Corrections

Involved Classes	Correction No.	Harmful	Fixed	Consequence
InnerDeclaration, CompositeDataType		✓		
ResourceSignature, ResourceInterface		✓		
ResourceType, ResourceRepository		✓		
SchedulingPolicy, ResourceRepository		✓		
ResourceInterface, ResourceRepository		✓		
InternalFailureOccurrence-Description, InternalAction		✓		
ExternalFailureOccurrence-Description, SpecifiedReliabilityAnnotation		✓		
FailureType, Repository		✓		
AbstractBranchTransition, BranchAction		✓		
ServiceEffectSpecification, BasicComponent		✓		
ResourceDemandingInternalBehaviour, ResourceDemandingSEFF		✓		
SynchronisationPoint, ForkAction		✓		
InfrastructureCall, Abstract-InternalControlFlowAction	19	✓	✓	−1 God Class, −10 Dependency Cycles
ResourceCall, AbstractInternalControlFlowAction		✓		

continues on next page

Table A.1.: Metric Occurrences in the PCM and Corrections

Involved Classes	Correction No.	Harmful	Fixed	Consequence
ParametricResourceDemand, AbstractInternalControlFlowAction		✓		
RecoveryActionBehaviour, RecoveryAction	21	✓		
SpecifiedQoSAnnotation, QoSAnnotations		✓		
QoSAnnotations, System		✓		
SpecifiedOutputParameterAbstraction, QoSAnnotations		✓		
LinkingResource, ResourceEnvironment		✓		
ProcessingResourceSpecification, ResourceContainer		✓		
CommunicationLinkResourceSpecification, LinkingResource		✓		
AllocationContext, Allocation		✓		
Specialized Relation (6)				
ForkAction, ForkedBehaviour	20	✓	✓∗5	−2 Container Relations, −89 Dependency Cycles
ForkedBehaviour, ForkAction	20	✓		
InternalCallAction, ResourceDemandingInternalBehaviour	20	✓		

continues on next page

Table A.1.: Metric Occurrences in the PCM and Corrections

Involved Classes	Correction No.	Harmful	Fixed	Consequence
RecoveryActionBehaviour, RecoveryAction	21	✓	✓	−1 Obl. Container Relation, −1 Dependency Cycle
RecoveryAction, RecoveryActionBehaviour	20	✓		
RecoveryAction, RecoveryActionBehaviour	20	✓		
Speculative Hierarchy (5)				
Expression, IfElse	9	✓		
ServiceEffectSpecification, ResourceDemandingSEFF	22	×	✓	+68 Dependency Cycles
ComposedStructure, ComposedProvidingRequir-ingEntity	23	×	✓	+1 God Class
InterfaceRequiringEntity, InterfaceProvidingRequir-ingEntity				
InterfaceProvidingEntity, InterfaceProvidingRequir-ingEntity				
Dependency Cycles without Container (13)				
EventChannelSourceCon-nector, EventChannel	24	✓	✓∗2	none
EventChannelSinkConnec-tor, EventChannel	24	✓		
AbstractUserAction		×		
ResourceTimeoutFailure-Type, PassiveResource	25	✓	✓	none

continues on next page

Table A.1.: Metric Occurrences in the PCM and Corrections

Involved Classes	**Correction No.**	**Harmful**	**Fixed**	**Consequence**
Interface		×		
CompositeDataType		×		
HardwareInducedFailure-Type, ProcessingResourceType		✓		
NetworkInducedFailure-Type, CommunicationLinkRe-sourceType		✓		
InternalFailureOccurrence-Description, SoftwareInducedFailure-Type		✓		
AbstractAction		×		
RecoveryActionBehaviour		×		
HDDProcessingResource-Specification, ResourceContainer		✓		
ResourceContainer		×		

Table A.1.: Metric Occurrences in the PCM and Corrections

B. Technical Foundation of the Reference Structure Approach

Although my approach is widely based on EMOF, not all the concepts that Section 6.3 proposes are supported by EMOF. The concepts that are already supported by EMOF are classifiers, properties of classes and dependencies to other metamodels. Concepts that are not supported are metamodel modules, layers, dependency restriction, feature models and extension relations, which Chapter 5 already covered.

This section is structured as follows. Appendix B.1 explains how metamodel modules can be supported by EMF. Appendix B.2 presents the graphical editor which supports the remaining concepts.

B.1. Metamodel Modules

A metamodel module can be realized as a metamodel file that is encapsulated in an Eclipse plugin. In EMF, dependencies of a class to another package or to a metamodel file that resides within the same plugin are not restricted. The current graphical tooling (Ecore diagram editor) and the tree editor, however, require an explicit declaration if the content of a metamodel file from another plugin is referenced. After such a declaration is put in place, the tooling adds the dependency to the dependency list of the plugin. From then on, it is allowed to add new dependencies to classes of that specific metamodel.

If a tool needs a particular set of language features, s/he merely has to deploy the metamodel modules that implement the features. Eclipse then automatically deploys further metamodel modules from dependency list of the plugin.

B.2. Tool Support: The Modular EMF Designer

The *Modular EMF Designer*[1] *(Modular Designer)* [KS18] is a graphical editor that visualizes metamodel modules, module dependencies, layers, and feature models. It also detects dependency violations and can perform move refactorings of classifiers. In the scope of my approach, the Modular Designer is used by metamodel architects.

Except for move refactorings, the editor is not intended to create or manipulate the internals of metamodel modules. This functionality is already covered by the standard Ecore diagram editor. In conjunction, however, both editors can be used to either create layered modular metamodels or refactor an existing metamodel into a modular and layered form that adheres to the constraints of the reference structure.

Figure B.1 shows a screenshot of the complete graphical user interface (GUI) of the Modular Designer (except for a part of the palette). The different parts of the GUI are: (1) the diagram pane, (2) the palette, (3) the model explorer, and (4) the properties view. Figure B.2 exemplarily shows the notational elements of a Modular Designer diagram. The diagram pane contains a container that in turn contains the layers and modules of a metamodel. The Modular Designer is intended to develop modular metamodel. Thus, the container is always labeled “Modular metamodel”, even if the metamodel that is displayed consists of only one module. The remainder of this section explains the notation and functionality of the Modular Designer.

Layers The metamodel architect uses the Modular Designer to view, create, delete, and name layers. An arbitrary number of layers can be created.

Metamodel modules The Modular Designer visualizes metamodel modules. New empty metamodel modules can be created via the palette. Existing metamodel modules can be loaded via the palette or by drag and drop from the model explorer. If a metamodel module is loaded into the diagram, all metamodel modules it depends on are also loaded automatically. A metamodel module is always contained

[1] The Modular Designer was developed in the scope of a bachelor’s thesis [Kec17] that I supervised.

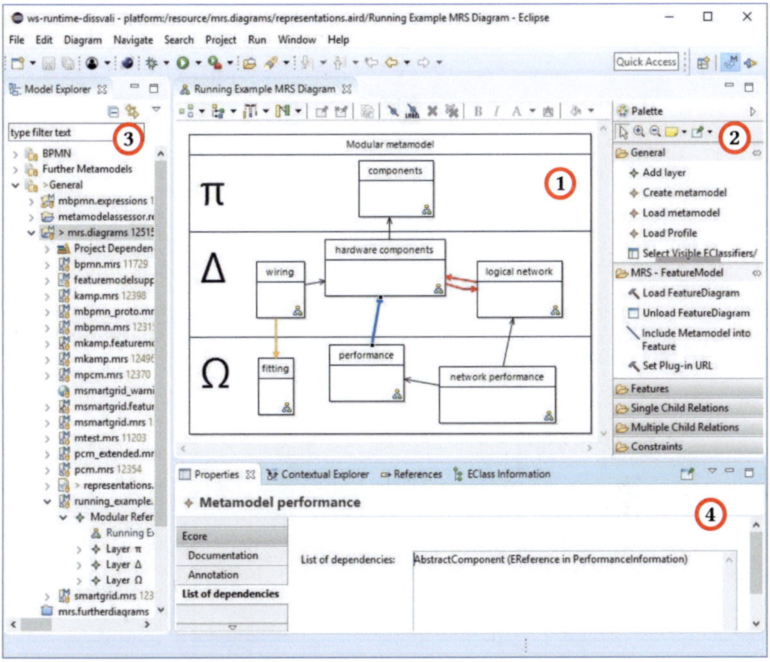

Figure B.1.: Screenshot of the GUI of the Modular EMF Designer

in exactly one layer. Metamodel modules can be moved between layers by drag and drop.

Module Dependencies The Modular Designer visualizes dependencies between metamodel modules. Transitive dependencies can be hidden on demand. This helps to make large Modular Designer diagrams clearer. Transitive dependencies may be omitted, as they are less important compared to non-transitive dependencies (see Section 6.3.3).

Profiles Like metamodel modules, existing EMF profiles can be loaded into a Modular Designer diagram. Profiles are visualized like a dependency between two metamodel modules with the exception that the name of the profile and stereotype is shown in guillemets.

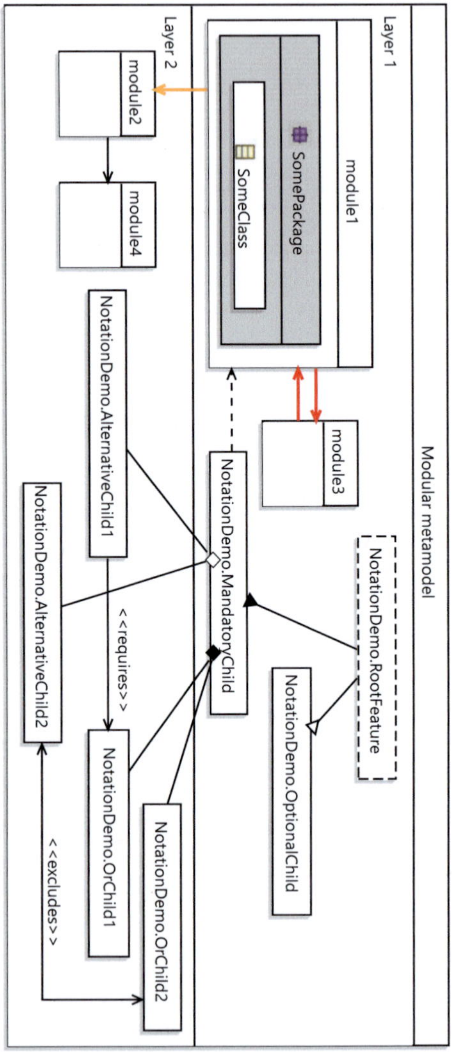

Figure B.2.: Notational Elements of Modular EMF Designer Diagrams

Dependency Violations The Modular Designer reports on module dependency violations. As seen in both figures, it highlights dependency cycles (in red) and violations against the layering (in orange).

Module Dependency Details The Modular Designer provides detailed information about the dependencies between two metamodel modules (which classes are dependent with what kinds of dependencies). This is shown in Figure B.1. The dependency from the Performance metamodel module to HardwareComponents is selected and therefore highlighted in blue. In the properties view (4) a text box lists all class dependencies that constitute the module dependency. It distinguishes between the following types of dependencies: attribute, superclass, reference, operation (return type and parameter), generic type reference (type parameter bound or type argument).

Move Refactoring The Modular Designer can perform move refactorings of classifiers and packages between metamodel modules. Usually, metamodel modules are shown as boxes with an empty compartment. The compartment is used to visualize packages and classifiers that should be moved. In Figure B.2, a package and a class are shown in the compartment of module1. Either the class or the package could be drag-and-dropped on the compartment of another metamodel module.

When the Modular Designer performs a move refactoring, it automatically updates all incoming dependencies from metamodel modules that are loaded into the diagram. If such a refactoring is be performed manually, all incoming dependencies break, and have to be fixed manually. There are some ways to circumvent this; however, the metamodel developer needs to know and link all metamodels with incoming dependencies. Having all related metamodel modules in a Modular Designer diagram is much more convenient, as the developer is relieved of tracking incoming dependencies.

Feature Nodes, Relations In addition to the layered metamodel module dependency graph, the Modular Designer enables to create and embed feature models in a Modular Designer diagram. The feature models are saved in model files that are separate from the metamodel module dependency graphs. This decouples Modular Designer diagrams from feature models, and it is possible to define multiple feature models for one metamodel module dependency graph.

The Modular Designer supports creating, renaming, and deleting feature notes. The root node is highlighted by a dashed border. The graphical notation is not yet fully developed and therefore differs a bit from the usual feature model visuals. Optional child relations are indicated by a little empty triangle as its arrowhead. Mandatory child relations are indicated by a little black triangle as its arrowhead. Requires and excludes relations are simple arrow connectors with requires or excludes in guillemet. Alternative feature sets are shown as a white rhomb on the border of the parent node. OR feature sets are shown as a black rhomb. The child features of the feature set are connected by lines to the rhomb. The metamodel modules that implement a feature are connected with a dashed arrow.

B.3. Readily Available Tool Support

As already mentioned, besides the Modular Designer, further tools are needed to work with the internals of metamodels. The metamodel tree editor and the graphical Ecore diagram editor are the main tools that are used to create, modify and delete metamodel elements. There are two additional Eclipse views, which are less well known, that can be used to explore a metamodel and retrieve information about its elements. The *Amalgam Contextual Explorer* view provides useful information about the incoming and outgoing dependencies of a class. Considering the Amalgam Contextual Explorer shows information of a class C, it provides the following information: classes that have a reference to C, superclasses of C, subclasses of C, inherited attributes and references, and all classes C is dependent on. Incoming dependencies are, however, only registered when they come from within the same metamodel file or from a metamodel file that is a dependency. The *Show Reference View* provides more detailed information about incoming references. Whereas the Amalgam Contextual Explorer shows all classes that have references to a class C, the Show Reference View does not list classes that inherited a reference C and do not have own references to C. For each class with references to C, it also provides detail of the references. It, however, has the same drawback as the Amalgam Contextual Explorer, as it does not register classes from metamodel files that cannot be reached by following dependencies. In conclusion, both views provide useful information when working within the same metamodel file. In modular metamodels, however, they are less helpful. Thus, the Modular Designer provides in-depth summaries for metamodel module dependencies.

C. Evaluation Tooling and Setup

In this section, I briefly present the tool that I implemented to automate the evaluation of the evolvability and the need-specific dependence and use. I call the tool the Modular Reference Structure validation tool (MRS validation tool). It hopefully proves useful to future research that has to evaluate metamodel utilization or Allen's metrics on metamodels. It provides a GUI to configure the analysis and define its inputs. It automates the processing of metamodel extensions and model files, the subgraph extraction and the transformation from subgraphs into hypergraphs. It passes the hypergraphs to the Architecture Evaluation Tool [JHH16; Jun16a] (AET). The AET then evaluates Allen's metrics on the hypergraphs. In the remainder of this section, I describe (1) the setup of the MRS validation tool, the AET and its dependencies, (2) the specific versions and revisions that I used for the evaluation, and (3) an overview of the functionality of the MRS validation tool and a brief user guide.

C.1. Installation

As the MRS validation tool is a very special purpose tool, there is no update site for comfortable installation. The MRS validation tool and its dependencies have to be installed manually. An advantage of the manual installation is the explicit control over the versions of the dependencies of the MRS validation tool. This enables a more exact reproducibility of the validation setup.

Eclipse The MRS validation tool and its dependencies are Eclipse plugins. I developed and used them with Eclipse Neon and Oxygen. I highly suggest using the Modeling Tools Package of Eclipse, as it provides many dependencies like the EMF.

AET All AET plugins have to be imported. These should be obtained from my fork[1].

Dependencies To get AET to compile, several plugins are required. The Generator Composition (GEKO) Framework has to be installed[2]. All Kieler Lightweight Diagrams have to be installed[3] (Ptolemy is not needed). The Xcore SDK and m2e (Maven Eclipse integration) have to be installed via the Eclipse releases update site. If any Maven errors occur, Tycho connectors have to be installed. Import all AET plugins.

MRS validation tool All plugin projects have to be imported from SVN[4].

Runtime Instance To enable the MRS validation tool to read model files, the respective plugins also have to be imported that carry the metamodel and the model code. Finally, an inner eclipse instance can be started. Within this instance, the MRS validation tool can be used.

C.2. Concrete Versions Used in the Evaluation

Results are expected not to change with future versions. To replicate the exact results, however, the following version and revisions can be obtained.

- Eclipse Oxygen.2 Release version 4.7.2
- EMF SDK version 2.13.0.v20170609-0928
- MRS validation tool revision 12607
- AET commit a842ce1a3824a131b87b6c2f87ff425055463db8
- GEKO version 1.0.0.201801100455
- Xcore SDK version 1.5.0.v20170613-0242

[1] https://github.com/MishaStrittmatter/architecture-evaluation-tool (last visited 23.08.2019)

[2] http://build.se.informatik.uni-kiel.de/eus/geco/snapshot (last visited 23.08.2019)

[3] http://rtsys.informatik.uni-kiel.de/~kieler/updatesite/release_pragmatics_2016-07/ (last visited 23.08.2019)

[4] https://svnserver.informatik.kit.edu/i43/svn/palladio/misha.strittmatter/ResearchProjects/MetamodelReferenceStructure/evaluationtooling/ (last visited 25.09.2019)

C.3. Using the Validation Tool

The GUI of my MRS validation tool can be started in the Eclipse toolbar by a button that carries an icon that shows a pair of glasses. Figure C.1 shows the GUI. The MRS validation tool supports several modes of operation. These are subdivided into modes that compare two metamodels and modes that analyze one metamodel only. The inputs that are required have to be specified in two ways. A project may be highlighted in the project explorer or up to two metamodels have to be specified in the lower two control groups. The control groups provide the PCM and mPCM as predefined metamodels. Alternatively, a modular metamodel can be referenced by providing a prefix. All projects from the workspace that start with the provided prefix are then considered as part of the metamodel. Dependent metamodel modules are automatically loaded. Therefore, at least the metamodel modules without incoming dependencies have to be captured by the prefix. How inputs have to be provided depends on the selected mode and is described in the info tooltip beside the radio button of the mode. All comparison modes require two metamodel versions to be specified through the two control groups. The modes perform the following functionality.

Extension Comparison The extension comparison evaluates a series of metamodel extension to extract affected classes. It then extracts the relevant subgraphs and transforms them into hypergraphs to evaluate Allen's metrics. This is performed for two versions of a metamodel. It requires the project that contains metamodel extensions that are each contained in an own folder. A metamodel extension may provide several metamodel files if it originally consisted of multiple metamodel modules.

Modification Comparison The modification comparison evaluates Allen's metrics on a subgraph that is determined by classes that are modified. A modification description consists of a list of classes that are affected by the modification. This mode is performed on two metamodel versions. It requires a project to be selected that contains the modification descriptions.

Model Comparison The model comparison evaluates metamodel utilization on two metamodel versions. It requires a project to be selected in the project explorer that contains models.

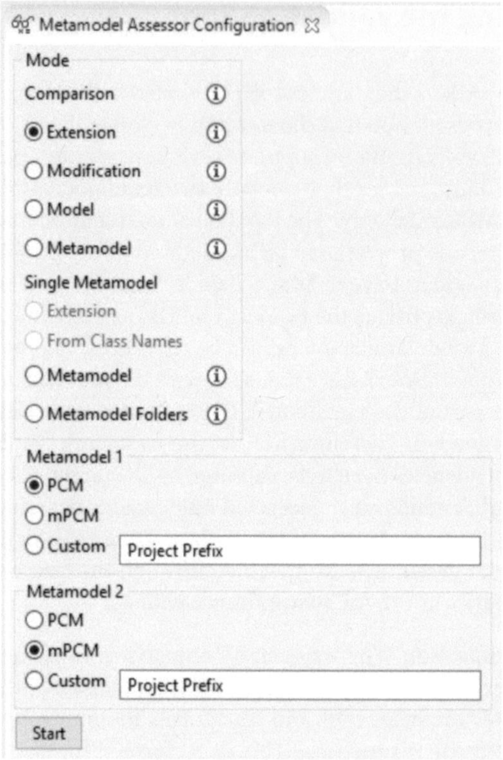

Figure C.1.: The GUI of the MRS validation tool

Metamodel Comparison The metamodel comparison does not work on subgraphs but on whole metamodels. It evaluates counting metrics, Allen's metrics, and performs a dependency analysis on two metamodel versions. No explorer selection is required.

Metamodel The metamodel mode performs the same functionality as the metamodel comparison mode, but only on a single metamodel. It only requires the projects that belong to the metamodel to be selected in the project explorer.

Metamodel Folders The metamodel folders mode performs the same functionality of the metamodel comparison on a series of potentially different metamodels. It requires a project to be selected in the project explorer that contains a collection of folders that contain metamodel files.

In the comparison modes, the input (extension, modification list, and models) has to belong to the first specified metamodel version. The MRS validation tool processes the input and also applies it on the second specified metamodel version. This means it is not necessary to reimplement the same extension for the other version or to recreate each model with the second metamodel version. However, this also means that when a metamodel extension, a list of modifications, or the instantiated classes of a model are processed, the MRS validation tool has to locate the affected classes or in the case of model analysis types in the second metamodel version. Usually, the MRS validation tool matches these classes one to one according to an exact match of the classes names. The MRS validation tool, however, also supports the handling of several special cases. If a class is split, an imply matching exception can match multiple classes in the second metamodel version. If several classes carry the same name or if the name of a class is changed, a distinguish match exception can be used to map the classes correctly. The matching exceptions are provided in a text file in the input project that is selected in the project explorer.

Bibliography

[ABT10] Thorsten Arendt, Matthias Burhenne, and Gabriele Taentzer. "Defining and checking model smells: A quality assurance task for models based on the eclipse modeling framework". In: *BENEVOL workshop*. 2010.

[AG13] Colin Atkinson and Ralph Gerbig. "Harmonizing Textual and Graphical Visualizations of Domain Specific Models". In: *Proceedings of the Second Workshop on Graphical Modeling Language Development*. GMLD '13. Montpellier, France: ACM, 2013, pp. 32–41. ISBN: 978-1-4503-2044-3. DOI: 10.1145/2489820.2489823.

[AG16] Colin Atkinson and Ralph Gerbig. "Flexible Deep Modeling with Melanee". In: *Modellierung 2016 - Workshopband*. Ed. by Stefanie Betz and Ulrich Reimer. Bonn: Gesellschaft für Informatik e.V., Mar. 2016, pp. 117–122. URL: https://dl.gi.de/20.500.12116/843.

[AGF13] C. Atkinson, R. Gerbig, and M. Fritzsche. "Modeling Language Extension in the Enterprise Systems Domain". In: *2013 17th IEEE International Enterprise Distributed Object Computing Conference*. Sept. 2013, pp. 49–58. DOI: 10.1109/EDOC.2013.15.

[AGG07] Edward B. Allen, Sampath Gottipati, and Rajiv Govindarajan. "Measuring size, complexity, and coupling of hypergraph abstractions of software: An information-theory approach". English. In: *Software Quality Journal* 15.2 (2007), pp. 179–212. ISSN: 0963-9314. DOI: 10.1007/s11219-006-9010-3.

[AKM13] Omar Alam, Jörg Kienzle, and Gunter Mussbacher. "Concern-Oriented Software Design". In: *Proceedings of the 16th International Conference on Model-Driven Engineering Languages and Systems - MODELS 2013*. Ed. by Ana Moreira, Bernhard Schätz, Jeff Gray, Antonio Vallecillo, and Peter Clarke. Vol. 8107. Lecture Notes in Computer Science. Springer Berlin Heidelberg, 2013, pp. 604–621. ISBN: 978-3-642-41532-6. DOI: 10.1007/978-3-642-41533-3_37.

[All02] Edward B. Allen. "Measuring graph abstractions of software: an information-theory approach". In: *Software Metrics, 2002. Proceedings. Eighth IEEE Symposium on*. 2002, pp. 182–193. DOI: 10.1109/METRIC.2002.1011337.

[Are14] Thorsten Arendt. "Quality Assurance of Software Models – A Structured Quality Assurance Process Supported by a Flexible Tool Environment in the Eclipse Modeling Project". PhD thesis. 2014. DOI: 10.17192/z2014.0357. URL: https://archiv.ub.uni-marburg.de/diss/z2014/0357/pdf/dta.pdf.

[ASB10] Colin Atkinson, Dietmar Stoll, and Philipp Bostan. "Orthographic Software Modeling: A Practical Approach to View-Based Development". In: *Evaluation of Novel Approaches to Software Engineering*. Ed. by LeszekA. Maciaszek, César González-Pérez, and Stefan Jablonski. Vol. 69. Communications in Computer and Information Science. Berlin/Heidelberg: Springer, 2010, pp. 206–219. ISBN: 978-3-642-14819-4.

[AT13] Thorsten Arendt and Gabriele Taentzer. "A Tool Environment for Quality Assurance Based on the Eclipse Modeling Framework". In: *Automated Software Engineering* 20.2 (June 2013), pp. 141–184. ISSN: 0928-8910. DOI: 10.1007/s10515-012-0114-7.

[Bac94] Paul Bachmann. *Die analytische Zahlentheorie*. Leipzig: Teubner, 1894.

[Ban+00] Jerry Banks, John S. Carson, Barry L. Nelson, and David M. Nicol. *Discrete-Event System Simulation*. 3rd ed. Prentice Hall, 2000. ISBN: 0130887021.

[BBM96] V.R. Basili, L.C. Briand, and W.L. Melo. "A validation of object-oriented design metrics as quality indicators". In: *Software Engineering, IEEE Transactions on* 22.10 (Oct. 1996).

[BC06] E. Bondarev and M.R.V. Chaudron. "Compositional Performance Analysis of Component-Based Systems on Heterogeneous Multiprocessor Platforms". In: *Software Engineering and Advanced Applications, 2006. SEAA'06. 32nd EUROMICRO Conference on.* IEEE. 2006, pp. 81–91. ISBN: 0769525946.

[BCE08] Hongyu Pei Breivold, Ivica Crnkovic, and Peter J. Eriksson. "Analyzing Software Evolvability". In: *32nd Annual IEEE International Computer Software and Applications Conference.* IEEE, July 2008, pp. 327–330. DOI: 10.1109/COMPSAC.2008.50.

[BCR94] Victor R. Basili, Gianluigi Caldiera, and H. Dieter Rombach. "The Goal Question Metric Approach". In: *Encyclopedia of Software Engineering - 2 Volume Set.* Ed. by John J. Marciniak. John Wiley & Sons, 1994, pp. 528–532.

[BCW11] Kacper Bąk, Krzysztof Czarnecki, and Andrzej Wąsowski. "Feature and Meta-Models in Clafer: Mixed, Specialized, and Coupled". In: *Software Language Engineering.* Ed. by Brian Malloy, Steffen Staab, and Mark van den Brand. Berlin, Heidelberg: Springer Berlin Heidelberg, 2011, pp. 102–122. ISBN: 978-3-642-19440-5.

[BE15a] Richard Braun and Werner Esswein. "Designing Dialects of Enterprise Modeling Languages with the Profiling Technique". In: *2015 IEEE 19th International Enterprise Distributed Object Computing Conference.* Sept. 2015, pp. 60–67. DOI: 10.1109/EDOC.2015.19.

[BE15b] Richard Braun and Werner Esswein. "Extending the MOF for the Adaptation of Hooks, Aspects, Plug-Ins and Add-Ons". In: *Model and Data Engineering: 5th International Conference, MEDI 2015, Rhodes, Greece, September 26-28, 2015, Proceedings.* Ed. by Ladjel Bellatreche and Yannis Manolopoulos. Cham: Springer International Publishing, 2015, pp. 28–38. ISBN: 978-3-319-23781-7. DOI: 10.1007/978-3-319-23781-7_3.

[Bec+14] Steffen Becker, Stefan Dziwok, Christopher Gerking, Wilhelm Schäfer, Christian Heinzemann, Sebastian Thiele, Matthias Meyer, Claudia Priesterjahn, Uwe Pohlmann, and Matthias Tichy. *The MechatronicUML Design Method - Process and Language for Platform-Independent Modeling*. Tech. rep. tr-ri-14-337. Version 0.4. Heinz Nixdorf Institute, University of Paderborn, Mar. 2014.

[Bet+17] Lorenzo Bettini, Davide Di Ruscio, Ludovico Iovino, and Alfonso Pierantonio. "Edelta: An Approach for Defining and Applying Reusable Metamodel Refactorings". In: *Proceedings of MODELS 2017 Satellite Event co-located with ACM/IEEE 20th International Conference on Model Driven Engineering Languages and Systems (MODELS 2017)*. Austin, Texas, USA: CEUR-WS, Sept. 2017, pp. 71–80. URL: http://ceur-ws.org/Vol-2019/me%5C_4.pdf.

[Bet+19] L. Bettini, D. Di Ruscio, L. Iovino, and A. Pierantonio. "Quality-Driven Detection and Resolution of Metamodel Smells". In: *IEEE Access* 7 (2019), pp. 16364–16376. ISSN: 2169-3536. DOI: 10.1109/ACCESS.2019.2891357.

[BG10] Erik Burger and Boris Gruschko. "A Change Metamodel for the Evolution of MOF-Based Metamodels". In: *Proceedings of Modellierung 2010*. Ed. by Gregor Engels, Dimitris Karagiannis, and Heinrich C. Mayr. Vol. P-161. GI-LNI. Klagenfurt, Austria, Mar. 2010, pp. 285–300. URL: http://sdqweb.ipd.kit.edu/publications/pdfs/burger2010a.pdf.

[BHP06] Tomáš Bureš, Petr Hnetynka, and František Plášil. "SOFA 2.0: Balancing Advanced Features in a Hierarchical Component Model". In: *Proceedings of the Fourth International Conference on Software Engineering Research, Management and Applications (SERA)*. Washington, DC, USA: IEEE Computer Society, 2006, pp. 40–48. ISBN: 0-7695-2656-X. DOI: 10.1109/SERA.2006.62.

[Bie06] Matthias Biehl. "APL-A Language for Automated Anti-Pattern Analysis of OO-Software". In: *CS846: Source Transformation Systems, Project Report. University ofWa terloo* (2006).

[BKR09] Steffen Becker, Heiko Koziolek, and Ralf Reussner. "The Palladio component model for model-driven performance prediction". In: *Journal of Systems and Software* 82 (2009), pp. 3–22. DOI: 10.1016/j.jss.2008.03.066.

[BL03] Dirk Beyer and Claus Lewerentz. "CrocoPat: Efficient pattern analysis in object-oriented programs". In: *Program Comprehension, 2003. 11th IEEE International Workshop on.* IEEE. 2003, pp. 294–295.

[Bra15] Richard Braun. "Towards the state of the art of extending enterprise modeling languages". In: *2015 3rd International Conference on Model-Driven Engineering and Software Development (MODELSWARD).* Feb. 2015, pp. 1–9.

[Bra17] Richard Braun. "Extensibility of Enterprise Modelling Languages". Doctoral Thesis. TU Dresden, Mar. 2017. URL: nbn-resolving.de/urn:nbn:de:bsz:14-qucosa-219873.

[Bro+12] Franz Brosch, Heiko Koziolek, Barbora Buhnova, and Ralf Reussner. "Architecture-based Reliability Prediction with the Palladio Component Model". In: *IEEE Transactions on Software Engineering* 38.6 (Nov. 2012), pp. 1319–1339. ISSN: 0098-5589. DOI: 10.1109/TSE.2011.94.

[Bro+98] William H. Brown, Raphael C. Malveau, Hays W. "Skip" McCormick, and Thomas J. Mowbray. *AntiPatterns: Refactoring Software, Architectures, and Projects in Crisis.* 1st. New York, NY, USA: John Wiley & Sons, 1998. ISBN: 0471197130.

[BSK15] Axel Busch, Misha Strittmatter, and Anne Koziolek. "Assessing Security to Compare Architecture Alternatives of Component-Based Systems". In: *Proceedings of the IEEE International Conference on Software Quality, Reliability & Security.* QRS '15. Acceptance Rate (Full Paper): 20/91 = 22%. Vancouver, British Columbia, Canada: IEEE Computer Society, 2015, pp. 99–108. DOI: 10.1109/QRS.2015.24.

[BT14] Erik Burger and Aleksandar Toshovski. "Difference-based Conformance Checking for Ecore Metamodels". In: *Proceedings of Modellierung 2014.* Vol. 225. GI-LNI. Vienna, Austria, Mar. 2014, pp. 97–104. URL: http://sdqweb.ipd.kit.edu/publications/pdfs/burger2014a.pdf.

[Bur14] Erik Burger. "Flexible Views for View-based Model-driven Development". PhD thesis. Karlsruhe, Germany: Karlsruhe Institute of Technology, July 2014. ISBN: 978-3-7315-0276-0. DOI: 10.5445/KSP/1000043437. URL: http://digbib.ubka.uni-karlsruhe.de/volltexte/1000043437.

[Bus+16] Axel Busch, Robert Heinrich, Jörg Henss, Martin Küster, Sebastian Lehrig, Misha Strittmatter, Max Kramer, Erik Burger, and Ralf H. Reussner. "Architectural Viewpoints". In: *Modeling and Simulating Software Architectures – The Palladio Approach.* Ed. by Ralf H. Reussner, Steffen Becker, Jens Happe, Robert Heinrich, Anne Koziolek, Heiko Koziolek, Max Kramer, and Klaus Krogmann. Cambridge, MA: MIT Press, Oct. 2016. Chap. 3, pp. 37–73. URL: http://mitpress.mit.edu/books/modeling-and-simulating-software-architectures.

[Bus+18] Kiana Busch, Dominik Werle, Martin Löper, Robert Heinrich, Ralf Reussner, and Birgit Vogel-Heuser. "A Cross-Disciplinary Language for Change Propagation Rules". In: *14th IEEE International Conference on Automation Science and Engineering (CASE).* IEEE, 2018, pp. 1099–1104.

[Bus+96] Frank Buschmann, Regine Meunier, Hans Rohnert, Peter Sommerlad, and Michael Stal. *Pattern-Oriented Software Architecture – A System of Patterns.* Wiley & Sons, New York, NY, USA, 1996.

[But+18a] Arvid Butting, Robert Eikermann, Oliver Kautz, Bernhard Rumpe, and Andreas Wortmann. "Controlled and Extensible Variability of Concrete and Abstract Syntax with Independent Language Features". In: *Proceedings of the 12th International Workshop on Variability Modelling of Software-Intensive Systems.* VAMOS'18. Madrid, Spain: ACM, Jan. 2018, pp. 75–82. URL: http://www.se-rwth.de/publications/Controlled-and-Extensible-Variability-of-Concrete-and-Abstract-Syntax-with-Independent-Language-Features.pdf.

[But+18b] Arvid Butting, Robert Eikermann, Oliver Kautz, Bernhard Rumpe, and Andreas Wortmann. "Modeling Language Variability with Reusable Language Components". In: *Proceeedings of the 22Nd International Conference on Systems and Soft-*

ware Product Line. SPLC '18. Gothenburg, Sweden: ACM, 2018, pp. 65–75. ISBN: 978-1-4503-6464-5. DOI: 10.1145/3233027.3233037.

[BV10] Manuel F Bertoa and Antonio Vallecillo. "Quality attributes for software metamodels". In: *Proceedings of the 13th TOOLS Workshop on Quantitative Approaches in Object-Oriented Software Engineering (QAOOSE 2010)*. 2010.

[CBW17] Benoit Combemale, Olivier Barais, and Andreas Wortmann. "Language Engineering with the GEMOC Studio". In: *2017 IEEE International Conference on Software Architecture Workshops (ICSAW)*. Apr. 2017, pp. 189–191. DOI: 10.1109/ICSAW.2017.61.

[CE00] Krysztof Czarnecki and Ulrich W. Eisenecker. *Generative Programming*. Addison-Wesley, Reading, MA, USA, 2000. ISBN: 0-201-63361-2.

[Čer+09] Ondřej Černý, Petr Hošek, Michal Papež, and Václav Remeš. *SOFA 2 Component System Developer's guide*. Nov. 2009. URL: https://sofa.ow2.org/docs/index.html.

[CG11] Hyun Cho and Jeff Gray. "Design Patterns for Metamodels". In: *Proceedings of the Compilation of the Co-located Workshops on DSM'11, TMC'11, AGERE! 2011, AOOPES'11, NEAT'11, & VMIL'11*. SPLASH '11 Workshops. Portland, Oregon, USA: ACM, 2011, pp. 25–32. ISBN: 978-1-4503-1183-0. DOI: 10.1145/2095050.2095056.

[CH03] Krzysztof Czarnecki and Simon Helsen. "Classification of Model Transformation Approaches". In: *OOPSLA 2003 Workshop on Generative Techniques in the context of Model Driven Architecture*. Last retrieved 2008-01-06. Oct. 2003. URL: http://www.softmetaware.com/oopsla2003/czarnecki.pdf.

[Cic+08] Antonio Cicchetti, Davide Di Ruscio, Romina Eramo, and Alfonso Pierantonio. "Automating Co-evolution in Model-Driven Engineering". In: *Proceedings of the 2008 12th International IEEE Enterprise Distributed Object Computing Conference*. EDOC '08. Washington, DC, USA: IEEE Computer Society, 2008, pp. 222–231. ISBN: 978-0-7695-3373-5. DOI: 10.1109/EDOC.2008.44.

[CK91] Shyam R. Chidamber and Chris F. Kemerer. "Towards a Metrics Suite for Object Oriented Design". In: *SIGPLAN Not.* 26.11 (Nov. 1991), pp. 197–211. ISSN: 0362-1340. DOI: 10.1145/118014.117970.

[CN01] Paul C. Clements and Linda Northrop. *Software Product Lines: Practices and Patterns.* SEI Series in Software Engineering. Boston, Mass. ; London: Addison-Wesley, Aug. 2001.

[Coa99] Peter Coad. *Java modeling in color with UML : enterprise components and process.* Upper Saddle River, NJ: Prentice Hall PTR, 1999. ISBN: 013011510X.

[Com+18] Benoit Combemale, Jörg Kienzle, Gunter Mussbacher, Olivier Barais, Erwan Bousse, Walter Cazzola, Philippe Collet, Thomas Degueule, Robert Heinrich, Jean-Marc Jézéquel, Manuel Leduc, Tanja Mayerhofer, Sébastien Mosser, Matthias Schöttle, Misha Strittmatter, and Andreas Wortmann. "Concern-oriented language development (COLD): Fostering reuse in language engineering". In: *Computer Languages, Systems & Structures* 54 (2018), pp. 139–155. ISSN: 1477-8424. DOI: 10.1016/j.cl.2018.05.004. URL: http://www.sciencedirect.com/science/article/pii/S1477842418300496.

[Com13] International Electrotechnical Commission. *IEC 61131-3:2013 – Programmable controllers – Part 3: Programming languages.* 3rd ed. Feb. 2013. URL: https://webstore.iec.ch/publication/4552.

[Com16] International Electrotechnical Commission. *IEC 62424:2016 – Representation of process control engineering – Requests in P&I diagrams and data exchange between P&ID tools and PCE-CAE tools.* 2nd ed. July 2016. URL: https://webstore.iec.ch/publication/25442.

[CU06] Munkhnasan Choinzon and Yoshikazu Ueda. "Detecting defects in object oriented designs using design metrics". In: *Proceedings of the 2006 conference on Knowledge-Based Software Engineering: Proceedings of the Seventh Joint Conference on Knowledge-Based Software Engineering.* IOS Press. 2006, pp. 61–72.

[Cue+10] Philippe Cuenot, Patrick Frey, Rolf Johansson, Henrik Lönn, Yiannis Papadopoulos, Mark-Oliver Reiser, Anders Sandberg, David Servat, Ramin Tavakoli Kolagari, Martin Törngren, and Matthias Weber. "The EAST-ADL Architecture Description Language for Automotive Embedded Software". In: *Model-Based Engineering of Embedded Real-Time Systems.* Ed. by Holger Giese, Gabor Karsai, Edward Lee, Bernhard Rumpe, and Bernhard Schätz. Vol. 6100. Lecture Notes in Computer Science. Springer Berlin Heidelberg, 2010, pp. 297–307. ISBN: 978-3-642-16276-3. DOI: 10.1007/978-3-642-16277-0_11.

[DCJ17] Thomas Degueule, Benoit Combemale, and Jean-Marc Jézéquel. "On Language Interfaces". In: *Present and Ulterior Software Engineering.* Ed. by Manuel Mazzara and Bertrand Meyer. Springer International Publishing, 2017, pp. 65–75. ISBN: 978-3-319-67425-4. DOI: 10.1007/978-3-319-67425-4_5.

[DDN02] Serge Demeyer, Stéphane Ducasse, and Oscar Nierstrasz. *Object-oriented reengineering patterns.* Elsevier, 2002.

[Deg+15] Thomas Degueule, Benoit Combemale, Arnaud Blouin, Olivier Barais, and Jean-Marc Jézéquel. "Melange: A Meta-language for Modular and Reusable Development of DSLs". In: *8th International Conference on Software Language Engineering.* SLE 2015. Pittsburgh, PA, USA: ACM, Oct. 2015, pp. 25–36. ISBN: 978-1-4503-3686-4. DOI: 10.1145/2814251.2814252. URL: https://hal.inria.fr/hal-01197038.

[Deg+17] Thomas Degueule, Benoit Combemale, Arnaud Blouin, Olivier Barais, and Jean-Marc Jézéquel. "Safe Model Polymorphism for Flexible Modeling". In: *Computer Languages, Systems & Structures* 49.C (Sept. 2017), pp. 176–195. ISSN: 1477-8424. DOI: 10.1016/j.cl.2016.09.001.

[Di +14] Juri Di Rocco, Davide Di Ruscio, Ludovico Iovino, and Alfonso Pierantonio. "Mining Metrics for Understanding Metamodel Characteristics". In: *Proceedings of the 6th International Workshop on Modeling in Software Engineering.* MiSE 2014. Hyderabad, India: ACM, 2014, pp. 55–60. ISBN: 978-1-4503-2849-4. DOI: 10.1145/2593770.2593774.

[Dij82] Edsger W. Dijkstra. "On the Role of Scientific Thought". In: *Selected Writings on Computing: A personal Perspective.* New York, NY: Springer New York, 1982, pp. 60–66. ISBN: 978-1-4612-5695-3. DOI: 10.1007/978-1-4612-5695-3_12.

[Dra+08] Rainer Drath, Arndt Luder, Jorn Peschke, and Lorenz Hundt. "AutomationML - the glue for seamless automation engineering". In: *2008 IEEE International Conference on Emerging Technologies and Factory Automation.* Sept. 2008, pp. 616–623. DOI: 10.1109/ETFA.2008.4638461.

[Dur+14] Darko Durisic, Miroslaw Staron, Matthias Tichy, and Jörgen Hansson. "Evolution of Long-Term Industrial Meta-Models - An Automotive Case Study of AUTOSAR". In: *40th EUROMICRO Conference on Software Engineering and Advanced Applications, EUROMICRO-SEAA 2014, Verona, Italy, August 27-29, 2014.* 2014, pp. 141–148. DOI: 10.1109/SEAA.2014.21.

[Dur+17] Francisco Durán, Antonio Moreno-Delgado, Fernando Orejas, and Steffen Zschaler. "Amalgamation of domain specific languages with behaviour". In: *Journal of Logical and Algebraic Methods in Programming* 86.1 (2017), pp. 208–235. ISSN: 2352-2208. DOI: 10.1016/j.jlamp.2015.09.005. URL: http://www.sciencedirect.com/science/article/pii/S2352220815000875.

[DZT13] Francisco Durán, Steffen Zschaler, and Javier Troya. "On the Reusable Specification of Non-functional Properties in DSLs". In: *Software Language Engineering.* Ed. by Krzysztof Czarnecki and Görel Hedin. Berlin, Heidelberg: Springer Berlin Heidelberg, 2013, pp. 332–351. ISBN: 978-3-642-36089-3.

[EAS13] EAST-ADL Association. *EAST-ADL Domain Model Specification – Version 2.1.12.* Nov. 2013. URL: http://www.east-adl.info/Specification.html.

[EBL11] Maged Elaasar, Lionel Briand, and Yvan Labiche. "Domain-Specific Model Verification with QVT". In: *ECMFA.* Springer, 2011. ISBN: 978-3-642-21470-7. DOI: 10.1007/978-3-642-21470-7_20.

[Ela12] Maged E. Elaasar. “An Approach to Design Pattern and Anti-pattern Detection in MOF-based Modeling Languages”. PhD thesis. Ottawa, Ontario, Canada, Canada: Carleton University Ottawa, 2012. ISBN: 978-0-494-93678-8.

[EMF04] EMF. *FeatureMaps.* draft. Eclipse Foundation, June 2004, p. 6. URL: `https://www.eclipse.org/modeling/emf/docs/overviews/FeatureMap.pdf`.

[ES06] Matthew Emerson and Janos Sztipanovits. “Techniques for metamodel composition”. In: *OOPSLA–6th Workshop on Domain Specific Modeling.* 2006, pp. 123–139.

[Fav03] Jean-Marie Favre. “Meta-model and model co-evolution within the 3D software space”. In: *Evolution of Large-scale Industrial Software Evolution Workshop (ELISA@ICSM).* Vol. 3. Royal Netherlands Academy of Arts and Sciences, Amsterdam, The Netherlands, Sept. 2003, pp. 98–109.

[FD05] M Fedai and R Drath. “CAEX – a neutral data exchange format for engineering data”. In: *ATP International Automation Technology* 1.2005 (2005), p. 3.

[FGH06] Peter H. Feiler, David P. Gluch, and John J. Hudak. *The Architecture Analysis & Design Language (AADL): An Introduction.* CMU/SEI-2006-TN-011. Carnegie Mellon University, Software Engineering Institute, Feb. 2006. URL: `http://www.sei.cmu.edu/library/abstracts/reports/06tn011.cfm`.

[Flo67] Robert W. Floyd. “Nondeterministic Algorithms”. In: *Journal of the ACM* 14.4 (Oct. 1967), pp. 636–644. ISSN: 0004-5411. DOI: `10.1145/321420.321422`.

[FM18] Adel Ferdjoukh and Jean-Marie Mottu. “Towards an Automated Fault Localizer while Designing Meta-models”. In: *MDEbug@MODELS, International Workshop on Debugging in Model-Driven Engineering.* 2018.

[Föh14] Christoph Föhrdes. “Simulation components for software quality simulation in Eclipse”. Master’s Thesis. Karlsruhe Institute of Technology (KIT), Germany, 2014.

[Fon+15] Jaime Font, Manuel Ballarín, Øystein Haugen, and Carlos Cetina. "Automating the Variability Formalization of a Model Family by Means of Common Variability Language". In: *Proceedings of the 19th International Conference on Software Product Line*. SPLC '15. Nashville, Tennessee: ACM, 2015, pp. 411–418. ISBN: 978-1-4503-3613-0. DOI: 10.1145/2791060.2793678.

[Fow+99] Martin Fowler, Kent Beck, John Brant, William Opdyke, and Don Roberts. *Refactoring: Improving the Design of Existing Code*. Addison-Wesley object technology series. Boston, MA, USA: Addison-Wesley, Reading, MA, USA, 1999. ISBN: 0-201-48567-2.

[Fow03] Martin Fowler. *UML Distilled: A Brief Guide to the Standard Object Modeling Language, Third Edition*. Addison-Wesley, Reading, MA, USA, 2003.

[FP10] Martin Fowler and Rebecca Parsons. *Domain Specific Languages*. 1st. Addison-Wesley, Reading, MA, USA, 2010. ISBN: 9780321712943.

[Fre+04] Eric Freeman, Elisabeth Robson, Bert Bates, and Kathy Sierra. *Head First Design Patterns*. Head First. O'Reilly Media, 2004. ISBN: 9780596800741.

[Für+09] Simon Fürst, Jürgen Mössinger, Stefan Bunzel, Thomas Weber, Frank Kirschke-Biller, Peter Heitkämper, Gerulf Kinkelin, Kenji Nishikawa, and Klaus Lange. "AUTOSAR–A Worldwide Standard is on the Road". In: *14th International VDI Congress Electronic Systems for Vehicles, Baden-Baden*. Vol. 62. 2009.

[Gam+95] Erich Gamma, Richard Helm, Ralph Johnson, and John Vlissides. *Design Patterns: Elements of Reusable Object-Oriented Software*. Addison-Wesley, Reading, MA, USA, 1995. ISBN: 0-201-63361-2.

[Gar+14] Antonio Garmendia, Esther Guerra, Dimitrios S. Kolovos, and Juan de Lara. "EMF Splitter: A Structured Approach to EMF Modularity". In: *Proceedings of the 3rd Workshop on Extreme Modeling*. Vol. 1239. CEUR-WS, Sept. 2014, pp. 22–31. URL: http://ceur-ws.org/Vol-1239/xm14_submission_3.pdf.

[GBB12] Thomas Goldschmidt, Steffen Becker, and Erik Burger. "Towards a Tool-Oriented Taxonomy of View-Based Modelling". In: *Proceedings of the Modellierung 2012*. Ed. by Elmar J. Sinz and Andy Schürr. Vol. P-201. GI-Edition – Lecture Notes in Informatics (LNI). Bamberg: Gesellschaft für Informatik e.V. (GI), Mar. 2012, pp. 59–74. ISBN: 978-3-88579-295-6.

[GBS12] Juan J. C. Gómez, Benoit Baudry, and Houari Sahraoui. "Searching the Boundaries of a Modeling Space to Test Metamodels". In: *2012 IEEE Fifth International Conference on Software Testing, Verification and Validation (ICST)*. Los Alamitos, CA, USA: IEEE Computer Society, Apr. 2012, pp. 131–140. ISBN: 978-0-7695-4670-4. DOI: 10.1109/ICST.2012.93.

[Gen+07] Marcela Genero, Esperanza Manso, Aaron Visaggio, Gerardo Canfora, and Mario Piattini. "Building measure-based prediction models for UML class diagram maintainability". English. In: *Empirical Software Engineering* 12 (5 2007). ISSN: 1382-3256.

[GGF09] I. García-Magariño, J. Gómez-Sanz, and R. Fuentes-Fernández. "An evaluation framework for MAS modeling languages based on metamodel metrics". In: *Agent-Oriented Software Engineering* (2009).

[GL03] Jean Gelissen and Ronan Mac Laverty. *ROBOCOP: Revised specification of framework and models (Deliverable1.5)*. Tech. rep. Information Technology for European Advancement, 2003.

[GMS05] Vincenzo Grassi, Raffaela Mirandola, and Antonino Sabetta. "From Design to Analysis Models: a Kernel Language for Performance and Reliability Analysis of Component-based Systems". In: *WOSP '05: Proceedings of the 5th international workshop on Software and performance*. Palma, Illes Balears, Spain: ACM Press, 2005, pp. 25–36. ISBN: 1-59593-087-6.

[Gra+08] Vincenzo Grassi, Raffaela Mirandola, Enrico Randazzo, and Antonino Sabetta. "KLAPER: An Intermediate Language for Model-Driven Predictive Analysis of Performance and Reliability". In: *The Common Component Modeling Example: Comparing Software Component Models*. Ed. by Andreas Rausch, Ralf Reussner, Raffaela Mirandola, and František Plášil. Berlin,

Heidelberg: Springer Berlin Heidelberg, 2008, pp. 327–356. ISBN: 978-3-540-85289-6. DOI: 10.1007/978-3-540-85289-6_13.

[Gre+15] Timo Greifenberg, Markus Look, Sebastian Roidl, and Bernhard Rumpe. "Engineering Tagging Languages for DSLs". In: *Conference on Model Driven Engineering Languages and Systems (MODELS'15)*. ACM/IEEE, 2015, pp. 34–43. URL: http://www.se-rwth.de/publications/Engineering-Tagging-Languages-for-DSLs.pdf.

[Grö+08] Hans Grönniger, Holger Krahn, Claas Pinkernell, and Bernhard Rumpe. "Modeling Variants of Automotive Systems using Views". In: *Modellbasierte Entwicklung von eingebetteten Fahrzeugfunktionen*. Informatik Bericht 2008-01. TU Braunschweig, 2008, pp. 76–89. URL: http://www.se-rwth.de/topics/~/rumpe/publications20042008/Modeling-Variants-of-Automotive-Systems-using-Views.pdf.

[GSS13] Samarthyam Ganesh, Tushar Sharma, and Girish Suryanarayana. "Towards a Principle-based Classification of Structural Design Smells". In: *Journal of Object Technology* 12.2 (2013).

[Gul07] Jon Atle Gulla. "Using Models in Enterprise Systems Projects". In: *Conceptual Modelling in Information Systems Engineering*. Ed. by John Krogstie, Andreas Lothe Opdahl, and Sjaak Brinkkemper. Berlin, Heidelberg: Springer Berlin Heidelberg, 2007, pp. 107–122. ISBN: 978-3-540-72677-7. DOI: 10.1007/978-3-540-72677-7_7.

[Hab+11] Arne Haber, Holger Rendel, Bernhard Rumpe, Ina Schaefer, and Frank van der Linden. "Hierarchical Variability Modeling for Software Architectures". In: *Software Product Lines Conference (SPLC'11)*. IEEE, 2011, pp. 150–159. ISBN: 978-1-4577-1029-2. URL: http://www.se-rwth.de/publications/Hierarchical-Variability-Modeling-for-Software-Architectures.pdf.

[Hab+15] Arne Haber, Markus Look, Pedram Mir Seyed Nazari, Antonio Navarro Perez, Bernhard Rumpe, Steven Völkel, and Andreas Wortmann. "Integration of Heterogeneous Modeling Languages via Extensible and Composable Language Components". In: *Model-Driven Engineering and Software Development Conference (MODELSWARD'15)*. SciTePress, 2015, pp. 19–31. URL: http://www.se-rwth.de/publications/Integration-of-Heterogeneous-Modeling-Languages-via-Extensible-and-Composable-Language-Components.pdf.

[Hah17] René Hahn. "Bad Smells and Anti-Patterns in Metamodeling". MA thesis. Karlsruhe, Germany: Karlsruhe Institute of Technology (KIT), Nov. 2017.

[Hap+14] Lucia Happe, Erik Burger, Max Kramer, Andreas Rentschler, and Ralf Reussner. "Completion and Extension Techniques for Enterprise Software Performance Engineering". In: *Future Business Software – Current Trends in Business Software Development*. Ed. by Gino Brunetti, Thomas Feld, Joachim Schnitter, Lutz Heuser, and Christian Webel. Progress in IS. New York, Heidelberg: Springer International Publishing, 2014, pp. 117–131. ISBN: 978-3-319-04143-8. DOI: 10.1007/978-3-319-04144-5.

[Hau+08] O. Haugen, B. Moller-Pedersen, J. Oldevik, G.K. Olsen, and A. Svendsen. "Adding Standardized Variability to Domain Specific Languages". In: *12th Intl. Software Product Line Conference, 2008*. Sept. 2008, pp. 139–148. DOI: 10.1109/SPLC.2008.25.

[Hau09] Michael Hauck. "Extending Performance-Oriented Resource Modelling in the Palladio Component Model". Diploma Thesis. Germany: University of Karlsruhe (TH), Feb. 2009. URL: http://sdqweb.ipd.uka.de/publications/pdfs/hauck2009a.pdf.

[HBJ09] Markus Herrmannsdörfer, Sebastian Benz, and Elmar Juergens. "COPE – Automating Coupled Evolution of Metamodels and Models". In: *European Conference on Object-Oriented Programming*. Ed. by Sophia Drossopoulou. Berlin, Heidelberg: Springer Berlin Heidelberg, 2009, pp. 52–76. ISBN: 978-3-642-03013-0.

[HBK18] Robert Heinrich, Kiana Busch, and Sandro Koch. "A Methodology for Domain-spanning Change Impact Analysis". In: *2018 44th Euromicro Conference on Software Engineering and Advanced Applications (SEAA)*. IEEE, 2018, pp. 326–330. DOI: 10.1109/SEAA.2018.00060.

[Hei+15] Robert Heinrich, Stefan Gärtner, Tom-Michael Hesse, Thomas Ruhroth, Ralf Reussner, Kurt Schneider, Barbara Paech, and Jan Jürjens. "The CoCoME Platform: A Research Note on Empirical Studies in Information System Evolution". In: *International Journal of Software Engineering and Knowledge Engineering* 25.09&10 (2015), pp. 1715–1720. DOI: 10.1142/S0218194015710059. eprint: http://www.worldscientific.com/doi/pdf/10.1142/S0218194015710059. URL: http://www.worldscientific.com/doi/abs/10.1142/S0218194015710059.

[Hei+17] Robert Heinrich, Philipp Merkle, Jörg Henss, and Barbara Paech. "Integrating business process simulation and information system simulation for performance prediction". In: *Software & Systems Modeling* 16.1 (2017), pp. 257–277. ISSN: 1619-1366. DOI: 10.1007/s10270-015-0457-1.

[Hei+18] Robert Heinrich, Sandro Koch, Suhyun Cha, Kiana Busch, Ralf Reussner, and Birgit Vogel-Heuser. "Architecture-based change impact analysis in cross-disciplinary automated production systems". In: *Journal of Systems and Software* 146 (2018), pp. 167–185. ISSN: 0164-1212. DOI: 10.1016/j.jss.2018.08.058. URL: http://www.sciencedirect.com/science/article/pii/S0164121218301717.

[Hei14] Robert Heinrich. *Aligning Business Processes and Information Systems: New Approaches to Continuous Quality Engineering*. Springer, 2014. ISBN: 978-3-658-06517-1. DOI: 10.1007/978-3-658-06518-8.

[Her11a] Lukáš Hermann. *User documentation of the SOFA 2 UML*. July 2011. URL: https://sofa.ow2.org/docs/index.html.

[Her11b] Markus Herrmannsdörfer. "Evolutionary Metamodeling". PhD thesis. München: Technische Universität München, 2011.

[Her17] Rüdiger Heres. "Vergleich von Metamodell-Erweiterungsmethoden in EMOF". Bachelor's Thesis. Karlsruhe, Germany: Karlsruhe Institute of Technology (KIT), Oct. 2017.

[Hin+16] Georg Hinkel, Max Kramer, Erik Burger, Misha Strittmatter, and Lucia Happe. "An Empirical Study on the Perception of Metamodel Quality". In: *Proceedings of the 4th International Conference on Model-Driven Engineering and Software Development.* Rome, Italy, Feb. 2016, pp. 145–152. ISBN: 978-989-758-168-7. URL: `http://www.scitepress.org/DigitalLibrary/PublicationsDetail.aspx?ID=9KRBAJDhYyc%3d`.

[Hin16a] Georg Hinkel. *Deep Modeling through Structural Decomposition.* Tech. rep. Karlsruhe: Karlsruhe Institute of Technology, 2016. URL: `http://nbn-resolving.org/urn:nbn:de:swb:90-576330`.

[Hin16b] Georg Hinkel. *NMF: A Modeling Framework for the .NET Platform.* Tech. rep. Karlsruhe: Karlsruhe Institute of Technology, 2016. URL: `http://nbn-resolving.org/urn:nbn:de:swb:90-537082`.

[Hin18] Georg Hinkel. "Implicit Incremental Model Analyses and Transformations". PhD thesis. Karlsruhe Institute of Technology (KIT), 2018. 475 pp. DOI: `10.5445/IR/1000084464`.

[HR17] Katrin Hölldobler and Bernhard Rumpe. *MontiCore 5 Language Workbench Edition 2017.* Aachener Informatik-Berichte, Software Engineering, Band 32. Shaker Verlag, Dec. 2017. ISBN: 978-3-8440-5713-3. URL: `http://www.se-rwth.de/phdtheses/MontiCore-5-Language-Workbench-Edition-2017.pdf`.

[HS18] Georg Hinkel and Misha Strittmatter. "Predicting the Perceived Modularity of MOF-based Metamodels". In: *Proceedings of the 6th International Conference on Model-Driven Engineering and Software Development* (Funchal, Portugal). Jan. 2018. URL: `http://sdqweb.ipd.kit.edu/publications/pdfs/hinkel2018a.pdf`.

[HSR19] Robert Heinrich, Misha Strittmatter, and Ralf Heinrich Reussner. "A Layered Reference Architecture for Metamodels to Tailor Quality Modeling and Analysis". In: *IEEE Transactions on Software Engineering* (2019). ISSN: 0098-5589. DOI: 10.1109/TSE.2019.2903797.

[Hub+17] Nikolaus Huber, Fabian Brosig, Simon Spinner, Samuel Kounev, and Manuel Bähr. "Model-Based Self-Aware Performance and Resource Management Using the Descartes Modeling Language". In: *IEEE Transactions on Software Engineering (TSE)* 43.5 (2017). DOI: 10.1109/TSE.2016.2613863.

[HW14] Markus Herrmannsdörfer and Guido Wachsmuth. "Evolving Software Systems". In: ed. by Tom Mens, Alexander Serebrenik, and Anthony Cleve. Berlin, Heidelberg: Springer Berlin Heidelberg, 2014. Chap. Coupled Evolution of Software Metamodels and Models, pp. 33–63. ISBN: 978-3-642-45398-4. DOI: 10.1007/978-3-642-45398-4_2.

[ISO01] ISO/IEC 9126-1:2001(E). *Software engineering – Product quality – Part 1: Quality model.* International Organization for Standardization, Geneva, Switzerland, 2001.

[ISO11] ISO/IEC 25010:2011(E). *Software engineering – Software product Quality Requirements and Evaluation (SQuaRE) – System and software quality models.* International Organization for Standardization, Geneva, Switzerland, 2011.

[ISO16] ISO/IEC 25023:2016(E). *Systems and software engineering – Systems and software Quality Requirements and Evaluation (SQuaRE) – Measurement of system and software product quality.* International Organization for Standardization, Geneva, Switzerland, 2016.

[JHH16] Reiner Jung, Robert Heinrich, and Wilhelm Hasselbring. "GECO: A Generator Composition Approach for Aspect-Oriented DSLs". In: *Theory and Practice of Model Transformations: 9th International Conference on Model Transformation, ICMT 2016.* Springer International Publishing, 2016, pp. 141–156. ISBN: 978-3-319-42064-6. DOI: 10.1007/978-3-319-42064-6_10.

[Jia+04] Yanbing Jiang, Weizhong Shao, Lu Zhang, Zhiyi Ma, Xiangwen Meng, and Haohai Ma. "On the Classification of UML's Meta Model Extension Mechanism". In: *UML 2004 — The Unified Modeling Language. Modeling Languages and Applications.* Ed. by Thomas Baar, Alfred Strohmeier, Ana Moreira, and Stephen J. Mellor. Berlin, Heidelberg: Springer Berlin Heidelberg, 2004, pp. 54–68. ISBN: 978-3-540-30187-5.

[Jul13] Klaus Julisch. "Understanding and overcoming cyber security anti-patterns". In: *Computer Networks* 57.10 (2013), pp. 2206–2211. ISSN: 1389-1286. DOI: 10.1016/j.comnet.2012.11.023. URL: http://www.sciencedirect.com/science/article/pii/S1389128613000388.

[Jun+14] Reiner Jung, Robert Heinrich, Eric Schmieders, Misha Strittmatter, and Wilhelm Hasselbring. "A Method for Aspect-oriented Meta-Model Evolution". In: *Proceedings of the 2Nd Workshop on View-Based, Aspect-Oriented and Orthographic Software Modelling.* VAO '14. York, United Kingdom: ACM, July 2014, 19:19–19:22. ISBN: 978-1-4503-2900-2. DOI: 10.1145/2631675.2631681.

[Jun16a] Reiner Jung. "Generator-Composition for Aspect-Oriented Domain-Specific Languages". Doctoral Thesis/PhD. Faculty of Engineering, Kiel University, Aug. 2016. URL: http://eprints.uni-kiel.de/33602/.

[Jun16b] Michael Junker. "Flexible Graphical Editors for Extensible Modular Meta Models". MA thesis. Karlsruhe Institute of Technology (KIT), 2016. URL: http://nbn-resolving.org/urn:nbn:de:swb:90-669277.

[Jür02] Jan Jürjens. "UMLsec: Extending UML for Secure Systems Development". In: *International Conference on The Unified Modeling Language.* Ed. by Jean-Marc Jézéquel, Heinrich Hussmann, and Stephen Cook. Berlin, Heidelberg: Springer Berlin Heidelberg, 2002, pp. 412–425. ISBN: 978-3-540-45800-5.

[KAK09] Jörg Kienzle, Wisam Al Abed, and Jacques Klein. "Aspect-oriented multi-view modeling". In: *Proceedings of the 8th ACM international conference on Aspect-oriented software development.* AOSD '09. Charlottesville, Virginia, USA: ACM, 2009, pp. 87–98. ISBN: 978-1-60558-442-3. DOI: 10.1145/1509239.1509252.

[Kan+90] Kyo C Kang, Sholom G Cohen, James A Hess, William E Novak, and A Spencer Peterson. *Feature-oriented domain analysis (FODA) feasibility study*. Tech. rep. Carnegie-Mellon University Pittsburgh PA Software Engineering Inst, 1990. URL: https://resources.sei.cmu.edu/asset_files/TechnicalReport/1990_005_001_15872.pdf.

[Kan17] Ilknur Kanatsiz. "Entwicklung eines durch ein Feature-Modell konfigurierbaren Palladio-Metamodells mit dem CORE Ansatz". Diploma Thesis. Karlsruhe, Germany: Karlsruhe Institute of Technology (KIT), Nov. 2017.

[KBH14] Samuel Kounev, Fabian Brosig, and Nikolaus Huber. *The Descartes Modeling Language*. Tech. rep. Department of Computer Science, University of Wuerzburg, Oct. 2014, p. 91. URL: http://www.descartes-research.net/dml/.

[KBK15] Johannes Kroß, Andreas Brunnert, and Helmut Krcmar. "Modeling Big Data Systems by Extending the Palladio Component Model". In: *Softwaretechnik-Trends* 35.3 (2015).

[KBL13] Max E. Kramer, Erik Burger, and Michael Langhammer. "View-Centric Engineering with Synchronized Heterogeneous Models". In: *Proceedings of the 1st Workshop on View-Based, Aspect-Oriented and Orthographic Software Modelling*. VAO '13. Montpellier, France: ACM, 2013, 5:1–5:6. ISBN: 978-1-4503-2070-2. DOI: 10.1145/2489861.2489864. URL: http://sdqweb.ipd.kit.edu/publications/pdfs/kramer2013b.pdf.

[Kec17] Amine Kechaou. "A graphical approach to modularization and layering of metamodels". Bachelor's Thesis. Karlsruhe, Germany: Karlsruhe Institute of Technology (KIT), 2017, p. 42. DOI: 10.5445/IR/1000078437.

[KKK13] Benjamin Klatt, Martin Küster, and Klaus Krogmann. "A Graph-Based Analysis Concept to Derive a Variation Point Design from Product Copies". In: *Proceedings of the 1st International workshop on Reverse Variability Engineering (REVE'13)*. Genua, Italy, Mar. 2013, pp. 1–8.

[KKW14] Benjamin Klatt, Klaus Krogmann, and Christian Wende. "Consolidating Customized Product Copies to Software Product Lines". In: *Softwaretechnik-Trends* 34.2 (May 2014), pp. 64–65. URL: http://pi.informatik.uni-siegen.de/stt/34_2/01_Fachgruppenberichte/WSRDFF/wsre_dff_2014-08_submission_w8.pdf.

[Kla14] Benjamin Klatt. "Consolidation of Customized Product Copies into Software Product Lines". PhD thesis. Karlsruhe, Germany: Karlsruhe Institute of Technology (KIT), Oct. 2014. URL: http://digbib.ubka.uni-karlsruhe.de/volltexte/1000043687.

[Koc17] Sandro Koch. "Automatische Vorhersage von Änderungsausbreitungen am Beispiel von Automatisierungssystemen". MA thesis. Karlsruhe Institute of Technology (KIT), 2017.

[Koz08] Heiko Koziolek. "Dependability Metrics". In: *Dependability Metrics.* Vol. 4909. Lecture Notes in Computer Science. Springer-Verlag Berlin Heidelberg, 2008. Chap. Goal, Question, Metric, pp. 39–42. URL: http://www.springerlink.com/content/n737771751296q23/fulltext.pdf.

[Koz10] Heiko Koziolek. "Performance evaluation of component-based software systems: A survey". In: *Performance Evaluation* 67.8 (2010). Special Issue on Software and Performance, pp. 634–658. ISSN: 0166-5316. DOI: 10.1016/j.peva.2009.07.007.

[Koz11a] Anne Koziolek. "Automated Improvement of Software Architecture Models for Performance and Other Quality Attributes". PhD thesis. Karlsruhe, Germany: Institut für Programmstrukturen und Datenorganisation (IPD), Karlsruher Institut für Technologie, July 2011. URL: http://digbib.ubka.uni-karlsruhe.de/volltexte/1000024955.

[Koz11b] Heiko Koziolek. "Sustainability Evaluation of Software Architectures: A Systematic Review". In: *Proceedings of the 7th Int. ACM/SIGSOFT Conference on the Quality of Software Architectures (QoSA).* Boulder, Colorado, USA: ACM, June 2011, pp. 3–12. DOI: 10.1145/2000259.2000263.

[Kra+12] Max E. Kramer, Zoya Durdik, Michael Hauck, Jörg Henss, Martin Küster, Philipp Merkle, and Andreas Rentschler. "Extending the Palladio Component Model using Profiles and Stereotypes". In: *Palladio Days 2012 Proceedings (appeared as technical report)*. Ed. by Steffen Becker, Jens Happe, Anne Koziolek, and Ralf Reussner. Karlsruhe Reports in Informatics ; 2012,21. Karlsruhe: KIT, Faculty of Informatics, 2012, pp. 7–15. URL: `http://nbn-resolving.org/urn:nbn:de:swb:90-308043`.

[Kra+15] Max E. Kramer, Michael Langhammer, Dominik Messinger, Stephan Seifermann, and Erik Burger. *Realizing Change-Driven Consistency for Component Code, Architectural Models, and Contracts in Vitruvius*. Tech. rep. Karlsruhe: Karlsruhe Institute of Technology, Department of Informatics, 2015. URL: `http://nbn-resolving.org/urn:nbn:de:swb:90-456541`.

[KRV08] Holger Krahn, Bernhard Rumpe, and Steven Völkel. "MontiCore: Modular Development of Textual Domain Specific Languages". In: *Objects, Components, Models and Patterns: 46th International Conference, TOOLS EUROPE 2008, Proceedings*. Ed. by Richard F. Paige and Bertrand Meyer. Springer, 2008, pp. 297–315.

[KRV10] Holger Krahn, Bernhard Rumpe, and Steven Völkel. "MontiCore: a framework for compositional development of domain specific languages". In: *International Journal on Software Tools for Technology Transfer* 12.5 (Sept. 2010), pp. 353–372. ISSN: 1433-2787. DOI: `10.1007/s10009-010-0142-1`.

[KS18] Amine Kechaou and Misha Strittmatter. "Modularizing and Layering Metamodels with the Modular EMF Designer". In: *Proceedings of the 21st ACM/IEEE International Conference on Model Driven Engineering Languages and Systems: Companion Proceedings*. MODELS '18. Copenhagen, Denmark: ACM, Oct. 2018, pp. 32–36. ISBN: 978-1-4503-5965-8. DOI: `10.1145/3270112.3270119`.

[Küh17] Thomas Kühn. "A Family of Role-Based Languages". PhD thesis. Dresden, Germany: Technische Universität Dresden,

Fakultät Informatik, Aug. 2017. URL: http://nbn-resolving.de/urn:nbn:de:bsz:14-qucosa-228027.

[Lan+11] Philip Langer, Konrad Wieland, Manuel Wimmer, and Jordi Cabot. "From UML Profiles to EMF Profiles and Beyond". In: *Objects, Models, Components, Patterns.* Ed. by Judith Bishop and Antonio Vallecillo. Vol. 6705. Lecture Notes in Computer Science. Springer Berlin / Heidelberg, 2011, pp. 52–67. ISBN: 978-3-642-21951-1.

[Lan+12] Philip Langer, Konrad Wieland, Manuel Wimmer, and Jordi Cabot. "EMF Profiles: A Lightweight Extension Approach for EMF Models". In: *Journal of Object Technology* 11.1 (2012), 8:1–29. ISSN: 1660-1769. DOI: 10.5381/jot.2012.11.1.a8.

[Lan74] Edmund Landau. *Handbuch der Lehre von der Verteilung der Primzahlen.* 3. ed. New York: Chelsea Publ., 1974. ISBN: 0-8284-0096-2.

[LDC18] Manuel Leduc, Thomas Degueule, and Benoit Combemale. "Modular Language Composition for the Masses". In: *Proceedings of the 11th ACM SIGPLAN International Conference on Software Language Engineering.* SLE 2018. Boston, MA, USA: ACM, 2018, pp. 47–59. ISBN: 978-1-4503-6029-6. DOI: 10.1145/3276604.3276622.

[Léd+01] Ákos Lédeczi, Greg Nordstrom, Gabor Karsai, Peter Volgyesi, and Miklos Maroti. "On metamodel composition". In: *Proceedings of the 2001 IEEE International Conference on Control Applications.* CCA'01. IEEE, Sept. 2001, pp. 756–760. DOI: 10.1109/CCA.2001.973959.

[Leh18] Sebastian Michael Lehrig. "Efficiently Conducting Quality-of-Service Analyses by Templating Architectural Knowledge". PhD thesis. Karlsruher Institut für Technologie (KIT), 2018. 514 pp. ISBN: 978-3-7315-0756-7. DOI: 10.5445/KSP/1000079766.

[Leh80] Meir Manny Lehman. "On Understanding Laws, Evolution, and Conservation in the Large-program Life Cycle". In: *Journal of Systems and Software* 1 (Sept. 1980), pp. 213–221. ISSN: 0164-1212. DOI: 10.1016/0164-1212(79)90022-0.

[Lev+14] Tihamer Levendovszky, Daniel Balasubramanian, Anantha Narayanan, Feng Shi, Chris van Buskirk, and Gabor Karsai. "A semi-formal description of migrating domain-specific models with evolving domains". In: *Software & Systems Modeling* 13.2 (May 2014), pp. 807–823. ISSN: 1619-1374. DOI: 10.1007/s10270-012-0313-5.

[LEZ14] Benoit Langlois, Daniel Exertier, and Boubekeur Zendagui. "Development of Modelling Frameworks and Viewpoints with Kitalpha". In: *Proceedings of the 14th Workshop on Domain-Specific Modeling*. DSM '14. Portland, Oregon, USA: ACM, 2014, pp. 19–22. ISBN: 978-1-4503-2156-3. DOI: 10.1145/2688447.2688451.

[LG10a] Juan de Lara and Esther Guerra. "Deep Meta-modelling with MetaDepth". In: *Objects, Models, Components, Patterns*. Ed. by Jan Vitek. Berlin, Heidelberg: Springer Berlin Heidelberg, 2010, pp. 1–20. ISBN: 978-3-642-13953-6.

[LG10b] Juan de Lara and Esther Guerra. "Generic Meta-modelling with Concepts, Templates and Mixin Layers". In: *2010 ACM/IEEE 13th International Conference on Model-Driven Engineering Languages and Systems (MODELS)*. Ed. by Dorina C. Petriu, Nicolas Rouquette, and Øystein Haugen. Oslo, Norway: Springer Berlin Heidelberg, Oct. 2010, pp. 16–30. ISBN: 978-3-642-16145-2. DOI: 10.1007/978-3-642-16145-2_2.

[LGL14a] Jesús J. López-Fernández, Esther Guerra, and Juan de Lara. "Meta-Model Validation and Verification with MetaBest". In: *Proceedings of the 29th ACM/IEEE International Conference on Automated Software Engineering*. ASE '14. Vasteras, Sweden: ACM, 2014, pp. 831–834. ISBN: 978-1-4503-3013-8. DOI: 10.1145/2642937.2648617.

[LGL14b] Jesús J López-Fernández, Esther Guerra, and Juan de Lara. "Assessing the Quality of Meta-models". In: *Proceedings of the 11th Workshop on Model Driven Engineering, Verification and Validation (MoDeVVa)*. 2014, p. 3.

[LH96] Sheng Liang and Paul Hudak. "Modular denotational semantics for compiler construction". In: *Programming Languages and Systems—ESOP'96* (1996), pp. 219–234.

[LP09] Maria Teresa Llano and Rob Pooley. "UML specification and correction of object-oriented anti-patterns". In: *Software Engineering Advances, 2009. ICSEA'09. Fourth International Conference on*. IEEE. 2009, pp. 39–44.

[LR06] Martin Lippert and Stephen Roock. *Refactoring in large software projects: performing complex restructurings successfully*. John Wiley & Sons, 2006.

[LR13] Kevin Lano and Shekoufeh Kolahdouz Rahimi. "Case study: Class diagram restructuring". In: *Proceedings Sixth Transformation Tool Contest, TTC 2013, Budapest, Hungary, 19-20 June, 2013*. 2013, pp. 8–15. DOI: 10.4204/EPTCS.135.2.

[LW94] Barbara H. Liskov and Jeannette M. Wing. "A Behavioral Notion of Subtyping". In: *ACM Transactions on Programming Languages and Systems* 16.6 (Nov. 1994), pp. 1811–1841. URL: http://www.acm.org/pubs/articles/journals/toplas/1994-16-6/p1811-liskov/p1811-liskov.pdf.

[Mar03] Robert Cecil Martin. *Agile Software Development: Principles, Patterns, and Practices*. Upper Saddle River, NJ, USA: Prentice Hall PTR, 2003. ISBN: 0135974445.

[Mar98] Michele Marchesi. "OOA metrics for the Unified Modeling Language". In: *Proceedings of the Second Euromicro Conference on Software Maintenance and Reengineering*. Mar. 1998, pp. 67–73.

[May+13] Tanja Mayerhofer, Philip Langer, Manuel Wimmer, and Gerti Kappel. "xMOF: Executable DSMLs based on fUML". In: *International Conference on Software Language Engineering*. Springer. 2013, pp. 56–75.

[McC76] Thomas J. McCabe. "A Complexity Measure". In: *IEEE Transactions on Software Engineering* SE-2.4 (Dec. 1976), pp. 308–320. ISSN: 0098-5589. DOI: 10.1109/TSE.1976.233837.

[Mén+16a] David Méndez-Acuña, José A. Galindo, Benoit Combemale, Arnaud Blouin, and Benoit Baudry. "Puzzle: A Tool for Analyzing and Extracting Specification Clones in DSLs". In: *Software Reuse: Bridging with Social-Awareness: 15th International Conference, ICSR 2016, Limassol, Cyprus, June 5-7, 2016, Proceedings*. Ed. by Georgia M. Kapitsaki and Eduardo Santana de Almeida. Cham: Springer International Publishing, 2016, pp. 393–396. ISBN: 978-3-319-35122-3. DOI: 10.1007/978-3-319-35122-3_26.

[Mén+16b] David Méndez-Acuña, José A. Galindo, Thomas Degueule, Benoît Combemale, and Benoît Baudry. "Leveraging Software Product Lines Engineering in the development of external DSLs: A systematic literature review". In: *Computer Languages, Systems & Structures* 46.Supplement C (Nov. 2016), pp. 206–235. ISSN: 1477-8424. DOI: 10.1016/j.cl.2016.09.004. URL: http://www.sciencedirect.com/science/article/pii/S1477842416300768.

[Mey09] Bertrand Meyer. "Touch of class". In: *Learning to program well with Object Technology and Design by Contract, AN INTRODUCTION TO SOFTWARE ENGINEERING http://se. inf. ethz. ch/touch* (2009).

[MG06] Tom Mens and Pieter Van Gorp. "A Taxonomy of Model Transformation". In: *Electronic Notes in Theoretical Computer Science* 152 (2006). Proceedings of the International Workshop on Graph and Model Transformation (GraMoT 2005), pp. 125–142. ISSN: 1571-0661. DOI: 10.1016/j.entcs.2005.10.021. URL: http://www.sciencedirect.com/science/article/pii/S1571066106001435.

[MGP03] MaEsperanza Manso, Marcela Genero, and Mario Piattini. "No-redundant Metrics for UML Class Diagram Structural Complexity". In: *Advanced Information Systems Engineering*. Vol. 2681. Lecture Notes in Computer Science. Springer Berlin Heidelberg, 2003, pp. 127–142.

[MH11] Philipp Merkle and Jörg Henss. "EventSim – An Event-driven Palladio Software Architecture Simulator". In: *Palladio Days 2011 Proceedings (appeared as technical report)*. Ed. by Steffen Becker, Jens Happe, and Ralf Reussner. Karlsruhe Reports in Informatics ; 2011,32. Karlsruhe: KIT, Fakultät für Informatik, 2011, pp. 15–22. URL: http://digbib.ubka.uni-karlsruhe.de/volltexte/1000025188.

[MHK99] Brian Keith Miller, Pei Hsia, and Chenho Kung. "Object-oriented architecture measures". In: *Systems Sciences, 1999. HICSS-32. Proceedings of the 32nd Annual Hawaii International Conference on.* IEEE. 1999, 10–pp.

[Mor+14] Antonio Moreno-Delgado, Francisco Durán, Steffen Zschaler, and Javier Troya. "Modular DSLs for flexible analysis: An e-Motions reimplementation of Palladio". In: *European Conference on Modelling Foundations and Applications.* Ed. by Jordi Cabot and Julia Rubin. Springer International Publishing, 2014, pp. 132–147. ISBN: 978-3-319-09195-2.

[Mos04] Peter D Mosses. "Modular structural operational semantics". In: *The Journal of Logic and Algebraic Programming* 60 (2004), pp. 195–228.

[MT04] T. Mens and T. Tourwe. "A survey of software refactoring". In: *IEEE Transactions on Software Engineering* 30.2 (Feb. 2004), pp. 126–139. ISSN: 0098-5589. DOI: 10.1109/TSE.2004.1265817.

[Nar+09] Anantha Narayanan, Tihamer Levendovszky, Daniel Balasubramanian, and Gabor Karsai. "Automatic Domain Model Migration to Manage Metamodel Evolution". In: *Model Driven Engineering Languages and Systems.* Ed. by Andy Schürr and Bran Selic. Berlin, Heidelberg: Springer Berlin Heidelberg, 2009, pp. 706–711. ISBN: 978-3-642-04425-0.

[Obj06] Object Management Group (OMG). *Object Constraint Language, v2.0 (formal/ 06-05-01).* 2006. URL: http://www.omg.org/cgi-bin/doc?formal/2006-05-01.

[Obj11] Object Management Group (OMG). *UML Profile for MARTE: Modeling and Analysis of Real-Time Embedded Systems, version 1.1.* 2011. URL: http://www.omg.org/spec/MARTE/1.1/PDF.

[Obj14] Object Management Group (OMG). *Business Process Model And Notation Specification (BPMN) – Version 2.0.2.* Jan. 2014. URL: http://www.omg.org/spec/BPMN/2.0.2/.

[Obj16] Object Management Group (OMG). *MOF 2.5.1 Core Specification (formal/2016-11-01).* Nov. 2016. URL: http://www.omg.org/spec/MOF/2.5.1/.

[Obj17] Object Management Group (OMG). *Unified Modeling Language (UML) – Version 2.5.1.* Dec. 2017. URL: http://www.omg.org/spec/UML/2.5.1/.

[Obj18] Object Management Group (OMG). *Structured Metrics Metamodel (SMM) – Version 1.2 beta.* Apr. 2018. URL: https://www.omg.org/spec/SMM/1.2/Beta1/.

[Pag88] Meilir Page-Jones. *Practical Guide to Structured Systems Design (2nd Edition).* 2nd ed. Prentice Hall, May 1988. ISBN: 9788120314825.

[Par72] David Lorge Parnas. "On the Criteria to Be Used in Decomposing Systems into Modules". In: *Communications of the ACM* 15.12 (Dec. 1972), pp. 1053–1058. ISSN: 0001-0782.

[Pes+15] Ana Pescador, Antonio Garmendia, Esther Guerra, Jesús Sánchez Cuadrado, and Juan de Lara. "Pattern-based development of Domain-Specific Modelling Languages". In: *2015 ACM/IEEE 18th International Conference on Model Driven Engineering Languages and Systems (MODELS).* IEEE. Sept. 2015, pp. 166–175. DOI: 10.1109/MODELS.2015.7338247.

[Pil18] Roman Pilipchuk. "Coping with Access Control Requirements in the Context of Mutual Dependencies between Business and IT". In: *Proceedings of the Central European Cybersecurity Conference 2018.* CECC'18. ACM, 2018. DOI: 10.1145/3277570.3277587.

[PS16] Parul and Brahmaleen Kaur Sidhu. "Model Smells In Uml Class Diagrams". In: *International Journal of Enhanced Research in Management & Computer Applications* 5.5 (May 2016). ISSN: 2319-7471.

[PSH18] Roman Pilipchuk, Stephan Seifermann, and Robert Heinrich. "Aligning Business Process Access Control Policies with Enterprise Architecture". In: *Proceedings of the Central European Cybersecurity Conference 2018.* CECC'18. ACM, 2018. DOI: 10.1145/3277570.3277588.

[Ras+15] Wolfgang Raskob, Valentin Bertsch, Manuel Ruppert, Misha Strittmatter, Lucia Happe, Brandon Broadnax, Stefan Wandler, and Evgenia Deines. "Security of Electricity Supply in 2030". In: *Critical Infrastructure Protection and Resilience Europe (CIPRE)*. Den Haag, Netherlands, Mar. 2015. URL: https://publikationen.bibliothek.kit.edu/1000056115.

[Rat13] Christoph Rathfelder. *Modelling Event-Based Interactions in Component-Based Architectures for Quantitative System Evaluation*. Vol. 10. The Karlsruhe Series on Software Design and Quality. Karlsruhe, Germany: KIT Scientific Publishing, 2013. URL: http://www.ksp.kit.edu/shop/isbn2shopid.php?isbn=978-3-86644-969-5.

[RDV09] Jose E Rivera, Francisco Durán, and Antonio Vallecillo. "A graphical approach for modeling time-dependent behavior of DSLs". In: *2009 IEEE Symposium on Visual Languages and Human-Centric Computing (VL/HCC)*. IEEE, Sept. 2009, pp. 51–55. DOI: 10.1109/VLHCC.2009.5295300.

[Ren15] Andreas Rentschler. "Model Transformation Languages with Modular Information Hiding". PhD thesis. Karlsruhe, Germany: Karlsruhe Institute of Technology, Apr. 2015. ISBN: 978-3-7315-0346-0. DOI: 10.5445/KSP/1000045910. URL: http://www.ksp.kit.edu/9783731503460.

[Reu+11] Ralf Reussner, Steffen Becker, Erik Burger, Jens Happe, Michael Hauck, Anne Koziolek, Heiko Koziolek, Klaus Krogmann, and Michael Kuperberg. *The Palladio Component Model*. Tech. rep. Karlsruhe: KIT, Fakultät für Informatik, 2011. URL: http://digbib.ubka.uni-karlsruhe.de/volltexte/1000022503.

[Reu+16] Ralf H. Reussner, Steffen Becker, Jens Happe, Robert Heinrich, Anne Koziolek, Heiko Koziolek, Max Kramer, and Klaus Krogmann. *Modeling and Simulating Software Architectures – The Palladio Approach*. Cambridge, MA: MIT Press, Oct. 2016. 408 pp. ISBN: 9780262034760. URL: http://mitpress.mit.edu/books/modeling-and-simulating-software-architectures.

[Reu01] Ralf H. Reussner. "Parametrisierte Verträge zur Protokolladaption bei Software-Komponenten". PhD. Thesis. Department of Informatics, University of Karlsruhe, 2001.

[Ris98] L. Rising. *The Patterns Handbook: Techniques, Strategies, and Applications.* SIGS, 1998. ISBN: 9780521648189. URL: https://books.google.de/books?id=HBAuixGMYWEC.

[Roq16] Pascal Roques. "MBSE with the ARCADIA Method and the Capella Tool". In: *8th European Congress on Embedded Real Time Software and Systems (ERTS 2016).* Toulouse, France, Jan. 2016. URL: https://hal.archives-ouvertes.fr/hal-01258014.

[Ros+15] Kiana Rostami, Johannes Stammel, Robert Heinrich, and Ralf Reussner. "Architecture-based Assessment and Planning of Change Requests". In: *Proceedings of the 11th International ACM SIGSOFT Conference on Quality of Software Architectures.* QoSA '15. Montreal, QC, Canada: ACM, 2015, pp. 21–30. ISBN: 978-1-4503-3470-9. URL: http://dl.acm.org/citation.cfm?id=2737198.

[Rum02] Bernhard Rumpe. "Executable Modeling with UML - A Vision or a Nightmare?" In: *Issues & Trends of Information Technology Management in Contemporary Associations, Seattle.* Ed. by T. Clark and J. Warmer. London: Idea Group Publishing, 2002, pp. 697–701. URL: http://www.se-rwth.de/topics/~rumpe/publications/Executable-Modeling-with-UML-A-Vision-or-a-Nightmare.pdf.

[Run+12] Per Runeson, Martin Host, Austen Rainer, and Bjorn Regnell. *Case Study Research in Software Engineering: Guidelines and Examples.* 1st. Hoboken, N.J: John Wiley & Sons, 2012. ISBN: 9781118104354.

[Sch+15] Matthias Schöttle, Nishanth Thimmegowda, Omar Alam, Jörg Kienzle, and Gunter Mussbacher. "Feature modelling and traceability for concern-driven software development with TouchCORE". In: *Companion Proceedings of the 14th International Conference on Modularity, MODULARITY 2015, Fort Collins, CO, USA, March 16 - 19, 2015.* Mar. 2015, pp. 11–14.

[Sch+16] Matthias Schöttle et al. "On the Modularization Provided by Concern-oriented Reuse". In: *Modularity*. ACM, 2016, pp. 184–189.

[Sch06] Douglas C Schmidt. "Model-driven engineering". In: *COMPUTER* 39.2 (2006).

[SH12] Misha Strittmatter and Lucia Happe. "Compositional performance abstractions of software connectors". In: *Proceedings of the 3rd ACM/SPEC International Conference on Performance Engineering (ICPE)*. Boston, Massachusetts, USA: ACM, 2012, pp. 275–278. ISBN: 978-1-4503-1202-8. DOI: 10.1145/2188286.2188337.

[SH16a] Misha Strittmatter and Robert Heinrich. "A Reference Structure for Metamodels of Quality-Aware Domain-Specific Languages". In: *13th Working IEEE/IFIP Conference on Software Architecture*. Apr. 2016, pp. 268–269. DOI: 10.1109/WICSA.2016.51. URL: http://ieeexplore.ieee.org/xpls/abs_all.jsp?arnumber=7516841.

[SH16b] Misha Strittmatter and Robert Heinrich. "Challenges in the Evolution of Metamodels". In: *3rd Collaborative Workshop on Evolution and Maintenance of Long-Living Software Systems*. Vol. 36(1). Softwaretechnik-Trends. 2016, pp. 12–15.

[Sie04] Johannes Siedersleben. *Moderne Software-Architektur: Umsichtig planen, robust bauen mit Quasar*. Heidelberg, Germany: dpunkt.verlag, 2004. ISBN: 9783898642927.

[SK03] R. Subramanyam and M.S. Krishnan. "Empirical analysis of CK metrics for object-oriented design complexity: implications for software defects". In: *IEEE Transactions on Software Engineering* 29.4 (2003). ISSN: 0098-5589. DOI: 10.1109/TSE.2003.1191795.

[SK16] Misha Strittmatter and Amine Kechaou. *The Media Store 3 Case Study System*. Tech. rep. 2016,1. Faculty of Informatics, Karlsruhe Institute of Technology, Feb. 2016. URL: http://digbib.ubka.uni-karlsruhe.de/volltexte/documents/3792054.

[SL14] Misha Strittmatter and Michael Langhammer. "Identifying Semantically Cohesive Modules within the Palladio Meta-Model". In: *Proceedings of the Symposium on Software Performance: Joint Descartes/Kieker/Palladio Days*. Ed. by Steffen Becker, Wilhelm Hasselbring, André van Hoorn, Samuel Kounev, and Ralf Reussner. Stuttgart, Germany: Universitätsbibliothek Stuttgart, Nov. 2014, pp. 160–176.

[SLT14] Daniel Strüber, Michael Lukaszczyk, and Gabriele Taentzer. "Tool Support for Model Splitting using Information Retrieval and Model Crawling Techniques". In: *BigMDE 2014: Workshop on Scalability in Model Driven Engineering*. CEUR-WS, 2014, pp. 44–47.

[SST13] Daniel Strüber, Matthias Selter, and Gabriele Taentzer. "Tool support for clustering large meta-models". In: *Proceedings of the Workshop on Scalability in Model Driven Engineering*. BigMDE '13. Budapest, Hungary: ACM, 2013, 7:1–7:4. ISBN: 978-1-4503-2165-5. DOI: 10.1145/2487766.2487773.

[Sta12] International Organization for Standardization. *ISO/PAS 17506:2012 – Industrial automation systems and integration – COLLADA digital asset schema specification for 3D visualization of industrial data*. 1st ed. July 2012. URL: https://www.iso.org/standard/59902.html.

[Sta73] Herbert Stachowiak. *Allgemeine Modelltheorie*. Wien: Springer Verlag, 1973. ISBN: 3-211-81106-0.

[Str+13a] Misha Strittmatter, Philipp Merkle, Andreas Rentschler, and Michael Langhammer. "Towards a Modular Palladio Component Model". In: *Proceedings of the Symposium on Software Performance: Joint Kieker/Palladio Days*. Ed. by Steffen Becker, Wilhelm Hasselbring, André van Hoorn, and Ralf Reussner. Vol. 1083. Karlsruhe, Germany: CEUR Workshop Proceedings, Nov. 2013, pp. 49–58. URL: http://www.kieker-palladio-days.org/.

[Str+13b] Daniel Strüber, Gabriele Taentzer, Stefan Jurack, and Tim Schäfer. "Towards a Distributed Modeling Process Based on Composite Models". In: *Fundamental Approaches to Software Engineering*. Ed. by Vittorio Cortellessa and Dániel Varró.

Berlin, Heidelberg: Springer Berlin Heidelberg, 2013, pp. 6–20. ISBN: 978-3-642-37057-1.

[Str+14] Daniel Strüber, Julia Rubin, Gabriele Taentzer, and Marsha Chechik. "Splitting Models Using Information Retrieval and Model Crawling Techniques". In: *Fundamental Approaches to Software Engineering*. Springer, 2014, pp. 47–62.

[Str+15] Misha Strittmatter, Kiana Rostami, Robert Heinrich, and Ralf Reussner. "A Modular Reference Structure for Component-based Architecture Description Languages". In: *2nd International Workshop on Model-Driven Engineering for Component-Based Systems (ModComp)*. CEUR, 2015, pp. 36–41. URL: http://ceur-ws.org/Vol-1463/paper6.pdf.

[Str+16a] Misha Strittmatter, Georg Hinkel, Michael Langhammer, Reiner Jung, and Robert Heinrich. "Challenges in the Evolution of Metamodels: Smells and Anti-Patterns of a Historically-Grown Metamodel". In: *10th International Workshop on Models and Evolution (ME)*. Saint Malo, France: CEUR Vol-1706, Oct. 2016. URL: http://ceur-ws.org/Vol-1706/.

[Str+16b] Misha Strittmatter, Michael Junker, Kiana Rostami, Sebastian Lehrig, Amine Kechaou, Bo Liu, and Robert Heinrich. "Extensible Graphical Editors for Palladio". In: *Symposium on Software Performance (SSP)*. Nov. 2016.

[Str+16c] Daniel Strüber, Stefan Jurack, Tim Schäfer, Stefan Schulz, and Gabriele Taentzer. "Managing Model and Meta-Model Components with Export and Import Interfaces". In: *BigMDE 2016: Workshop on Scalability in Model Driven Engineering*. CEUR-WS, 2016, pp. 31–36.

[Str11] Misha Strittmatter. "Performance Abstractions of Communication Patterns for Connectors". Study Thesis. Karlsruhe Institute of Technology (KIT), Germany, Jan. 2011.

[Str13] Misha Strittmatter. "Feedback-Driven Concurrency Improvement and Refinement of Performance Models". Diploma Thesis. Karlsruhe Institute of Technology (KIT), Germany, Mar. 2013.

[SV06] Thomas Stahl and Markus Völter. *Model-driven software development : technology, engineering, management.* Ed. by Jorn Bettin, Krzysztof Czarnecki, and Bettina von Stockfleth. Chichester: John Wiley & Sons, 2006. ISBN: 9780470025703.

[SW00] Connie U. Smith and Lloyd G. Williams. "Software performance antipatterns". In: *Workshop on Software and Performance.* 2000, pp. 127–136. DOI: 10.1145/350391.350420.

[SZS10] Kawther Saeedi, Liping Zhao, and Pedro R. F. Sampaio. "Extending BPMN for supporting customer-facing service quality requirements". In: *2010 IEEE International Conference on Web Services.* IEEE. July 2010, pp. 616–623. DOI: 10.1109/ICWS.2010.116.

[Tri08] Adrian Trifu. "Towards Automated Restructuring of Object-Oriented Systems". PhD thesis. Fakultät für Informatik, Universität Karlsruhe (TH), Germany, 2008.

[TT07] Adrian Trifu and Mircea Trifu. *SISSy: Catalog of Detected Problem Patterns.* 2007.

[VC15] Edoardo Vacchi and Walter Cazzola. "Neverlang: A Framework for Feature-Oriented Language Development". In: *Computer Languages, Systems & Structures* 43.3 (Oct. 2015), pp. 1–40. ISSN: 1477-8424. DOI: 10.1016/j.cl.2015.02.001. URL: http://www.sciencedirect.com/science/article/pii/S1477842415000056.

[Vép+06] Éric Vépa, Jean Bézivin, Hugo Brunelière, and Frédéric Jouault. "Measuring model repositories". In: *Proceedings of the 1st Workshop on Model Size Metrics.* Genoa, Italy, Oct. 2006. URL: https://hal.inria.fr/hal-01272259.

[Völ11] Steven Völkel. *Kompositionale Entwicklung domänenspezifischer Sprachen.* German. Aachener Informatik-Berichte, Software Engineering, Band 9. Shaker Verlag, 2011. ISBN: 978-3-8440-0328-4. URL: http://www.se-rwth.de/phdtheses/Diss-Voelkel-Kompositionale-Entwicklung-domaenenspezifischer-Sprachen.pdf.

[VS10] Markus Voelter and Konstantin Solomatov. "Language modularization and composition with projectional language workbenches illustrated with MPS". In: *Software Language Engineering, SLE* 16 (2010), p. 3.

[WBK14] Felix Willnecker, Andreas Brunnert, and Helmut Krcmar. "Predicting Energy Consumption by Extending the Palladio Component Model". In: *SOSP'14 Symposium on Software Performance: Joint Descartes/Kieker/Palladio Days 2014.* 2014, p. 177.

[WL99] David M Weiss and Chi Tau Robert Lai. *Software product-line engineering: a family-based software development process.* Vol. 12. Addison-Wesley Reading, 1999.

Index

List of Figures

List of Tables

The Karlsruhe Series on Software Design and Quality

Edited by Prof. Dr. Ralf Reussner // ISSN 1867-0067

Band 1 **Steffen Becker**
Coupled Model Transformations for QoS Enabled Component-Based Software Design.
ISBN 978-3-86644-271-9

Band 2 **Heiko Koziolek**
Parameter Dependencies for Reusable Performance Specifications of Software Components.
ISBN 978-3-86644-272-6

Band 3 **Jens Happe**
Predicting Software Performance in Symmetric Multi-core and Multiprocessor Environments.
ISBN 978-3-86644-381-5

Band 4 **Klaus Krogmann**
Reconstruction of Software Component Architectures and Behaviour Models using Static and Dynamic Analysis.
ISBN 978-3-86644-804-9

Band 5 **Michael Kuperberg**
Quantifying and Predicting the Influence of Execution Platform on Software Component Performance.
ISBN 978-3-86644-741-7

Band 6 **Thomas Goldschmidt**
View-Based Textual Modelling.
ISBN 978-3-86644-642-7

Band 7 **Anne Koziolek**
Automated Improvement of Software Architecture Models for Performance and Other Quality Attributes.
ISBN 978-3-86644-973-2

Band 8 **Lucia Happe**
Configurable Software Performance Completions through Higher-Order Model Transformations.
ISBN 978-3-86644-990-9

Band 9 **Franz Brosch**
Integrated Software Architecture-Based Reliability Prediction for IT Systems.
ISBN 978-3-86644-859-9

Band 10 **Christoph Rathfelder**
Modelling Event-Based Interactions in Component-Based Architectures for Quantitative System Evaluation.
ISBN 978-3-86644-969-5

Band 11 **Henning Groenda**
Certifying Software Component Performance Specifications.
ISBN 978-3-7315-0080-3

Band 12 **Dennis Westermann**
Deriving Goal-oriented Performance Models by Systematic Experimentation.
ISBN 978-3-7315-0165-7

Band 13 **Michael Hauck**
Automated Experiments for Deriving Performance-relevant Properties of Software Execution Environments.
ISBN 978-3-7315-0138-1

Band 14 **Zoya Durdik**
Architectural Design Decision Documentation through Reuse of Design Patterns.
ISBN 978-3-7315-0292-0

Band 15 **Erik Burger**
Flexible Views for View-based Model-driven Development.
ISBN 978-3-7315-0276-0

Band 16 **Benjamin Klatt**
Consolidation of Customized Product Copies into Software Product Lines.
ISBN 978-3-7315-0368-2

Band 17 **Andreas Rentschler**
Model Transformation Languages with Modular Information Hiding.
ISBN 978-3-7315-0346-0

Band 18 **Omar-Qais Noorshams**
Modeling and Prediction of I/O Performance in Virtualized Environments.
ISBN 978-3-7315-0359-0

Band 19 **Johannes Josef Stammel**
Architekturbasierte Bewertung und Planung von Änderungsanfragen.
ISBN 978-3-7315-0524-2

Band 20 **Alexander Wert**
Performance Problem Diagnostics by Systematic Experimentation.
ISBN 978-3-7315-0677-5

Band 21 **Christoph Heger**
An Approach for Guiding Developers to Performance and Scalability Solutions.
ISBN 978-3-7315-0698-0

Band 22 **Fouad ben Nasr Omri**
Weighted Statistical Testing based on Active Learning and Formal Verification Techniques for Software Reliability Assessment.
ISBN 978-3-7315-0472-6

Band 23 **Michael Langhammer**
Automated Coevolution of Source Code and Software Architecture Models.
ISBN 978-3-7315-0783-3

Band 24 **Max Emanuel Kramer**
Specification Languages for Preserving Consistency between Models of Different Languages.
ISBN 978-3-7315-0784-0

Band 25 **Sebastian Michael Lehrig**
Efficiently Conducting Quality-of-Service Analyses by Templating Architectural Knowledge.
ISBN 978-3-7315-0756-7

Band 26 **Georg Hinkel**
Implicit Incremental Model Analyses and Transformations.
ISBN 978-3-7315-0763-5

Band 27 **Christian Stier**
Adaptation-Aware Architecture Modeling and Analysis of Energy Efficiency for Software Systems.
ISBN 978-3-7315-0851-9

Band 28 **Lukas Märtin**
Entwurfsoptimierung von selbst-adaptiven Wartungsmechanismen für software-intensive technische Systeme.
ISBN 978-3-7315-0852-6

Band 29 **Axel Busch**
Quality-driven Reuse of Model-based Software Architecture Elements.
ISBN 978-3-7315-0951-6

Band 30 **Kiana Busch**
An Architecture-based Approach for Change Impact Analysis of Software-intensive Systems.
ISBN 978-3-7315-0974-5

Band 31 **Misha Strittmatter**
A Reference Structure for Modular Metamodels of Quality-Describing Domain-Specific Modeling Languages.
ISBN 978-3-7315-0982-0
